For Ken!
from –

The author's personal experience with addictive behavior has inspired deep introspection and a broad investigation of philosophical and spiritual propositions. His agrarian origins, formal education, and years in the investment business provide authentic grounding for this intimate account. He presently spends a good deal of time on the prairies near his childhood home, while otherwise traveling the world with enduring passion.

Dedication

To all who have faced difficult truths about themselves, especially those still searching for a way to serenity.

James Clare

COMPELLED BY DESIRE

AUSTIN MACAULEY PUBLISHERS™

LONDON • CAMBRIDGE • NEW YORK • SHARJAH

A CIP catalogue record for this title is available from the British Library.

ISBN 9781787105843 (Paperback)
ISBN 9781787105850 (E-Book)

www.austinmacauley.com

First Published (2018)
Austin Macauley Publishers Ltd.
25 Canada Square
Canary Wharf
London
E14 5LQ

Acknowledgments

I am grateful for my friend Margaret, who spent countless hours reviewing and constructively commenting on this work.

Part I
Wanting Identity

Chapter 1

Through the window of the yellow school bus, blurred by the icy flakes of sleet that streamed across it almost horizontally, recently harvested wheat fields were turning white with the first snowfall of the season. It was a cold and dreary November day that seemed to seal the termination of summer, and it matched my mood entirely, without aggravating it in the least. In fact, I was not conscious of anything external to my own despair, the ache that clutched my heart and kept me on the verge of tears. I only stared out the window so I wouldn't need to face anyone inside the bus. While the rest of the world was still in a state of shock over the assassination of John Fitzgerald Kennedy, which had occurred exactly one week previously, I was not affected in the least by it. No, I had just lived through my own assassination, the complete annihilation of my social life. I had actually cried in front of my entire ninth-grade class: cute little red-haired Janie, Brenda who typically greeted me with a warm smile, my one and only male friend Jimmy, and big Dwight, the tough and lanky son of a rancher, who rode on the same school bus and always greeted me man to man. I'd only ever grasped at the slenderest of social reeds, and now they were gone, obliterated.

There was only one aspect of my circumstances for which I felt the slightest gratitude: it was Friday and I would not have to face anybody until Monday morning, except members of my immediate family who would remain mercifully unaware of my horrible humiliation. Meanwhile, I relived the moments during which I had walked unsteadily back to my seat, profoundly aware that behind me was the awful setting in which the final ruin of my already tenuous dignity and self-confidence had occurred. I met each recurring mental image of my classmates with a gut-wrenching wince and suppressed their unbelieving and ill-omened facial expressions as quickly as I could.

It had all begun on Monday morning, following the death of President Kennedy on the preceding Friday. Mr. Benson, our literature teacher, had given us an assignment to report on the event factually and to describe its significance for the country. We were expected to give a five-minute presentation to the class and mine had been scheduled for this afternoon, four days away at the time. An excruciating visceral contraction had seized me as I envisioned standing in front of everyone and giving a talk, certain I would be violently and uncontrollably nervous, dreading the odd, misfit image I would surely present along with my paper which could only lead to future ridicule and further social exclusion.

Over and over, those fears had swamped me as I sat silently through the one-hour bus trip home that afternoon. After three months in his class, I was quite sure that the skinny, gangly, pale-faced Benson had it in for me somehow, although I was far too timid to have caused any disruption in his class. In elementary school I had proven to be intelligent enough, I had no physical impairments, I was a fit healthy young man and, as far as I could determine, I was actually quite good-looking. Perhaps he despised my shy and awkward social demeanor. I searched for some characteristic, something about me, that invited a bullying response, not only from him but from two high school seniors as well. The latter's abuse was openly physical, while Benson's was confined to deprecating glances, terse greetings, and abrupt impatient replies to the few questions I dared to ask.

But I did not search for an escape. Terrifying as it had been, I made it through a 4-H Club public speaking event about four years ago. The memory fueled a grim determination to forge ahead. Being older now, the fear looked childish and I believed I must conquer it. As the days ground slowly toward Friday, I wrote and rewrote my presentation, until I thought it was quite good. I read it over with considerable satisfaction several times on Thursday night, all the time pushing to the shifting perimeters of my consciousness the formidable task of delivering it. More than twenty students had already presented their versions of the event. Several were visibly nervous, but they got through it. So would I.

I quite successfully kept it out of my mind until I got to school and Jimmy asked if I was ready. I replied that I was, with an air of confidence, but from that point on I was conscious of the approaching hour. Other than Jimmy and a few of the girls, I viewed everyone in the class as potentially hostile. My appetite was curtailed at lunchtime and I entered the classroom with rapidly escalating trepidation. When Mr. Benson came in, his navy blazer and khaki slacks hanging loosely on the extremities of his bony frame, I tried to catch his glance for some reassurance of friendliness, to no avail. My heart pounded in my chest, I had great difficulty sitting still while ten other students presented their work, and I was beginning to feel the need to go to the washroom. Finally Mr. Benson, sitting in a spare seat in the first row to leave the front of the room for presenters, glanced at the sheet he held in his pallid skeletal hand, pinned me with leaden lifeless eyes, and said, "Richard, what have you got for us?"

Amidst the dense throbbing in my ears his voice sounded as though he called from the inside of a barrel. I rose from my seat in a trance, an automaton with rigid intentions to read what was written on the paper I held with my vibrating hand until I reached the end, beyond which point I envisioned myself safely back in my seat with the nightmare behind me, come what may. At the side of the big oak teacher's desk, where others had stood, I turned and began to read.

"Doesn't your paper have a title?" he interrupted.

"The Assassination of John Fitzgerald Kennedy," I no doubt mumbled while backtracking to the top of the page with my eyes, and I began to read the text again. I felt even more disoriented, but struggled to hang on to the stability that my own familiar words promised to provide.

"Can you speak up?" he interrupted again, his voice abrupt.

I felt myself quake, like a small train on a section of uneven track. A wave of vertigo washed over me and I felt unsure that I was standing upright, but I continued reading, "As the president dismounted from the plane into the bright sunshine…"

"Excuse me, dismounted? One dismounts from a horse. Can you think of a better word?" I felt that Benson was deliberately taunting me.

He had not interrupted others like this. The torment was not going to stop. The end of the ordeal as I had envisioned it was receding. My shallow well of courage and resolve was dry. A wave of hopelessness engulfed me; I knew I could not come up with a different word. Feeling helpless and utterly vulnerable, naked and feeble in front of everyone, I realized I could not go on. Tears rose in my eyes as I looked pleadingly at my tormentor. There was nothing, no more of me to hide behind. I didn't care what happened; I was finished, no more to lose. The tears ran down my cheeks and my nose needed wiping. I used the back of my hand.

"You can sit down," Benson said matter-of-factly.

I didn't catch his next words, but as I approached my desk the rest of the class began to rise and leave the room. I left the room in a stupor, wanting nothing but escape. I skipped the last class of the day, leaving the school and walking around town in a daze until the buses came to take us home. Heavy sorrow filled my chest and swelled upward in surges of pressure behind my eyes. But more tears did not come.

Although I felt a little safer now, isolated in my seat with the passing roadside distracting my eyes, hopelessness still gripped my arms with tingling numbness and swamped my head like some nauseating intoxicant. I sensed that I could sink into a morass of gloomy wretchedness and find some comfort there. Overwhelmed by the misery welling from my heart, I pleaded silently for answers to a vague notion of Jesus to whom I had prayed on my knees as a child. But a long history of similar earnest imploring had never once resulted in a release from my pain, and I was suddenly consumed by a sense of betrayal. A raw urge to fight pulled me back from the brink of giving in to hopelessness, and my dejected state of mind was transformed into one of rage.

In the core of my being, in the lowest reaches of my abdomen, intense indignation percolated, until a volcano of wrath simmered on the verge of eruption. The bus was no place to let my anger out physically, so I redirected it mentally, toward a perceived source of my unacceptable misery. "Now I lay me down to sleep. I pray thee God thy child to keep…" What the fuck was that all about? I seethed at the very notion of this self-induced hope in some external source of relief, this contrived sense of security, the belief that there was any kind of benevolent being looking out for me. Ludicrous! Fucking God was a trickster at best, or an evil deceitful monster to whom the concept of fairness must be a kind of jest, or He was nothing at all, a non-entity that was no more than the figment of simple and ignorant imaginations.

The rage sustained me and gave me new strength. I felt braced by some primal energy, a deep-rooted will to survive. It vanquished the hideous reality of the present, numbed the emotional turmoil that threatened to destroy me, and trumped any remnant of faith in a benevolent universe. If ever I were going to rise above this dismal existence and overcome the victimization I suffered so frequently, I would have to go it alone.

I felt bitter contempt when I thought of the economically deprived status my parents had been willing to endure, probably the primary cause of my failure to gain social acceptance. My whole being reacted with revulsion at the circumstances into which I'd been born. Deep in my gut, an unshakable faith in some far-off notion of self-assured justice began to take shape. Within that lonely but hopeful vision, I saw that someday I might look down with pride and vengeance upon this whole ugly quagmire of twisted incongruity.

Over the next few miles, that conclusion provided a bit of mindless peace and relief. Gradually, however, I began to follow another train of thought. Despite the fact that external circumstances often seemed entirely unreasonable, even unacceptable, I really wondered about myself. Reflecting upon my fifteen years of experience with life to this point, it seemed to me that I had been born with fear and anger, because I could not remember when they did not, from time-to-time, permeate my senses, besiege my state of mind, and otherwise dominate my existence. My anger was generally pervasive, although it ranged in intensity between dormancy, irritation, and rage. It waited, innate, ever-present but unassigned, until it found something upon which to focus. Once that happened, it gained specific expression and felt justified. My fear was persistent and typically generic as well, until my mind found specific application for it. In its latent aspect it was a kind of general insecurity. In its active state it became debilitating terror. Believing those feelings were unique to me, I had never discussed them because I couldn't trust anyone to understand. In that respect, I had lived alone, shouldering a heavy emotional burden, isolated in a state of stern self-reliance.

It is possible my troubles originated with the notion of a separate 'self' which depended for its survival upon the world around it. From that perspective, fear may have been appropriate because my existence was threatened by any shortfall I perceived; anger may have been a tool, useful in procuring items essential to my survival. In any case, they were always present, inevitably influencing me in ways that far exceeded the demands of those two practical primal purposes.

Too often I was compelled by the need to overcome deeply perceived deficiencies in my make-up, to push myself unreasonably. I was thus driven by fear, and loathed being driven. My anger rose to a pitch when my objectives were frustrated and internal rage became habitual. I writhed with a sense of panic at my perception of a hostile world and became insanely constricted. Then I reacted with self-loathing to consequent instances of stuttering hesitation, because I felt stymied by a lack of inner courage.

A few more miles passed by; in another ten minutes I would be home. Home, I thought. In spite of the foregoing, my life was not all bad. There were days I enjoyed as much as anyone. My parents rarely placed restrictions on my activities. As a child, I'd had the run of five acres around the farmyard. Later on, when I could wander that far, or saddle a horse, I enjoyed unrestrained exploration of our three hundred and twenty acre farm, plus thousands upon thousands of acres of untouched native prairie and undulating sand-hills. I reveled in the vastness of the countryside, the wildlife I spotted, and the silence that seemed to ride on the wind. Some days I spent in complete solitude, the circumstances in which I felt most comfortable. There were the family gatherings as well, when we visited my cousins at Christmastime and they came to the farm on other holidays. Certainly those had been high points in each year. Even so, as this day had proven, the negative side outweighed the positive far too often and, if one could actually weigh them, perhaps on balance.

Chapter 2

I was born in eastern Montana, in nineteen forty-nine, and raised on a small mixed cattle and wheat farm. Although my name is Richard Nelson, only my mother and teachers ever consistently called me Richard. The nickname, Rick, was by far the most commonly applied by my father, friends, siblings, and cousins. Ricky and Richie I wholeheartedly detested, while I secretly hoped the seldom-used appellation, Rich, contained within it a prophecy, the latter primarily because my family lived a simple rural agrarian life, much of it pre-industrialized and rather peasant-like. Horses were still a common form of transport when I was very young, with horse-drawn sleighs and buggies, and they remained an integral part of the cattle operation long after I left home at age eighteen. We went without the conveniences of running water, indoor plumbing and even electricity until I was more than six years old. Consequently, my parents worked hard physically, just to survive, and we spent a great deal of time outside.

I think the distinguishing characteristic of life on the prairies was harshness. During the long winters the thermometer could dive to minus forty degrees and stay there, winds howling and snow drifting as high as buildings. It seemed that we waited a long time for summer. When it did arrive, so did the mosquitos and horse flies. Then in July and August temperatures could soar to above one hundred degrees, and the parching wind nearly always blew. I didn't realize it then, but the vegetation was relatively harsh, too. Thistles grew thick in the cultivated fields, so that walking required boots, though I often ran barefoot. On the natural prairie, cactus thrived, thorny rose bushes grew wild, and porcupines waddled along until they climbed clumsily into a purple birch tree. Snarled clumps of sagebrush with velvety powder-blue leaves sweetly perfumed the ever-present breezes, while the smell of a dead animal, especially a skunk, could waft pungently for weeks. A grove of tall poplars shading the perimeter of a slough, the music of frogs and crickets from beyond the dwarf willow at the water's edge, and the sight of a mule-deer buck bounding off to avoid the intrusion: such circumstances presented an irresistible invitation to my inquisitive nature. But exploring such a setting was not the effortless amusement promised by an initial glance. The thick tangled undergrowth was crisscrossed with gnarled deadfall. Mosquitos swarmed and whined as they were disturbed. To reach the open water, one was often forced to cross boggy outlying depressions, making sopping sloshing feet a part of the endeavor.

I didn't perceive the conditions as being extraordinarily challenging. But one needed a certain toughness to ignore the scraping and stinging discomforts, and an inner constitution that was impervious to protracted struggle, fatigue, or a trickle of blood. Those qualities were modeled effectively by my father who once waited a month, until harvest was over, before reporting a sore swollen hand in which he had broken four small bones.

My mother was self-sacrificing and loving. My father was self-cherishing but responsible. I'm sure they had their struggles, such as getting beyond the death of their first child, a little girl who only lived ten weeks. I was born a little more than a year after that tragedy, and eighteen months ahead of my first surviving sister. I have been told, jokingly, I tried to kill her by throwing a box of laundry detergent into her crib – two-year-old competition for attention, my mother believed. Though it probably was an early manifestation of substantial insecurity, childishly uninhibited, I expect I had in mind a vague idea of 'getting rid of her' rather than 'killing her' which would nonetheless have relieved me of enormous torment over the years.

It is difficult to distinguish between old photos, the historical accounts of others, and my own experience as the source of memories. For example, I am aware that I entertained myself with my tricycle, tying a rusty red wagon behind it and trying to get our Border Collie to hop aboard and sit still; I built corrals and established a farm of my own, with sticks pounded into the dusty ground that served as our barren grassless yard; I played at the edge of the garden while my mother worked at keeping the weeds under control, and I sat beside her in the old Ford truck while she hauled grain from the combine. I know my aunt stayed with us at those times to babysit my sister or, when my mother was expecting my second sister, took her turn at hauling grain through harvest while I rode along with her.

But there are only a few things from my early childhood for which I retained my own distinct mental images. I remember my dad's black riding boots, the ornate leatherwork he did, and the familiar aroma of his roll-your-own cigarettes – my distant hero. One time I tripped along with him as he walked back west to check on some calving cows. One cow with a newborn calf became aggressive and moved threateningly toward us, toward me more specifically, which is not surprising since I would have been the more foreign of the two intruders in her eyes. My dad threw a lump of dirt, hit her, and she veered off. My initial reaction was one of security and awe, having been saved by my idol, but it didn't prevail. Some aspect of the incident left me feeling uncertain about his whole-hearted commitment to protecting me. I was dismayed by a subtle but perceptible hesitation on his part. Doubt was born, and lingered.

I am familiar with the historical account of riding-double with my cousin, Carolyn, the day she panicked, wrapped her arms around me from behind and pulled me off a horse. My face was wrecked when it absorbed our fall onto the hard dirt road. Some weeks after a doctor advised my parents to delay my starting first grade, to avoid psychologically damaging 'scar-face' ridicule from other students, it healed completely without any scarring. My actual memory of the incident is vague, however, and perhaps, as much as any other reaction, I enjoyed the attention.

Not long after I started, I began riding my horse the three miles to school. I climbed on in the barn at home and ducked as I passed through the door. I ducked again to enter the barn at the schoolyard, and dismounted with my lunch-pail in hand by crawling off and down the planks that separated the stalls. It was an immense source of pride from the beginning. Soon a neighbor boy in my class began riding, too. We shared a mile and a half of road each day and were happy companions for that time. Sometimes my parents gave me a ride to school and I walked home with some of the neighbor kids. Because of the roadside sloughs and other attractions it often took two hours or more, but the adults were too busy to worry about us. I have always been consciously grateful for those enduring experiences of immense space under a limitless prairie sky, and the timeless unfettered freedom that permitted our complete and immediate immersion.

I remember the time my father pulled me to school on a toboggan behind his saddle horse because the snow was too deep for vehicles. It tipped over repeatedly and just as often I fell off, getting snow in my face and down my neck, while the lunch my mother had packed for me was destroyed. I felt a great sadness that focused on his apparent disregard for my mother's kindness, and distrust for my father surged. My sister told me, many years later, she remembered him beating me repeatedly, quite viciously she thought, but I don't remember any of that. I do know I didn't receive much affection from him. One day, when he was on his way out the door, I said something he must have found especially amusing. He reached over without altering his forward momentum, rubbed the top of my head affectionately, and continued on. My eyes filled with tears of elation and my heart swelled in my chest with the notion that things would be different. But it did not happen again.

I have a happy memory of my mother playing 'store' with me when I stayed at home with the mumps. Everything she needed in the kitchen that day she had to buy from me. I knew

21

she enjoyed it, too. I remember my paternal grandmother cursing my mother's housekeeping while she was in the hospital having one of my siblings. It was an indiscretion that earned her a scrap of animosity that never dissolved. I know I liked to play with matches and lit a fire that nearly burned down the farm one day. About forty years later my mother apologized for beating me over that. I guess she felt really bad about it for all those years, but I don't remember any part of it. Perhaps I found it easy to forgive her because I understood the fear she must have felt. My mom worked incredibly hard for a small woman and I often felt sorry for her. Of course, my dad worked really hard, too, but he gradually became an object of frustration, dread, and bitterness. Sometimes that was interwoven with admiration, goodwill, and yearning for his affection, but never sympathy.

While my life was unfolding otherwise, there was one source of pain so great that consciousness of it had to be suppressed. I don't know to what degree my memory can be trusted, but it seems I wet the bed from the day I was born until I was ten years old. I don't know if it was that long, but I am sure it imprisoned me in a tomb of my own mind. I was free to move about physically, but I felt I couldn't move about emotionally. I couldn't engage with anyone emotionally, to share my agony and let it out. As a consequence, I spent much of my childhood in an emotional crypt. Little got in and nothing got out.

It was impossible to feel like meeting the world when I woke up in a cold damp bed that smelled like piss, knowing that my mother would have to change the sheets again, knowing that my parents had tried desperately to find a solution: talking with the doctor, buying this and that kind of medication, and exploring various behavioral ideas. I felt sorry for them. I remember my father shaking his head in despair and disgust when my mother related another occurrence, which, out of compassion for us both, she didn't always do. The wetness caused my legs and hips to ache from the cold and my whole body suffered a chilled numbness. Mentally, I had to shut the door on it or I couldn't have faced anybody. I don't remember my parents scolding me, or outwardly doing anything that would make me feel unloved, but I guess I didn't need that. I doubt that I ever considered myself as lovable anyway. I couldn't consider myself at all really, because the self-disgust would be too enormous and would wash me away.

At some point I concluded that my penis was defective and blamed it for the bed-wetting. I think I came to this conclusion after a memorable trip to visit my cousins in the city. My parents accepted my aunt's invitation to stay overnight and, as we were heading off to bed, my mother asked nervously if I had gone to the bathroom. At that point my uncle looked at me and threatened in a low but deliberate tone, "If you're going to wet the bed maybe I should tie a string around it." Mortified is the only word I can use to describe my reaction. I immediately felt drained of physical strength. I felt fear for and disgust at my pathetic little penis. At the same time, I felt embarrassed for my mom and dad, embarrassed in front of everyone, so lonely and alienated at being singled out from the other kids.

I don't remember anything more specific, except that I didn't sleep much, if any, that night and I was glad when people started to get up, so the conscious nightmare of my uncle's words and the lonely fearful vigil of remaining awake could end. I have no recollection of playing with my cousins. It was as though nothing else happened, no meals, no games, no laughs, nothing, just the words of my uncle and those eight or nine hours of hell when everyone else was asleep. That may have been the night that I began to scoff at the significance of my nightly prayers to a loving and caring Jesus. Maybe the disgust I had for myself and my penis reached a saturation point and I began loathing the concept of God, just to spread it around.

In spite of that too frequently distressing disorder, I enjoyed solid occasions of wellbeing. Family evenings of playing cards and other games around the kitchen table were satisfying and comfortable interludes. I especially enjoyed playing softball during breaks at school and even more when I could join the men during community gatherings. Those took place at the one-room schoolhouse, with its large yard, ball diamond, and horseshoe pits. In spite of my Protestant father's narrow-minded (thankfully mostly private) intolerance for our Catholic neighbors, the closeness of the community lent those events the feel of family gatherings. As the afternoon inevitably ran into early evening, all the members of our immediate acquaintance became melded together as one, parents and kids laughing and playing and eating together beneath the benevolent infinity of the prairie sky. Even the desperate need to prove myself and be seen at the top of the heap, which subtly plagued me in smaller circles, all but dissolved in the full presence of my known universe.

The highlight of my growing-up was undoubtedly our semi-annual cattle drive. From age seven, I rode my own horse, chasing cattle for two days over twenty-one miles of rugged native prairie. There were no roads for the entire trip and only four barbed-wire fences. Hundreds of cattle, the amalgamation of small herds belonging to a dozen local farmers, trudged out in the spring and back home in fall, leaving an easily recognizable trail that led to the wire gates in the fences, then on again through a vast landscape that was otherwise untouched by man. It was as it had been for millennia 'out there' and I was innately drawn to it from the beginning, with a deep appreciation. There was magic in the twittering poplar groves with their pungent scent of decay and renewal. The ground cedar formed a soft carpet beneath the horses' feet and it sweetly perfumed gentle breezes. There were stretches where relentless west winds had eroded the surface, creating gigantic blowouts and piling the sifting sand into drifts fifty feet high. My trusty mare geared down and powered her way to the crest, from which I surveyed an expanded view of the wonderland that surrounded us while she caught her breath. Then she seemed to intuitively back-pedal, as she allowed her body to slide in perfect control, down, down with an avalanche of sand to the eroded bottom again.

We stopped at midday to eat the lunch my mother had packed for us and to let the cattle graze for a while. It felt truly luxurious to stretch out on the soft ground, carefully on a bed of cedar rather than cactus, and to quench the thirst born of trail dust and the hot dry air that often cracked men's lips to bleeding as the day wore on. While tough, often somber, and rarely sympathetic, the men were nevertheless generous and kind-hearted. I felt at home in my boots and hat and, if a day passed without my father finding too much fault with me, it was as good as it could get.

Old Tom was a long-time friend of my father's and he always volunteered to drive the truck for us, over forty miles around the perimeter of the hills, to meet us at our destination which was an extensive set-up of corrals at the entrance to the sixty-thousand acre ranch where the cows and calves spent the summer. I especially recall the trips home, after the horses had been loaded and the evening had cooled with the sunset. I sat between Old Tom and my father and stared drowsily as we bounced along, the headlights searching in the darkness for the prairie trail. The comfort of the heater flooded over my tired face and purged the chill that had crept into my body. The not unpleasant cloud of roll-your-own cigarette smoke filled my nostrils and I listened to the baritone conversation of sages as I drifted into an exhausted and secure oblivion.

Even so, within the lonely confines of my mind and my most readily accessible memory, I had an unremitting propensity to emphasize the negative. I believe a seething cursing rage first completely engulfed me one very hot August day. I was inside the metal hopper of the combine, perched awkwardly upon a metal guard that obstructed my work, which was chipping stinking congealed grain away from the auger which ran beneath the guard. It had not been cleaned out following the previous harvest, when it would have been much easier to do.

To make matters worse, I had planned to play that day with a visiting male cousin of my age. My mother had announced her plans to construct a tent with our help, which included my two sisters as well. On the verge of those plans being realized my father had compelled me, in the imploring voice he engaged to satisfy his purposes, to change my course by saying, "Rick, I don't suppose you'd climb in and clean out that hopper for me?" My whole body had quaked with despair. But there was no valid protest in the face of work on the farm. Nor, for the same reason, could my mother have intervened with a reasonable plea.

For several hours I listened to the playful voices of those engaged at their novel project, while the temperature must have hit a hundred and twenty degrees inside the hopper. Sweat streamed down my face and back as I pried and picked away clumsily at my miserable task. Hatred of my father soared to new heights and I cursed with a vocabulary I didn't realize I possessed, employing combinations and permutations that were as original as the new tent. In some perverse way it appeased the livid fury that racked my being.

When I turned ten years of age, my parents encouraged me to join the 4-H Beef Club. My dad and I picked one of the better steer calves out of the herd in September. I fed it, groomed it, got it accustomed to wearing a halter, and spent many hours leading it around the farmyard. By spring, he had grown to nine hundred pounds and was as tall as me; he knew how to stand square on all fours and hold his head up adjacent to mine. It was from that stance that he reached over and rasped his huge tongue across my cheek, like a giant friendly dog.

In a way I was a tough boy, because you needed to be tough on the farm. Becoming attached or showing emotion was for women. But I was pretty lonely, too, except for my grandfather who represented a friendly harbor for me. I often stayed with my grandparents in town and helped Grandpa with projects in their back yard. He was a carpenter, but he also worked as a janitor at the schools in town. I worked as his little helper there as well, safe and happy, never doing anything wrong in his eyes. Because of my father's prickly attitude toward religious differences, visits from school friends on weekends or after school were not encouraged. I had my horse of course, and the dog, but they were part of the furniture. The calf delighted me with his unusual display of affection and made me laugh inside.

That's why I felt so bad at the end of achievement day, when I had to lead him up the ramp into a giant cattle liner because he'd been purchased by some people who would turn him into beef. It didn't help that the club had enjoyed a tour of a packing plant a few months prior to that, including the killing floor where the animals fell in a heap, got their throats cut, and had their hides removed. So, although I held my tears like a tough guy until we got home, I rushed into my bedroom, buried my face in the pillow, and cried and cried. Agony racked my body with each recurring realization that I had betrayed a trusting friend. I pulled my knees to my chest and I felt my heart would burst. As though it had no value at all, I'd severed the bond. I had been expected to sever the bond, as though it had no value. It didn't seem right to me, but I concluded that the problem must somehow reside in the wrongness of my excruciating pain. I thought perhaps I had to shun its existence or fail at becoming a man. But I'm not sure about that. I'm only certain that it formed an intensely emotional touchstone somewhere deep in the core of my being.

It may have been a suitable preparation, as events were to unfold, because later in that year my grandfather became ill and was taken to the hospital, they told me. I wanted to see him but they said I couldn't. Then everyone was wailing and sniffling and buzzing around, hugging each other, and I guessed that he must have died. I couldn't imagine that he had actually died, that he would not be around anymore. That seemed quite impossible and I hoped there was some mistake. In any case, I noticed that only the women seemed to be crying and, maybe because I'd had some recent practice, I proved myself a man and swallowed the awful heavy emptiness that wanted to well up in my chest. In a few days they all left in the afternoon for grandpa's funeral and to bury him in the ground. I really wanted to see him once more before he was gone forever and I did cry at that point, a burst of repressed sadness and the conviction that my separation from my grandfather was being unfairly imposed. Maybe I felt that he had abandoned me as well. I just didn't know how to think about it. It seemed a great void of not knowing had just swelled to an abyss and everything seemed very bleak indeed. Every time I became close to something, it ended in a painful tragedy.

Back in my room, suffering in solitary agony and crying into my pillow again, the obsession that God was no more than a bad joke festered. It was difficult to remember the good times with my grandfather. I didn't feel a part of the family. My enormous and inappropriate sensitivities were eventually tucked away, as if in a tomb. But I felt the heaviness of the world would never let me up again. In the private recesses of my existence, I embraced anguish and sorrow for the little boy that had ceased to exist, and there also, I nurtured my budding distrust in a loving, fucking interventionist God.

Around the time I turned eleven years of age, one of my uncles gave me a single-shot .22 caliber rifle. Whenever I could, I escaped over the rise to the west of our farmyard and spent the day wandering the hills, looking for a jackrabbit and living with my own thoughts. During the winter I trudged through knee-deep snow regardless of the temperature. Sometimes I walked so far that I feared my exhausted legs would not carry me home. Sometimes I saddled my horse and the dog followed along, but I never craved the company of other human beings. My thoughts, which often ranged across grandiose possibilities for my future, recurrently retained as a backdrop the subtle desire to impress my mother.

The anger I carried deep inside surfaced one day as I was trying to start a small gasoline engine I had been working on as a project. My father was proficient as a mechanic, usually doing his own engine repairs and overhauling equipment, so I came by the inclination naturally. But the engine would not run and, after countless adjustments and pulls on the starting rope, I became frustrated, to the point of fuming, and I was swearing a blue streak of foul language by the time my father came by. In a quiet and rather friendly tone, that may even have been empathetic, he said, "You had better not let your mother hear you talking like that." The incident was made memorable by his sudden presence and by his manner, in which I caught a fragment of understanding. That was the sort of thing that lingered and returned to my consciousness as I roamed the hills in solitude.

Fear, manifesting as self-doubt, proceeded from my seemingly inborn notion of a hostile world. One very memorable instance epitomized that phenomenon: the 4-H Club's annual public speaking competition. For weeks I worked at writing my speech, which had to do with a particular type of canoe used by the West Coast natives of North America. I memorized the words and proudly practiced the delivery with my parents, without giving much thought to the conditions surrounding its actual presentation. As we headed toward town, I felt a mild anxiety that increased with each mile, but it was not stifling even when we arrived. In the hall I became still more frightened and, after we had been seated awhile, I began to tremble inside and my hands grew sweaty. As my time approached, my limbs became numb and my head felt like it was gripped by a vice. On the stage, my legs shook violently and it seemed that my head and mouth were shaking, too.

I don't know if I repeated all the words, or if anyone could hear them beyond the distraction of my quaking shuddering body. Most everyone said I had done well except Mary Ann, a school friend who was a year older than me and with whom I was infatuated. I felt safe with her because we had shared moments of closeness, even brushing our cheeks together once while practicing for a Christmas concert, and she always greeted me with a warm smile. She said, "You seemed really nervous."

I nodded my head in voiceless agreement, thinking 'nervousness' a very desirable impression. I hoped she suspected nothing of my terrified reality, and the absurd nature of my tremendous fear. Why was I like that?

It was the bare absurdity of it all that I struggled with in the days to come. Thankfully, there were no neighbors and no roads for twenty miles south and west of our farm, just the vast open prairie. I needed to lose myself in the solitude and the security I experienced under the boundless sky. I needed the stillness of the earth and the silence.

The awakening of sexuality provided solace, an avenue of escape through masturbation. I sensed from the beginning that it was wrong, but made no effort to stop. I only had to hide the fact, which increased my sense of separation. One day my mother glanced at me oddly and I perceived shame in her eyes, as though she knew what I was doing. I didn't connect masturbation with male-female bonding, because sex was dirty and I found the very idea repulsive, people engaging in an act that I had observed among animals. I refused to allow carnal images of my parents to form in my mind. I remember riding along on my horse and entertaining myself with fairy-tale images in which Princess Anne and I had fallen in love. I vowed that I would never impose upon her a demand for sex. I felt the same way about my pretty little friend, Mary Ann. My mother's Victorian reserve and seeming denial of sexuality had some influence perhaps, as my visions of romance took shape within this sphere of innocence. Masturbation remained outside that sphere.

I believe I was probably born with mental circuitry that included the assumption of innocence, and that knew no shame. How and when could I have begun to imagine that I had any unacceptable defects? Probably the bed-wetting cracked the veneer. Certainly, sexual urges and masturbation were messy unsettling phenomena that disturbed my sense of purity. As life became more difficult and complex, those sources of distress were joined by others and I became increasingly stymied by a sense of shameful inequality. The ground I stood on lost its firmness.

My mother used shame as a weapon to counteract my father's verbal and emotional bullying. When my parents were struggling with each other, the role of 'victim' was a common and effective strategy for both. But the same ploy had no potential to work for me because, consistent with some vague formula, I deserved what came to me. Even though I wandered innocently and confidently into situations, my father invariably launched a devastating pre-emptive undermining of my self-worth. At the end of a day of working on the farm, for example, when I returned to the house with a feeling of accomplishment and expected to experience a special partnership with my dad, I often discovered before long that I had committed some unforgivable error, some brainless omission, or made a mindlessly stupid decision. Criticism ran rampant and I could do nothing right, nothing met with more than minimal acceptance, nothing was ever received with enthusiasm, praise or gratitude. My naturally innocent and optimistic state of mind was smashed – not punctured with a sharp stab, but ground to a pulp. His most persistent, intense and relentless attacks took place at the supper table, and there were nights when a growing boy, with a ravenous appetite born of a long physical day, abandoned a partially eaten meal and ran to his room with tears of shattered pride streaming down his cheeks.

My conscious awareness escaped to another plane, blotting out as effectively as possible searing flashes of that which could not be tolerated as reality: the sorry faces of my sisters, little brother and mother. What can you do when all self-esteem has been sucked out of you by the one you hoped to impress, when the deflation goes so deep that nothing is left? How does some fucking moral code, or a sense of shame, stack up against the only soothing connection possible and remaining, a sexual association with one's self? It was a stroke of mercy that there wasn't a mirror in my room forcing me to witness my own pathetic reflection. The spirit of innocence that had surrounded my dreams was replaced by something like casual irrelevance. I concluded that it must all be irrelevant, because if I took it seriously I would die. If I had no escape to another plane of existence, I would never stop crying or screaming or punching the God-damned walls. I had to crawl inside myself, into my own mind and being, spinning my own emotional cocoon and closing out the images others must have formed of me. As innocence, and the simple right to feel okay, went down the drain, fierce hatred replaced them: hatred for my father, certainly, but hatred for God, too, by extension in some way. I was the victim of betrayal, indirectly oppressed by some duplicitous trickster that permitted my father to treat me as he did. It seemed I was without defenses in a spiteful and unsympathetic universe.

Still, the hope of receiving love, encouragement and acceptance from my dad was not completely extinguished. My resentment toward him intensified and deepened and I saw him as an obstinate, unreasonable, and malicious son-of-a-bitch. But I experienced less personal injury from his cruel nature. He was, after all, mean with my siblings as well, sometimes criticizing and picking away at our friends from school, and when he frustrated our plans to visit cousins at Christmas, for example, he punished everyone, including my mother.

I knew my mother loved me, as far as that went, but I couldn't talk to her about the inner, intimate stuff. I couldn't imagine penetrating the walls of relative purity that no doubt shielded her comprehension. I perceived my relationship with my mother as one of general acceptance, not as a forum for sharing emotional pain. Consequently, my emotional world was turned completely inward. The result was an ever-hardening sense of being isolated and unique. I learned to live two separate lives. To the outside world I was bold, victorious, self-confident, and arrogant. Inside, I held on desperately against discovery. I craved affirming gestures and recognition. When in the presence of adults, from the fuel deliveryman to my teachers, uncles and neighbors, I craved acknowledgement of my existence and a friendly smile. I grasped desperately for others to mirror my acceptability. That need pre-empted everything else, to the degree that I could never initiate a greeting, or even be the first to smile, for fear of the awful possibility that people had changed their mind about me. I felt I couldn't live up to the image I wished them to have of me, certainly not based on my secret reality, and I lived with an unceasing anxiety that they sensed that.

Deep in my heart, I regarded my present reality as only temporary and I maintained an attitude of stern audacity and defiance. In a special compartment that was completely divorced from my existing circumstances, in a kind of futuristic apparition, I envisioned the day when a currently inaccessible God, a universal force of fairness and retribution, would set things right. I intuitively knew there would be a link to some unknown power that would transport me beyond this mundane life of unremitting suffering. I was confident of being placed, eventually, in a position of unqualified superiority.

I therefore existed on three levels: my private and personal world, that inner and safe but distasteful reality that I retreated to; my struggling relationship with the outside world, where I endured persistent hardship and sought fleeting fragments of approval; and the third, a misty vision in which I would someday rise above these other two, aloof and exalted, far above and beyond the miserable putrid status quo.

Chapter 3

Female sexuality entered my awareness gradually. My first clue came from a young female schoolteacher who, after responding to an invitation for dinner at the farm, followed me out to look at my tree house. I couldn't help noticing, as she squatted in the corner of the cramped and shaky structure, that she wore no underwear beneath her skirt. The bushy patch between her legs seemed pronounced at close range and, in the center beyond the curly hair, it appeared pink and fleshy. That snapshot image lingered in my mind, which subsequently entertained itself with more thoughts about sex. I regretted that I had not taken a more determined look.

Then one day a group of us were walking the three miles home from school and we stopped at the neighbor's yard. It was a girl my age who initiated the idea that we have a look at the differences between boys and girls. First, her brothers unveiled their contribution and then she and her sister pulled their pants down. I thought it was very interesting indeed, but did not have the courage to participate in the demonstration. Fear gripped me, possibly the awful embarrassment of bed-wetting combined with the more recent dark aspect of masturbation. I sensed that, had I joined in, a bit of my terrible loneliness might have been dissolved. I noticed with considerable envy that the whole event seemed rather ordinary for them, without much mystery or inhibition. As I walked on alone however (because ours was the last farmyard on the road) I rationalized my decision to remain aloof. I simply placed the others, and that kind of base behavior, beneath my superior sense of morality.

But that rationalization didn't hold. I began to detest my assumption of innocence. The very idea brought with it antipathy and contempt; that someone would think there was nothing wrong with them infuriated me. Evil lurked in everyone and they would not admit it. For the most part, evil, as I perceived it, was sexual desire. Sexual desire lurked in everyone, but they denied it. I began to reason in my private moments that there may be more truth and authenticity in depravity than in respectability. I felt motivated to expose the fallacy of innocence and to destroy it.

After I graduated from eighth grade at fourteen years of age, I started catching a bus each day to attend a larger high school in a town fifteen miles from the farm. With that change, my social insecurity quickly became a stifling hurdle. The year began with humiliating and sometimes abusive initiation ceremonies that, in my view, were staged for the entertainment of everyone but the new victims. From the beginning two larger boys, who were in grade twelve at the time, chose me as their preferred target for bullying. With his stooge buddy restraining me, Rod Brown would repeatedly beat my shoulder with one knuckle protruding from his fist, zeroing in on a point which numbed and pained my whole arm. It became effectively paralyzed as I suppressed the desperate impulse to cry out in helpless anguish. I staggered in a kind of vertigo, fighting the nauseating weakness that enveloped me, as I rejoined the school population after those attacks, sometimes returning to a classroom after being cornered in the men's room. I didn't possess the courage or have the predisposition to lash out in my defense, perhaps because I had been accustomed to accepting abuse at home without recourse. Nor did I have the common sense to report the activity to my parents, grandmother or teachers, because I dreaded the implicit disclosure of my cowardice. Only through some flickering but indomitable spirit deep within me, was I able to hang on; and the conviction that all this was only temporary, not my reality. At the same time, within the solitary confines of my bus seat on the journeys home, I vaguely longed for some sort of merciful rescue by something unseen, but that ray of hope grew continually dimmer.

This was the time of the horrific incident administered by the teacher, Mr. Benson, in my ninth grade literature class, coinciding with the assassination of President Kennedy. My botched presentation, the humiliation of crying in front of the class, and the consequent conviction that my social standing had been destroyed took me to the brink. During the weekend that followed that event, because I was completely unsuccessful at suppressing the bitter reality of it, unable to look upon it as an isolated experience, the outcome of my deliberations was a pivotal adjustment in my attitude. I began to view the world, and my position in it, as though I had nothing more to lose.

Monday mornings began with basketball practice, which I usually looked forward to, but had dreaded all the way to school that day because I knew Mr. Benson was filling in for our regular coach. As we changed in the locker room off the school's new gymnasium, I secluded myself in the remotest corner I could find, hoping to avoid any taunting comments concerning last Friday's hideous display.

After some warm-up exercises, we were divided into opposing teams for a practice game. Benson, who was on the side opposite mine, was taller than everyone else on the court and more practiced at the sport as well, but I knew that wouldn't stand in the way of his being an aggressive and even mean opponent. I had always despised his haughty existence; today I hated him. He had the ball and was dribbling across the centerline, full speed, probably intending to go all the way just to show us that we couldn't stop him. He glared at me intimidatingly as I moved in to interrupt his advance. While deftly dodging to avoid a direct collision, he threw a bony elbow toward my head. Governed entirely by reckless abandon, I simultaneously dodged his elbow and stuck my foot out to trip him. I was amazed and startled at the effect. His arms stretched ahead of him as he sprawled into our end zone, his knees and

36

elbows seemed to rattle against the hardwood floor, and he skidded to a stop on his side, groaning.

My shock turned to fear of his physical reprisal as he rose to his feet. The glare in his eyes intensified. I stood my ground as he rushed toward me with his fist drawn fully back. I would definitely lose a fistfight, given his long reach, but it would be social suicide to run.

"You son-of-a-bitch…" he spit through his rage, with little distance left between us.

"Leave him alone, asshole," big Dwight drawled without ceremony as he threw his sinewy ranch-hand's arm across Benson's chest. The teacher stopped abruptly and stood looking into the eyes of a young man who outweighed him by fifty pounds, one who could cause serious injury in a scrap, and would without hesitation.

We went back to playing basketball for the balance of the allotted time. At the end of the day, as we were getting on the school bus, I finally found an opportunity to thank Dwight for his intervention.

"He'd have killed me." I admitted the uneasiness that had been floating to the surface all day.

"That bastard deserved what you did to him," he chuckled.

I felt the ecstasy of retribution, through and through. I believed I had restored some of my lost dignity, and I reveled secretly at the proof of Dwight being on my side.

Rod Brown and his cohort seemed to adjust their tactics after that day as well. Bullies are really cowards, if only their victims knew it, and to stay clear of trouble personally, they began deliberately stirring up animosity between others, entertaining themselves with the ensuing fights they had perpetrated.

My thought-life, while I was out walking or riding in solitude where I had the space to create a more equitable world, was preoccupied with those events. Rod Brown caused a lot of physical pain for me, but more difficult to deal with was the humiliation I endured. I brooded and fantasized that, launched from beneath the table, my fist had broken his nose; I came up from behind him and crushed his shoulder with a baseball bat; I laid in wait and shot him in the kneecap or thigh with my semi-automatic .22 rifle, and then tormented him further, prolonging his agony. Punishment under the law discouraged me from converting that satisfying mental activity into gratifying physical reality. Meanwhile, an attitude of poisoned antagonism became embedded in my character.

I think my father sensed that I was having trouble fitting in at the new school when he encouraged me to sign up for fourteen-and-under hockey. I have no doubt his intentions were entirely good. He must have known it was an onerous commitment: frequent practices in town fourteen miles away, games out of town when he accepted a turn at transporting members of the team, and the expense of equipment. I had not grown up wearing skates, as many of the town-kids had, and I found the practices brutal. It seemed the coach pushed me especially hard, perhaps with the hope that I could catch up, but his assistant, Rod Brown, seemed to find pleasure in my poor performance. Some games I did not get on the ice at all and I sat on the bench regretting that my father's efforts to help me were being disappointed. One night on the way home he expressed his frustration with volunteering when I was not even allowed to play. He was kind about it, seeming to empathize with my position, and I felt bad that he had not been rewarded for his willingness to help out. He suggested that perhaps we should drop out and I agreed. As much as I had longed to be a part of it, I knew I couldn't and welcomed the end of a doomed experiment.

It was during the summer holiday following my first year of high school that a visiting cousin, a year younger than me, invited me to inspect and touch her vagina. It was infinitely more appealing than the teacher's bushy gash, with its little pink button and still sparse population of bristly black hairs. That left me with a heightened interest in a shadowy world. I feared my reaction wasn't normal because I didn't develop a powerful instinctive urge to stick my penis into one of those things, as preoccupying as the image was. I definitely wanted to touch it again, and her firm budding breasts, too, and she didn't have an objection to that, sometimes pretending to be asleep while making herself available.

Unfortunately, the lack of follow-through to a natural conclusion may have contributed to an extremely distressing incident I had after school started again: a classmate came round to my grandma's house when I was there alone, and, after kissing me, laid back on the bed while pulling me down on top of her. As much as I would have liked to do it that time, I had no reaction, not even the hint of an erection. I felt numb with vague anxiety and confusion. It felt good to rub against her and I thought of erections I'd experienced at other times, inconveniently while sitting at my desk in the classroom, for example. I did not know what was wrong and interpreted the problem as yet another defective aspect of my existence. I continued to masturbate while imagining that I was doing it with a girl, hoping to change the course of things.

Otherwise, circumstances improved a lot by the time I entered my second year of high school. Rod Brown, after taking six years to pass four grades, had finally graduated. Because I had dropped out of hockey, I was eligible to join the school basketball team where, in spite of the fact that I was five feet eight inches tall, I found it much easier to fit in and make some good friends. The team consisted mostly of others who were bussed to the school, as I was, from the country and several outlying villages. I occasionally looked on with envy and resentment as others played baseball, but they were the same exclusive clique of guys from town that played hockey, so I kept my distance.

On two completely separate and exceptionally memorable occasions, I received invitations from classmates to join them and their brothers for Saturday night outings. Both included several guys in my age group and their older brother who drove the car. In the first instance we travelled fifty miles to the nearest city to see a movie, then went to the new A&W drive-in afterwards for hamburgers and root beer. On the second occasion we spent a day at the annual fair and rodeo. Each time,

I remember feeling enormously grateful to be invited along because both families were in a social status above that of my own. One owned the immense ranch that shared a fence-line with us and the other operated a very large grain farm. But they were not boastful in the least and included me as an equal in every aspect, even expressing an interest in my family and our farm, however inferior it was to theirs.

I was a little nervous, wondering if they were about to make some embarrassing comparisons, so I kept my answers to their enquiries very brief. At the same time, I searched in the seemingly stultified void of my mind for meaningful comments to make and questions to ask of them, desperately convinced that I should have more to say. Trying to contribute as much as possible, I smiled and pretended to keep up with the conversation. But it seemed I was out of tune with the topics, not up to speed, and I did not feel that I was truly a part of things.

Those were by no means the only times my insecurity manifested itself in suffocating shyness. It happened frequently when an adult greeted me and asked a friendly question, except in the case of our closest neighbors and Old Tom who was often around the farm and had a special way of making kids feel warm and accepted. This time though, it felt like I had failed a test, that they must have considered me rather slow, even mentally impaired. The struggle I had with fitting in baffled me. I had consistently achieved the highest marks in my small elementary school class, typically scoring one hundred percent in math and geometry tests. The guys I travelled with those nights must have remembered that I had repeatedly won first prize in 4-H judging competitions and got the highest marks on the written examinations for knowledge of the beef industry, the only tests of intelligence on achievement days. In the days that followed, however, even though I gratefully counted the excursions as forays into a higher plane of existence, as a precious step up the societal ladder, I had to suppress nauseating images of my social ineptitude. Once again, in order to escape the unpalatable present, I had to look to the future and trust that my reality was yet to be.

My family's attendance at church was mostly irregular and I was never thrilled with the monotonous event. Even so, the fact that I fainted and fell back into the pew on several consecutive Sundays as the congregation stood collectively to sing was not a premeditated strategy. I had never lost consciousness otherwise, but I most certainly suffered severe dizziness on those occasions, intense enough to be disconcerting for everyone near me. With little resistance from my parents I was granted a reprieve and, from then on, while the rest of the family entered the little white church, I trundled off to the pool hall. I knew that's where I would catch up with a new acquaintance named Darren. He and his family had only recently moved there from the city, because his father had taken a job as chief administrator in the town office. Darren was a clever, good looking guy with an animated smile, a year younger than I was but infinitely more advanced in the art of life, and I was never entirely sure I could trust him. But I didn't have an abundance of friends, which is why I tolerated the regular loss of a few dollars playing small-stakes pool with him. We had a good time together and he often spent the money on cokes for us anyway. Besides, it was the cost of acquiring a vital skill, and I was thrilled by the grown-up atmosphere of the old billiards parlor.

When much younger, I had often frequented the same establishment with my father, a combined pool hall and barber shop as the twirling red, white, and blue cone on the corner of the building still indicated, because that's where we went to get our hair cut. It had seemed then that we were entering a magical and mysterious place, because only men were allowed to enter and the opaque glass in the large front window blocked the view from the street. There was a long glass counter framed with varnished oak to the right of the entrance. Beyond it, the owner side-stepped and snipped his way around his elaborate adjustable chrome and leather barber's chair that always made me feel so small, but never vulnerable. His clippers, scissors,

41

and razors were lined up at the base of a mirror which took up the whole wall behind him. The fragrances of shaving soap, hair tonic, and aftershave permeated the air of his enclave. He had an assistant, too, a paraplegic man whose squeaky voice made him difficult to understand, but who was so friendly and welcoming that all the men obviously loved him.

The lighting, down the length of the huge room, was dim, becoming spectral in the far reaches. Individually shaded bulbs hung low over a half dozen large billiard tables, while cigar and pipe smoke hung thick as a cloud above the glow. The smell was sweet, agelessly masculine and exquisite. The floorboards creaked in muffled tones as pool players prowled along the perimeters of the tables in search of the perfect shot, while onlookers kept their voices low in quiet reverence for their sanctuary. Only the distinct smack of cue balls making contact with their targets rose noticeably above the low hum of the electric lights. Occasionally one of men acknowledged me, in passing, and made a chuckling comment about how I was growing. I felt safe there. You just had to smile and be quiet; it was not a kids' place and no one expected anything of you. That was back in the days of innocence, but it still felt as homey as it ever had.

I started smoking cigarettes in that year, too, whenever the opportunity arose, and it soon became an obsession that influenced the planning of my days. We were too young to smoke in the pool room, but Darren and I smoked behind the school during breaks and after school when I stayed in town with my grandmother, which I did more often as the year went on. When home at the farm, I began to 'go for walks' in the evening, in pitch darkness except for a brilliant umbrella of stars, with the sole purpose of having a cigarette.

It was during one of those before-bedtime strolls that I passed by the un-curtained window of my sisters' bedroom, just as they were both completely undressed from the waist up. It was a tantalizing glimpse that caused an obsessive preoccupation and a monumental struggle to resist the temptation to catch a repeat performance. Fear of embarrassment, should my parents catch me in the act, was the sole deterrent and the reason I chose a different route in the future. I eventually started smoking in my bedroom with the door closed, as though my non-smoking mother remained oblivious. Neither of my parents ever said anything about it and I didn't care that much if they were aware of it or not.

Another landmark event took place when I turned sixteen and got a driver's license. I borrowed the old farm truck for the day and, to celebrate the occasion, Darren and I managed to purchase a case of beer through the local bootlegger. We headed directly for a secluded, abandoned farmyard to do some serious drinking. After a bottle or two, the incredible effect of the alcohol set in and we began laughing hysterically. All the weighty inhibitions I had labored under for so long suddenly vanished and I felt free at last. It was a very warm day and before I finished the third beer I became sick and threw up. But I felt all right shortly after that and we drank some more. The laughter soon returned and even getting sick seemed hilarious. Shortly after the beer was gone, I drove Darren home and left for the farm. I stopped the truck and vomited again on the way. No one else was home and I went straight to my room where I passed out immediately. I slept right through and still felt a bit groggy when I awoke in the morning, but my thoughts quickly settled on the amazing experience I'd had. The harsh physical effects were overshadowed completely by the longing I had to again experience the mental and emotional relief, the sense of ease and comfort that had prevailed.

Although he had left the school at the end of my first year, Rod Brown continued to manipulate others into fighting with me and a few of my friends. Promoting a sort of low-intensity gang warfare, he perpetrated lies and stirred up bitterness between kids from the town and those from out-of-town, or used his 'big guy' influence to encourage other forms of harassment, such as happened the afternoon I parked my dad's car in front of the local café while I went in to get drinks for my date and me.

My girlfriend remained in the car, which I had carefully washed and given an extra shine for the occasion after wrangling it from my father with great difficulty. As I opened the door to exit the café, I was filled with gut-wrenching horror. Brown had persuaded Greg, a fellow in my class, to smear a thick streak of mud across the windshield and he was stooping for another handful. In a rage, I let the drinks fall to the ground and threw myself at my newest antagonist. I punched frantically at his face until he grabbed me and we fell down wrestling, groveling in the muddy street, each of us trying ineffectively to land blows to the other's head, until a mature member of the community came along and broke it up. Brown sat smirking in his car with his cronies, enjoying the show he had created. It took a lot to overcome my fear and it was very much contrary to my inner nature, but I clashed repeatedly with my contemporaries, just to defend myself or express outrage over some perpetrated act like that. Though I dreaded each encounter and never once believed afterwards that I had fought a good fight, there was immense self-satisfaction in knowing that I had fought back.

At the same time, the curse of impotence continued to frustrate my hopes in another department. Necking in the back seats of cars, when girls made it obvious they were willing to go much further, had resulted in demoralizing awkwardness. I think the self-loathing at the time, and the devastating fact that the girls moved on to other guys pretty quickly, helped to refine my repressing of intolerable reality. It all seemed so impossibly stupid and dismal. That's how I felt when one of them invited me to a dance and then shunned me for someone else after I had borrowed my dad's car and driven fifty miles to meet her. Of course, I pretended all was well and tried to project a macho exterior to the only people who might have helped me through it, my parents, when I got back home earlier than expected. Deep inside, I shed angry tears of despair. A few months later my grandmother, after confirming that I knew of that particular girl, reported that she had been diagnosed with leukemia and was not expected to live. Not long after that, I received the news of her death as evidence that there may at least be a God of retribution.

I became separated from the accepted social and cultural norms of my small community and invented a world in which I could live comfortably by myself. I developed contempt for those things I thought others must have been relying upon for a good life, because I couldn't fit into their world. A companion for my angry contempt was increasing arrogance. I rebelled against the traditional values of society, began to cast them off, and no longer measured my actions against them. I began to view laws and other social guidelines as applicable to all the dull and unimaginative creatures that couldn't see the ugly reality around them. Just as I had concluded regarding innocence, I saw only naivety and stupidity at the base of it. I, the new master of my destiny, would leave all those restrictions behind and seek my own unrestrained experience of reality. In that way, I began compensating for debilitating insecurity (an inferiority complex, I suppose) by smothering it with a bitter and unprincipled ego, a sort of superimposed superiority that was tainted by a comforting undercurrent of vindication.

Sadly, it was Mary Ann, my erstwhile little friend, who became the first victim of this new attitude. I had not seen much of her in the intervening years because she did not attend high school after eighth grade. That was common among the majority of our neighbors, who persisted with a peasant-like belief that higher education wasn't of much value to a farmer, even less so for a farmer's wife. Our family was different in that regard because my mother had graduated from a teachers' college and taught school for a few years. She took our education very seriously, a fact for which I have always been thankful.

It was a Halloween night and I had driven my sisters and some of the neighbor kids into town. It was natural that Mary Ann and I were drawn toward each other. I was truly delighted to see her again. Later in the evening we were alone in the car together. I knew it was unlikely she had had anything to do with men, only travelling around with her parents and having a

45

strictly rural exposure. Despite my many frustrations, I knew I had infinitely more experience with romance and sexual matters. I kissed her and she responded with shock rather than enthusiasm. In line with my new insight into reality, I responded with contempt for her naivety rather than respect for her innocence. At the same time, I decided I needed to resort to more finesse, if I were to make anything of the situation – to gain any practical experience, that is. Looking at things that way, her being naïve was actually a plus because it placed me in control, and I seemed to instinctively possess a brazen aptitude for capitalizing on such circumstances. That aptitude was further enhanced by a talent for subtle intimidation, resulting from complete mental elimination of any and all options contrary to my will.

I had first tested my tactics on the toboggan hill with my sisters when I was nine years old. Reacting to a self-centered craving to make my own mark in freshly fallen snow on a trackless slope, I suggested I would take the first run alone to test it out for their safety. Not very sophisticated, but it seems to have launched me on a course of management through manipulation nonetheless.

After Mary Ann and I talked a little while, I asked if I could hug her. She said that would be all right and demonstrated less resistance. I kissed her again and her lips kissed back a little that time. As we experimented with variations of those exercises, I managed to put my hand over one of her quite substantial breasts. Then I managed to get under her clothes and make direct contact with them. I wasn't feeling romantic or aroused really, although I liked touching her, and I had no thought that we would ever be a couple. In the larger scheme of things, I had already advanced to a higher social stratum. I was mostly motivated by the notion of practice, the idea that it would be useful on future occasions. Before long, she suggested we should leave to find the others, which we did. The pleasant mutual attraction that had been so precious to me in the midst of a lonely childhood seemed to have been tainted. On balance, I didn't regret it because I believed I had achieved a measure of proficiency in an arena that was a source of embarrassment and desperation. The only cost was recurring spasms of something akin to disgrace.

I had been introduced to the sport of curling during my first year in high school. I liked it and did it often enough to become good at it, partly because the games were always after school or in the evening and it had provided a good reason to stay in town with my grandmother. By grade twelve I was acting as the skip of a team that represented the school in district playoffs. I was proud to be the leader and to feel the loyalty of my three team members. We won our first two games and advanced to the semi-finals. Because the bonspiel was held in another town, we had hotel rooms for the night. Darren was my roommate and, in line with our newly established priority, he had managed to purchase some wine from the bootlegger. Being a novice drinker, I ignored the fact that our third game was scheduled for the evening and went along with Darren's suggestion that we have a few sips. Right from the beginning, because of the irresistible benefits, I had no desire or inclination to stop drinking once I'd begun. The delayed effect of the wine ensured that I was quite drunk by game-time and we proceeded to lose badly because of it. I regretted the outcome and felt ashamed in the presence of my teammates the next day, but it did nothing to reduce my enthusiasm for alcohol. I merely decided I would be more careful in the future.

My use of the family car resulted in frequent arguments with my father, from whom it was nearly impossible to get a straight answer. Eventually, to avoid impossible negotiations as the weekend approached, I began to get commitments from him early in the week: if I worked on the farm at certain jobs that needed doing, he agreed to let me have the car for the coming Saturday night. He was only ever as definite as was required to satisfy my harping distrust and to get the work done. As the week progressed, my reminders of our agreement brought vaguer and vaguer replies. At week's end, when the work was done, I confronted the mushy hurdles he invariably constructed with utter disbelief. Attempts to gain clarity were exasperating to the point of insanity, as he slipped from side to side with fresh and creative objections. Those skirmishes were always eventually expanded to include my mother, who inevitably took my side, and together we could corner him sufficiently to squeeze out permission. When he did relinquish his grip, it was always with undisguised reluctance accompanied by some degrading comment that lingered excruciatingly while I drove away with tears of hatred and betrayal in my eyes. Perhaps he harbored forebodings related to my drinking which generated a heightened concern for his property. Certainly, his infuriating duplicity undermined any natural concern I had for it.

In the summer following my eleventh school year, I went to work for a bachelor uncle, my mother's oldest brother, on his farm. As well as receiving my first direct monetary compensation, I was rewarded over and over again with the first compliments I'd ever received for jobs well done. Some aspect of my relationship with my father came up one day, not that I divulged very much, and my uncle said, with surprising bitterness in his voice, "He is a little man!" I didn't like hearing him say that, but I concluded there might be some truth in his words as I thought about it later.

My father remained an enigma to me, dropping occasional crumbs of hope, like the time I borrowed my uncle's pick-up and met the rest of my family for a picnic on a pleasant Sunday afternoon. I hadn't been there five minutes when my father casually offered me a cigarette, as though he and I had smoked together for years. I declined the offer in a state of well-disguised shock but regretted declining it later. It might have cracked the ice that had been getting thicker and thicker between us.

I was puzzled another time, too, when I got up quite late after using the car the night before, only to hear from my mother that one of the tires was flat and my father was changing it at that very moment. I panicked when I remembered that I had left a bottle of whiskey in the trunk and went out immediately with the objective of damage control. My hope that it was somehow hidden from his view was in vain. He was putting the jack away and had to lean right over the bottle of bright amber liquid to do so. I said nothing, waiting. In a perfectly calm voice, this time as though we had been drinking buddies for years, he said, "You had better not let your mother see that." Those surprising events suggested he was willing to treat me as an equal. I sometimes wondered if the problems and misunderstandings that came between him and I weren't primarily because he was a poorer communicator than me.

The good grades I had achieved in my first eight years of school had dropped to depressing levels during my first three years in high school. My mother had tried helping to little avail and in the first months of grade twelve, instead of attending classes, I hunted geese in the mornings and sharp-tailed grouse in the afternoons with my friend Darren. We had both adopted the attitude that smoking, drinking, hunting, and chasing after girls were more important than school. Darren was a year younger than me, with his graduation nearly two years away, and his future was not looming before him as immediately as mine. That is essentially the way Mr. Rowling, the new school principle, approached the subject when I finally turned up for classes one day and he invited me into his office.

My mother had described Rowling as a wonderful man and she believed we were very fortunate have him around, that he would bring positive new direction to the school. Only slightly taller than I was, with wavy but thinning light brown hair that gave way to grey at the temples, and a nicely cut beige suit that conformed perfectly with his trim build, Mr. Rowland seemed easily in a class above other men I'd known. His amiable demeanor and lack of pretense put me at ease immediately, and I was even further relieved as I realized his intentions were not coercive or admonishing. Instead, there was solemn purpose in his voice, a weighty pragmatism that instilled within me a sense that I was being spoken to as an equal, as though he and I had something in common and were engaged in a mature discussion of matters that had consequence.

With utmost sincerity in his blue-green eyes, Mr. Rowling looked at me directly and said, "I don't know what it is you would like to do with your life, but you are quite capable of choosing any career that appeals to you. You are a very bright young man and could easily qualify for university if you were determined to do so. Have you thought about that?"

Suddenly embarrassed by my lack of effort and the fact that my marks were all in the fifties and sixties, I admitted sheepishly that I had not given it any thought.

"Do you think you would be happy spending the rest of your life in this town?" he asked with genuine concern. Then, probably detecting the answer to his question in the forlorn expression that reflected my self-searching, he added, "A university degree would open untold doors for you and I personally hope you will consider the prospect."

With that, the brief meeting ended, but his genuine regard for my wellbeing lingered and awakened something within me. There were the efforts my mother had made as well, and several instances when my grandmother had commented on my moving on to something better someday. It had not occurred to me before that those around me were quite concerned. I concluded they were right and quickly adopted a new vision for myself. Almost all my efforts were suddenly directed toward schoolwork and, by Christmas, things were looking better. I carried this new priority into the next five months and focused on little else, so that, by the end of the spring term, I had an 'A' average.

I got past my high school graduation by complying with tradition and choosing an escort for the ceremonies, a girl I didn't care much about. After we had been drinking for a few hours, we sneaked off to the privacy of the back seat of the car. Before long she was expressing further interest in me by frantically rubbing her pubic area against my leg. Dreading another embarrassing situation and having no intention of admitting my infuriating impotency, I mumbled that I loved her too much to have sex with her. Some women, I was reasonably sure, could be expected to place more importance upon expressions of love than they would upon sexual satisfaction. But I sensed this lady shared a lack of interest in our combined future that was comparable to my own and would never count herself among that number. Fortunately, more partying was an acceptable alternative to both of us.

Chapter 4

My application to attend university in the fall had been mercifully accepted and, for the summer, I got a construction a job in a different town. While there, I met Jo-Anne. Before long I was explaining how I loved her too much to have sex with her, then leaving after an evening together and feeling anxious that she would be forced to dump me. I didn't want that, because I really did like her a lot, like a really close friend. I'd gotten to know her parents as well, and I felt very much at home with them, as though I truly belonged in a family for the first time. Maybe she actually believed me.

Jo-Anne's father was a big reason for my feeling welcome in their home. Edwin drank a lot and always invited me to drink with him. I admired the fact that he was a World War II veteran who had served as a navigator on Lancaster bombers and flew many missions with the Royal Air Force Bomber Command. He often recounted his four years in England with immense fondness when he was drinking, including the revelry and the girlfriends that were a natural component of a precarious existence, as though it was an aspect of his life that had rendered all the balance of it mundane. Although he treated me like his best friend, he was sometimes a little unfair to Jo-Anne's mother, Aldi, who I liked a lot as well. But I considered their relationship none of my business.

I left for college in the fall and only saw Jo-Anne a few times through the school year, during Christmas and Easter breaks, for example, but we remained committed to each other. While away at university my drinking accelerated, with new pals who were enthusiastic partiers, and I had Edwin to get into the beer with when visiting Jo-Anne. It felt like I was doing a good job of growing up. The summer found me working near home again and we picked up where we left off, spending all available time together and still not having sex, a source of frustration that separated me from life as I believed it ought to be. I had learned to repress things that were humiliating, however, and that's what I did, most of the time.

Then one day it happened. My penis wasn't completely erect and it probably didn't take more than five seconds, but I could tell that she felt loved and I felt like I'd been freed from a life sentence for which I'd been wrongly convicted. I took her home later that night because I had to work the next day. I woke up the following morning and 'choked the old chicken' once more, in a private celebration of my freedom. Then we started doing it everywhere, including standing up one night as I dropped her off at her parent's house. In the fall, she decided to get a job and rent a room in a house near the college. That worked really well until her prudish landlady evicted her one day, for having a boy around too often, and she decided to move to another city where she had the opportunity to study drafting. She had substantial talent for drawing and it made good sense that she should further her education.

Though I felt a little guilty admitting it, her leaving was liberating, a chance to really spread my wings, and I didn't miss having her around for long. But I did have a lot of sexual energy and it propelled me in ways that sometimes surprised me. I began searching out a darker side of life, almost certainly a rebellion against the innocence projected by my aloof Victorian mother, innocence I condemned as falsely claimed by anyone other than her. I went to strip bars, prowled neighborhoods where welfare, alcohol, and drugs dragged people down, and hung around the red-light district. There was something deeply intriguing, even mentally freeing, about these shadowy, gritty, sluttish hinterlands of society. Certainly, I intended remaining anonymous, as much as possible completely invisible, but inside I enjoyed immense relief from a long-suffered sense of inferiority. I didn't view those people as lesser beings, but rather as a reflection of the darker side of all beings, that part of human existence which I believed most people suppressed and denied to the rest of the world. They mirrored the tarnished and foreboding aspect of my character I had never been able to share with anyone because I feared I was different. Here was some basic honesty at last and I experienced a comforting kinship as I witnessed the undisguised suffering and degradation. There remained only one complicating thread, running back through my miserable childhood and adolescent years, a tiny residual of my nearly eradicated notion of God. I made a conscious decision, with the purposefully shallow conclusion that, if there was in fact a God, He seemed to serve only one function: that of waiting for something enjoyable to develop and then putting a damper on it. I had no further use of the concept. I would henceforth be looking out for myself.

That was more or less the time that I began actively living two quite distinct lives, slipping back and forth almost seamlessly. It was easy and quite natural for me to compartmentalize things because of my long history of keeping feelings to myself and presenting outward appearances that had nothing to do with my internal being. While I obsessively craved a cruder side of life, with compelling sexual undertones, and drank to excess several times a week, I attended my university classes regularly, mixed with my fellow students, and was elected to a position of vice-chair on the student body. I thought of the latter as my normal side.

On the side of crudity I ran into Brenda, a slightly emaciated thirty-year-old woman who was a touch unhinged and who engaged in sex with as much feeling as most people experience while washing dishes. To be fair, I don't think my technique was up to rousing her from her lethargy. I knew very well I needed practice, and broadening my experience was the extent of my interest in her. After about two weeks, she claimed she was pregnant and I was the father. I was pretty sure two weeks was insufficient time in which to draw such a conclusion, and I was even more disgustedly convinced that Brenda wouldn't have been able to identify the father with any certainty if she did become pregnant. I told her that and never heard from her again.

It was shortly after my association with Brenda, and immediately following several consecutive nights of prowling around seedier districts of the city, that I became uncomfortable with my behavior, mainly the discrepancy between my compulsive sexual cravings and some hazy perception I had of normalcy. I had been wondering if I was seriously abnormal, perverted even. I knew where the college counseling services office was and my sense of desperation was enough to overcome my usual hesitancy toward discussing anything personal. The receptionist led me to the office of a young man who, on first impressions, put me at ease and made me glad I had come.

In answer to his general question regarding what might be troubling me, I said, "I think I am too sexual. I spend too much time with sex on my mind, looking at women as sexual objects, and seeking out sexual experiences."

His response was, "You are a young man and that is not uncommon. It isn't something you need to worry about."

I thought he was too brief, either because he was uncomfortable with the subject or didn't understand me. I thought he should have asked for some details. I said, "I think I am more obsessed with it than I should be and I wonder about masturbating as well."

"Masturbating is normal," he replied, "and I doubt that you are more obsessed than other young men in your age group." He was evidently not inclined to delve any deeper into it.

I was not satisfied that I had been heard, but I decided that was enough said for now and left. I was satisfied that I had made an effort to address what I considered a problem, but I really thought my preoccupation with sex was beyond normal. Rather than a physical need, it seemed more like a mental craving, but I had not been comfortable trying to explain that. In the end, I construed the visit to the counselor as permission to continue on with even less regard for my own trifling conscience, and angrily converted his lack of concern into further contempt for social boundaries.

When Jo-Anne came to visit me on a weekend, so happily preoccupied with the notion of our reunion, she came face-to-face with a guy who feared that an unconditional welcome might implicitly limit his newly discovered experiential universe. The fear was translated into a nasty approach I developed for maintaining distance. The insecurity I felt regarding my manhood was also a factor and I felt it necessary to convince her of the quality of man she might be taking for granted. Behind the pretense of ruthless honesty, I greatly embellished for her the vast sexual experience I'd amassed since she'd gone away. As I sat across from her in the car and listened to her heartbroken cries of anguish, I concealed my regret and the compassion that welled up inside me. At the same time I was absorbed, in a detached way, with my observation of another person reaching the painful touchstone of my own reality. The punishing emotional damage I had just inflicted I associated with my own past suffering. As from an enormous cesspool of rage and hatred, originating with my sense of victimization in childhood, a vindictive expression of frustration had inadvertently erupted in a ruthless perpetration of misery for another, a person I believed I loved. I had acted in a previously unthinkable fashion, and the true underpinning of it had been some vague, all-inclusive notion of getting even. Unhappily, it was only possible to do that with someone who had become emotionally involved with me, who loved and trusted me.

At last, to soothe her pain and blunt the remorse I felt, I assured her I was sorry and restated my commitment to her. Our emotional connection over the balance of the weekend and the passion of our lovemaking were enriched by an underlying current of making-up. She returned to her studies and I to mine.

When summer came again, I went to see Jo-Anne and secured a job in the town where she lived. We were together nearly every day and decided to be married before I went back for my third year in university. I don't remember giving any thought to long-term commitment or the termination of my experimental promiscuity. Maybe I did it to escape my lifelong feeling of loneliness. Jo-Anne left for home to prepare for the wedding while I stayed and worked a few weeks longer.

The people I worked for, tradesmen engaged in housing construction, were both gracious and generous. They held me in high regard and offered me a long-term position with the promise of a partnership in the firm, but my plans were for soaring higher than that. I declined in favor of further education.

On the way home to join my future wife and attend our wedding, I picked up a couple of enticingly attractive unattached French girls who were hitchhiking across the country. A few hours down the highway, during which time the effervescent pair had virtually captured my senses, they asked me to join them on their journey. Their persistence was hypnotic and my compulsive mind connived to find a way to make it work. I dropped them off and said good-bye at the last possible junction. But I continued to replay, over and over in my mind, an erotic version of a trip that regretfully would not be. The impossibility of explaining such a diversion to Jo-Anne's family, and mine, had stood in the way. After the fact, I saw the decision as a token of my future responsibility. When I finally stood face-to-face with a beaming Jo-Anne, I felt ashamed of giving our important reunion too little prior thought.

The men I'd worked for surprised me and honored me once more by showing up at my wedding. In the midst of that day, just as I had reacted to other aspects of it, I swelled with pride and importance and thought 'look at me now.' I did not possess sufficient maturity to observe and thankfully accept the generous goodwill and kindness people had bestowed upon us. But it was a glorious day in any case, all too short, and I had spent it basking in a wondrous blaze of limelight.

Over the next year, I grew to like living together a lot and we enjoyed a good friendship. We enjoyed a married social life, much of it in the pubs, and it was nice to visit family as a couple. We agreed that the military fellow who lived next door with his attractive wife was a little weird, particularly after he showed me photos of her wearing a skimpy lift-up bra that didn't cover her nipples. Indeed, she was a beauty and I looked at her a little differently from then on. In my heart, however, I felt saddened at his apparent lack of respect for her. I suppose my decent moral reaction was a function of my own contented circumstances. Except for a rather senseless trip west with two male friends in search of summer employment, from which I returned about six weeks later, we carried on without incident into my fourth year at university. Jo-Anne worked while I attended school.

I didn't have a job lined up following graduation in the spring, so I took a Realtor's Association course and sold houses. I discovered I possessed a talent for sales, talking people into things, and in a short time I was doing a surprisingly good business. In spite of my full life, however, I was soon challenged with fidelity to my wife. Propelled by an obsession with sexual experience and quite unimpeded because of the flexibility of my employment, my eyes searched compulsively for opportunities. I came in contact with a religious college girl who did nothing to adorn herself or arouse sexual interest, but she had a guileless submissive quality that invited bold intrusion. I created some story about impotence and told her she could help me through sexual playing. I felt I was challenging her religious resistance to the dark side – to sex, that is. On the first occasion, we fondled each other for a while and she gave me her phone number. I arranged to take her out and we went to a park where we began fondling again. She said she had her period and couldn't have intercourse so she volunteered to give me a hand-job. I couldn't afford to develop things further, being married, and didn't call her again.

Sometime later, I picked up a hitchhiker on the highway near the edge of town, took her for breakfast, and offered her the use of the shower back at the apartment because she smelled of too many days without one. I never forced myself on women and I was always somewhat amazed after having sex with them that they were so willing. I simply didn't bother with much socializing and left little doubt about the nature of my interest. In this case, after she showered and we began a little kissing on the couch, she suggested it would be better if we moved to the bed, which we did. It was thrilling to engage clandestinely like that, no names or complications, just unfettered human connection through the medium of mutual sexual satisfaction. All that remained was a sense of gratification for the benign conqueror. I took her back out to the road, wished her well, and hurried home to wash the sheets and erase any traces of a visitor before Jo-Anne returned from work.

That brief but intensely satisfying incident would reside with my shadow-existence, safely concealed from view to all who would condemn it. I had heard people speak of things they'd done that were far more humiliating or socially unacceptable than things I had done, sometimes boasting with misplaced pride, sometimes laughing at their own peculiarities, and I wished that I could be that open and relaxed. But I couldn't, because I depended upon a too lofty image of respectability, the foundation of which had always been weak and trembling. It was the same inhibition that stood in the way of my joining the neighborly 'show and tell' event at age eleven.

I don't remember the particulars of our married sex life, but we shared a close friendship and had a vibrant time socially with wonderful acquaintances. In a way, we enjoyed growing up together and facing a world of opportunities. I remained restless, however, and reached out in several directions with respect to my future. I was always full of energy and left no stone unturned on many fronts. At some point, I learned that I had the personality of an achiever. I might have been happier, and better able to contribute to the happiness of others, if I'd been given a more passive disposition.

About mid-summer I was accepted into an M.B.A. program at a prestigious Eastern university and we started making plans to relocate. I loaded the car with things we planned to leave with Edwin and Aldi, including houseplants, and headed out on my own. Part way, the highway became the main street of a smaller city and traffic slowed down. I spotted a girl sauntering slowly along the sidewalk as though she had nowhere to go, looking a little forsaken, I thought. Always the opportunist, I edged to the curb and asked if she would like a ride. She got in and we stopped at a drive-in for root beer.

I don't exactly know how the conversation got there, but she said, "You want to ball me, don't you?"

I'd never heard that expression before but asked, "Would that be OK?"

She said without much enthusiasm, "I don't mind."

Once we got around to it, she said she needed to hold onto my penis to stop it going in too far. That definitely intensified the sensation for me but, as I dropped her off, it was with some sadness that I realized she may have agreed to do it because she was desperate for a friend. I didn't want to bully anyone or cause a distressing loss of wellbeing. I could relate to that kind of pain and I truly hoped she wasn't too alone as she disappeared in the rear-view mirror.

I drank too much beer with my father-in-law that night and returned the next day. We bought a tent-trailer to pull behind the big Ford car that Edwin had turned over to us, visited my parents and younger siblings for a few days, and headed off for the two thousand mile journey. I remember leaving the farm, the horses grazing in the pasture beside the road, and thinking I may not see my old mare again. Of course, there was a lot more than that behind the tears that welled in my eyes and the choking feeling in my throat. In elevated moments, I loved the place with its miles of open space, where I had ridden horseback and hunted with so much freedom. I loved my mother, too, and hoped that life would be good to her. I never did get very far along the list though, in thinking fondly of those closest to me. My young brothers admired me and would have liked more of my attention and affection. In that respect, I guess I was like my father, sadly unable to give it. I felt pulled down by the weight of a life that hadn't been much fun so far. To some extent, I had bad luck to blame, but primarily, it seemed,

I just hadn't been much good at it. Perhaps my tears were those of farewell to that phase of my life. After entertaining that thought for a few miles, I was cheered by the prospect of new horizons and the open road.

The drive took us across the open prairie until it gave way to a greater abundance of trees and then thick forest as we neared the Great Lakes. It was all new to us and we delighted in camping each night of the five leisurely days it took to reach our destination. We often stopped to take photographs of the scenery and to enjoy the views. In the evenings we prepared elaborate meals on the grill and ate outdoors in pleasant surroundings. Once we arrived, we parked at a local campground while I registered for the upcoming term and we searched for a place to live. The unfolding of life seemed so simple and our compatibility throughout was remarkable.

Before long we established a new routine in which Jo-Anne worked at the drafting job she'd secured with a professor of engineering and I applied myself to course work, often from early morning to midnight. I was not without the recurrence of strong impulses that resulted in my walking or driving around in a kind of compulsive daze occasionally, through neighborhoods where throngs of young female students lived, for example, and the girl I hired to assist in the typing of papers and reports was a nearly salivating temptation. But, as much as I remained open to the exhilaration that accompanied such adventures, nothing happened. Regular married life seemed right and satisfying, an opinion I emphasized in more than one conversation with men I met, quite naturally speaking with enthusiasm in support of my current status. We made new friends, especially during pub night on Fridays, and we spent time together exploring the countryside and lakes within a day's drive of the small college city.

The large old frame house, in which we rented the second floor apartment, was owned by a very old and grumpy lady who kept to herself, with the window shades drawn. A few days passed with no sound at all from below and that seemed unusual, so I decided to wander around the outside to determine if she had gone away, or worse. As I peered through a small slit in the curtains, I saw her slumped in her rocking chair with her tongue sort of bulked up between her lips. I detected a trace of that unmistakable odor, too, whether human or animal. 'Worse,' I concluded, still staring at the first dead person I'd seen. There wasn't anything very eventful about it, just dead, I thought. The tough guy in me needed to circumvent an emotional reaction and I went back upstairs to call the police, responding with a deadpan expression to Jo-Anne's alarm.

Toward the end of summer break, Jo-Anne was suffering with abdominal pain and the doctor put her in the hospital for monitoring and then treatment of an infection. I visited her for a few hours the following day. The next day, which was exceptionally hot and muggy, I took a drive up to one of the many lakes in the area to rent a boat and do some bass fishing. Sometimes the strangest, most unexpected things happen, and this was one of them. The man who operated the rental business set me up with a small outboard and began giving me directions to a good area. His daughter, pretty and seventeen or eighteen, I'd say, chimed in and suggested she knew the way and would go with me. I never thought of myself as either roguishly handsome or a virile knight in shining armor, but I became convinced and quite confident that something about me stirred up female interest. Continuing with that line of thought I concluded, in a general way, that physically attractive people had a far greater likelihood of attracting painful experiences than those of more drab, dumpy, or common appearance, those more apt to be overlooked by self-seekers who harbored shallow, narrow, and ignoble desires.

Anyway, she was a perfectly pleasant companion who sat in the bow while I controlled the little aluminum fourteen-footer from the stern. We talked comfortably the whole time and, while she suggested trying this spot and that, I fished but didn't catch anything. Because of the warm day and because I preferred the close-to-nothing feeling, I'd worn a loose pair of shorts with nothing under them, which I kept falling out of and did little about as I sat facing her. I still don't know how women react internally to a view of that nature, but it didn't seem to bother her. She, in turn, had an airy top with no bra covering her well-developed little torso and short shorts. I simply enjoyed the blending of her natural allure with the general pleasantness of the day and the glassy-calm of the lake. It all had a dreamy quality and I was reluctant to bring it to an end. She then told me her grandmother lived in the city and asked if I would give her a ride back there so she could stay with her that night. I thought little of it, except that I welcomed spending more time with her. I think she must have seemed younger in my eyes than I appeared older in hers because, although I was much aroused by her presence, I did not develop any intention of getting sexual with her. Uncharacteristically, I only perceived in her an innocence that I preferred to preserve rather than violate.

It surprised me that her parents had no objection to their daughter jumping in with a stranger and heading off to the city. On the way we decided to catch a movie at a drive-in theatre and chose *The Godfather* which I'd seen before but she hadn't. I asked if her grandmother was expecting her and she said it didn't matter what time she got in. I didn't mention the bit of guilt I felt over not visiting my wife in the hospital that day, primarily because I'd not told her I had a wife. Regardless of where it led in the end, I thought that news would undermine the hour-to-hour quality.

During the movie, things got a little more intimate. We kissed, and the touch of her fresh cool lips was compelling; we kissed more deeply and I found she had no objection to me touching and caressing her breasts and nipples. Below her waist was off limits though, I discovered, and she demonstrated no interest in what was going on below mine. I didn't resort to manipulative insistence, content enough to honor her boundaries and avoid infringing further on the sanctity of my marriage at the same time. I kissed her briefly in front of her grandma's house, shared from my heart that she was a very beautiful girl, informed her that I thought our age difference too great, and told her this would be good-bye. That punctuated an otherwise picture-perfect day with its only regrettable moment. I filed it away as though it were a precious gem I could gaze upon with delight from time-to-time.

Jo-Anne recovered in a few days and the only ripple we experienced between us occurred a few weeks later, while camping at the edge of another small pristine lake with several classmates and their wives or girlfriends. Rob's wife, a sexy little nurse named Linda, and I were still sitting at the campfire after everyone else, including Jo-Anne, had turned in for the night. I don't think we'd been preoccupied with an erotic kiss very long when I realized my wife was standing behind us.

"So that's the way it is!" she said with a tone of warning and abruptly returned to the camper. I felt a sense of dread at the time, but it was simply forgotten. Perhaps it was the liquor, easily recognized as a catchall cause of misbehavior, an uncontestable excuse that usually curtailed further comment.

The next eight months of school went by in a flash and toward the end of the term I secured a position with a longstanding and prestigious investment firm in Manhattan. My academic standing of third place among my fellow graduates hinted at unobstructed success and I was anxious to begin an exciting new life. Nevertheless, I yielded to my wife's desire to make the long drive back to visit family first. I remained miserable for most of the two thousand mile trip and spent nearly all of it with a can of beer between my legs. I hoped my attitude would not be too hurtfully obvious, especially to my mother, but I foresaw that I must merely endure a month of family and social activity that I now associated with a dull bygone existence.

The day we arrived, in early May, it became clear that my father was planning the annual twenty-mile, two-day cattle drive across the great sand hills. That was not a dull chore at all, and I looked forward to it with an eagerness heightened by nostalgia. I phoned a friend who I knew would be excited and invited him and his wife to the farm for those few days, so he could join us in the tradition-packed event. He drove two hundred miles and arrived on the evening prior to the appointed day. All was set.

I had awakened with all the excitement of a child on Christmas morning and greeted my father as I joined him and other family members at the large kitchen table for breakfast. "Well, I don't know," he responded to my inquiry regarding the readiness of plans. "Maybe we should wait." I don't remember the excuse he proposed for waiting because I was already reacting to a pattern that I had lived with from my earliest memories through to eighteen years of age when I left home: his long-standing propensity to balk at fulfilling plans that had transported my mother, my siblings, and myself to the brink with joyful anticipation. Like a bolt of lightning, I recalled his repeated obstinacy with respect to our annual plans to spend Christmas Day visiting our cousins. He invariably found some excuse to sink all of us into a state of crying despair because we were suddenly not going.

My state of mind snapped back with boiling fury to his repeated broken promises regarding my use of the family car as a teenager. They, too, had invariably been retracted on the basis of some vague shift in circumstances. The details ceased to matter and, once again, I became enraged at his painful withholding of positive regard, his denial of love, his betrayal of trust.

The path my mind followed that morning was short and well worn. In the presence of my friends, my wife, my siblings, and other members of my family, it led inexorably to that infuriating place where the little boy cried in despair. Instead, however, the adult swore, raged, and wanted to beat the shit out of his old man. I called him outside but he didn't come. My mother came through the door and into the yard in his place, and commented on my swearing, "So, that's the way you've learned to talk." Her voice intoned the old familiar connotation of shame, which I ignored, and we briefly discussed our exasperated acquaintance with the pattern.

Meanwhile, the effect on my father had been sufficient and he reluctantly reset his course for moving the cattle that day.

He did not utter solicitously, "I'm sorry, son; I'm really happy that you are visiting and I'm glad I can contribute a little something that will make your stay enjoyable." He only hollered from the back of his crow-hopping mare, as he spun her toward the herd of still directionless cows, "We'll have to get moving if we're going to make the corrals by nightfall." He successfully evaded the most trifling note of affection. Thus we began the cattle drive. Before we were far along in the day's eight-hour trek, the easygoing conversation of the trail prevailed. My dad seemed to put it all behind him without regret, but I could not get free of a nagging sense of loss, and the wish that things had been different. My mother's diary for that day contained the exclamation, "What a shemozzle!" and continued without further entry for four days after that, conspicuously inconsistent with the fact that her eldest son was visiting for the first time in almost two years.

Back and forth we went between families: picnics, relatives, and big family dinners with mine; drinking, joking, camping, and fishing with Jo-Anne's. Four weeks slipped by quickly and without further notable incident. In early June, we returned to New York, and I to my new career.

Chapter 5

The entire elegant upper floor of the office tower was occupied by executive offices and the underwriting department, the source of new public offerings. On the floor below, still richly appointed, were the trading operations: corporate and government bonds, institutional sales, currency exchange, short-term interest-bearing instruments, and retail sales. Below that the company occupied another two floors that were comparatively austere with respect to design and furnishings. They accommodated the 'back office' where hundreds of employees were engaged in processing and clearing trades, accounting, customer correspondence, record keeping, and payroll. It was a large, conservative, and successful firm, in a time when dedicated loyalty was expected from highly educated career-minded employees. My first year would be spent gaining familiarity with the areas of operation, learning on the job. When the time was right, the company could then effectively and strategically set a course for their future benefit and mine.

My rotation began with the back office and a stretch of tedious engagement with people whose jobs entailed nine-to-five repetition. Many of the employees seemed disgruntled with their lot and envious of the money paid to the 'big shots' upstairs. Others grumbled about company policy and strategy, often without much insight for the bigger picture, I thought. I went for drinks a few times, with those who made a habit of it, but I sensed they didn't trust me, a future big shot perhaps. Nor did I think affiliating with people who knocked upper management constructive to my career. But I needed to learn the trade and there were interesting aspects, such as accompanying two other men, at the close of business each day, to the enormous vaults below the office tower. I was captivated by the vast horde of securities, including stock certificates that were occasionally first-issue for century-old corporations, and bearer bonds that were essentially as liquid as cash. Because of the flow of business, from stockbrokers, to the trading floor, to the back office, the latter maintained a close working relationship with clerks on the floor. On several occasions, I spent most of the day on the floor of New York Stock Exchange, immersed in the intricacies of business tradition and the excitement of the moment.

Most of the employees on the two lower floors dressed casually and, even compared to the few supervisors who did dress up a bit, my sadly tasteless western jackets and garish ties were not greatly out of place. But I was soon to move upstairs, and I hoped my wardrobe would be graciously overlooked by men for whom luxurious three-piece pinstripes were relaxed everyday attire. Things would have to change as my budget permitted. Meanwhile, other circumstances contributed to my comfort level. First, all promising new business graduates were treated respectfully and, because 'learning' had been our primary focus for years, the proficiency with which we often grasped new processes further encouraged a good opinion. Much of the office activity was well below the level of neurosurgery and, when we gathered together at the pub to celebrate our new lives in the fast lane, it felt like winning could well be an easy walk. Second, there were at least as many females providing secretarial and administrative support as there were males in lofty money generating lead roles. Evidence suggested that all the women had been screened for presentability as well as capability, which created a pleasant atmosphere indeed. They were always especially convivial and helpful, and many participated in the regular drinks-after-work gatherings, particularly on Fridays. It didn't take long to develop a social life which drastically interfered with returning home in the evenings, especially early evening. The heady experience of abundant female company, coupled with my disinclination to quit drinking once I'd begun, resulted more and more frequently in my missing dinner because "I had to work late."

Infatuated with the terrific prospects for sexual gratification, I suddenly viewed my marriage as an anchor that would preclude other thrills and frills likely to befall a rising star. Late in the evenings, I frequently found myself standing outside on our apartment balcony, drinking alone, and idly scrutinizing a thin middle-aged lady across the way as she undressed in front of her curtainless bedroom window. I often finally went to bed long after Jo-Anne had. That, as I saw it, was the initial wretched step in establishing that our marriage wasn't working. I needed to create some distance between us, a wedge. I felt miserable about hurting her and her parents, all of whom had been so generous and kind to me. I had to squelch ugly feelings of shame over the obvious fact that she had worked to support us, while I had been investing time and money in our future. I thought of my mother's heartache upon hearing the news of our separation. Nevertheless, I fabricated other frustrations and emphasized the presence of headaches that, in reality, could only have resulted from excessive drinking. I had, as my hazy objective, the notion of manufacturing a life that was so miserable for us she would welcome my departure.

In the end I told her I needed to move out for a while. With acquaintances, especially Peter and Cindy Kane, who had remained good friends since our college days back home and who now lived nearby, I assumed a cool nonchalance while I explained that it just wasn't working out between us. Jo-Anne's father, with whom I had long enjoyed a close friendship, flew down and asked us to meet him, as though there were a serious crisis unfolding. I suggested that it was all a very casual arrangement, leading to this point and henceforth, which made it impossible for him to depart with any meaningful understanding. I had manipulated my way to freedom without a trace of hard evidence against me. I knew I had caused a lot of pain for those I loved and who had been my best friends in the world. I did my best to subdue the disgrace of it all, rather than drown in it, but I sensed I was crossing a line that I had merely tested with my transgressions to that point.

It was Saturday mid-afternoon when I left the meeting with my wife and father-in-law. I drove to a tavern a few miles away, where I sidled onto a stool at the bar, feeling that I needed to consolidate my thoughts. I ordered a scotch and soda, took a first sip, and glanced around the drab mostly empty interior. Two stocky men were drinking glasses of beer they parked on a small round terry-cloth-covered table while taking turns at eight ball. A slim girl with glasses and long rusty hair sat alone at the opposite end of the bar – not my type.

"Another one?" the bartender asked.

"Sure, why not?" I droned.

Her jeans fit well enough over her pretty little butt, I noticed as little rusty-hair sashayed to the ladies room. When she came out again, she picked up her drink and occupied the stool next to mine.

"You don't look like you're having a great day," she suggested.

"Could be better," I growled. "What are you up to?" She had a cute nose and bright blue-green eyes.

"Nothing really. You hungry?" she asked.

"I am, a little." I decided to cooperate. She was a welcome distraction.

"I am," she said. "We could get a pizza and go to my place, just around the corner from here."

With that, I tipped back the last of my scotch and we left. Judy told me a little about herself. She was a country girl, from up north. I soon thought of her as pleasantly down-to-earth, very casual and unrehearsed. Uninhibited, too. "Fuck me! Fuck me!" she liked to moan and yelp as we did it, and I believe it helped her get a little more than she might have gotten otherwise. I hung around with her for a while, even took a weekend trip to view the fall colors near her hometown and to visit her mother.

Peter and Cindy Kane joined us for that drive in the country. Even though Peter had long been and remained a good drinking buddy, it surprised me a little that the recent shake-up of loyalties seemed to go almost entirely unnoticed. While Judy was still in the restroom, I asked Cindy if she'd talked to Jo-Anne lately, hoping that she'd been a friend, been there for her a bit. When she replied, "No, we were never that close really," I saw that they'd only been together because their husbands had. The thought crossed my mind, causing some momentary consternation, that women must seek meaningful relationships with their male partners, while men are more apt to be content with the recreational companionship of other men. My reflections were pleasantly interrupted by Judy's reappearance and I resumed my enjoyment of a carefree day.

The bond trading desk, as it was referred to, consisted of an elongated divider that supported banks of phone-line buttons that lit up to attract traders' attention. The divider itself was about two feet high and each side was a mirror image of its opposite. Traders sat next to each other in comfortable swivel chairs and were able to access the phones by reaching the short distance across their individual desk space. The arrays of communication buttons, each of a dozen traders having a separate but identical display directly in front of him, consisted of some ninety-seven separate lines. The phones didn't ring individually; instead the buttons flashed individually and a non-specific low beep-tone sounded with each incoming call. Some were direct lines to major competitors, such as banks and other brokers; others were regular phone lines used by retail salesmen or less frequently active industry participants. This arrangement included corporate bond trading, government bond trading, short-term commercial paper, treasury bills, and currency trading.

That was my next assignment and, sitting next to Patrick Ross, I could feel the pulse of these giant over-the-counter markets. Quick and precise decisions demanded acute awareness and cunning. Responsibility and accountability were scrutinized by seasoned associates, enforced with brutal honesty. Renegotiation was not an option and the numbers were often very large. The most successful traders maintained shrewd vigilance over huge positions, allowed no insight into their thoughts during conversations, and kept those they dealt with on a knife-edge. Intimidation, the ability to disarm and create confusion in the mind of another, was an envied talent. It became a character trait these men carried beyond the work they did, and certain people found their style alluring, enticing, and endlessly entertaining. I became a devotee on my first day.

Patrick Ross was both enigma and idol to trainees who spent time on the corporate bond desk. Following mornings of non-stop action, he took ninety-minute lunches, during which he savored the singular consumption of three very dry three-ounce martinis, exchanged dry humor, irony, and wry wit with his 'groupies,' then returned to the office, lit up a fat Cuban corona, and carried off an impression of total competence amidst, admittedly, the much quieter pace of an afternoon. I coveted a similar image.

Occasionally encroaching on this smoky masculine lair (for the traders were all male) were secretaries seeking information, because they were serving clients themselves or putting together reports of trading activity and bond price levels for other departments. They were situated about twenty paces away, on the opposite side of a space occupied by a dozen institutional salesmen and their large personal desks. Their objective for entering the foggy warren was rarely social, but rather a venture in search of security quotations, 'quotes' as they were referred to. That is what brought Lori to Patrick's side one afternoon. He leaned back in his chair and met her eyes lazily.

Lori, having ample prior exposure, hoping to get away unscathed, gingerly stated her request. "Can I have a quote, please?"

He smirked as he droned, "Better to have loved and lost, than to have never loved at all."

It seemed to momentarily set her mind adrift, anchorless and exposed to a sea of beaming male faces, all delighted by their colleague's drollness. But it wasn't exceptional, and the crimson blush on Lori's face faded quickly as she smiled prettily. "Good one, Patrick. Twenty-year, eight percent, AT&T's, please?"

"Ninety-eight and a half, ninety-nine, firm up to five million," he replied pleasantly, and turned in my direction with a twinkle in his eye.

These people enjoyed coming to work every day, personalities meshed and flourished, and I reveled in every minute of it. But the martini lunches left me with late afternoon jitters, and I often spent the last hour of the workday willing the clock toward cocktails at five o'clock. My interest in Judy was quickly diluted by the magnetic social life that spilled over from the office. As I listened in on conversations, I often felt I was hardly 'in the game' yet, hardly up to it. Jack Grimm, an average looking government-bond trader, seemed always to have an erotic tale from previous nights at the bar, weekends for sure. I thought he was tastelessly boastful about his escapades: "She liked T in A," he grinned, and, "like a Hoover," he described another lady, terms I barely grasped, while I continued to secretly view my own behavior as depraved. Another trader, tall, dark, and handsome to be sure, told of a girl following him into the washroom at a party and giving him a blowjob. I reacted internally with pity and disgust at the image of her degrading desperation. What would lead a girl to do that?

Alternatively, Patrick, I soon learned, despite his being divorced in the previous year, was not cut from that cloth. I had only just moved on to the research department when news broke that he and Lori had been seen together outside the office, and six months later, they were married. I knew very well I was more like Jack Grimm except for talking about it afterwards.

The main bank of elevators opened to a view of the pretty girls who rotated throughout the day at a large reception desk. It occupied a central position in the grand foyer, with glossy black and white tiles fanning in checkerboard fashion to the perimeter, where elegant chairs and settees of classic European design had been tastefully placed, but never utilized. Debbie with the short blond hair was as pretty as any, despite the few extra pounds that her workstation effectively concealed. She always had a smile and something to say when I passed by, so I viewed it as inevitable when she ended up in the basement apartment I'd moved into. We'd been partying after work, it was on her way home, and, a mutual decision, we decided the night was still young.

Or, the common-sense hesitancy she might have at least half-heartedly displayed was easily eroded by my conniving and willful insistence. Next morning, I saw things differently. Neither a misplaced desire for romance nor an obsession with sexual gratification justified the depravity. The encounter had been rendered hollow by an excess of alcohol and a dearth of romantic spirit, a grasping happenstance that cheapened the dignity of a previously agreeable relationship. What was I thinking?

Monday morning, as I said hello one-by-one to Petra, Francine, Rita, and Nicky – the four party girls who worked as secretaries in corporate research – I concluded with relief that no one had heard about Debbie and me from Friday night. If one of those four had known, they all would, and they'd have made it obvious with some sneering hint. I liked them a lot because they could be relied upon for fun-loving camaraderie after work, always rich with smutty hilarity and sexual innuendo, and they surrounded me with something like fondness, but they could be loose cannons back in the office. The bar I went to with them was not the same one the bond traders frequented, different ballgame, and there was no kinship between the men in the two departments.

The insight I was gaining into investment industry research, seeing how the firm's stock trading recommendations were generated, did not instill respect or confidence. Cynical comments I'd heard from bond traders suggested the research department was nothing but an advertising arm for new product from underwriting, or pushed stock that large customers needed to move, or never issued a sell signal on loyal corporate underwriting accounts. Easily inclined toward suspicion, I was predisposed to seek evidence that discounted the work these experts were turning out. It was not difficult to find and I developed an arrogant and enduring contempt for the department and its head, a PhD economist.

"Fundamental analysis!" Horst Mueller scoffed, in reference to traditional research methods for predicting company earnings and forecasting economic conditions in an industry.

It was the first time I visited his cramped, stuffy, paper-strewn office, and the man on the other side of the tornado-struck desk was shockingly uncharacteristic of the firm. His suits, if in fact he had more than one, fit sloppily, with a baggy shapeless appearance; his shirts bulged to the point of bursting over his distended middle as he slouched in his chair; his hair was in disarray and looked unwashed; his unstylish glasses were grimy and smudged; there were food stains on his otherwise lackluster ties. In sum, he was a visual representation of the contempt in which he held the establishment, within the confines of which he presently worked.

Mr. Horst Mueller had been hired to fulfill a perceived demand for something called 'technical analyses.' Stockbrokers said they were receiving inquiries, more and more often, for a technical opinion. Arguing that it was an essential component of being a full-service brokerage firm, they had pressured management to do something, as abhorrent as the concept had been for the traditional research department.

Mueller explained how he used charts and historical patterns of price movement to predict future market behavior. "It's based on a belief in market psychology, something that exists independent of accounting fundamentals," he said. "I know it is referred to as superstitious voodoo by these educated experts, and summarily dismissed. But a strong argument in favor of technical analysis is that fundamental news is known so quickly and so generally that, except for insiders, it is of little value to traders. They need some other method of forecasting price direction, and this works. The tools I use have actually been around for decades."

I listened carefully to his words, because he seemed so sincere and credible. Although I thought his unkempt style unlikely to serve him well, I was genuinely interested in his contrarian views, and I sensed that his disestablishmentarianism, his loathing of things formal and official, might give him an edge.

Just as I was leaving his office, Horst Mueller said, "You should talk to Noel Hyman – just moved into a space across from bond-trading. He's setting up a commodity futures trading operation. Same as my stuff, pretty foreign to this outfit but they are finding they need to offer a broader range of services in order to hold onto the business they have. You can talk to him about the importance of technical analysis."

The next day, I stopped to introduce myself to Noel Hyman. I had done some theoretical research on price relationships between cash-markets and the corresponding futures-markets while in university, and I looked forward to linking that with the reality of the commodity futures business. Mr. Hyman was a portly gentleman, late fifties, with glasses and light brown hair that might have been curly before it receded too much to be described as such. He greeted me with a kindly smile and introduced me to Moira, his pleasant looking assistant. As he briefly explained that he had just moved from Chicago and described the business he planned to do, I thought of the enormous potential there must be in the industry. I mentioned the prior work I'd done and Noel made it clear he was open to expanding his operation once it was firmly established. "Credibility," he said, "will be my greatest challenge. These people aren't familiar with this business and they don't trust me yet. It's the same with Horst Mueller; have you met him?"

"Yes, just yesterday. Interesting guy," I said. "He suggested I talk to you about technical analysis."

Noel smiled modestly. "Our clients use it all the time. There are serious fundamental analysts in the commodity business, but it's nearly impossible to gain an information advantage on the rest of the world, for example, in vegetable oil, let's say, when a drought is threatening the soybean crop in Brazil and the canola crop in western Canada is receiving record rainfall."

It was nearly five o'clock on Friday afternoon when I left Noel's office, and John Sargent, a member of the trainee fraternity to which I belonged, was ready to go for a drink. I'd become acquainted with John during liquid lunches with the bond traders and we had become good friends, primarily by virtue of our similarly contemptuous and nonconformist attitudes. Despite his being no older than twenty-five, he had thinning grey hair, almost white, without which, his eccentric personality may have appeared concocted.

On a Saturday morning, I decided to visit Jo-Anne at her new place. It was a few months since we parted ways and I hoped to be as kind as possible, without stirring up any hope of us getting back together. She didn't seem at all thrilled to see me. But I greeted her amicably. "Hello, how have you been?"

"I met a very nice man," she replied bluntly in response to my superficial query. "He took me on a trip to Europe and we just got back last Friday."

"I'm happy for you," I said with sincerity. My guilt was assuaged. "That must have been exciting. What did you do?"

"We really enjoyed touring the French wine growing regions," she said, and added, "And I never knew how good sex could be."

I didn't doubt her claim, and I understood the spite behind her sharing it with me. At the same time, I believed I could not tolerate an extended visit of this nature.

Just before I left, she said, "I am moving back west. There isn't anything here for me and I miss my family."

I was saddened by her announcement, because the huge distance seemed to symbolize the termination of our friendship, which I had never wished for. "I'll always wish you well, you know, and your parents, too," I said, meaning it. Just as strongly, though, as I walked away, I felt relieved, because it represented a guarantee of my uninhibited freedom.

Drinking with Peter Kane on weekends became habitual and, possibly wanting to make it a foursome again, Cindy suggested I should meet the nice looking woman who had just taken an apartment down the hall. Marisa, a lovely lady, very stylishly dressed with a gracious and refined manner, came over for a drink and we learned she worked as a teacher and vice-principal at a nearby Catholic School. In answer to my question about getting to know her better, she thought perhaps we could go to a movie one evening. Wednesday, we decided. I couldn't have known, until she started sniffling a little and finally sobbing, that Barbara Streisand and Robert Redford in *The Way We Were* was an unfortunate choice for a lady whose pilot-husband had just run off with a stewardess. She was therefore a little love-starved and, although she later thought I was a bit crazed and that Peter and I shared an abnormal enthusiasm for alcohol, we spent most weekends together. I'm sure it was a welcome distraction for her and she was soon joining us with enthusiasm, including a round of strip poker one evening, which was her idea as I recall the event.

I was surprised at the way she insisted I rub my pubic area against hers, until she whimpered pleasurably and emitted little closed-mouth squeals while enjoying an orgasm. I found it arduous and I had to struggle against the bruising discomfort caused by her aggressive pressing against me. In the middle of the day, sometimes jokingly in the midst of a visit with Peter and Cindy, she would boldly drag me off to her place and the bedroom. But I always thought of her as a beautiful lady, and the remorse I experienced when she kept wonderful Italian dinners waiting for me was heartrending and emotionally numbing. I don't know if she really believed I had been working late at the office.

On days when I had no reason to leave the downtown scene after work, I was like a rogue warrior, conquering and possessing new territory as though its availability, or my powers to claim it, were time-sensitive. Perhaps I subconsciously sought, in that empty realm, a kind of cumulative vanquishing of my own horrible inadequacy. Sometimes they were girls from the office and sometimes they were new acquaintances from the bars. But, unlike those who boasted openly the next day, I had been nourishing a concealed hunger and frequently fretted over jeopardizing my public image. Not until my year as a trainee came to an end and I was transferred to a branch office, because one of the stockbrokers had suffered a mental breakdown in the market crash of 1973 to 1974, did I pull myself out of that futile and gloomy, but irresistible, rut.

My departure was cause for celebration and the farewell drinks on Friday night made me quite drunk by eight o'clock. Because Marisa was out of town visiting her parents, I phoned my friend Judy and drove over to her place. On arrival, I tried to parallel-park in a spot too small, slammed into the parked car behind me, swore, and drove away to find another spot. It was bad timing that a policeman lived right there, saw what happened, and reported it along with my license plate number. I didn't even find another parking spot before they caught up with me and charged me with driving while intoxicated and the more serious offence of hit and run, which would almost certainly leave me walking for a while and could interfere with my Investment Dealers Association license. I spent the night at Judy's, too drunk to do anything but eventually pass out, and the rest of the weekend I was tormented by the prospect of a dismal future.

I showed up for court Monday morning and an unlikely chain of events unfolded. I noticed the door to the public prosecutor's office and took a chance on talking with him. At first, he objected on the basis that he couldn't discuss a case like this. Then, he relented somewhat and heard me out: how I was in serious trouble with a new job assignment, how I'd just been licensed with the securities industry, and how being unable to drive would prevent me performing my business duties. He didn't commit to anything and dismissed me, but when I rose and stood in front of the judge an hour later, His

Honor mumbled with the prosecutor about the charges being reduced. He then spoke to me sullenly about the seriousness of what I had done and asked me if I had a drinking problem. I said I didn't think so. Next, he announced a very lenient fine of five hundred dollars for leaving the scene of an accident and suspended my license for six months, except during working hours and provided I was engaged in a work-related activity. I left the court still anxiously aware of my narrow escape, viewing it – fleetingly, at least – as a wake-up-call.

I phoned the office and explained my predicament to my drinking companion, Patrick Ross, who graciously agreed to drive my car and belongings several hundred miles to meet Marisa. She and I had made plans to take a trip out west before I assumed my new position. I thought perhaps this was how a squirrel must feel when leaping for his life from tree to tree ahead of a forest fire. I appeared to be escaping but I felt that something behind me had been destroyed. We flew to San Francisco, where my sister and her husband lived. By coincidence, my parents were visiting them at the same time. It was the first time I had seen any of my family since I left Jo-Anne and I had to remain rather aloof with respect to my personal affairs. My nieces were there and my youngest brother. They must have held back some honest child-like questions about their aunt and sister-in-law. Fortunately, my brother-in-law had a camper in the back yard and invited Marisa and me to sleep there, somewhat removed from the pressures of moral decency. It was because of their remarkable talent for staying out of things that no family member ever remarked on my thoughtless tornado-like existence.

From there we scheduled a train ride, because it seemed romantic and offered a view of the mountain scenery. I enjoyed the bar service. A day later, we met up with a few of my undergrad university friends and my second brother, Dennis, and his fiancée. Marisa did become a little irritated with my drinking on the train and she finally reached a common-sense breaking point when my brother and I passed out for the night after drinking tequila. It was only early evening and everyone but the two of us carried on with the plans we'd had for dinner and dancing later. The next day she informed me that she was going back east alone and that there was no point in calling her anymore. It was the first time someone had dumped me, post-adolescence, and although I planned to mitigate the loss with new companions as soon as possible, I felt resentful toward her, indignant, as though she had taken something that belonged to me. I had lost control by allowing myself to become the 'dumped' instead of the 'dumper' and I would bear a grudge toward her for that. The disingenuous phone calls I made over the next months, with the objective of re-establishing my advantage, were futile.

Chapter 6

Meanwhile, I settled into my job at the branch office. The shrunken equity balances I discovered, as I studied the list of accounts, explained the distressed exit of my predecessor. Phoning each one and introducing myself, I was greeted variously with despair, skepticism, and anger. There were only a few that had survived the market slide with significant resources. Mr. Feldman, a cantankerous sounding man who possessed enough innate skepticism to have sidestepped the general demise, still had over one hundred thousand dollars in his trading account.

I called and introduced myself, discovering quickly that Feldman was not interested in socializing. "Just find something that will make some money in this mess and get back to me."

The man seemed willing to do anything, except buy into some self-destructing blue-chip stock or dull utility bond, the phony recommendations of dutiful company men. Maybe this is where the technical types could help, I thought, and dialed the phone.

"Mueller here."

"Hi Horst, Rick Nelson here." I smiled at the man's lack of ceremony.

"Well, pal, how are things in the trenches?" He seemed glad to hear from me.

"Pretty ugly, but I've got a bit of a gunslinger with a hundred grand in his margin account. Says he'll do anything that makes money," I said hopefully.

Mueller didn't hesitate. "Sell Chrysler Corporation convertible bonds."

"Jesus, Horst, short Chrysler? I know everything's collapsing, but the research department has retained a 'buy and hold' recommendation on that stock!" I was masking my enthusiasm for his contrarian suggestion.

"When they raid the whorehouse, sonny, they take all the girls. That stock has broken out of a 'head and shoulders' formation on the price-chart and it's going to drop by thirty percent. The convertibles are sitting ducks for a drop from ninety-six to sixty dollars." He hadn't been popular while predicting this bear market, and he continued to enjoy undisguised contempt.

"So this wreck isn't over yet?" I wanted to hear more.

"I'll let you know when it's over. Stay in touch." Click, the seedy sage was gone.

Full of fresh-faced zeal, I called Mr. Feldman with the suggestion. Without hesitation, he growled, "Good, sell fifty thousand of it," and hung up.

I was somewhat startled at his casual reliance on my proposal, the new guy on the block. To establish the position, I called Patrick Ross on the corporate bond desk. "I need to sell short fifty thousand par value of the Chrysler six percent convertibles."

"Done, ninety-five and half," he replied, and then chuckled irreverently, "That'll be popular."

As Mueller had predicted, the security slid precipitously and the client covered his short position in less than a month with a twenty thousand dollar profit. I knew Patrick had taken a little slice for the bond desk. "Nice one," he said.

I had earned a nice cut, too, while Feldman was audibly overjoyed. "Pretty good. What's next?"

But that episode was not typical of my approach. I was usually low-key and conservative in dealing with the clientele I'd inherited. I was confident from the beginning, too. I collected a sizable commission check after placing with clients a sizable chunk of a nice safe government bond issue. When an elderly couple asked me to come round and take a look at some additional holdings they had, after I'd sold them ten thousand dollars in bonds, I was humbled by the trust they so readily placed in me. They had spent a working lifetime buying a few shares of different companies from time-to-time and stuffing them in a safe-deposit box. It all sat on the kitchen table in front of us and, as we sorted through certificate after certificate, I listed them and made a rough calculation of value. Their trusting innocence resonated deep in my heart and my chest swelled with a sincere desire to do the right thing.

The sum was more than a quarter million dollars – despite current low stock prices, enough to buy five houses of the type we sat in. They had more than they needed without this money as both received good pensions and they had no debts. Somehow that fact reinforced my aspiration to do the right thing, to honor people who were vulnerable only because they expected others to possess their own high standards. I said I would talk to people with more experience, and I did. I received sound conservative advice and left most of the securities as they were. Integrity was worth more than money.

The bear prowled and ravaged, devastating savings and financial dreams, destroying the retirement plans and security of the aged. Back at head office, two stock brokers I'd known committed suicide because of severe losses suffered by people who relied on them as professionals. It had become more than their self-respect could handle. In the seventies that still happened. Even so, I thought their reactions were too desperate and severe. I couldn't imagine killing myself over lost money whether it had been mine or belonged to others. Noel Hyman, in the brief time I'd known him, had impressed me with his sincerity and apparent concern for people around him. I felt like talking to someone like that.

"Noel Hyman," he answered, with a welcoming and positive inflection, overcoming his characteristically subdued and barely audible voice, as though his words needed additional thrust to get them out. Chronic respiratory complications, exacerbated by years of heavy cigar smoking, he had explained.

"Noel, Rick here. Just thought I'd check in this morning, see how things were going. I heard about the two guys who did themselves in there."

"Yes, and then Tom McRae shot himself last night. That's the third from this office now and it's pretty glum around here today." Noel sounded troubled.

All of them fine middle-aged men: one had jumped to his death from an overpass into rush hour traffic, the second left the car running in his garage a week ago. But Tom McRae, known for doing the largest business among the thirty-six retail-brokers in the office, was all the more respected for his pleasant, even-tempered, and kind deportment. No doubt a factor in his huge success, his friends believed his integrity and nobility had been a factor in his death as well.

Joel continued, "They say, near the top of the market, when everyone was still very bullish and convinced of another big move up in stocks, he had taken huge amounts of his clients' money and put it into call-options on a few strongly touted companies. When it all turned down with a vengeance, they suffered serious losses very quickly. He had invested a lot of his own money in the same way. Nobody knew how much pressure he was under. I guess, after watching this for eight months, enduring and sharing the agony of his customers, people who had trusted him to make good decisions for them, he could see that the money was gone and wouldn't be recovered even if there was run-up in the market."

"Christ, imagine. Time just ran out, and hope, too." I exhaled, feeling like I was floating above a deep chasm, and then inhaled to tentatively recoup, "It's like old-time navy captains going down with a sinking ship. It seems these guys really get caught off guard with a bear market. It's as though no one remembers what can happen from one big clean-out to the next."

"Well, you're right," Noel said. "Stock markets get into up-trends that last a long time. They start off quite unnoticed and edge into higher ground with relatively little public participation. Over time, ten years or more, as they continue to drift higher and participation broadens, they develop a momentum that is very convincing and there is a dramatic increase in public awareness and word-of-mouth stories about the money being made. There is an increased focus by the press and a huge swell of schemes to make it easier for the public to invest in whatever great thing is happening. It doesn't matter that the incentive for these schemes is the lining of promoters' pockets. People just turn over greater and greater amounts of money to the market. Over the next few years, the ever-broadening phenomenon acquires an image of being unique. At this point, the few remaining skeptics are laughed into obscurity."

He continued on, "Governments, because this fresh status quo is so politically beneficial, hold forth promises of everlasting prosperity and trumpet the new age in which the realities that threatened the old one are now safely history. Regulations are relaxed to allow the fullest possible realization of benefits for the public, and for the investment industry whose objectives are innocently assumed to be the same; central banks adjust to the amended and much improved economic order and permit the banking industry to engage their assets more liberally; and the press transforms its formerly brief and circumspect reports on business into broad public forums where financial heroes and heroines are paraded before an audience greedy for clever advantage. The illusion of certainty leads to another deadly practice: leverage. People start to borrow money to increase their profits. And so it grows of its own momentum, and it seems, more and more, that there never was another world but this one of increasing prosperity. That is especially true for the brokers themselves who are making six and seven figure incomes, more than most ever dreamed of, and spending accordingly, so that an end to it all is not only undesirable but outside their vision of reasonable possibilities.

"Inevitably, going back to tulip-mania in Holland, the South Sea Bubble, and the roaring twenties, the end comes. When it does there is blood in the streets. Things don't change very much. You should read a book called *Extraordinary Popular Delusions and the Madness of Crowds*, written by a guy from Scotland in the eighteen hundreds, but it still applies."

In a way, Noel had delighted in sharing this callous reality; I could see that. Behind it was his subtle contempt for the traditional investment industry.

"That book sounds interesting. I'll look for it," I said. Noel could really go on and on, but he knew what he was talking about. I was thrilled with the added insight, things you don't learn in school. I asked, "Am I to assume the same doesn't happen with futures brokers?"

Joel responded with fondness for his business. "There's so much volatility in commodities, bull markets and bear markets are happening all the time, and leverage is normal practice. You only need about five percent in equity to carry a position, so futures traders are used to it. It's a different game and there isn't enough time between one big swing and the next to forget the reality of it. Traders go broke all right, but no one is surprised about it. Whoops, I've got another call here."

"Thanks, Noel. See you later." I leaned back in my chair, stretched my feet up onto the desk, and let the growing aspiration to be a commodity futures broker wash over me. Above the crowd, that's what I wanted, and the image in my mind was just that.

In the hours after work I remained creative and bold in achieving other objectives as well, but more clandestine and far less constrained by a moral compass. Over the half year I spent at that location, I had three female encounters that were typified by some ongoing social exchange, and a few others so brief that names were hardly exchanged. Just more girls and, I assume for them, just another guy. But my technique had improved during my time with Judy and Marisa and, in response to a perfectionist bent, I continued to explore more effective ways of giving women orgasms. Certainly I wanted to leave them satisfied and happy that they had met me, but I also needed a sense of control, to physically possess them at some deeper level, to be remembered. Most of all, however, it seemed rather difficult, even impossible, to bring women to orgasm with plain old-fashioned intercourse and the motion required was often in conflict with my preferences. So I worked on different manual approaches and began experimenting with oral sex. Once they were satisfied I considered myself freed of that obligation, as well as any accusation of selfishness, and could proceed to fully satisfy my own desire.

A trip back to New York resulted in another crazed and purposeless evening with the four girls from the research department. I had repeatedly engaged in inebriated tangles with two of them, Petra and Nicki. The third, Rita, was fun but had no allure for me, and the fourth, Francine, held a lot of allure but was married, although kissing each other, with our friends partying all around us, had become a pleasant and ostensibly innocent expression of the nice feeling we shared for each other. We'd been up to some of that when the whole group decided to go to a private party. I wanted to stop on the way at the one-bedroom flat belonging to Patrick and Lori Ross where I'd been invited to sleep on the couch while I was in town. Wanting to avoid any interruption of a good time, I asked Francine if she'd like to accompany me in one cab and let the others go directly to the party in another. Petra, who felt it her place to act as a kind of advocate or team-coach regarding such matters, encouraged Francine with a sly little giggle and off we went.

In the seclusion of the cab our kissing resumed in earnest. Alone in the elevator our bodies connected through our clothing and the rest of the world quickly dissolved in a passionate frenzy. In the apartment, we wasted no time getting to the bedroom. We undressed without a word and fell at once into a sweet hot maelstrom of mutual desire. Beyond the world of intensifying pleasure, from the very edge of consciousness, I heard the door open.

"Hello?" Lori Ross queried.

I froze; Patrick's wife would not be open-minded about this and Patrick would have to back her up. "Give us a few minutes to get out, Lori. Best if you didn't know who was here."

My first reaction was to shield Francine from office gossip. Noble to place her first, I suppose, but then these circumstances weren't as exceptional for me. I heard the door close and I knew we were alone again. We were still horizontal and I kissed her gently, clinging hopefully to a moment I knew was lost.

"Another second," she whispered, "and I would have been in heaven." My voice quaked with my own despair and affectionate empathy. Practically speaking, I suppose it was lust that brought us together. But we had liked each other a lot, over a long period of time, and it had only been regard for her marriage that kept us apart. In a world with no social constraints, it was simply love, arisen in a universe of emptiness. Its manifestation, a dreamily pure primal expression, had been suspended. For a long time, I gloomily filed that chapter under unfinished business. However, I began to wonder if its lingering allure wasn't the consequence of its suspension. Perched forever on the threshold of erotic make-believe, our intimacy remained unblemished by egocentric mauling.

Before I left for my out-posting once more, I stopped to see Noel and Moira. Noel was on the phone so I visited with Moira, a bubbly lady with a charming English accent, fair complexion, medium-length strawberry-blonde hair, and emerald-green eyes that served as the birthplace of an easy-going smile. Responding to my enquiries, she said she had begun working with Noel a week after arriving in Chicago four years ago, from Tilbury, England, an ocean port on the Thames just east of London. "A grimy little dock-town," she added. "The reason I don't exactly speak the Queen's English."

"So, you moved to New York with Noel? How do you like it?" I asked.

"I don't think either of us like it as much as Chicago, but here we are," she replied. "It seems this is a terrific opportunity, though Noel is under a lot of pressure to get the bleed'n business going. He thinks you're going to come and work with us. Are you?"

"I'd like to," I answered, just as Noel's call ended. She had said all I needed to hear concerning my future.

Noel, following the briefest of preliminaries, immersed me in a hasty introduction to the commercial application of commodity futures, touching on subjects which included generic commodity merchandizing, hedging versus speculation, and basis-trading. I would need practical exposure to grasp it all, in more than a very general way, but I became more enthused about all of it.

Following a pause in another largely one-sided conversation, he said, "If you are quite certain this is what you want, I will begin persuading management to have you transferred back here. I think you will do very well in this business."

During my ninth month at the branch, I noticed an uncomfortable itching in my urinary tract and closer inspection revealed a greyish discharge. With dread, I made a doctor's appointment, found out I had contracted gonorrhea, and picked up the prescribed penicillin. Two days later I was invited to dine with a young lady who lived a few doors down the hall from my own apartment. It was an enchanting evening and, when things began to develop romantically, I had to make an embarrassing ethical decision. I warped the truth, telling her that I was afraid I might have an infection and was going to get things checked the next day, that I did not want to take a chance on giving anything to her in the meantime. Anxious that my pronouncement would bring a rapid end to a promising beginning, I chuckled with disbelief when she said, "The wait had better be worth it."

I went back to my place thinking, 'One of these days the price for my degenerate behavior is going to be more severe.' Nearly swamped with nausea, I thought back to the pubic-lice Jo-Anne and I were treated for just after our journey east for my graduate studies, probably the hitchhiking girl. Jo-Anne had agreed to blame it on the camping trip and public restrooms. Self-loathing, in no way a stranger, seeped into my consciousness. But it was earned this time, self-made; I'd become physically contaminated as well as emotionally self-doubting. To make matters worse, I'd just denied myself access to my surest source of wellbeing – sex. I poured a stiff scotch, and then another, and arrived at a kind of theoretical oasis just before passing out for the night.

Three weeks later, Noel called to report management's approval of his plans for me. Once they found someone to assume my current position, I could make the move back to New York and begin my career as a futures broker, probably another month or two.

The treatment for my infection was successful and sexual involvement with my neighbor had resumed where we left off. Now I had to tell her that I was moving and that I thought there wasn't a future for us, a prospect which caused me painful reluctance because she had been an especially caring and enjoyable companion. When I finally broached the subject she reacted with greater sadness than I'd prepared myself for. I held her for a long time and promised I would call.

I didn't like the sadness of parting, the sense of loss that welled up in my throat and behind my eyes. I didn't like seeing the suffering mirrored in the eyes of someone who had been trusting, kind, and loving toward me. I wished a part of me could remain there, just happy, traveling along in a traditional and contented life. But I knew I was on my way, had to be, and I didn't want strings attached. Severing bonds of affection and betraying another's blind hope, despite the heartache, was required sacrifice along the road to a loftier destiny.

Part II
Without Constraint

Chapter 7

Back in New York, I dove into building a career around the commercial use of commodity futures. Noel Hyman turned out to be a master mentor and I soon discovered my former academic investigation of the futures markets was of little practical value, beyond increasing my general awareness.

Noel said, "I want you to understand the purpose of the business from a client perspective, the reasons people and corporations direct capital and human effort toward trading these markets in the first place. It will be a necessary component in your efforts to develop business. Some of the ideas involved are conceptually challenging and you need to find ways of presenting them effectively.

"Excuse me if this sounds like a lecture," he smiled, and continued, "For starters, unlike most other markets, one can just as easily sell a commodity futures contract, to initiate a position in his account, as he can buy one. Selling, as an opening trade, creates a 'short position' and, in order to get out of it, he has to eventually buy it back. It is the reverse of the usual form of trading in which the trader first buys and then sells. But these are contract markets and they deal with future delivery, the promise to do something at some specified time in the future. Obviously a transaction that will take place in the future, just as one occurring in the present, must consist of both a buyer and seller. That is true whether it is a contractor's agreement to build a house or a farmer's to deliver five thousand bushels of corn six months from now. The other side must have agreed to take possession of the house, or the corn as the case may be, and pay money for it, in the future. The contractor and farmer are 'short,' meaning they owe the product, until the transaction is complete. The buyers are 'long' in a position of eventual ownership. A further conceptual leap is required to become comfortable with the fact that thousands of these contracts trade on organized exchanges, where buyers and sellers effectively meet but never see each other. Academically, economic theorists have assumed that free-market prices are established at a point where the buyer and seller agree, proposing the notion of equilibrium. In fact, buyers and sellers do not agree at all, with respect to the level of market. Quite the opposite, in fact, prices are established where, for whatever reasons, the buyers thought or feared it would go higher and the sellers thought or feared it would go lower. They may have been motivated by a thorough analysis of supply and demand, the guidance of an astrologer, a rational need for the transaction in operation of their business, the desire to make some money through speculation, or sheer panic at the threat of an unsustainable loss for which this transaction appeared to be a painful but necessary resolution. Whatever the motives of individual traders, trading is very much an impersonal exchange; there is no cordial agreement, except that each did what he did in that moment, with no resulting or residual personal obligation to each other. Commercial traders can thus buy and sell to suit their specific needs, perhaps offsetting the future sale of something they have in stock by selling a futures contract, or offsetting some future need for an ingredient by buying a futures contract. This is called 'hedging,' taking a temporary position in the futures market as a substitute for a pending transaction in a cash, or actual, market."

Noel jumped from there to elucidating the concept of 'basis-trading,' assuring me it was an integral part of the business. I glanced at Moira, who had been present all along but seemed to have tuned-out with this shift in topics.

She declared, snickering, "That bit is beyond me, but I'm glad you guys know what we're doing here, so I don't have to worry about it."

I knew she was being modest, because Noel had told me once before that she had a very good grasp of the system, including: order entry and reporting procedures, client records and position statements, procedures for reconciling positions, and what it took to rectify imbalances. "In other words," he had said, "Moira understands the day to day operations, communications, and client service aspects of the office, all the indispensable support functions, which allows her to run the show by herself for a few days when I need to be away."

"What about speculators? Where do they come in?" I asked, feeling I wanted to get the whole picture.

"Speculators can trade both ways just as easily as commercial traders, placing bets on the market rising or falling. They add volume, or liquidity, to the markets, without which the large commercials couldn't operate in them. Some speculators make a sound career of trading for profit and become very rich. For others, the vision of successful speculation can be an excruciating delusion. The promise of easy-money, draped in apparent simplicity, draws them headlong into desperate straits, sometimes financial ruin," Noel said, as though it was a warning. Then he added, "It's best for a broker to stick to his customer business and not trade his own account."

"You never speculate in your own account?" I asked.

"I don't even have a futures account in my name. I've seen others do it and it just distracts them from good customer service, the thing that generates their income. It just causes problems," Joel cautioned me again.

"Are futures referred to as derivatives?" I strayed to another subject.

After some thought, he answered, "They aren't usually included under that term. Strictly speaking, I guess they are because they are derived from some underlying tangible item. But they aren't in the category of instruments that gets such bad publicity and close attention from regulators. Options on equities, once the smoke clears on this current debacle, will be scorned again; certainly options on futures contracts attract suspicion. But none of those are as whacky as currency and interest rate swaps and other derivatives that are not traded on organized exchanges."

Enough for one session, we turned to the quote screens to see what the markets had been doing. Noel asked Moira about several phone calls she'd taken.

"Franz wants you to call him," she said, and Noel began to dial the number of a long-time client who owned a flour milling business.

"Where do you live, Moira?" I asked, because I was interested.

"I bought myself a little condominium in Brooklyn. It's a darling little place in a lovely neighborhood. The subway runs near there, so it's convenient, only thirty minutes to work," she answered.

"I haven't made it over to Brooklyn yet," I said for no reason, just as Noel finished his call and began listening in.

Moira said, "Well, if you do make it over, here's my number. Feel free to knock me up."

Noel's hand flew to his brow and he looked down, shaking his head with mock mortification, belly laughing. I howled with laughter, too, at the divergence in meaning, and at Noel's exaggerated response.

Moira looked on in bewilderment, though quite sure she was about to be enlightened. Too naturally relaxed to fear ridicule, she only wanted in on the joke. "What now? C'mon, Noel, let's have it then."

"Moira, if you knock someone up over here, you make them pregnant," Noel said, still enjoying his mirth.

"Oh," she joined in the laughter, "that's not what I meant. But I think I've said that on other occasions. No one ever said anything before."

"We feel responsible for you. You're very lucky I've learned to put up with things like that." Noel was caught between a deadpan smirk, trying to convey the hardship he endured on her account, and fond amusement.

I loved working with those two people. Our personalities and lifestyles could hardly have been more diverse, but a warm and genuine conviviality permeated nearly every minute.

Life was soaring on all fronts and the flickering optimism I'd once clung to, amidst the grip of bewildered self-pity and rage, gave way to self-importance, even haughty conceit. I was making a little more money and had taken an apartment downtown, ten minutes from the office by subway. Because we had re-established our previously ruffled friendship, I travelled out to spend time with Marisa occasionally, but mostly partied downtown. And I'd only been back in town for two months when I met Yvonne.

We met at a winter festival where I was keeping myself warmed with tequila concealed in a hollow, capped, red plastic walking stick. I was travelling with a male friend and she was accompanied by a female friend. We paired off at some point and went back to the girls' hotel room where our friends began groping each other rather liberally. As it became evident that we would spend the night with them, Yvonne explained to me that she was a virgin and wanted to remain that way. She was a very pretty petite blonde with the loveliest demeanor, and I had no thought of disrespecting her request. In fact, sustained by a state of noble tenderness, my attraction toward her grew ten-fold and I became certain of a longer-term interest. Perhaps she would be the key to my establishing a decent respectable life. We snuggled through the night and kissed quite a lot, while our infatuated friends bounced and moaned in the bed across from us.

Her caring and honest nature soon became apparent and I believe my initial demonstration of respect convinced her of my own good character. Back in the city, we continued to see each other platonically. I met her blue-collar father, her mother, and brother. They were a respectable Catholic family in a respectable neighborhood and they bestowed upon me the admiration I usually elicited as a rather good looking, clean cut, well-educated young man.

I don't know when I told Yvonne of my previous marriage, or whether she ever told her family about it, but I think it should have been a red flag for her. After a short while, and certainly before she would have preferred, she lovingly gave into my arguments that not having sex was somewhat unnatural for me. That was especially true, I believe I reasoned in some convoluted fashion, since I had been previously married. We became a couple in the eyes of her family and our acquaintances. We spent weekends with other couples at their cottages; she often stayed at my place; we exchanged gifts, some of which were the nicest and most appropriate I'd ever received. She put her heart into it.

One evening, she joined me at our favorite pub and I introduced her to my work colleagues and drinking buddies. Patrick Ross, that perceptive fellow for whom I had much respect, looked at me sullenly and said, "You'll be the ruin of her."

I sincerely hoped I wouldn't be, because I really cared about her. But I cared about my freedom as well, and continued to pick up one-night stands and frolic with the girls in the office where I was (in my opinion at least) a rising star. She was shocked and hurt when she discovered a list of six or eight phone numbers I had clumsily not stored away. Mercifully, there was no record of my several recent one-night encounters, whose names I couldn't remember. She wanted to talk, but I had a way of stifling conversations that threatened to probe too deeply. I just didn't leave myself open, or participate beyond claiming a vague sort of independence. Yvonne persisted in the relationship because, in her heart, she had made a much larger and more enduring commitment.

Using some of my commission income from the branch office job, I purchased a few hundred shares in an oil company near the bottom of the market. Just like my personal optimism, it quickly soared to several times its former level. I took the profit and I spent most of it flying Yvonne to Acapulco for a holiday. We were in love and we had a euphorically romantic time exploring the sea and surrounding environs.

As spring arrived, we started riding bicycles together and explored the miles of city trails. Nearly every Saturday morning we stopped by a large open food market and strolled leisurely up and down the aisles selecting culinary delights for the rest of the weekend. Governed by my passion to leave nothing untried, I crewed on a thirty-eight foot racing sailboat a few times, and I signed on for flying lessons that summer.

My desire to achieve the broadest possible experience of life, without regard for inherent usefulness, material benefit, or social promise, was insatiable and resulted in my thorough commitment to adventurous endeavor. Three or four days per week, right after work, I drove out to the airport flight training center to satisfy my objective of being a pilot. Moira found the idea intriguing; Noel thought it might be immature fantasy; Yvonne seemed delighted with anything.

Ground school was relatively easy, a chance to exercise my math skills and learn some interesting things about clouds. In two months, after twenty hours in the cockpit of a Cessna 150, with an instructor sitting beside me in the right seat, I was assessed ready to fly solo. With each instance of accelerating down the runway and reaching rotation speed, then applying steady back pressure to tilt the ailerons, I joyfully anticipated liftoff, that precise moment when the wheels left the ground and I knew I was flying. It was a profound sensation of freedom, quite impossible to describe to my friends, except to say I really had left the world behind. But I don't think they understood.

I found out soon, though, the security of having a trained pilot sitting beside me, with his own set of controls if he should need them, contributed to the relaxed purity of my experience. Moments of substantial angst, often followed immediately by profuse perspiration, can seize the trainee solo pilot as he completes circuit after circuit of touch-and-goes (as the repetitive round and round, up and down pattern over the airport is referred to). But the exhilaration was still there, and lingered when each session was at an end and I strolled coolly into the training center.

"How's the flying coming?" Patrick Ross leaned back in his chair one morning as I passed by the bond-trading area.

I was proud of the image, actually flying airplanes, being a pilot, and I was inwardly thrilled to answer his question, while doing my utmost to project nonchalance. "Well, alright I think. Takeoffs are easy enough; straight and level flight, banks, turns, they're pretty good. I still have a little trouble with the landings though."

"Otherwise, Mrs. Lincoln, how was the play?" Patrick failed to contain the grin that forced itself over his entire face. I doubled forward laughing at his satirical analogy, covetous of his quick and droll wit.

I was still chuckling to myself when I entered the trading room and said good morning to Noel and Moira.

"What's tickling you this fine morning?" Moira asked.

It never seemed that I was very good at relating stories, but I passed on the entire exchange I'd had with Patrick Ross. The brief half-laugh from Noel was obviously more of a courtesy than it was an expression of appreciation. I suspected he would rather I severed links with that unsavory crowd, and his dismissive remark, "I don't know about those guys," supported my hunch.

Moira, meanwhile, was puzzled. "Come on, guys, what does he mean, the play?"

After I explained the historical circumstances to her, Moira snickered reservedly and said, "Oh, I get it. I'm not up on everything that's taken place this side of the pond." Then she added with a giggle, "He is witty, that Mr. Ross, isn't he? Sharp as a tack. I wish I had more of that; it adds a bit of fun. Too bad for the old Lincolns, though, wasn't it?"

I adored her quaint accented declarations and laughed aloud. Noel enjoyed that part, too, shaking his head as though forced to tolerate a great nuisance. In spite of the light-hearted conclusion, however, I wasn't yet free of Noel's initial subdued and nuanced response, primarily because I believed he had a remarkable instinct for character. Seemingly deep within me, I experienced some archetypal call to greater maturity, or nobility. The sensation lingered a long time and influenced my associations in the office, though it had no impact on the unwholesome aspects of my out-of-office life, which, in New York City, seemed safely concealed.

Usually, only the most inspiring and exciting diversions could distract me from the magnetism of drinking and sexual carousing. But I did discover one source of social balance, however dubious, in the form of three new male friends and their partners. They were avid partiers, turning drinking into refined ritual. Two had cottages on lakes up north, they loved getting together for ski trips, and our house parties frequently ended with entertainment that called for nudity. We had such a laughing good time together that, after several years, I still didn't know exactly what most of them did for work, what their families looked like, what religion they grew up with, or which political party they backed. Throughout, Yvonne was my partner and close friend, and I can't remember once being disappointed with her ability to mix lady-like behavior with uninhibited enthusiasm.

At the same time, I was immersed in my career and Noel was pleased with my performance, greatly satisfied with his handpicked protégé. Conceptual emancipation gripped the industry, freeing it of traditional constraints, and new financial derivative markets sprang to life. Futures on foreign currencies began to trade at the Chicago Mercantile Exchange. The company was particularly interested in the pragmatic application of a new long-term government bond contract, initiated by the Chicago Board of Trade, and I jumped to the leading edge of the issue. We went after prospective mining and forestry clients, as well as agricultural production and food processing. The solid old firm had deep roots in these industries and doors opened easily. Although I worked zealously right from the beginning, the rapid success I experienced was a miracle of timing as well. The seventies were characterized by a worldwide commodity price boom and it set the stage. Connections I established with business interests in the west of the country were quick to bear fruit, in the form of new clients.

My sexual exploits were less frequent and confined to one-time encounters, some more memorable than others. Fortified by alcohol consumption, I couldn't resist a lady I met in the pub one night after work. The electricity passing between us was too compelling and, because neither of us could take the other home, we got a hotel room, expensive but worth it. One-night stands could be like that. She was fun and beautifully at ease. We kissed goodbye as I put her in a cab, no last name and no phone number. Her generous parting words hung in the air – "You can park your shoes under my bed anytime" – uncluttered, entirely memorable, and no clinging obligations.

I travelled out west on business quite a lot, and often extended the trips into ski weekends or visits with friends and family. It was while staying in hotels that I had several more gem-quality one-night encounters. Some were married, but I decided that was none of my business. In a smaller city, at more of a motel than hotel, an attractive woman was sitting in the lobby as I stopped at the front desk. As I waited for the clerk, I turned and caught her pleasant smile. We began a casual exchange which led to eating dinner together, and that led to a few drinks afterwards, which led to my room. I had become quite familiar with the female body and, before we said goodbye, Cindy volunteered that she was unlikely to forget those few hours. She told me she wasn't the type of girl who did that kind of thing a lot, and said she was thrilled, pleasantly alarmed, at how it could be.

Nor would I soon forget, just as the memory of a nice childhood birthday party lingers. I had forgotten that I gave her my business card, until I was sitting at my desk in the midst of a busy office reading her letter some weeks later, physically aroused once more by her charming openness. "I am sitting in my comfy chair, removed some distance from my family but in the same room, dreaming that we are together, naked and making sweet love again. I often remember, and I just wanted you to know how wonderful it still is for me that we loved for even a little while. Warmly, Cindy." There was no return address or phone number, just a whisper of desire.

Either consciously or instinctively, I remained open to serendipitous sexual opportunity, constantly scouting as it were. I think females, by comparison, are more often impulsive about it, rather than consciously seeking. It doesn't require much of the right energy, however, to shift their latent sexual desire to a state of pondering the idea, and then, to increasing degrees of concurrence, ending with enthusiasm. That's how I remembered the transition concerning the girl whose letter I held in my hand.

Later that week, over a martini lunch with the bond traders, four of us decided we should take an excursion to Europe. John Sargent, Patrick Ross, Jack Grimm, and I landed in London and had a beer-drinking lunch with a friend of ours who now worked in the City, as London's financial district is known. The strong beer and my excitement over the trip must have tipped me into a foggy compulsive daze, from which I didn't fully recover for the whole two weeks. London was a blur except for the carpet saleslady I met in a bar and the embarrassment of being asked by Jack Grimm if I could "shut up for a while." Patrick Ross admonished, "Try to get hold of yourself." My memory of the yappy performance to which I'd subjected them is imprecise. My visit to the lady's flat is vague as well. Upon leaving, I told her I was taking a tour of the Continent. She invited me to call when I returned, which surprised me a little because I think we managed to have sex without getting excited.

The next day Jack Grimm, the fellow who reported his sexual triumphs on a daily basis at the office, elected to stay behind and we three troupers flew to Barcelona to begin using our Euro-Rail passes. I remember a little of the extensive collection of his life's work at the Picasso Museum, and spending time near the imposing Barcelona Cathedral. I recall inspecting several casinos, which were too rich for our wallets, in San Remo on the Italian Riviera. I wish I had a clearer recollection of the spectacular Mediterranean Coast, as it appeared from the dining car window while we enjoyed more than one tastefully presented mouthwatering multi-course meal. In other words, I wish I had drunk less alcohol and remained more attentive, less flippant. I was too inclined to view the trip as a reconnaissance mission, thinking I'd come back later for real.

By the time we arrived in Rome, I had "got hold of myself" a little more and was fascinated with the Coliseum and St. Peter's Basilica. We spent a good long time at each of those sites. Walking the streets was memorable as well, and I bought a nice three-quarter length mackintosh there, to wear over my suits on cold, drizzly workdays back home. I have a lasting overall impression of young Italian women, too – stirringly attractive features and enticingly stylish. We headed back through Pisa and finally to Gare du Nord, the train station in central Paris. We checked into a small, very elegant hotel near Place Vendome; 'boutique' might be a good description. It was tranquil as well, except for an American woman who first, in a loud raspy voice, ordered a dry martini and then, in a loud indignant and belligerent voice, complained about the French waiter not recognizing the term. I didn't want to be associated with her; she hadn't 'got hold of herself,' I thought. The British say one is not demonstrating self-possession. A person who is self-possessed is composed, poised, in control of his speech and actions.

We found the Louvre and beheld the Mona Lisa; then we strolled around Notre Dame Cathedral and along the Seine. Then I decided, feeling somewhat at odds, I would part with my pals and enjoy my own romantic connection with the grand and ancient city of style and fashion. I wanted to free myself, to roam in harmony with my serendipitous nature, though I could not explain my intentions in those terms, nor would they have been well received.

I followed my street map and arrived at the Avenue des Champs Elysees. I slowly ambled along in a state of carefree wonder, perhaps my first experience at being romantically immersed in unfamiliar and freshly different surroundings. At the same time, feeling safely alone amid the throng, my mind was free to ramble like it had as I trudged through the snow hunting rabbits in my early teens. That I lacked self-possession, which meant that I sacrificed dignity, was immediately obvious. I occasionally became quite air-headed and really didn't keep myself under control, especially regarding the pointless and untimely words that jumped out of my mouth. When I was talking to prospects, either clients or women who I wanted to have sex with, I managed my image carefully as a means of achieving my ends. But the responsibility of continuously operating at such a pitch struck me as tiresome. "That is my problem," I thought. "I approach life as though I am just visiting this planet, anonymously, and even the most serious endeavors are only turns in a game I'm playing."

"He went to Paris, looking for answers…" The Jimmy Buffet tune drifted in and soothed my restless state of mind as I walked back to the hotel in the early evening. Not far from the entrance, a quite stunning lady smiled and asked me if I would like company. Her accent alone was bewitching and I wished to detain her a while, with no intention of paying for sex. She seemed rather refined, composed, and asked a few questions of me in a manner I would not have expected from a prostitute. Certain that I didn't want Patrick Ross to walk in on me, as his girlfriend Lori had a few years ago, I opted for being upfront. I told her I'd love to spend time talking with her but I wasn't interested in anything beyond that. I asked her if I could buy her a drink and she said, "Oui, Monsieur, I think that would be nice." We had a delightful talk during which I learned that she was a university graduate. I wondered if a Parisian view of extramarital sex placed it beside other commonplace activities, such as dining out, substantially enriching its overall image and acceptability, compared to the 'sex is evil' Anglo-Saxon Puritan version. We sat and talked an hour before my friends came into the lobby. Patrick shot me a raised eyebrow, perched above an indulging grin, as I escorted the pretty lady into the street. Then, we three left to find an interesting place for drinks and dinner.

My friends had done nothing to produce the strangely forlorn state that engulfed me upon awakening next morning.

In response, however, I booked a flight back to Gatwick under the pretense that I wanted to see more of London, which I did, but the carpet saleslady was on my mind as well. She agreed to meet in the late afternoon at Leicester Square. She was relaxed and chatty. I considered her physically attractive and enjoyed our hours walking together about the fine old city. Her happy frame of mind fully matched mine. Nevertheless, by about ten o'clock that evening, it was obvious that nothing very passionate was stirring between us. No reason, it just was not. We'd had a nice time and parted pleasantly.

On the British Airways flight home we partied all the way. The back of the plane was designated smoking and I think the flights were more apt to be lively in those sections. Anyway, that's where I was when bowled over by an electric surge between a pretty flight attendant and me. I didn't foresee it going anywhere, because I knew that Yvonne might be waiting for me at the gate, and the female stealing my immediate attention was performing a job that required self-restraint. But the mutual attraction wasn't disguised either. After we landed, as I walked up the ramp toward the terminal, she caught up to me. "I've written the name of my hotel for you," she said with her sweet accent. "I'm here for two days and would love to see you." We walked side-by-side and spoke in animated tones but, as much as I wished there were two of me, I envisioned Yvonne, excited to see me, glowing with happy expectation. My distaste for deflating that moment held sway and I broke away just in time, most reluctantly.

It was nice to have a steady partner awaiting my return and to slip back into the recreational life that revolved around us. Yvonne shared excitedly that she had tickets to *The King and I* starring Yul Brynner and she wondered in the next breath if I wanted to spend a weekend at the Stratford Shakespeare Festival in Ontario, because Brian Bedford and Maggie Smith were playing lead roles in *Richard the Third* and *Macbeth* – life-enriching events. My reaction was wholehearted and immediate and I felt very grateful for the lovely petite blonde sweetheart that was so totally devoted to our partnership.

The next day found me thinking about all the women that crossed my path as though they were a threat to our peaceful co-existence. Why didn't it happen to my friends? I don't believe I had any physical qualities that made me more attractive, and no other advantage would be evident at a glance, such as money, if I had any, or intelligence. I concluded, rather unsatisfactorily, that the research department girls thought of me as no more than a male slut, primarily because I acted like one – had been one, in fact. It was odd that they hadn't minded taking turns over the last year.

But the women I merely crossed paths with, what about them? It had to be a more subtle projection of something they wanted. The title to the book *As a Man Thinketh* popped into my mind. Was that it? Did it happen because my propensity to think about it and be open to it was evident? Maybe my crazy uninhibited attitude was actually attractive, a wild-man who had an unconstrained appetite and aptitude for instant romance and sexual play, with no strings attached. I remembered a line in a Merle Haggard country song: "Ladies love outlaws." Well, at least outlaws could be relied upon to ride off into the sunset. I let it go and joined Yvonne for a pleasant bike ride through Central Park.

Chapter 8

A few weeks later I left for Denver on another business trip. The hotel I stayed in had a pleasant pool and garden area that served an adjacent block of luxury condominiums as well. On a warm evening, after a busy day and some rousing partying the night before, I ordered a cool glass of beer by the pool and said hello to the only other person out there, a not unattractive lady, probably a little older than me, who had been enjoying the sun. In truth, she would have been easy to ignore. She let me order her a drink and volunteered the information that she lived in one of the condos. She was quite self-effacing, not timid, but in a way that implied long compliance, very agreeable to visit with. She shared that her live-in partner was on a trip in Eastern Europe; she didn't miss him, she told me, and she said life was difficult at times because he was very religious.

I was getting hungry and, in answer to my invitation, she said she would love to join me for dinner. The waiter seated us side-by-side in a cozy alcove and, while we ordered and ate, we talked until the good wine and intimate chatter dissolved most barriers between us. As a consequence I said, "You know, Debbie, I've really enjoyed getting to know you, and I'm not at all tired of being with you." But because she seemed rather defenseless, in an innocent childlike way, I added, "But if you prefer to say goodnight now, I'll go to my room and read for a while."

"Do you want to hear something that will sound a bit strange?" she asked.

"Go ahead," I cheered her on.

"I feel like a bit of a traitor telling you this, but my partner doesn't like sex, not for the last three years."

"Well, what do *you* think about it?" I was a bit lost for words.

"I guess I haven't thought about it much, until tonight, and now I can't stop thinking about it. I think he's crazy."

I grinned inwardly; she'd probably think I was crazy, too, thinking of little else much of the time. "Does that mean you want to come up to my room and spend more time together?" I believe her smile originated in her reclaimed free will.

"For a little while, if you don't mind."

I closed the door behind us, followed her down the hall and into the large, well-appointed room, took my shoes off, and lay back on the bed. She slipped her shoes off, too, and turned to see me pat the area beside me as an invitation. It might have been the scene of a wedding night, virgin and worldly gentleman. I kissed her tenderly and whispered, "You're very pretty you know," because that's how she appeared in that moment. She offered her lips again and I determined that I wanted her to have a night that would not soon fade from her memory. We stood and undressed and, still standing, pressed the length of our bodies against each other. I traced my fingers lightly down her back and grew more excited with her body's responsiveness. I enjoyed the anticipation of pleasing her and thrilling her. We tossed the bed covers back and, as we lay there again, I slowly applied every tender, titillating maneuver that came to mind. Her body trembled when my tongue teased her nipples and shuddered at a kiss of her inner thigh. She gasped with ecstasy at the first stimulation of her sexual center; her hips moved as though I was already inside her, then for a few minutes I was. Her body became awash with shifting shades of red and pink, completely alive. The night was young, so I saved myself and focused on her desire until she crossed over the magic line. "Oh my God, that's never happened to me. I didn't think I could." We began again a little later and, because I was 'conducting the entire symphony,' I don't know whether I

111

enjoyed her pleasure more or my own. The second time I felt completely altruistic in sharing the bliss of sexual release.

We lay there, staying close to each other. I dozed in and out a bit. Then she rolled away and put her feet on the floor. I asked if she was leaving and she replied, "That's what I've been thinking about. He may call, but I've decided I don't care right now. I want to stay with you, if that's OK." She slowly turned her head and looked at me, that distinctive expression of innocence completely unaltered.

"I'd like that," I assured her, and a few hours later we made love again.

We had breakfast together. She said thank you a dozen times in different phrases. I said, "You're very beautiful," and meant it. I kissed her goodbye and watched as she walked through the gardens and past the pool, toward what I feared was her prison. Because of her comments in that regard, I thought it prudent to leave no contact information; she offered none either. Her erotic adventure, and mine because of her, would sustain a primal connection between us.

Seated on a plane with a three-hour flight in front of me, I asked myself what it was that made intense one-night encounters so rewarding. What was the big deal? Was it the completely unpremeditated romance? Was it because the experience was always an exciting first? The answer was 'yes' to both of those questions, especially for me, because I craved the heady effect of newly discovered romance and I persistently pursued the novel and unusual, just as I loved travelling to new places and trying new sports. Romance faded, giving way to inhibiting entanglement; familiarity eventually resulted in contempt and stifled creativity. One-night stands offered liberated physical intimacy and generous tenderness inspired by a narrow projection of faultlessness. Those points, however, were in essence hardly more than an intellectual case in support of the activity, as though I was trying to convince someone else of the benefits.

Something more fundamental to the occurrence of those brief but intense and seemingly chance meetings, I sensed, originated beyond the level of cerebral consciousness. Sexual energy is a powerful force; few would argue with that assertion. But it is more powerful than the conscious mind can know. It arises as a primal instinct and it seems impossible that it could be effectively fenced-in. It defies possessiveness and selfish grasping, and yet humans work overtime at enforcing the constructs they invent to control it. Its waxing and waning, its ubiquitous bursting forth, exemplify its impermanent and unstable nature. It is founded deep within our inter-being. A phrase I'd read somewhere, "interdependent co-arising," somehow illuminated the spontaneous occurrence of desire between two people who've only just met.

I know many of my friends and family members would scoff at my contention that the sensation is love, and I don't claim to know much about love, but it isn't hate, intolerance, or ill-will. It sees only the best in another person, makes no judgment of past transgressions, asks no questions based on prejudice, and implies no future obligation. What is there about it that isn't love? Answers to that question can only be found within the context of human constructs, moral and legal. I once read a statement made by a judge in a Delhi courtroom: "Premarital sex is immoral and against the tenets of every religion." That statement, I thought as I read it, is immoral because it promotes the pain and suffering that is inflicted by the attempts of religion to place brutally unrealistic demands upon innocent people who are overpowered by a force beyond their control. How much of the world's heartache is the direct result of arbitrary conditioning and a denial of human reality? Sexual energy will manifest in sexual activity; that is its purpose. Most of the significance assigned to sex is derived from the phenomenon of its continually breaking loose of man-made attempts to confine it. Why is it so important to confine it, especially among consenting adults?

Sensual ecstasy is very much like a wave on the ocean, beginning from nothing and relying on the confluence of unseen conditions. Without interference or inhibition, it will increase with harmonious impulse and of its own accord. It will rise to a level commensurate with its own latent energy and crest in its own time. When it has fulfilled its manifestation, it will become one with all the water around it and be as if it never was. There wouldn't be many waves, and the spontaneous beauty of the sea would be lost, if all those same molecules had to agree to come together each time, within prescribed constraints.

All mature consensual sex must be Eros love unless, within a marriage for example, physical desire is secondary to obligation. The meaning of the word love is subject to personal interpretation and colossal social distortion. The meaning of Eros love is romantic allure, carnal desire, and blissful ecstasy, a rare and precious jewel. No wonder a single romantic encounter that turns out well is so memorable. I mentally rummaged through relationships I had participated in for notable lengths of time – Jo-Anne, Marisa, even Yvonne – and found I couldn't recall the thrill or the specific sensations of lovemaking, the novelty and romantic excitement, I mean.

All aspects considered, though, I had to admit that my life was wonderful if only I could content myself with parameters as they were outlined by society; my relationship with Yvonne, friends, career, and life experiences were more than I could have imagined only a few years prior. There remained only one irritant: my salary had only risen from eleven thousand per year at the beginning, four years earlier, to twenty-one. I had a taste of commission income in the six months I spent at the branch office and I calculated that a reasonable payout on the business I was currently generating would be about fifty thousand per year. I know the company took the view that the business I generated was a return on their investment in my career and compensation for the risk they had taken with this new venture, but outside contacts had roused my interest with more lucrative ideas. Because the clientele I'd established was largely in the west and rather distinct in its make-up, I was confident it would follow me into different arrangements, especially if I were to relocate.

Admittedly, there was risk and it would be a major disruption in all my affairs, but I saw it as much more than career advancement. The idea grew and grew in my mind until it was no longer an issue of money. I envisioned, rather, the launching of a new life, the opportunity to experience another plane of existence. It was the sort of opening that was reserved for the quick and nimble, a reward that could only be captured by a man who'd remained free of restraining entanglements. Above all else I prized my freedom.

Yvonne was still going to teacher's college and would have to stay behind. That meant a clean break in our relationship, without me having to appear a ruthless bastard and face her directly. Although we'd spent nearly three years together, I don't think I ever envisioned a future for us, or honestly considered the issue. I really cared about her and I sincerely wished to avoid causing her any heartache, perhaps because I recognized I couldn't inflict it without incurring emotional damage myself. Close friends were sincerely concerned and asked me about it; I mumbled that it wasn't a big deal. I mumbled to one friend that I thought I might not see her anymore and he suggested, supportively, that she was rather plain. Although I have since realized with some regret that she was not at all plain, that statement carried inordinate weight in ensuing debates I had with myself concerning our future. That is how little my thoughts were tied to any internal code and how vulnerable I was to whim and the opinions of others.

I had to discuss my business alternatives face-to-face before abandoning the present ship. That meant another flight out to Denver. I didn't have a specific set of criteria for deciding upon this new relationship, other than maximizing the income I would receive after compensating somebody for putting up the capital and clearing the business I conducted through the commodity exchanges. Otherwise, it would be a process of elimination based upon factors of which I was not yet aware. I had a good first day of discussions with two of my three possible alliances, ending in dinner with one of them. The offers each of the men had laid on the table without reservation were very good and I ended the workday with plenty of optimism for my future.

I thought I'd peek into the second-floor cocktail lounge before retiring alone for the night to my spacious four-star city-center hotel room – a last chance gander. As it turned out, the extraordinarily attractive lady with the long kinky brunette hair, enjoying a drink with her closer to average friend, was even more prepared for adventure than I. When she glanced my way, the effect of her large, dark, indulgent eyes and well-tanned classic visage altered my course immediately. I smiled briefly and selected a table about twelve feet away. I ordered a scotch and, perhaps ten minutes later, her friend departed for the ladies' room.

Following the briefest exchange across the space that separated us, she asked, "Would you like to join us?"

"Certainly," I answered, and made my way to an empty chair beside her. She was positively stunning.

With each new development, she persisted in altering my previous conclusions regarding women and the latency of their romantic aspirations. Feeling as though I'd been far away during the brief conversation that laid the foundation of our acquaintance, I shook off enough of the debilitating enchantment to gain a fragment of self-control. "Yes, I'm staying here," I answered her question. "Are you?"

Her friend was halfway across the lounge, then only a few feet from the table, at which point she said, "I think I'll leave you two. I should be getting home. " Moments later she vanished beyond the door.

"I don't have a room here, but I would stay," she replied as though there had been no interruption. She told me her name was Carrie. As my second scotch arrived, I asked her if she'd like another drink.

"No, let's not drink anymore," she said without delay. "Can we just go up to your room?" Her unabashed singleness of purpose cleared my mind of all but dreamy infatuation. I fell in love as we rode up the elevator making small talk without any physical contact. She went into the washroom and I lay back on the bed, contemplating her striking appearance and how comfortably blissful I was in her presence.

When she returned, she'd removed a small jacket and her ample breasts were apparent for the first time under her blouse. Otherwise, she still wore a mid-thigh length skirt. She lay on her back beside me and I lightly stroked her arm and hand. She told me she worked in an office downtown, answering the pointlessly rhetorical question I immediately regretted asking. I quickly redirected my attention to the moment at hand.

Then she turned on her side, moved nearer, and brought her lips close to mine, so that all distance between us melted. Our first kiss lingered, very gently. I moved my hand down along her side and caressed her back. I was moved and encouraged by her milky soft acquiescence. Soon my hand stroked down past her skirt to her bare leg and then upward, slightly under the hem of her skirt. She whimpered with passion and shivered a little and my senses withdrew from all but Carrie. Her eyes summoned another kiss, her sweet wet lips parted, softly, and then our tongues met. I moved my hand, caressing lightly, along the outside of her leg to where her panties would have been. Nothing obstructed the path of velvety smoothness as it curved and inspired a feathery caress of her firm buttocks. A low soft groan of submission arose from my abdomen and she whispered, "Our clothes are in the way."

Our bodies met full length, warm and wanting. Her breasts were marvelously shaped, magnificent, and she arched in pleasure when I teased her with the tip of my tongue. Her excitement was calm rather than frantic, knowing and assured, as she took me in her hand and said, "I want you now." My one and only conscious thought, as the sweet fragrance and bewitching feel of her engulfed me and swirled through my senses, was to preserve our blissful union indefinitely. We moved slowly, lost in an instinctual dance of love. Pleasure resonated in our throats. She breathed deeply, then more abruptly, and whimpered sweet notes of lustful yearning. I felt I was on fire and always very near the edge. She began to let out tiny muffled screams; my body convulsed and my mind reeled. From deep inside she gave a final scream of ecstasy that trailed gradually into a happy giggling celebration of fulfilled desire. As the small aftershocks in my taut body subsided, I lowered myself into her waiting arms and felt a tear of pure ecstasy roll down my cheek.

We held each other and tenderly shared the lingering glow. We talked in whispers and only a little, about nothing really. Answers to all those questions we didn't ask could only steal the exquisiteness of the moment. Although I think love's sad feelings linger longer, happy feelings might be stronger, and in that moment I felt happy feelings of love for her, as much as I ever have felt.

In a luxurious state of exhaustion, I must have fallen sound asleep in a very short time. I awoke some hours later and reached for Carrie, her subtle perfume fresh and still permeating my senses. The bed was empty and the lights were turned out. "Carrie?" I said quietly, knowing there wouldn't be an answer. Nor did I have any contact information or a last name, and that was all right. Let it remain, like priceless crystal or a beautiful cut diamond, flawless and uncommon; her life circumstances were entirely extraneous and better left that way, I contemplated in the dark. I was going home the next afternoon anyway. The fact that she was truly knockout gorgeous, and probably knew it, may have inspired her to seek sex outside her marriage; I could understand that, the notion that it's a waste not to make use of such attributes. That's why I never said no to a sexual opportunity – not that I had her allure, but that it felt somehow wasteful. In her case, she had honed the art of one-night romance to near perfection. Damn, she was beautiful. I hugged a pillow that still held the scent of Carrie and slept a few more hours.

I had lunch at a nearby restaurant planned with my religious sister and her promiscuous husband, and I had that third meeting to attend beforehand. I swung my feet onto the floor and flicked on the light. There was a note on hotel letterhead: "Good Morning, Sweetie. Here's my number at work. Lunch before you leave?" Oh yes, there was no doubt about the answer to that question. My delight at the chance to see her again was entirely authentic and completely free of any fixated strings. I was quite confident of her attitude being the same. Last night was just so damn perfect that a few more minutes would be a touch of honey-sweet icing on the cake. I'd call and explain my previous commitment and invite her to join us. To parade a remarkably pretty lady before my brother-in-law would be an unplanned extra. I'd wait until nine o'clock to call her and arrange to meet her a little before noon if I could. I had to check out at eleven, so more lovemaking was out. Just as well, as I'd probably have cancelled lunch, maybe even my business appointment, for that opportunity.

Everything went according to plan and I caught a glimpse of her before she came in. She smiled her lovely smile when our eyes met and we shared a brief but deliberate kiss as we turned toward the bar. Fifteen minutes later, as my sister arrived, I knew that Carrie was an administrative manager at a mid-sized engineering firm; she held a Bachelor's Degree in Sociology; she would have loved to stay last night but explaining that to her husband would have been difficult; she had every intention of continuing her marriage; she was glad to see me again and had trusted me enough to leave her phone number. I was thus assured of no strings and assured her likewise. We had a pleasant lunch and I enjoyed listening to her predictable conversational agility. With utmost discretion she took several opportunities to place her hand affectionately on my leg under the table and, while my brother-in-law was engaged pulling my sister's chair back so she could get to the restroom, Carrie pressed her hand into my groin, only once, but to last for eternity.

I took a cab to the airport, checked in, found my window seat, and buckled up. I glanced out across the tarmac, unseeing. Carrie pervaded my thoughts; my nervous system and the blood coursing through my body still seemed gently bathed in the aftermath of our rendezvous. I reached for a magazine from the seat pocket in front of me and examined its contents. "Eros and Psyche" seemed distant enough from the mundane world I resisted rejoining, and I flipped through the pages to find the article with that title. The legend, as it unfolded, resonated deeply with my thoughts. It went something like the following.

Eros, the Greek God of romantic and sexual desire, was of primordial origin. Primal Gods, those without prior cause, included Chaos (formlessness), Nyx (night), Erebus (deep darkness and shadow), and Tartarus (the abyss). Erebus and Nyx parented Hypnos (sleep) and Thanatos (death). Eros sprang from the ethereal union of black-winged Night and the infinite deep of Darkness. On his golden wings, swift as the whirlwinds of the tempest, erotic Eros mated in the deep Abyss with dark Chaos, winged like himself, and thus emerged our human race. Gentle Psyche was born among that newly created mortal race. Eros, powerless over her extraordinary beauty and his own sensual nature, crossed the great gulf between God and man, and took her as his consort.

Glancing at glossy depictions of Eros' form, reflections upon sensuous masculinity, alluring sexuality, and untarnished dignity permeated my thoughts. I was spellbound by the simple vital validity that seemed inherent in this ancient mythology, especially metaphorical images originating as early as the sixth century B.C.E. in which Psyche's uninhibited and passionate spirit was illuminated in the butterflies that attended her. Psyche, synonymous with the ancient Greek word for 'butterfly,' variously refers to a deification of the human soul, spirit, breath, life, or animating force.

Unfortunately, extraneous complexities linked to her earthly heritage led to trouble that threatened the idyllic connection between Eros and Psyche. But Zeus, in his infinite wisdom and (somewhat uncharacteristic) compassion, solved the problem by granting Psyche immortality. The sexy pair resumed their blissful coexistence and out of their unbound ecstasy was born a daughter, Voluptas (physical pleasure, bliss).

I sat a long time, just dwelling in the synchronicity of that ancient otherworldly conception of reality and the otherworldly encounter that still enchanted my conscious mind. I felt I could see clearly beyond the struggles man created for himself, to the parameters of existence as they actually are. "Zeus, help me!" I prayed. "Remove the manmade shackles that crisscross the horizons of my mind and dull my spirit like a giant spider-web splashing across my face on a sunny morning in a pristine forest."

Chapter 9

I made a choice between the three different options for clearing my business. I discarded the partnership arrangement proposed by a large client, because it meant a conflict of interest with another large client. I rejected forming a stand-alone satellite operation with a link to a larger broker because of the administrative burden. It was thus by default that I joined another quite conservative firm, somewhat smaller, but with a handsome commission payout agreement. Only a week later, early in 1978, I left my first real job after a little more than four years, and launched myself on a new path. I experienced no regret over leaving New York behind for a return to my roots in the west.

I placed some bets on my future when I splurged on a new townhouse, outfitted it with new furniture, and leased a new Chrysler Cordoba. One of the staff, a blue-eyed, frizzy-haired blonde named Sharon, and I flew off to San Francisco and checked into the Marriot at Fisherman's Wharf for the weekend. Although the unique and historic city generated some fascination for me, and we ventured out to take a streetcar ride one sunny day, we spent the majority of our time more intensely engaged in an inebriated carnal frenzy. It had soon become apparent that our interests in drinking and sex were all we had in common, and I felt hung-over from both aspects on the flight home, with no remaining aspirations for the relationship.

I rented single-engine Piper or Cessna airplanes and hopped off to drum up new business through seminar presentations, to visit established clients, and to party. The 'flying broker' – clients liked the catchy image. Business boomed and my share of commissions climbed to fifty-five thousand dollars in the remaining ten months of that first year.

In the bar after work, chic little Brenda, also from the office, explained why Sharon hadn't been right for me. "Not stylish enough, no flair," she said, and invited me back to her place. I never said no to an offer like that, unless I had a better one, but I really can't say that either was my type.

Late in that first year of my new situation, the markets turned extremely volatile. I had some very high flyers among my list of clients, with substantial positions on the company's books, and some were experiencing huge losses. I maintained frequent contact with most of them, three or four times a day, and a close connection developed as a consequence. I therefore felt bad in a personal sense, with respect to losses that had already taken some to the edge of bankruptcy. I feared, too, that my business was at risk of shrinking irreparably. The mental and emotional strain was enormous, day and night.

The capital requirements for the brokerage firm, typically hefty because of the leverage inherent in the commodity futures business, were exaggerated in the wild markets by inordinately large margin calls, which clients traditionally had twenty-four hours to meet. The firm's chief executive officer in New York, who had apparently gone into shock over the increased demands on his capital, phoned the office manager, Fred Wilson, and asked, "Does this Richard Nelson guy know what he's doing?" Fred was a glib, immaculately dressed man who had risen to the position of vice president and feared for his job on the best of days. He relayed the CEO's question to me personally, and I nearly went into shock when he suggested I should trim back the positions as an interim solution. My clients were under enough pressure as it was, and so was I.

Suddenly, the company I worked for had become the enemy, demonstrating a lack of trust and representing an additional threat to my business. My thoughts turned quickly to Jay Noland, a man in Wilson's position, but at a much larger firm called Beckert and Company. They had a long history in the futures business, and he had repeatedly paved the way. "Any time you want to come on board with us, just call; sixty-percent commission payout and direct access to the trading floors."

It was Friday afternoon and, as soon as Fred Wilson left my office, I called Mr. Noland. By Monday morning all was in order for the transfer of positions and I was sitting behind a new desk, calling my clients to expedite the paper work. The whole business of switching under such conditions had been a high-stress process. But all of it had gone smoothly enough, with the exception of Fred Wilson, who dug in his corporate feet at paying me the commission I was due.

I called Noel Hyman, with whom I had maintained regular contact, to update him on the move and mentioned the problem with getting paid. "Don't fight it; don't get upset. Just call him every day and ask where the money is, two or three times a day even. They owe it, and it is the last thing he wants to be reminded of, especially in light of the fact that his firm couldn't handle the business."

I started right away. "Hello, Louise; is Mr. Wilson there?" Again and again, "Hi Fred, how are you? I was just wondering if that check is in the mail." Sometimes I left a polite message with Louise during his lunch break.

"For Christ's sake, what the hell is this?" he said before the week was out, upon taking my third call for the day. "I'll have a check delivered, just don't call anymore." I grinned and called my cunning old mentor.

"Hey, I've got some news, too," Noel said. "These guys have lost their enthusiasm for this business. It doesn't fit into their way of doing things, so I'm making plans to close this operation down and move back to Chicago. You should think about doing that, too." Chicago was Mecca to all futures traders. Nowhere but up, I smiled, as my mind whirled at the prospect of vanishing limitations.

The time was the inflationary late seventies and, in spite of the recent turmoil, I was smack in the middle of the business that benefitted the most. By late 1979, my income had edged beyond ten thousand a month. I rented out the townhouse and took a fashionable apartment downtown, primarily because partying made it difficult to commute, mornings as well as evenings.

During the winter I skied most weekends and took a few weekdays off for it as well. I worked resolutely at the sport and my skill level advanced accordingly. Whenever it worked out I booked into picturesque mountain lodges with female skiing companions, which added enticing romantic appeal, if not always a romantic conclusion. Back when I was still getting to know Yvonne, my girlfriend for the last three years in New York, she had talked a lot about skiing. I hadn't even tried it back then, but my habitual insecurity had painted an intimidating image of lithe young men frolicking with racy young women in cozy fireplace settings, all of which most certainly led to unrestrained sexual activity, and all of which had seemed beyond my reach. I was once again driven to great and exasperating lengths to reach a goal that, in the end, only scattered my illusions.

Nineteen-eighty promised to be a good year and I kicked it off by attending a market analysis seminar and trading course in Beverly Hills. It seemed every market participant I met was convinced that someone, somewhere, could reveal the secret to making a lot of money in the markets. Several large clients, all active traders, accompanied me on this expedition. The course content was stimulating, and so well presented that the allure of making easy money led to thoughts of opening my own personal trading account. I remembered Noel's advice to the contrary. It seemed to me, however, that not to try my fortune in this arena was a betrayal of my intellect.

Over a drink at the Beverly Hills Hilton, where we were staying, one of the men coyly admitted that a friend had lent him his Playboy membership card when he'd mentioned he would be in L.A. He was not a man one would expect to have such a card, even on loan, which contributed greatly to our instantaneous and unanimous support for his suggestion. The only notable impression I have of that experience concerns a fortune telling palm-reader, an exotically garbed, heavily perfumed, long eye-lashed, middle-aged woman – in all respects my vision of a gypsy. She first took the hand of the man with the membership card, a slightly built avid jogger who wore a short-sleeve sport shirt, dress slacks, and loafers – my vision of a bookkeeper. Within seconds she emitted a deep mooing sound and said, "Cows, lots of cows." In fact, he was the well-disguised general manager and very large shareholder of a fifty thousand head cattle feed yard. The accuracy of her perception left me feeling anxious when she took my hand next. "Oh, ho, ho," she bayed insolently, "I see some wild scenes, mirrors above the bed." Naturally everyone roared at the outlandish exclamation. I laughed with them, inwardly thankful that it was easier to minimize the truth in these surroundings than it would have been in some rural setting, for example. I was not proud of the murky after-hours life I led and I did not want my stage-character tarnished with the brush of moral depravity.

Yvonne stayed in touch by phone. Upon graduating she announced that she had secured a teaching position in Denver. I know she believed that we would resume where we left off, as I had not informed her otherwise. Not long after she arrived, I was forced to tell her that I had met someone else (perhaps three others, but I didn't elaborate) but that I had every desire to remain friends. I knew she was devastated, heartbroken, in spite of her comparatively stolid self-control. We did maintain a close contact, we got together with mutual friends when they came to town, and we skied together quite often.

When my production levels earned me a bonus cruise to the Greek Islands and Turkey, I asked her to join me. We flew first class to Athens, where we embarked first class on a cruise ship superbly staffed by friendly Greek personnel. The food was sumptuous, the hospitality to rave about, and the weather perfect. We cruised upon the turquoise Mediterranean Sea, into the crater of the volcano that created the Island of Santorini. Anchored there, we rode donkeys up the coarse stone steps and along the winding narrow streets into the whitewashed town.

We wandered the ancient cobblestone streets at Mykonos. There I bought a charming watercolor of small fishing boats resting on the sandy shore at ebb tide, just as they had for millennia. We climbed along the rocky trail to inspect biblical ruins at old Ephesus. We enjoyed fresh grilled exotically spiced swordfish and sipped wine at an outdoor café on the pier in Istanbul.

But we did not make love. I'd lost my previous passionate attraction for her. It seemed that suppressing the flow of affection and adoration that was in my heart had anesthetized my physical desire. Because going down that road had meant overcoming a lot of painful guilt, my return was blocked, as though a bridge I had crossed no longer existed. I took a picture of her sitting rather forlornly on a sculpted stone seat beside the Temple of Olympian Zeus in Athens, looking very pretty, but a little wilted, and not her wholesome and bubbly self anymore. For a long time, I felt wretched whenever that image replayed itself.

My business kept growing and I finished my second year of business independence with an income of one hundred and twenty-seven thousand dollars. Halfway through the third year I recorded three months in a row of more than thirty thousand dollars of income per month. I was thirty years of age, proudly thinking my life was finally on track. When a government man from the Department of Agriculture called, requesting that I deliver a presentation on "the application of commodity futures" at an upcoming farm and ranch convention, I responded with this new confidence.

"I have a budget," he said, "and you would be compensated, at least for travel expenses."

"I am honored, certainly," I replied, "but I'll have to spend time preparing for it and the facility is an hour away, meaning it will occupy an entire working day." My business would not suffer in my absence, but still, I thought. "Who is the guest you are paying the most and how much is it?" I asked.

He said, rather immodestly it seemed, "A renowned psychiatrist from New Jersey is speaking on the topic of business stress and we are paying him a thousand dollars plus expenses."

I said, "That sounds good."

"Are you serious?" he asked, and then replied to the silence, "I'll have to call you back to confirm it." An hour later he called and confirmed it.

I considered it a bit of free money and immediately decided, rather uncharacteristically, to treat my father and mother to a little vacation. They had not travelled very much, except to visit relatives, and I thought they ought to. We flew to Phoenix, where we went to the dog races. My dad and I bet heavily on the long shot, a big dog wearing the number eight. We cheered and howled with excitement as he stretched ahead of the pack, muscling the other hounds out of his way, and won by five lengths.

We rented a car and toured leisurely through the desert, past Flagstaff, and into Las Vegas where we had tickets to hear Neil Sedaka at the Riviera Hotel. Jay Noland, the office manager at Beckert and Company, had suggested providing big Danny, a casino official, with a bottle of Crown Royal. "He'll take care of you," he said. Danny promptly led us past a waiting queue of a hundred and fifty other patrons, through an adjacent door, across the still empty red-carpeted auditorium, and sat us at a table in front of the stage. "I can put in your order for drinks. What'll you have?" he smiled at my mother, nightclub suave and virile. Following a moment of pensive hesitation, to be certain she wanted to ask the question, my mother tilted toward me, "Are you involved with the mob?"

Her innocent question, containing as much motherly concern as personal alarm, broke through my haughty veneer and I burst with laughter. I don't think that completely quelled her disquiet but it must have suggested the absence of imminent peril. We laughed a lot, enjoying a trip we could talk about for years to come. It was a small gesture that inadvertently purchased me enduring benefit, an entirely good and selfless act I often reflected upon as my best return for money spent.

One day, when he forgot his tennis racket, I lent a friend my Cordoba to retrieve it. He collided with another vehicle; the insurance company wrote the car off, and the lease was dissolved. I invited Sherry, the highly intelligent, very pretty, and extraordinarily voluptuous young lady who now served as my assistant at work, and frequent companion after work, to come car shopping with me. I hadn't decided what I wanted and I valued her opinion on style.

As soon as we entered the showroom, I spotted the newly created, elegant but sporty Eldorado Biarritz on display. It wasn't at all what I had in mind, because I had not known of its existence. After asking what it was, however, and then sitting in it, I asked how much it cost.

"Oh, I think this might be a little more than you planned on spending. It sells for thirty thousand dollars," the salesman smirked too self-assuredly at his two naive prospects, still in their twenties and wearing cut-off blue jeans and tee-shirts.

Indignantly dismissing him, I asked to speak with the sales manager. "When can I take this car home?" I demanded.

"How will you pay for it?" he asked, with a little more respect than his salesman.

"With a check," I replied. It was only one month's income and the car was a dream, Sherry agreed.

After less than a week in my possession, Sherry and I took the Eldorado for a drive in the country and the transmission gave out. It had to be towed back to the dealership, and I realized I would be forced to take a loaner the next weekend to attend a family gathering. My plans for proudly parading this new symbol of my success had been ruined and I was incensed, raging over the fact that I'd spent thirty thousand dollars for a lemon. No matter what rewards I reaped from my success, I acquired no acquaintance with feelings of gratitude, except where the rewards served as a demonstration of success. I was frequently elated with the evidence that I was really going somewhere, but I always looked to the future, to reaching greater heights. I found no contentment in the present, and was thus perpetually on the verge of self-pity, ready for any obstruction or frustration to push me into a mire of bitterness and cynicism.

At my whim and invitation, Sherry accompanied me on the weekend trip to my brother's pleasant acreage home about five hours from the city. The two of us had an easygoing intimate relationship that made her presence seem quite natural to me, and I was pleased and proud to have a beautiful girl at my side. I thought very little of anyone's opinion regarding my unorthodox relationships. On Saturday afternoon, five of us – Sherry, my brother, a close friend of mine, his wife and myself – enjoyed an afternoon drive through the fall countryside. A delightful conviviality was aroused by liberal beer consumption, establishing a tone that pleased me a great deal, particularly because I hoped to establish a warmer and more harmonious bond with my sometimes unnervingly acrimonious brother.

Then my born-again sister, who I perceived as a flamboyant thief of any limelight, and her husband, whose bloated character always nettled me, arrived on the scene. It had always been in her nature to intrude unannounced for fear of missing out on something. This time, however, she threatened not only to disturb the atmosphere but also to undermine my emotional purpose. I maintained a seething self-control while we ate dinner. As we had more drinks, and the evening wore on into the night, I lost control and finally used some exceptionally foul language to express my suppressed feelings and judgments. My brother intervened and threatened me. The party ended and we all went to bed. The next morning, not a word was uttered in the way of accusation, admission or apology, and the trip home vanished in obsessed mental efforts to rationalize my actions. Inevitably, the only course open to me was hoping the memory was worse than the reality. Once again, I had to face the future as though nothing regrettable had happened, a process that increasingly depended on sex and alcohol for its success. Sometimes, leaving it all behind seemed the only possible solution, in a geographical sense, that is, nothing self-destructive. In fact, I had always found relocation very desirable, longed for it even, especially when it could be cloaked in the image of a giant leap forward.

Playing directly into my impatient yearnings, Noel Hyman called, wanting to talk more seriously about the opportunities he saw in Chicago. I flew there and met with him and the other partners at Holloway and Associates, the firm he had joined. The door was opened for another exciting advance in my persistent upward climb, which seemed at the same time well deserved, predestined, and worthy of any cost. Although it was another leaving behind of life as I could hardly have imagined it only three years previously, I began announcing my decision as soon as I returned. Sherry was personally saddened, as we had spent a lot of time together, but I appeased my guilt by launching her in her own business with some clients that didn't fit into the mold of my future. By the end of 1980 my taxable income totaled two hundred and eighty thousand dollars, and I compensated her further by doubling her income in recognition of the loyal and professional support she had provided.

I had also become close friends with the office manager, Jay Noland, and his sincere blessing counted for a lot. It puzzled me a little that he and another fellow in the office, a quiet but amiable stockbroker named Ben, didn't drink alcohol. They always arrived early at my parties and didn't stay very late, but they were exceptionally gregarious and noticeably tolerant of everyone else's excessive drinking. They were present at the party I arranged to honor friends and fellow workers just before leaving Denver.

"You never drank at all?" I asked Jay.

"Oh yes, far too much for a while. I had to give it up before it destroyed me," he answered with a calm modesty, the twinkle never leaving his eye.

I thought it was very sad, and could not envision myself coming to that point. "What about Ben, same thing?" I asked.

"I can't speak for Ben," Jay said, "but I'm sure he wouldn't mind telling you, if you're interested."

I was not interested. In fact the subject had made me a little uncomfortable. I noticed that Yvonne had arrived and I crossed the room to welcome her. She gave me a card in which she had written, "You were my first love and I shall always love you!" I don't know if I read it that night, really read it, I mean. I was soaring pretty high with the booze and raucous social interaction I enjoyed so much.

I read it the next day, though, and I've reread it, either the actual card or in my mind's eye, many times since. She appeared to have gotten beyond the burdensome emotional residue of our past, but I still was not free of remorse. A few women had inspired momentary visualizations of a shared future, but those mental meanderings always ended at an emotional dam displaying the inscription, "You can't betray the fact that Yvonne is the one you should be with!" It was a condition that I found acceptable, nonetheless, because I much preferred my bachelor life over any complex alternative. It worked as a strangely beneficial emotional catalyst, generating a last defense against slipping haphazardly into other entanglements.

I had just recently turned thirty years of age, my conscience had little remaining impact on my decisions, and my state of mind was in a full departure from reality. In a moment of misty awareness and sorry reflection, I found Yvonne's lack of self-preserving intuition entirely baffling. Why couldn't she have seen what I was like? But then, I reflected, I could be a very nice boy, with the noblest of loving intentions, though they soared far beyond my capacity to follow through. A silent lingering remorse, for the betrayal of her innocently misplaced devotion, coursed deeply through my being and merged with that old touchstone of agony: the day, at ten years of age, I sacrificed my loyal, trusting 4-H calf to his death.

Chapter 10

I left Denver on Friday afternoon and drove through the weekend. The Biarritz was a pleasure to drive; the miles slipped away and the back of the luxurious leather seat reclined to nearly level when I needed a nap. I handed the keys to a parking attendant and checked into the Chicago Union League Club Sunday night. Monday morning I was sitting at a new desk, this time on the mezzanine floor of the office tower known worldwide as the Chicago Board of Trade.

I felt certain I'd arrived. The dismal past was of little account and a golden future lay before me. Frank Sinatra's words resonated: Chicago was my kind of town. The men at Holloway greeted each other boisterously – "Hi, Big Guy" – and I liked that. It was an ego boost that implied unquestioning respect and admiration. It was alright, even desirable, to be called a big shot, but not at all good to be a "jurg-ov," a dismissive term, with its own derogatory inference, that was applied to any uncooperative or adversarial loser. "New crop" could refer to grains or other commodities that had a seasonal break in production, as distinct from "old crop," or it might be a reference to all the young college girls who showed up for summer jobs as clerks and runners. Money seemed to permeate the very air we breathed, while wry guffaws peppered moments of happy bliss. A bar on the ground floor of the building, Sign of the Trader, poured very large gin or vodka martinis and one single-malt scotch on-the-rocks went a long way toward dulling the pain of a losing day or spurring on the elation of triumph.

I arranged to rent a large apartment in the gentrified near north, roughly fifteen minutes by cab from the office at LaSalle Street and Jackson Boulevard, and began to carve a life for myself. I did bring one increasingly important aspect of my life with me: my newly acquired habit of speculating for profit in the futures markets, trading with my own money in an attempt to accelerate my accumulation of wealth. The motivation wasn't only money, but rather the vague idea that someday I could be free of all restraints, including the need for dealing with clients. I'd simply take money from the markets in great gobs and report to no one. I'd be able to expand my cultural horizons, increase my knowledge of the arts, and become a more refined person, larger than the one I'd been unable to accept so far.

My geographical relocation to the planetary center of the commodity business had in fact been greeted by my clients as a very hopeful state of affairs. They would now be dealing through a broker who had more intimate and rapid access to pertinent market information. I felt a strong nostalgic affiliation with my clients and I was happy about their perception of the benefits. I sincerely hoped the improved profitability they expected would materialize. But that happiness was small in comparison with the silent self-centered optimism I reserved for my own grandiose objectives.

My dabbling in the markets to date had led to thirteen thousand dollars in losses, small potatoes in light of my income, the fact that it was all an income-tax deduction, and my haughty view that it was merely the cost of tuition. There were other costs, however, primarily associated with the all-absorbing preoccupation that having a position in the market seemed to cause me. It was difficult to concentrate on conversations while my eyes were diverted by every tick on the electronic quote screen. Irritability and anxiety led to greater coffee consumption, more frequent smoking, and a reluctance to pick up the phone and provide service to clients. The closing of the markets brought some immediate relief, but the added pressure of the day was revealed in my impatient desire to have a drink and lose myself in the most readily available distraction.

Before the first week was out, a giddy drinking session ended in bed with an office staff member, Maria, for whom I had no broader interest. It is remarkable that, despite the encounter being repeated once or twice, she must have regarded it as an ordinary extension of partying, just as I did, because her attitude toward my frolicking with her good friend Cynthia, several weeks later, was wholly supportive and our work relationship remained unaffected. For me, sensitivity to the feelings and reactions of others was displaced by the heaviness of my own insecurities, and the self-absorbed frantic pace I maintained to surmount them.

Those were the days of rampant inflation, when formerly respected economists and government officials were assailed by accusations of runaway fiat currency devaluation. Providing leadership in the 'hard money' camp (those who advocated a return to a gold-backed monetary system), The National Committee for Monetary Reform sponsored a convention of thousands of like-minded anarchists. It was held in New Orleans and I joined several clients there for the weekend. Many of the presenters were truly exceptional and I learned I wasn't alone in my skepticism for, and ill will toward, the establishment. At night I assailed the company expense account by entertaining my guests at Antoine's, arguably New Orleans's finest restaurant. Following that, I believe we were probably fortunate to have avoided any violent physical repercussions over our brash and rowdy conduct in the French Quarter. The next morning, foggy tendrils from the night filled me with ominous clammy-skinned foreboding as a good client from out west, a pillar of his community and family man, related how one of the hookers we dragged home had stolen his wallet with his ID, money, and credit cards. Despite his being ten years my senior, the remorse that washed over me seemed a just punishment for my risky and thoughtless compulsiveness. But one had to get over such things and, as the final day unfolded, we laughed over a few drinks and made wry references to the previous night's highlights. By the time we headed for the airport we had declared our commitment to do it again next year.

Two weeks later, on the night before I was to leave on a business trip to visit prospective customers in Calgary, Alberta, we were sailing along the tri-state expressway in my Eldorado with Maria driving. Cynthia, who worked in the office as an executive secretary for the managing director, and I suddenly become infatuated with each other and fell into a bout of erotic kissing in the seat next to her. I didn't know I was attracted to Cynthia before that, but it was like an electrical circuit had been established. Nothing more happened that night, however, and the girls took my car home, planning to drive me to the airport the next morning.

We met for breakfast, drank too much champagne and orange juice, and they drove me to Chicago's O'Hare. The company always flew us first class and that meant the drinks kept flowing. I missed my connecting flight in Winnipeg because I passed out on a row of seats in the airport while waiting for it. I didn't regain consciousness until two Royal Canadian Mounted Police officers, a man and a woman, roused me. When they asked me for identification I realized my wallet was missing. The inconvenience of my situation infuriated me and, in a still drunken state, I obnoxiously accused them of stealing it, repeatedly, as though I would gain some kind of leverage over my unfortunate circumstances. The only leverage that materialized was their grip on my arms as they escorted me from the airport, placed me in the back seat of a police car, hauled me from the car into the station downtown and, finally, into a cell that I realized later was the drunk-tank. When I began banging on the bars and loudly asserting that I was an American, the duty officer warned me politely to be quiet. When I continued and they grew tired of it, two of them came in and handcuffed my hands behind my back.

When I woke up the next morning and found myself lying on concrete with a floor drain staring me in the face, severely cramped and still painfully handcuffed, I finally grasped the humiliating circumstances I had created for myself. By the time the door opened and I was led into the reception area, given my overcoat and briefcase and shown the door, I was more submissive. "No charges. You're free to go," the officer said dryly, accurately concluding that my punishment would continue for the day without me being a further nuisance to the RCMP. Most of my cards were in the wallet I'd lost but I found a credit card in my briefcase, along with my passport, and that allowed me to book another flight and resume the trip as planned, with the exception of the meetings I had missed on that first day. They needed rescheduling: "Other business had inconveniently popped up and delayed me."

I suppressed that mortifying incident into a segment of my memory that could have been labeled 'stupefied'. It is lamentable that I gained nothing from it in the form of insight or a decision to change my ways regarding alcohol consumption. I did, however, resolve to stay away from office girls and try to preserve a respectable professional image. Inadvertently supporting that resolution, an acquaintance introduced me to Connie, a very pretty girl with short blonde hair and lots of preppy style. She was an aspiring accounting professional whose father was a senior partner in a major law firm. She lived some distance from downtown and, because I liked to stay and party after work on Fridays, it became a pattern for me to show up at her place on Saturdays and spend the remainder of the weekend with her. She was a delightful lady and we began to spend many fine days together. It was Connie who inspired me to acquire a membership at the Art Institute of Chicago where I enjoyed countless hours of peaceful solitude amidst the marvelous collection of European Impressionist works.

My routine was interrupted briefly when my pal John Sargent called on a Monday morning and said he wanted to get away for a weekend. Four days later he and I met in Las Vegas. Touring the Grand Canyon seemed like a good idea and we booked a helicopter to do that on the Saturday afternoon. A typical outing with John: we took a quick cruise above the vast gorge, landed, stepped out to listen to a brief synopsis, and headed back to Vegas for a drink. Not that I was drawn with intense interest to the Grand Canyon, but I would have preferred spending a little time, a solitary moment or two, in reflection. I enjoyed having my own thoughts, even if they were no more than contempt for the over-indulgence of the masses. It disturbed me even further that I participated in these unfulfilling weekend getaways with John, rather than decline his impetuous suggestions, because of my inability to stop grasping after a superficial image of importance. John had somehow convinced me of the authenticity of his empty conceit, despite my dislike for his personality, and I wasn't standing on firm enough ground to refute it. I think a lot of people sort out this kind of thing for themselves during adolescence.

Connie envisioned a future for us, I'm sure, and invited me to her parents' place in the country for Christmas dinner. She invited me to stay there Christmas Eve as well, but I thought that would mean too much social exposure and I stayed in town. With the notion that Christmas Eve is a good time to meet another lonely heart, I went in search of entertainment in the bars along Rush Street. I started a conversation with a girl a little younger than me who sat by herself. I soon learned that her family rejected her, or she rejected them, on the basis of radically different lifestyle choices. She appeared a bit dreary and slovenly, lacked interest in most subjects, and seemed bent on getting drunk. But I developed a sad empathy toward her, with deference for her outsider status, and she had the most humongous tits. She was pleased with the invitation to go back to my place and, once there, became livelier. She said she needed a shower and didn't object to my joining her. I know we had sex a few times, continued to drink, and didn't get enough sleep to prepare me for the social encounter I'd agreed to the next day. I remember her enormous breasts, the huge tinted areas around her nipples, and the tension I felt while trying to edge her out so I could get to dinner on time. I think she had nowhere else to go and I felt kind of wretched about that. I might have spent the day with her, as a sympathetic gesture, if I hadn't had another obligation.

I felt wretched while driving to Connie's parents' house, too, imagining the respectable household I'd soon be in the midst of, in contrast to the night I'd just had. I'm sure my breath reeked of stale booze and my eyes were like angry red roadmaps. But she smiled graciously, her father and mother were genteel, and her siblings were thrilled to meet me. After a lavish and sumptuous dinner, Connie and I retired to the family room where she said I looked very tired and asked if I'd like to lie down. I declined her offer and soon began dozing off with my arm across her shoulders, my head falling forward, a condition I tried ineffectively to avert with jerking nods. Such a pitiful image must have been awkward for her, but it was never mentioned. She was too polite, and my abhorrence for discussions of that nature simply warned against it.

In February 1981, my friends Bob and Karen Hawk called and invited me to spend a week skiing in the Alps, at Verbier, Switzerland. They were now stationed in Saudi Arabia because Bob had accepted a banking placement there. Switzerland was a good halfway point. They'd be there in two weeks and I was immediately thrilled with the idea of joining them. I thought nothing of leaving on short notice and called Yvonne in Denver to see if she would like to go, offering to pay her share of the accommodation, since we had all been such close friends a few years back. She was a little surprised, but only a little and quite readily accepted.

The ski resort was thousands of feet above the Rhone Valley and a gondola soared from a townsite below to deliver visitors at the quaint mountainside village of Verbier. The village was the base of alpine operations, but the luxurious chalet Bob had rented was still further up, about two thirds of the way down the actual ski area. That meant we took a chairlift to get to it the first time and, for the rest of the week, arrived and departed with our skis on. Just above us was a small cluster of outdoor cafes and bars. We often stopped to rest there and to enjoy delicious raclette, heated cheese of the same name, scraped off and spread over small new potatoes. We sat in the sun for a while, over glasses of beer or wine, and then continued down the vast open runs or along the outer edge where we could see the historic Rhone River, a gleaming ribbon nine thousand feet below, coursing through the lush green valley where spring was already well advanced. Completely relaxed with our skis planted on the gentle incline, jesting and laughing while the high altitude sun warmed our backs, sharing wine skins full of heart-warming Chianti Classico, it seemed life was indeed ours to behold.

Every day was glorious, some perfectly sunny and clear, some when the mountain was partially shrouded in cloud and visual conditions became mysteriously flat. Joints were occasionally passed around, but I never cared for the effect of weed and declined. Besides, as we edged to a halt in front of the chalet at the end of a day, the wine had done its job preparing me for the evening meal and a night of partying.

Maid service regularly restored the place while we were out and our resident cooking staff prepared the most wonderful and abundant dinners for us in the evenings. Although we had the option of skiing down to the village under the lights, partying in the pubs there and catching a short chairlift back, eight of us staying in the chalet made self-contained social evenings more than viable. On at least two occasions, Bob Hawk led the party into a complete removal of our clothes, as I recall, and on my last night there I became seriously inebriated. I don't remember the last few hours of it, but I slept in the next morning and missed the bus that would have delivered me to Geneva and my flight home.

I considered waiting another day, but finally decided I had to expedite my return. I hired a taxi, which cost several hundreds of the strongest currency in the world at the time, the Swiss Franc, because the Swiss subscribed to a hard money philosophy. That fleeting business-related lament soon gave way to the more familiar sense of impending doom that often accompanied serious hangovers. It was a form of terror that, rather than leading to physical retreat or flight, caused internal flinching and the pitiful craving to escape from one's own shameful existence. I got to the airport too late and would get no credit for the missed flight. I purchased another flight from Geneva to Chicago and waited, knowing I had just spent a dream week in the Swiss Alps but unable to feel it, just enduring until I could get on the plane and pass out again. I thought of my friends back at the chalet and, though I would later recall many wonderful moments, I wished that I had departed in a more dignified fashion, that I had been more mindful and caring while saying goodbye to Yvonne who, once again I perceived, was disheartened that we remained no more than platonic friends.

Back home again, driving out to see Connie, I looked forward to the fact that she loved to position her body with elbows and knees on the bed and receive me as I kneeled behind her. She encouraged me to slam my hips against her buttocks which must have been a thrill for her, and most certainly added to my physical enjoyment. But my enthusiasm was often overcome by a sour acrid odor. I couldn't determine the exact origin and didn't say anything for fear of upsetting her. I even held my head off to the side in a desperate attempt to evade the pungent intrusion on my indulgence. It was a blot on our togetherness. I liked her and hoped a resolution of the problem would come about before I lost interest.

Because I believed I would eventually be rich and dwell in a world of adventure and culture, I thought it prudent to maintain my physical wellbeing and develop my character. If I partied heavily one or two nights, I often felt quite wrecked and tried to compensate with good food, abstinence, and constructive activities. I signed up for karate classes on Mondays and Wednesdays, as I had done in Denver. Those days of the week were appropriate because I was usually recovering from the weekend and there wasn't as much going in the evenings anyway. I played squash regularly, as a member at the Chicago Union League Club. Responding to an enduring fascination, I was drawn to musicals and live theatre events, such as the Broadway production of *Peter Pan* at the Arie

Crown Theatre, which I thoroughly enjoyed with Connie that season.

In May I accompanied Ken Wearing, upon his request, to a grain marketing conference in Memphis. Ken was a fine old Welsh gentleman of medium stature, with an abundant mane of silver hair, heavy rimmed spectacles, and a very unassuming demeanor. He was a professional who lived and prospered within all the guidelines of respectability. That alone left me feeling slightly off balance, but he was a kind man as well and soon dispelled my discomfort. There was no apparent reason that he should have invited me; perhaps he meant to share some of his insight into surviving in the industry all those years. I was honored to travel with him and the initial respect I had for him grew, although he talked very little about himself. Perhaps he, like others that I viewed as mentors, such as Noel Hyman, thought I could be influenced to live within guidelines of respectability myself.

Sometimes I thought people had a very good opinion of my potential, probably based on my sound education, my aptitude for the business, and my rather rapid rise in income, but they saw me undermining the foundations of my success with behavior that would eventually make it unsustainable. I could see that their conclusion was valid, assuming I desired success within their humdrum social framework. My assumption, however, which I could not expect people to understand, was that I possessed a level of intelligence that would carry me well beyond an average material success and permit me to enjoy a life of unrestricted anarchy, with regard to social norms. I suspect, if I had been honest with these men, they would have described my ideas as unrealistically egotistical. But I hadn't been versed in the practice of sharing my innermost thoughts and would never have trusted anyone to pass judgment on them. So I kept my aspirations to myself.

I behaved myself on that trip, eating meals with Ken at scheduled times, mixing with other attendees, and going to my room when I needed a break, or in the evening when the day was done. During the few hours I spent walking around outside the convention facility, I found the civil old southern city quite fascinating and I discovered their annual celebration, Memphis in May, was to take place the following week.

Sherry, the memorable young lady who'd been my assistant and social partner a year ago in Denver, had recently expressed a desire to visit and I immediately thought of it as a wonderful setting for our reunion. It turned out to be exactly that, a perfectly sunny weekend in that fabulously genteel old cotton trading port on the Mississippi River. Sherry told me about her experience during the last year with a would-be sugar daddy from New Jersey, an older man who had opened negotiations with a very expensive ring and offered her a life of leisure. She'd already broken the connection, sold the ring, and was now looking for an opportunity to start a family. We had a very easygoing relationship, the sexual component being especially rich, but she suffered no illusion regarding my family aspirations. In turn, I was completely unaffected by her additional carnal activity. She cherished sensual pleasure and sensual pleasure was an integral aspect of our friendship, very much like fine dining. I guess that's why images of Sherry's firm and voluptuous form, and many of our shared erotic moments and maneuvers, have survived with more resilience than those of any other continuing encounter.

On a June weekend, Connie and I flew to Boston where we joined my friend John Sargent, who now lived in Toronto. The flamboyant heavily-perfumed redhead he had on his arm was characteristic of John's bold defiance and haughty manner. We hired a driver and limousine for the day, toured the Bowery and beaches, ate too many chicken lobsters, and drank a lot of wine and champagne. That was a good time we thought and cost a mere thousand dollars each, or maybe two. Quite often we thought we were having fun, and 'thinking it' was doubtless the primary ingredient. There was little accumulation of fond memories, such as happens with married couples and within families, and not always much to reflect upon afterwards. But living on the edge, beyond the norm, outside the box, has its own rewards. And there is nothing comparable to spending money without restraint if one is seeking a sense of superiority.

A few weeks later Connie and I had a row following dinner downtown and we went home separately. I can't remember the issue and I expect I fabricated it, willfully staged it, and then proceeded to obstinately exaggerate the importance of it, all because I was ready to move on and wanted to offload some of the responsibility and guilt. The next day I awoke to a flood of empty remorse. I had let go of a special person who truly cared for me and I had jettisoned an opportunity to raise the bar of my own existence. The two thoughts that eased my troubled conscience most were these: I sincerely felt she wasn't missing out on much and I fully expected she would soon realize that.

Chapter 11

For the rest of the summer I took up golfing with friends Troy and Dave from the office. I rented airplanes and did a bit of flying out of Midway Airport, even once to Toronto for a wedding. I occupied the company's regular season seats, with Troy and Dave, whenever the Cubs played at Wrigley Field. Partying with those two men or not, I stayed open to romantic opportunities, and I tried to figure out how to make a lot more money. There were always more ladies, but none that I wanted to exchange my freedom for. As for making money by speculating, I was often frustrated and my disappointing efforts drained the equity from my account more than once. I had a guaranteed minimum income of ten thousand dollars per month and the commissions I generated were always beyond that, so I was flush with cash. But I desperately sought to trade my way to independence, to get beyond needing an income. As well, in gloomier moments, I felt no assurance that my ongoing income was secure despite its robust growth. A completely self-reliant man is predestined to fear his limitations, I concluded. No matter how buoyant my present circumstances, I was subtly but relentlessly driven by some menacing undercurrent.

Chicago, however, especially on weekends, offered endless distractions. I felt very much at home in the city, enjoying my uninhibited, unattached lifestyle, and the months vanished in a fun-filled blur. Troy, Dave, and I enjoyed several days milling through the crowds at 'Taste of Chicago' with casual opportunities to hear performers like Willie Nelson and John Prine. We were all three attracted to the Rush Street bar scene and evenings frequently turned into incidents, some hilarious, others regrettable. Troy became obnoxious with a bartender and suffered a broken nose; Dave was nearly decapitated vomiting out the door of a moving Checker Cab; I got us evicted because of the thunderous vulgar language I used when two other men joined our table and one proposed a philosophy to which I was strongly opposed, for that night at any rate.

Troy, who leased a membership and traded on the floor of the Chicago Mercantile Exchange, had knowledge of the cattle feeding industry and connections in the Texas Panhandle. I had the same in Colorado and had established a foothold in Alberta. We decided to join forces in developing more business in that industry by offering the firm's trading expertise in the cattle and grain futures markets. Over several months we travelled together on three separate occasions. We spent a week driving many miles across the prairie in the Amarillo and Lubbock areas, between feed yards, and met a good number of owners and managers. Next we flew to Calgary and began a thousand mile loop that included a broad swath of cattle feeders in the prairie south and several others that were situated in the northeast parkland. The initial prospecting part of our plan ended with trip number three on the plains north of Denver, around Greeley.

The people we met were generally in a distinct class. They wielded large amounts of money typically backed by multi-million dollar lines of credit and placed tens of thousands of head of cattle on feed at their feedlots. They therefore took huge positions in the market without knowing what the feeding costs would be or what they would receive for a final sale price. Many were custom lots that fed others people's cattle for a fee, 'yardage' it was called. Still, someone was taking enormous risk. Gambling was the only name for it and they reveled in their freedom to bet as big as they liked. They wanted no government interference, while many other agricultural producers did. They were members of a fraternity that stretched north and south over the whole western great plains of North America. Perhaps the bold character of the industry sprang from the vast sagebrush peppered grasslands where wraithlike

146

herds of antelope drifted among vaporous heat waves, under cloudless azure skies. Although we were presenting ideas of managing risk and controlling financial exposure, men in that industry often delighted in the discovery that futures markets provided easy access to even greater leverage. I had grown up in a small corner of that expansive landscape and, although I had not desired to remain there, I wondered if I hadn't taken from it an uncontrollable urge to roam, and an aversion to being fenced in.

It was mid-November when Cynthia and I arranged to meet for a drink after work. We had known each other well over a year now, worked in the same office, met in the midst of others for drinks after work, and had not forgotten our single sensual encounter in the car on the night before my ill-fated flight to Calgary. The exhilaration of a passionate kiss is not easily erased and the stirring of one's sensory desire can only be resolved through troublesome repression or the gratifying allowance of its full manifestation. We were no doubt on a course for the latter. She walked across the room toward me, to the bar where I half-stood and half-sat on the edge of a tall barstool, and we kissed deeply because that is what we had been waiting to do. Pulling back a little, we beamed with desire into each other's eyes and then let our bodies press together again through a buffer of fall clothes.

Over a drink, we assured each other of our firm resolve that this would not become public knowledge. It was commonly understood at Holloway and Associates, by unwritten decree of the managing partner, Darcy Eckhart, that sexual relations between employees would have to cease, or one of the parties would have to find work elsewhere. I knew of several that hadn't ceased, but they were between married men with key roles and female members of the staff. Careful discretion kept them from Eckhart's view, helped by the fact that he usually left for home before the office closed, well before those nighttime liaisons were resumed. Possibly, I thought, he simply chose to avoid uncomfortable confrontation by averting his attention.

I found Cynthia's body at least as lovely as I'd imagined and our lovemaking was exquisitely enjoyable. Afterwards, I gazed at her face and along the length of her naked body, as I propped my head on a vertical forearm, a tranquil and divinely lovable woman. We could hardly wait to be together again and talked of going away for a weekend. The fact that she lived with a partner was a source of comfort because substantial restraint was thus built in. A few moments later we enjoyed our mutual desire once more. It always fascinated me that the details of a one-night stand became etched in my memory, while sex in an ongoing relationship was only generally memorable. I suppose, if we had ceased after that first encounter, I would have retained an indelible imprint.

Concerning my financial goals, the bond market was in a dive and I took a short position because the technical analysis I followed said it was going to seventy-two from eighty-five. I made a bet with John Sargent that it would hit seventy-eight before December fifteenth; the loser would buy the winner Christmas dinner in London, England. It crashed even sooner than I had anticipated, so I closed out my position at seventy-two for a forty-two thousand dollar gain and booked a flight to London so John could buy me a nice dinner. I'd make sure of that.

We met at JFK in New York on December twenty-first and took the same flight to Heathrow. We were a few days early for Christmas and I wanted to visit a great-aunt and other distant relatives with whom my mother had stayed in touch for many years. John agreed to accommodate that wish. Upon our arrival we rented a car and drove west through the countryside to Taunton where they lived. I enjoyed a delightful visit and established a satisfying connection with my maternal ancestry. My great-aunt was bed-ridden but very chipper and bright, and very grateful for my coming all that way to see her. I left feeling I'd done something intrinsically good, quite outside the self-centered box that usually confined me. John shot me a sideways glance of incomprehension when I attempted to express that sentiment. I ignored his contempt, quietly nourishing my heartfelt reaction to the visit until we arrived back at the Castle Hotel, where we planned to stay for another night.

In the evening, we went to a small pub for something to eat and a few glasses of beer. There was a small lively group there who obviously knew each other well. They were playing musical instruments, singing and laughing, and soon included us in their revelry. Because it was a very good party, when the time came for the pub to close we invited them back to the expansive but homey lobby-parlor at our lodgings. The law provided that, because the hotel was our residence, we could invite these dozen guests, order liquor, and celebrate as long as we liked. In spite of the brief interruption, the party continued almost seamlessly and we left the tab open for our new friends. I don't remember what the final tally was, but the music, hilarity, and warm camaraderie were priceless.

Once again, as we drove back to London in the morning, pleasant waves of nostalgia left me feeling thankful for meeting those people, as though I had partaken in something vital and untainted, another encounter that was quite outside my routine. This time I didn't bother exposing it to John's snobbish condescension. We talked instead of the feature engagement and decided on the dining room in the Four Seasons Hotel at Park Lane, as the choice of restaurants was limited on Christmas Eve.

Once there and seated, I proceeded to spend as much as I could of his money. Two single malt scotches set the tone and were followed by a starter of Scottish smoked salmon and Caspian Sea caviar with a silky dry white wine, a luscious garden salad with a tart cheesy house dressing prepared at our table, rich and succulent Chateau Briand accompanied by a bottle of wonderfully robust Bordeaux, then another bottle. Dessert and a bottle of nineteen forty-eight Napoleon Port topped things off nicely. The entire meal had been spiced with cynical wit, arrogant laughter, and friendly joshing sarcasm, four hundred and fifty pounds worth, about eight hundred dollars.

Being a little inebriated by the time we stood to leave, we were drawn to a brilliantly lit ballroom where a party of stunningly gowned women and tuxedo clad men seemed engaged in an affair of grand sophistication. The fact that they were all black and we were white seemed of no importance as they welcomed us in and suggested drinks all around. I suppose, because it was quite late in the evening, the event had developed a casual tone. I remember the ladies, several of whom we danced with, being of extraordinary beauty and exhibiting nearly divine comportment. At some point we learned we were partying with the contestants of a 'Miss Black' beauty pageant, as to the dominion of which I am at a loss. We stayed and visited a little while with the very good-natured people who had first welcomed us among them. Eventually, I am very pleased to recall, we gratefully and respectfully took our leave.

From that point onward the liquor claimed my conscious awareness and the events of the night became obscure. The next morning, I struggled with a foggy image in which two prostitutes had departed unhappily, objecting to being laid-off, instead of laid, or something like that. "Merry Christmas," we exclaimed with more cynical laughter, as a new day began around noon with champagne and orange juice.

Back in Chicago I spent the last week of 1981 engaged in arduous mental gymnastics, the purpose of which was to come up with a workable philosophy for speculation and to identify parameters that would limit my losses and let the profits accumulate on a consistent basis. I was encouraged by the solid gains I'd accumulated during the bond market decline and intended to build upon that. I looked forward to 1982 with invincible optimism in that regard.

I awoke New Year's Day with a numbing hangover and a disgusted recollection of New Year's Eve. One of the brokers, a young fellow who only started trading in the last year, had invited us to the new house he'd recently paid cash for, the result of some surprisingly dramatic gains in the market. After drinks in the office and drinks at The Sign, as we affectionately abbreviated it, it didn't take me long to consume more alcohol than was appropriate at a party which included the wives of my more discreet fellow workers. I don't remember the nature or extent of the altercation that unfolded, but someone had called a taxi for me as a consequence.

On the way home, I asked the driver to find me a hooker. He knew where to go and soon a tall lanky black girl with a little leather skirt that barely covered her crotch joined me in the back seat of the Checker Cab. Smiling sweetly, she opened her fake-fur collared coat, wiggled her modest bosom a little and flipped the loose halter top up, exposing them for my inspection and arousal. With that she asked if I wanted a blowjob. "How much?" I'm sure I slurred. She said, "Fifty dollars."

I briefly considered the possible embarrassment of the driver, who seemed quite clean cut and about sixty, but took my wallet out of my sport-jacket pocket and paid her the money. She went to work immediately and effectively. As she moved her head up and down, though, her right hand moved along my left side toward the pocket into which she had obviously observed me returning my wallet. I immediately committed myself to two objectives: I would not interrupt her efforts to please me sexually and I would frustrate her efforts to get my wallet. By squeezing my left arm in tight, I made certain of the latter until the former was accomplished. I knew she was a thief. I knew her first plan had failed and I wanted to end our encounter as quickly as possible. I clutched my wallet, which she had gone after more aggressively, and said, "Quit! You've already been paid the amount you asked for. Stop the car," I said to the driver. She seemed unhappy with her mouth full of sperm and spit it all over my only partly pulled-up pants. Then she got out and, spitting a further stream of hostile verbiage, slammed the door.

Recalling an image like that was a bad way to start the day. The relief that no one I knew witnessed the event, except for whatever happened at the party, was hardly compensation for the ever-widening gap I perceived between the things I did and the person I wished to be. Only my long practice at stuffing things could clear away the cloud; that and placing the blame on alcohol, as though drinking was a valid excuse, some extraneous cause that left me with a temporarily misguided personality over which my authentic and superior personality had no control.

Since I had closed out my profitable position, the bond market had rallied back to eighty points. It looked to me like it would turn down again. I took another short position, a substantial one, hoping for a quick addition to my gains. A week went by and bonds rose to eighty-two, which translated into a ten thousand dollar loss in my position. Still feeling bulletproof, I did nothing about it, despite a bond trader's warning comment that it looked "quite strong." Being a natural contrarian, I turned that into an excuse to hold on. Next week they moved higher again, disturbingly. I couldn't bring myself to take the loss and protect my capital for fear of looking undisciplined, or worse, stupid, if it turned down right after I got out.

That is the point at which it is easiest not to look, so when Ken Wearing asked me to join him in Denver for another agricultural marketing convention, I thought of the pleasant interval we'd had in Memphis and accepted his invitation. That's what it was again, a pleasant interval. I spent the time listening to presenters and dining with Ken and some of his industry acquaintances. I didn't even call people who I knew would like to have a drink and I didn't call Sherry Mason, who lived nearby.

Once again, I thought there may be some kind of benevolent conspiracy behind it all, with the intention of constructively influencing me. As we took our first class seats for the return flight, Ken nodded discreetly to indicate the presence of Jesse Jackson across the aisle. With similar discretion I glanced toward the reverend. Almost simultaneously I began to follow a train of thought in which his presence was somehow linked to my need for character development.

Soon after that trip, Cynthia and I juggled our lives around a trip to Las Vegas for a long weekend. Our time together was pleasingly romantic and Vegas was the perfect place to ignore the outside world. On the Saturday night, following a show that was a distant relative of the Folies Bergere of Paris and which ended around one in the morning, the raucous enjoyment of a half-dozen men and one woman at a craps table attracted me. I decided to try my hand at dice. I had only fifty dollars in my pocket but considered it a good way to limit my losses. I didn't lose very often, however, and the chips piled up. Over the next three hours I intermittently cleared the black one hundred dollar chips off the table and put them in Cynthia's purse. When we did turn away, to leave behind a frowning croupier, we discovered there were seventy of them. I'm sure I must have considered that a good omen and the next day we talked about living together.

"That would mean resigning my position at the firm to avoid conflict," she said with some misgiving. She showed little reluctance for breaking up her relationship at home because, she told me, it had not been intimate for many months. Despite that, I admitted to myself that a little doubt and jealousy was creeping in. In the end, however, I was happy to wait and we continued to enjoy our weekend escape in a state of near perpetual bliss.

When the markets opened Monday, bond prices were higher again. The money I'd made in Vegas only made it easier to hang on to the losing position, which was now costing over twenty thousand dollars. In the following days, I sometimes left the office during market hours, just to take a break from the nerve rattling tremors that coursed through my upper body. All I had to do was remove the position and the damage would be controlled. But I could not face the possibility that I would be duped into covering at the top and have to watch while my ideas were vindicated but my money was left on the table, and along with it, my pride. I wondered about the three men who took their own lives over the money they lost trading in options trading during the 1974 stock market crash. Is that what they'd gone through, a kind of emotional paralysis that entangled them in a chasm of lost identity so dark they willingly gave up life itself?

Each time I had returned to the office, bonds were up some more. Finally the markets closed for the week. I was down twenty-nine thousand dollars. The same bond trader came up from the floor and walked past my desk, this time with sympathy in his voice. "Jesus, man, don't give it all back." With the little courageous defiance I could muster, I smiled to hide my suffering and left to get a drink. "A double," I said, which is what they normally poured at The Sign, so I got a real mind numbing start. I shook out my fortieth cigarette of the day, lit it, and drew deeply. I'd come up with a solution before Monday.

Troy and Dave came in before I finished my second scotch. They were more concerned about the cold and grey Chicago weekend we had in front of us. "Where can we go to get warm?" Troy asked rhetorically with his mild Texas twang. I immediately thought of Las Vegas, not to escape the dreary city so much as to get away from my own thoughts. My suggestion gained immediate interest and an hour later we had flights booked for that evening and we were hailing a cab for O'Hare Airport.

We checked into the Riviera, my haunt of default over the years, and I headed for a craps table. Between that and blackjack, between gambling alone and with Troy, I soon had the need of more money. To my surprise and egotistical delight, the line of credit I'd established there four years ago, but never called upon until now, was still available. Vegas hotels cooperate fully in that respect for good reason of course. By Sunday when we departed I had drawn down six thousand dollars, two of which I'd lent to Troy and Dave. So I'd lost more than four thousand dollars.

The light-headed effect caused by continuous alcohol consumption and almost no sleep was sufficient anesthesia for the flight and cab ride home. But once alone in my apartment, staggering reality engulfed me. At the same time my body,

154

rendered too weak and vulnerable already, informed my mind that it could not handle enough alcohol to drown the agonizing awareness. Cornered in a private Armageddon, or rather by the tendency of my mind to amplify and project situations that were indescribably horrendous, and the hopeless inclination to abandon all ideas of business success and retreat to the hills and anonymity, I made the decision to close out my position at Monday's opening. It was a relief to have made the decision: the suffering would end and life would continue, if on a plane beneath my previous vision. I slumped on the couch and considered how a winning trip to Las Vegas had encouraged me to suffer greater losses in the bond market and now, how a losing trip would result in stopping further losses.

The market opened higher again; I viewed it as a final and personal insult. I'd already placed the exit-order though and, with an aching gut, resigned myself to whatever punishment was forthcoming. I wondered if I hadn't been filling in for the older boys who bullied me back in high school. Why would I inflict such punishment upon myself? After the markets closed that day, I walked the city streets until I arrived at the door of the dojo where my karate class was held. The rigorous workout helped temporarily, but I was not feeling well and I booked an appointment for a physical check-up the next day with old Doctor Ruben.

"Your blood pressure is one-eighty over one-ten," the doctor said. "Dangerously high." He prescribed some medication and asked about my lifestyle. I admitted I smoked and drank a bit.

He said, "We have to get it down. You are a healthy young man, except for this, and it's too bad you are treating yourself this way."

He was a kind old man and very wise. I thought of my healthy outdoor upbringing and what good health I'd always enjoyed. Here I was, not yet thirty-three, and taking medication for high blood pressure.

My liaison with Cynthia reached full bloom during the annual Holloway post-Christmas company party, a full weekend in Fort Lauderdale. Everyone from the office, about a hundred men and women, flew off together without spouses and partners to drink, frolic, and unwind in the sun. So it wasn't unusual that Cynthia and I got together at night under a palm tree. It was unexpected that she would begin wailing away with the enjoyment of an orgasm, well within hearing distance of our workmates. Later on, a half dozen revelers burst into the room she shared with her friend Maria to find us in bed together. Having little chance of disguising the truth, we sat up and accepted the cans of beer they opened for us.

Mid-morning of the next day, Dave and I rented a twin-hull sailboat and took Cynthia and Celia, another young lady from the office, for a pleasant cruise up and down the gently rolling coastline. During that outing I learned that I had used courser language than I remembered with one of the firm's senior partners the night before. He was a man I liked more than admired, but I liked him for the kindness he'd always expressed and I sincerely regretted that I might have been inconsiderate. With the kind support of Cynthia and Dave, I decided to go directly to him and offer my heartfelt apologies, which I did as soon as we beached the boat. That evening, most of us left for the airport and went back to work Monday morning.

Only chuckling good humor, from a few brokers who'd become drinking buddies, was ever expressed regarding either incident. Except for Noel, that is, who invited me for a drink mid-week and got right to the point.

"Are you screwing Cynthia?" he asked. "Because the managing partner will take a dim view of that." That was extraordinarily blunt for Noel, but I saw it as justified from at least two angles. First, he had been a large part of my growing up in the industry and he took that seriously, much like a parent would. Second, he was the partner who had brought me into the firm and he saw my actions as a threat to the harmony he enjoyed there.

To justify my actions and lift them out of the gutter, I told him that my relationship with Cynthia was more serious than that. It really was, in a way, because I'd continued to be infatuated with her for several months. Having made such a declaration, I needed to live up to it. A few weeks later she informed her boss that she would be leaving at the end of March because we planned to live together.

A group of brokers had scheduled a ski vacation in Banff, Alberta, two weeks hence, and arranged a block of accommodations at the Banff Springs Hotel. An acquaintance, who knew I liked to ski, invited me to join them and I accepted without hesitation. It happily coincided with a Cattle Feeders' convention I wanted to attend in Denver, which would make some of the trip a business expense.

The skiing was excellent and we returned most often to the rambling mountain terrain at Lake Louise, where three mountain faces and countless runs offered endless thrills, while spectacular vistas of the Rockies clothed in snow captivated my attention each time we halted for a break. The evenings were occupied with fabulous dining, several times at the elegant old railroad hotel, followed by remarkably civilized drinking. It was a memorable adventure and I felt good about a few new friends I'd made.

I flew from there to Denver and the convention. I had requested the attendance of one of the Mercantile Exchange floor brokers and a fellow I worked with daily, Terry, with the intention that he could boost my sales effort. Not every firm offered clients direct contact with the trading floor and he could give them a first-hand explanation of the inherent benefits. Meanwhile, I'd known some of the participants for a few years now and I knew how a few of them liked to party. I had my many friends in that town as well and looked forward to a reunion with them. Like a tidal wave, it all seemed to gain momentum. By the time Terry arrived a day later, I was thoroughly distracted. Following a second night of drinking and more evidence that I had no specific plans for him, he informed me that he would not be staying for the last two days. He had moved his return flight ahead and was leaving for the airport right away.

Only as I watched him go did I realize how I'd neglected to take advantage of his generosity and had actually abandoned him socially. Terry was a highly respected partner in the company and had always been supportive and friendly toward me. I remembered standing at the bar in Sign of the Trader one afternoon a few months back, explaining to him the self-serving philosophy I'd adopted from a book called *Looking Out for Number One*. I thought of the uncomprehending expression on his face and his words: "I don't know, I wonder if that will result in a fulfilling life."

For the balance of my time at the convention, a too large part of me was impatient to get back and try to apologize for an indiscretion that could only harm a respectable friendship, and my standing among other partners in the firm.

When the month reached its end, there were farewell drinks for Cynthia after work and more drinks to salute our future together. Fairytale overtones were interwoven with undertones of legitimacy. She was, after all, quite a striking girl and very bright, and people tended to view decisions of that nature as being the outcome of careful consideration and firm resolve. My immediate internal experience consisted of two quite different phenomena: I enjoyed the high-minded romantic implications and simultaneously suppressed cerebral eddies of reprehensible hypocrisy.

Chapter 12

On a Friday night, a week before Cynthia came to live with me, I stopped by The Sign for a few scotches. Finding no one there to socialize with, I decided to walk toward home and stopped at one of the many stand-up bars in the Rush Street area for a few more. Generally making an evening of wandering, I walked west toward Halsted Street and a bar I'd not been in before. I sat at a small table by myself and soon engaged in light conversation with two black ladies at a table next to me. One of them was probably in her early forties, well dressed and nicely coiffed, quite conservative. The other was much younger, smartly dressed as well, and perfectly striking in her general appearance, very chic and very sexy. They were outwardly friendly and had the most agreeable personalities. I was generally interested in hearing more from them and, of course, physically attracted to the younger.

Before long I joined them and soon after that I discovered that the younger had aspirations of dancing and theatre and the older had it as her mission to assist in any way she could with that career. What luck, a few weeks ago I had met a fellow who said he was some kind of scout for that very industry. We had enjoyed each other's company while sitting at a bar and I remembered we'd exchanged business cards.

I'd had enough to drink by that time and I decided to make the most of this coincidence. I mentioned my acquaintance and said I could refer them to him. If I implied that there was anything more I could do for them, I do not remember it. Nor do I remember how we made the decision to go back to my place. I only very vaguely recall that the elder of the two wished that I could see the younger dance. I know I served them drinks and started to play some music to which the lovely girl started dancing. I remember verbalizing my sentiments regarding her extraordinary beauty and commenting upon her apparently very ample bosom.

"Do you want to see them?" her friend asked. With no hesitation I acquiesced and the next minute she was dancing in front of me with her top removed. I was mesmerized by the exquisite abundance of her form, the most beautiful silky body I had ever laid eyes upon. We were there quite some time before we both had removed all our clothes and were dancing together. She'd simply tossed the remaining items, skirt across the room, then pantyhose which landed behind the couch, as though she had been waiting a long time for this free expression. I recall that her friend, who stood against the wall with her drink, wouldn't join us and I recall that the younger had no objection at all to me fondling and fawning over her magnificent velvety breasts.

It saddened me somewhat to remember that we eventually went into the bedroom, followed by her seemingly voyeur older friend, and ended up on the bed, whereupon I became sexual with her and attempted to enter her vagina. She very suddenly squealed, as though fear gripped her in that moment, quickly got up, scurried around the apartment grabbing her clothes into a small bundle, ran to the bathroom, and closed the door. Once she came out they left immediately. I believe neither left with animosity toward me; that the dancer despised her older friend for betraying her in some way; that the elder believed she had somehow failed in her mission and regretted that the trust of her young protégé had been jeopardized. That is all pure conjecture, of course, as the whole episode baffled me from beginning to end.

The next morning, I awoke with a frightful vision of what had happened. I thought, first of all, that the one who was not dancing probably cleaned the valuables out of my apartment, beginning with my wallet. I soon discovered the wallet to be completely intact in the pocket of my discarded pants and realized almost as immediately that I had little else worth stealing. Then I began to doubt my memory. As vivid as the image was, it all seemed most unlikely to have occurred. Perhaps I'd dreamed the whole adventure. There were empty glasses on the coffee table, however, and the bottles of liquor were still on the counter. In a moment of inspired delirium, I pulled the couch away from the wall. There on the floor lay the shrunken rumpled form of her discarded pantyhose. It had happened just as I remembered. I was then left wishing that I had remained on amiable terms with the lovely pair, that I had gotten their phone numbers and could see them again to pass along that business card. I doubted very much that my friend the scout would have discovered a more attractive young lady in the interim.

Cynthia moved her things into my apartment and we began to live a normal life. I went to work and usually came home shortly afterwards. Even when I didn't, Cynthia often joined me, for dinner or partying. Sometimes we met for lunch at the Berghoff Restaurant, a persistent favorite with extraordinary corned beef on rye; or another preferred restaurant, Gene and Georgettes, for a delectable steak in the evening.

It was pleasant to crawl into bed with a beautiful partner at night and simply enjoy casual togetherness. I enjoyed the fact that Cynthia passed her spare time with various crafts and put together some nice meals for us at home. I relished the femininity in her methods and in the results. She arranged a small party and made a cake for my thirty-third birthday. She wanted to attend an Emmylou Harris concert and I was thoroughly grateful that we did. Although trading my own account remained an exasperating irritant for me, and often undermined otherwise good days, I rediscovered something precious in the concept of cohabitation.

In a moment of misguided magnanimity, I came up with the idea of a house party and invited everyone from the office. A dozen could be counted as good friends and they brought with them a cordial glow. Some showed up because of social obligation and didn't stay long. A few got a little drunk beforehand and chose our particular party by default. Finally, a small troublesome contingent came along late in the evening, the belligerent ones who had drunk enough to permit the manifestation of latent animosities. Haughty disregard for pleasantries and a few tactless remarks were a prelude to one of them falling on a four-foot square coffee table and smashing through it. Naturally, I hadn't expected this, but a person with my record for disregarding the sensitivities of others should not leave himself open to retaliation. Around midnight my landlady, with whom I had always been on good terms, called for the third time about the noise level and informed me that the combination of loud music and traffic in the common stairway must cease or I would face an eviction notice in the morning. I took her seriously, made an announcement of some force, and soon things were winding down. The morning following, as we began cleaning up the mess of empty glasses and dirty ashtrays, Cynthia said she'd had fun. On balance, I was not glad we'd done it.

Partly because I hoped to lessen my reliance on agriculture and place more emphasis on the financial markets, I promoted the idea that I could add some business through several contacts I had in the United Kingdom and France. My contact in London was Albert, who had shared a flat with me back in New York and who had a good position with a major UK bank. The fellow in Paris was a man originally from Montreal whom I'd met while working in New York as well. I was also motivated by the desire to visit London and Paris again and, although I didn't need to use the company expense account to do it, I considered it justified and no one wanted to cause a fuss by objecting, to me directly in any case, although I'm sure there were doubts.

It wasn't the first time I had been boldly assertive with some flimsy notion that I knew was just inside the limits of suspicion for those who had to approve of it. I had two phenomena in my favor: the partners were largely of Midwestern agricultural origin and had little familiarity with the New York-London world of international finance; and they were largely decent people who expected I did know something about it and believed I must have a solid plan, with a realistic expectation that their money would be well spent. In short, they trusted me.

I flew to London's Gatwick Airport and, as planned, met Albert at his office in the City. He suggested I not book a hotel room because we'd go to his house, where he lived with his wife and two-year-old twins, for dinner and the night. We discussed some of our previous experience together on the way to his home. I renewed my acquaintance with his wife, whom I'd met in New York before they were married. She served a lovely meal and we discussed the play we would attend that evening. A babysitter arrived before we left and I was provided with a parting glimpse of the sleeping twin boys, to which I reacted with an appropriately adoring smile. Perhaps it was exaggerated because I remember the relief I experienced in my facial muscles when I relaxed them afterwards.

The theatre experience was pleasant and "Anyone for Denis?" provided amusing insights into the daily circumstances of Margaret Thatcher's rather easy-going spouse, Denis. I didn't catch many of the quickly murmured colloquial phrases that led to outbursts of laughter from my hosts and the rest of the audience. I tried to disguise my lack of comprehension by wearing a smile, as a substitute for pretending to laugh. Once again my visage was strained by a dishonest projection. I supposed one's face could probably endure a great deal of continuous amusement, happiness and laughter, if it were involuntarily manifested. When elation is pasted on artificially, however, persistent effort is required and the resulting discomfort is similar to that caused by wearing shoes that are too small.

I had not been enjoying myself and realized it. Upon leaving the family's home the next morning, in spite of my continuing discomfort, I expressed my gratitude for their hospitality. It had been generously offered, if in some degree a response to obligation. On the way into town Albert asked about my plans for the day and described his own in a way that left no opening for discussing the services I'd referred to over the phone a few weeks prior. There wouldn't be any discussion. Well, I had to admit it: he never said there would be. He'd only politely expressed that he and his wife looked forward to seeing me, and perhaps they had. But, knowing the door to doing business was closed, I was suddenly gripped by self-loathing over the trust I had betrayed.

I checked into the first hotel I could find with a room available and asked the concierge about trains to Dover, the hovercraft service from Dover to Calais, and thence, a train to Paris. I had even less reason to hope for success in Paris than I'd had in London, but I could hardly abort the entire mission and admit my folly. I would have to play it out over time somehow, as though my initial plan had been a sound bet that merely unfolded without effect.

The hotel was close to Leicester Square and I walked south from there, finding my way to Trafalgar Square. By the time I passed beneath Nelson's column I was deeply immersed in imaginings that belonged to times gone by, and the awkwardness of my present predicament slipped from my consciousness. Thoughts of Nelson's brilliant seamanship and heroic death in the moment of victory for 'King and Country' left me feeling contempt for the present and I discounted the people I worked with and their narrow perspective. He had secured British supremacy over the seas and set the course of history. I sneered inwardly at the significance people assigned to the petty activities that made up their lives and the many pompous self-images that were based on personal wealth and reputations founded in small circles.

I turned right and then, a block or so further on, left again and followed the broad steps down to the Mall which runs west from there, between St. James Park on the left and several stately royal residences on the right, including Marlborough House and St. James's Palace. My freely drifting state of mind slipped from reverence at the grandeur of the open space before me, and the centuries of history that had left their imprint on it, to begrudging scorn for the lesser royals who, without either merit or duty, inherited their lives of pomp and circumstance.

When I came to Stable Yard, a small roadway at Clarence House, and noticed before me preparations for a mounted ceremony, my thoughts were elevated to admiration again.

My English mother's high regard for British sovereignty, especially Queen Elizabeth II, always seemed to transport her to a higher perspective, to a realm beyond loathsome political wrangling and the exasperation inherent in current affairs. It seemed to be a source of wellbeing, safe and sound, simultaneously exultant and pragmatic, lying between the mundane triviality of everyday life and the slippery ungraspable imaginings of religion. Its good effect derived partly from the reduced importance of the 'self' when it is exposed in the light of human history, legend, and myth. Perhaps more important, a true sovereign illuminated the importance of nobility and dignity in human life and, by extension, the senseless futility of a self-absorbed existence. I stood awhile in the shadow of the spectacular Queen Victoria Memorial sculpture, long enough to observe the changing of the guard, that most revered of traditions, in the forecourt of Buckingham Palace.

I strolled east from there, past St. James's Park again, but on the south side of the small lake, until Westminster Abbey caught my eye. I considered the wide variance in personalities associated with all the monarchs entombed there, from noble and high-minded to viciously self-serving. For many, their station had not been enough, in itself, to free them from sickening egoism. Power and wealth may have exacerbated a latent condition. Wasn't that true with me? My insecurities had been lessened as I climbed ever higher on flimsy social and economic ladders. At the same time, the ruthless tyrant in me had taken the reins more assuredly, until I seemed to be precariously perched atop a design that was supported by my efforts alone. I envisioned myself riding a very tall unicycle and I suddenly felt vulnerable, lest the path turn bumpy or an adverse breeze arose.

That strange resurgence of self-doubt stayed with me while I inattentively passed Westminster, the Houses of Parliament, and Big Ben. The urge to complete the trip, to return home and take hold of my life, overwhelmed me and I headed back to the hotel. I decided to arrange the earliest possible connections for Paris and put that futile leg of the misplaced undertaking behind me as well.

The meeting the following day left me with no hope of further business development, just the reality I had expected. My flight home was scheduled for early that same evening and, although I experienced a modestly gratifying sense of romantic familiarity with the charming old city over the intervening six hours, I remained anxious about getting back to Chicago. Waves of alarm waxed over me, as though I'd left a faucet running in a sink with no overflow outlet; and even in waning, as though I'd forgotten to lock an outside door.

Cynthia was happy to see me and had a little welcome home ceremony planned. She knew I liked watercolor paintings and presented me with a very pleasing one done by a local Chicago artist, an impressionist view of the Seine in Paris entitled "Pont Neuf." I wish I had shown more gratitude for the obvious personal thought and significant expense behind the gift. Worse, instead of honoring this unsuspected display of sophistication, I crudely discounted the value and authenticity of the gift. Only much later was I able to recognize the missed opportunity for greater mutual enjoyment of that moment. But I wasn't overtly unpleasant either, because the notion of having sex with her, which had arisen in the taxi from the airport, had increased to the point of craving. Nearly a week had lapsed. In her immediate presence, her curvaceous form and beautifully girlish expressions became a mouth-watering preoccupation.

Once in bed, all formality and reserve vanished and the mutual sexual energy we enjoyed with predictable regularity launched us into a tingling wonderland. Intense physical contact with another human being was a panacea for the insecurity that had pervaded my being over the last few days. I reveled in the nearness and feel of her body against mine. Her silky femaleness drove me wild and her squealing orgasm pushed me beyond awareness of anything but the roaring hot sensation of my own release.

In the aftermath, she reminded me that my friends Bob and Karen Hawk, who had returned from their stint in Saudi Arabia, were visiting the following weekend. She hadn't met them and said she was looking forward to that. We curled together spoon-like and I slept a comfortable sleep because, at least for the moment, I wasn't alone. The next morning I went to work and, in response to queries about my trip, some bold and some discreet, I avoided elaboration by mumbling that it was good and only time would tell.

Drinks began to flow immediately following the Hawks' arrival Friday afternoon, vodka martinis for old times' sake. Bob and Karen loved to party and, by the time we had finished the home-cooked steak dinner, I was flying high. I decided to take everyone on a cruise of the city, despite wise opposition from Cynthia and my friends. Strangely, the battery in my Eldorado was too weak to start the engine. In retrospect, I wondered if there wasn't something of a higher order looking out for me. In the moment, however, I was furious at my plans being derailed. In a frustrated rage I began wrenching the quite large passenger door open against its hinges, as though I would like to tear it off to punish the car for its inoperable condition. I think Bob managed to calm me and we finished the evening with another drink, although my memory is foggy.

The next day, I discovered that the car door sagged slightly as it was opened, and no longer closed completely flush. That kind of thing had to be ignored, even grinned at over champagne and orange juice, while a rhetorical wondering of what had happened to the battery provided a shallow pretense of rational behavior, and bridged the abyss of my temporary insanity.

We went out for a nice brunch, walked along Michigan Avenue past the old Water Tower, and then strolled back toward Butch McGuire's pub in the Rush Street area. The early October day was beautifully warm, and we decided more of it should be spent out-of-doors. We went home, picked up a few bottles of wine and some mats to sit on, and wandered through Lincoln Park to the beaches on the shore of Lake Michigan.

By the time the sun went down we were quite alone and I was fairly inebriated again. I don't know how Bob and Karen had progressed from naked partying to sharing themselves sexually with others, and I don't know what logic Bob used to convince Cynthia to go for a stroll with him. I do know I was taken by surprise when Karen started making herself physically available to me. She had a nice body with very large breasts which I thought would be nice to fondle, and they were I suppose, but much less firm than I would have imagined if I'd had any prior thoughts about them at all. The act of having sex with her struck me as an unexpected duty and I had little natural enthusiasm for it. I'd always considered her a fun-loving sister rather than a potential sex partner. It was therefore an awkward and clumsy attempt that failed to gain sufficient momentum. I felt that I should have been able to complete the circle, so to speak, and meet her apparent desire. That episode, as well, would need to be forgotten.

Bob and Karen left before noon Sunday and, later that day, Cynthia wanted to talk. She was sufficiently distraught that she had overcome her hesitancy to upset me and spoke directly. "Bob expected that I would have sex with him. He told me you guys had always shared partners and that you would have no problem with it. He said that you would probably have sex with Karen." She paused for my reaction and, when I hesitated, she continued, "I'm not that kind of woman. I told him I wouldn't do it and I didn't. Did you have sex with Karen?"

"No, I didn't," I said while still formulating the rest of my response. I didn't want to discuss past relationships because I didn't think that would help smooth things over. I never liked hearing about the former affairs of my current partners because it always aroused jealous insecurity and a sense of intrusion, as though someone was taking a shortcut across my property. The subject was further complicated by the fact that I didn't want to belittle my friends, who I had portrayed to Cynthia as sophisticated New Yorkers. Bob's family were long-time owners of a home in the Hamptons and his friendship therefore represented a partial fulfillment of my aspirations. Rather than console my partner with the simple truth that I had never, not ever, shared partners with Bob, that, like her, the idea was contrary to my beliefs, that, even in this very moment, I continued to feel insulted by his actions, I said with a conceited smirk, "I've known Bob and Karen a long time and we've had some interesting parties. Bob always likes to get naked and Karen seems to enjoy it."

"Well, I don't think I want to be a part of it," Cynthia said with tears in her eyes. I felt very uncomfortable sitting there and, with a tender stroke of my hand across her back and shoulders, a gesture meant to relay sentiments that ranged all the complex distance from loving empathy to condescending dismissal, I went to the fridge for a beer.

Our partnership wavered further when a trivial disagreement provided me with the foundation for an insanely angry resentment that led to my stabbing a knife in the coffee table which, in turn, resulted in her temporarily moving out. I spent the time with another girl, a casual encounter I'd enjoyed recently. Cynthia spent a night seeking comfort in the arms of a married man she knew from the office, Rob Simpson. I still worked with Rob, and I knew in the moment I learned about it that I could never accept facing him every day while living with someone he had screwed.

Cynthia came over; we had too many drinks and started to get sexual; my anger surfaced in rough foreplay, at which she exclaimed, "You're hurting me!" I was immediately reminded of the affection we once shared, knew I couldn't get back there, and our relationship ended in an unhappy shambles. Her friend Maria continued to work in the office and not a word was ever spoken in reference to our parting, by the managing director or anyone else. I had my place to myself again and heard no more of Cynthia, while Rob Simpson and I drank together and partied with other women.

Chapter 13

One afternoon Troy returned to the office after a session on the trading floor and told me a friend of his in Texas could provide us with tickets to the National Rodeo Finals. As I had never been to Oklahoma, the idea quickly became a plan and off we flew to Oklahoma City. The place was idyllic, the perfectly authentic setting for a grand old rodeo. Thistles tumbled along broad dusty streets before a stiff hot breeze. Sad country tunes flowed from the open doors of restaurants and rowdy crowds spilled onto the sidewalks from bursting honky-tonks. Hats and boots, denim and silk, lean men, buxom ladies, senior, junior, and senorita, the party was on. Troy and I had both grown up in cattle country and we enjoyed a special closeness while sharing our enthusiasm for the raw western atmosphere. I briefly considered my eastern friend, Jack Sargent, and the sniggering contempt he would have shown. The whole setting was in-tune with the 'real me,' I concluded, as we headed toward the grandstand to get good seats for the afternoon show.

The best of the best cowboys wrangled with livestock that had proven the toughest and ugliest over years of breaking men's bones. Cowgirls in tight jeans and colorful billowing blouses sat sleek swift horses like they were born there. And yet, the greatest heart-stopper was an instance of crowd response during the bull-riding event. A man named Samson, not as big in stature as many, a black man, and one of fantastic ability, had just stayed glued in perfect style to a particularity nasty animal for the required eight seconds. When the horn sounded he seemed in no hurry to abandon ship, to grasp at the earliest opportunity for safety by crawling on the back end of a wrangler's horse. Instead he waited for the perfect moment, still in flawless control, and let the monster launch him into the air. He landed on his feet and tossed his oversized hat high above his head in a celebration of triumph, the ultimate ride.

I was caught in a private state of amazement and a moment passed before I noticed the apparently unmoved crowd. The silence was deafening, stunning in its implication. I'd never been much of a spokesman for social equality, an issue quite outside my immediate concerns, but the lack of it was almost putrid. I asked Troy if the absence of applause was due to prejudice and he said, "That's the reason. They don't like to see their boys outdone like that, not in rodeo."

I wanted to stand before Mr. Samson, who came from the Bronx I believe, to tell him what a remarkable thing he had done, what courage I believed he must have, and what a conception of racial parity he had just aroused if only for me among that sullen crowd. At the same time I was grateful that my pale face blended in so well and that I would not be called upon to defend those thoughts publicly. We met up with the man to whom we owed thanks for the tickets, celebrated with plenty of whiskey, enjoyed a grand steak dinner, and mentioned not a word of Samson's prodigious bull-ride. But it stuck with me.

In the last months of 1982, Dave and I attended an Emmylou Harris concert with Troy, at his insistence. I had some mediocre gains and suffered a few more frustrating losses trading my own account, and I sold the townhouse I had bought in New York. I flew to Calgary in mid-December and drove a rental car a thousand miles to visit clients in Western Canada, over copious amounts of Christmas cheer. Finally, at the end of that jaunt, I headed back home to the farm in Montana to share the holidays with my parents and siblings.

Early in 1983 I sold the Eldorado, partly because I didn't need a car in the city and, even more, because the stereo had been stolen twice. The first time it happened I was aghast at discovering the roughly one-square-foot empty cavity, and infuriated by the inconvenience. Over the next week, I suffered the wretched and wearisome sense of invasion that tends to follow such events, a reaction I considered quite natural, but for which I received no sympathetic indulgence from native Chicagoans who seemed inured to it through long experience. The $1,700.00 replacement was covered by insurance, but I paid a similar amount for a new alarm system. I also paid to have the driver's side door adjusted slightly, caught in a strong wind, I told them. Two weeks later, my new alarm sounded and I went to the parking lot to discover the door opened. Satisfied that the alarm had deterred the thieves, I locked the door and went to bed. In the morning I was confronted once more by a large cavity. The thieves had been sufficiently astute and well informed, having broken into the car and set off the alarm, to open the hood and quickly disconnect it. They had then run off only to return later and perform their work without the noisy interruption. The men at work were not surprised at my story, and told me matter-of-factly that the dealership to which I had gone with my problems had a long record of ordering used parts, even dispensing addresses for thefts-to-order.

That event seemed to herald a decline in my positive attitude toward city life. I'm sure, however, an accumulation of personal escapades that were revolting to gaze upon, combined with a subliminal desire to end the oppressive futility of speculating, provided at least an equal impetus in my desire to escape. In any case, I merely experienced the longing at that point, and did nothing more about it than sell the car. I found I wasn't soaring as freely, though, and began to spend more time reading at home. One night I strolled out alone and enjoyed a rather intimate Doc Watson concert in a tiny acoustic club down the street. Seated right in front of the small stage, I minded his daddy's guitar when Merle passed it to me at the break. Their ordinary humility impressed me. Life could be abundant, I thought, and modest good quality went deeper inside than pompous display.

John Sargent called one day from Toronto. He'd been talking with a banker in the Cayman Islands and thought we should go down there and investigate the possibility of living on a Caribbean island, especially one that had a reputation as a tax haven. I thought that was a great idea and we made reservations for the next week, including flights, beach house, and a meeting with an advisor at a Swiss bank. John was bringing his noisy red-haired girlfriend, so I called Sherry Mason in Denver and invited her to the party. Even as I dialed the phone, I smiled in anticipation of her fresh and happy participation as we discovered a new environment together. I knew we would have lots of fun in bed, which generated a titillating buzz, but my longing to spend time with a good friend was at least as compelling.

My initial impression of Georgetown, Grand Cayman was streets lined with banks and curbs lined with Bentleys, and I found no reason to revise it. Either it was sufficiently accurate, or I simply enjoyed the uncluttered apparition. In any case, relative affluence was evident everywhere and the languid destitution too often found in the Caribbean seemed entirely absent. In the first days there we rented a jeep and explored the island, which didn't take very long. We met with our man at the bank. He gave us the forms required to set up a corporation and suggested that storing a gold-hoard in Canada was probably the safest bet in the world. We spent relaxed hours on the exquisite beaches and snorkeled above the coral reef, which encircles the island a considerable distance offshore and crests only a few feet below the surface. We dined out in lavish colonial style, reveled in the polite polished British ambiance and made plans for a deep-sea fishing excursion.

On a perfectly calm morning under a magical azure sky, with gentle swells folding upon the giant reef and leaving the inner waters completely undisturbed, the thirty-six foot recreational trawler purred through the only navigable gap in the coral and out upon the turquoise sea. The captain and owner of the boat, following his recent retirement from a business career in New Jersey, had developed a degree of seamanship and was presently perched before the upper helm a dozen feet above us, proudly in charge of the expedition we had contracted for. Oscar, his first mate, was a Cayman local who had made his living sailing the oceans of the world for thirty-five years as a merchant seaman. Against his naturally dark skin, salted, weathered, and dried until it resembled grainy black leather, his sparse white whiskers gleamed and highlighted a broad toothy grin. When he leaned closer to impart pithy anecdotes of the sea or a clairvoyant footnote regarding the mythic marlin, his dark irises sparkled with zest for life from their craggy settings. Oscar and I quickly developed an especially hearty, easy-going connection. Perhaps it was mutual identification with reckless adventure, or the proclivity for an icy far-away stare. I felt immensely privileged.

Once we were out a mile or two, Oscar set us up in the swiveling seats with long fishing rods and baited lures. In a very short time, I got a bite. The reel whined as the creature took more line. "Keep tension," he said to me. "Wahoo, wahoo," he grinned, just before the tension suddenly went out of the line. "He's running toward us. More throttle, take the slack," he hollered up to the captain. But the captain delayed, the tension never returned, and Oscar murmured with undisguised contempt, "Gone, too late." For several hours we cruised slowly, trolling. We drank some of the beer we'd put on ice, ate some of the lunch they'd packed for us, and caught a few smaller fish. One was a four-foot barracuda which Oscar said would be alright to eat at this time of year, though at other times they could be toxic. He told of a merchant crew that ended up quite disabled from eating one in the wrong season.

Sherry looked lovely in her bikini and seemed relaxed and happy for a nautical novice. A few more luxurious hours drifted by. Then quite suddenly our tranquility was interrupted and I still don't know if the captain understood the full implication of the message he relayed from the bridge, "Looks like the barometer is falling pretty fast, seems to be a squall coming from the east and these rollers are getting bigger."

The first mate's face clouded over and he scampered up the aluminum ladder. Almost immediately he uttered, "No good, man. We need to get going." His smile returned as he came back down but his terse instructions to secure everything on the deck had an unsettling tone. Then his smile turned to a devilish grin. "We've come west fifteen nautical miles," he said, looking at me. "We're not going to beat it, man. This could be a bit of hell."

For a half hour we powered smoothly toward our original point of departure, the high afternoon sun gradually rotating from starboard to stern. The wind in our faces gained a little more force and the swells had grown to four or five feet from peak to trough. Our sturdy vessel, although suddenly feeling diminished in proportion to our surroundings, still seemed more than capable. In a short time, though, we were being tossed around more vigorously and Oscar suggested to John, his girlfriend, and Sherry that they might be more comfortable below in the cabin. He suggested I wait a bit, maybe join them later. I was glad of that and, having seen the comfortable cabin when I visited the head, I wasn't anxious about my friends.

It got rougher, maybe eight to ten foot swells that began to crest as we ploughed through them. Heavy spray washed across the deck more frequently and I hung on as he told me to. "He cannot do it," Oscar yelled and scampered up to the bridge again. His words were lost on the wind but I saw him signal with his thumb and the captain came down. He had surrendered the controls to his first mate. The captain's tanned complexion had turned ghostly and he blurted to me that he was going below. As the turbulent sea raged all around us, his hand flicked forward in a palm-up gesture that invited me to precede him.

In the knife-edge tension of the moment, with a white knuckled grip on the aluminum railing at the side of the ladder and my splayed feet grasping for stability, I came face-to-face with the notion of hiding from the reality. A wild abhorrence convulsed through me, and drove me to choose the visible terror. I glanced at the upper bridge where the first mate swung like an inverted pendulum from my ten o'clock to two o'clock. Oscar's left hand parted with the wheel just long enough to wave me up, as he yelled over the roar of the engine and howl of the wind, "Hang on tight, man."

I began to climb, deliberately swapping the grip of my hands, one for the other, and edging my feet step by swaying step. Craving more stability, I kept my belly tucked tight against the rungs. As I drew nearer my destination, the pelting sheets of seawater that had blurred my vision on the main deck became little more than a misty spray. I crawled between the hand-railings, which looped above the ladder on either side, securing it to the flat metal surface. Standing up, I heeded his yelled instructions to wrap my arms around the horizontal protective railings that encircled the four-by-four foot platform.

I noticed with alarm that the cork-like oscillation of the craft sometimes sent the small bridge, with us on it, well out and over the water on either side. I saw that the swells had grown so tall that, when in the troughs, the crests hovered above our heads even though we stood more than fifteen feet above the surface of the water. I'd never imagined anything like the exhilarating sense of surrender that engulfed me. I knew with certainty, regardless of the outcome, that my present position was fate, and all-inclusive. There was no past and no future, only lavish life, abundant in the present moment.

His grin was genuine. I smiled in return and yelled, "Are we going to make it?"

He flashed an intrepid smirk. "Maybe not."

I hoped my friends below were doing all right. I believed, if they could see what I saw, that they would have chosen to ride it out down there. I also knew, if I had to perish at the bottom of this raging monster, I wanted to see it happen and I wanted to ride it to the end next to the man at the wheel. I noted the beads of sweat that formed on his forehead, dripped from his eyebrows, and rolled down his cheeks. The day remained warm, perhaps more humid than before, and the sun still beat directly upon him as he labored to keep us upright. Initially his efforts had appeared almost frantic, but I soon identified a highly systematic, though still desperate, pattern.

As a titanic roller approached, or as we headed into it, he met it headlong and the prow soared upward with a force that bent my knees, raising us to the crest for a full view of the tempest. With the march of time briefly suspended, we stood high above the gaping bottle-green cavern below, perhaps twenty-five or thirty feet, surrounded to the horizon in every direction by the hungry roiling sea. In that short interval, with his right hand on the spinning knob that was bolted to the wheel, applying a burst of full throttle with his left, he spun the craft ninety degrees. That prepared us to slide quite softly down a forty-five degree watery slope. The alternative was diving into the yawning trough bow-first, with the certainty of being partially submerged, destabilized, probably capsized by the next wave, and sunk.

Safely at the bottom most point, he efficiently directed us toward home again in preparation for the next wall of emerald brine. In a seemingly endless and futile battle, the sinewy untiring master mariner kept us from being swamped and we made deliberate headway.

As alarming as our circumstances were, taken as a whole, there was monotony inherent in the process. Excitement gave way to impatient endurance. Perhaps it was impatience at having to endure an elevated level of excitement. In any case, when he relayed his first sighting of land, I met the announcement with anger at having to endure what might be another hour. In the same moment I was rocked by sudden shuddering dread that we would not make it. That perturbing ambiguity persisted until he pointed out the line of foamy turbulence that signified the giant coral reef.

"We must strike the gap straight-on. If we land on that reef we will be smashed like an egg," Oscar hollered with more apprehension in his eyes than I'd noticed to that point. I'd been given something specific to worry about. My focus became fixed on the diminished crashing of waves and the relative calm that lay beyond the gap, and on the spumy turbulent surfaces above the coral that denoted the gap's deadly extremes. The scene appeared to welcome us with a frothy menacing smile.

I became fully engaged again, gripped by the exactness of his endeavor and the resolve of the man at the helm. Nearer and nearer we came with our laboring progress. When we rose upon a swell and could see it, sometimes the gap was off our starboard bow, sometimes to port. When we were only a few hundred feet out I yearned to put it all behind us and struggled against the urge to avert my eyes. Finally, we lumbered through the middle, masterfully. In the comparative calm I relaxed my aching arms. We exchanged glances that simultaneously reflected immense relief and lingering habitual doubt, haunting dregs of the fear that had been so long suppressed.

"Better let them know it's alright to come up now," he motioned with his thumb. The physical effort was conspicuously trivial as I stepped down the eight or ten rungs of the ladder to the main deck. I knocked at the closed hatch and hollered, "We made it." One by one, pale and obviously distraught, they clamored into the sunshine. "Everyone was sick," Sherry said, on the edge of tears. Then she forced a smile and grabbed my hand for reassurance. John Sargent was not happy at all, and chortled a string of profanity. His red-headed partner was unusually quiet and not pleased either. The captain merely grumbled about the mess his cabin was in. He walked over and stood before the still closed door to the main wheelhouse, only a few steps above the main deck. Oscar, descending from the upper bridge, acquiesced, "Take the helm." They exchanged no other words.

Oscar came over and stood next to me, each of us with a hand resting lightly on the stern railing. "When we get to shore, we got to clean the barracuda. You can get the cook at the beach house to make you steaks tonight. I'll take some home for the family." His tone was wholly unaffected, his smile subdued as though we'd been through an ordinary day of fishing with less than satisfactory results.

"I'll never forget it," I said, with welling gratitude and deep respect.

"I know," he replied, and his eyes went to seaward with a far-off gaze.

On the way back to our lodgings I discovered that no one else shared my beholden keenness for eating barracuda. I offered it to one of the maids and she seemed pleased to have

178

it. We went out for a nice dinner, where I heard a few more glum tidings of their confinement and refrained from trying to relate my experience. The next day we caught our flights home.

In the comparative solitude of my window seat I felt relieved to have the first opportunity to reflect more deeply upon the experience and my reaction to it. As I gazed across the sea of clouds below, I felt surprised at how little I had concerned myself with dying. Maybe it was because I placed too little value on the here and now, I thought, certainly not because I had faith in a glorious hereafter.

Only when I recalled the setting in which it had taken place, the great out-of-doors, vast and natural beneath an unrestricted sky, open to the cosmos, was I able to recognize the comfortable familiarity. What I first saw as an isolated intrepid response to a life-threatening situation had also been a welcome connection with my formative years. The experience had been ominous, emotionally strenuous, physically arduous, and it generated a fear for the end of life itself. Many times I had encountered conditions of that intensity while far from home on horseback, often in times of suddenly severe weather. I identified it as the childlike sense of pride that arises when a young man perceives himself to be responding to the world like an adult.

Because it had all taken place in a completely comprehensible crucible, its contents entirely revealed and finite, there had been no extraneous source of distress. Once the crucible had dissolved, there was no lingering attachment. The whole episode was fantastically satisfying to look upon. I experienced a powerful yearning to live like that, without strings attached, instead of feeling trapped in a life of perpetual entanglement. A wave of nostalgia for the open prairie came over me and I envisioned myself in a happier state, with more room to move and breath, away from the unwholesome city. I planned to explore the countryside when I returned, to see if I could escape.

Chapter 14

That spring there were several trading and market seminars and a number of clients came to town for them, and that inevitably led to extravagant dining and excessive partying. I took a few of them to see the musical "Oklahoma" which rather easily appealed to their western tastes and whetted their appetites for a bit more big-city culture. I'd recently attended a matinee performance of "The Wiz" and, although initially skeptical of the good reviews, I found it to be a truly delightful and creative adaptation of the classic old tale. In a whimsical moment I tossed the suggestion out to them and found myself procuring tickets for the next evening's performance at the Arie Crown Theatre.

Having taken the perceived social risk, I was relieved and delighted when one of my cattle feeding clients, admittedly a dignified gentleman that seemed completely governed by his own good judgment, openly expressed his elation and gratitude. Had he not led the way with his unencumbered enthusiasm, some of the other men might have pooh-poohed an event so novel to them. But Daniel Wilson, a man well under six feet in height who paid minimal attention to personal grooming or style and never drew attention to his own significant accomplishments, often stood out among others and provided leadership.

It was not enough to say that I liked him, nor was it especially important that I wanted to please him. Self-serving sentiments of that nature, toward someone who is contributing substantially to your income, are hardly uncommon. Completely independent of our business relationship, I had great admiration for his character. In fact, I feared him. I feared that he could see the truth about me, that I was a fraud, and my business integrity was thinly sustained by little more than a transitory self-interest. His life seemed grounded in the welfare of family, community, and humanity, and he exhibited a kind of nobility that far exceeded narrow religiosity, while I was driven by selfish clamoring and guided by nothing beyond my own ego-centered identity.

It didn't help either that, in Denver about a year previous, in the inebriated final hours of an evening at a convention and in the midst of a hotel room in which a half-dozen of us had congregated, I'd sunken into a drunken sobbing pit of self-pity over my disadvantaged beginnings and the struggles I'd faced in making something of myself, a crying jag, I think it is commonly labeled. I could only hope that others' memories were deadened to the embarrassing episode by their own liquor consumption. I doubted that, however, and I had to continually suppress a lingering image of the inquiring, but mercifully non-judgmental, look that I'd seen in Daniel Wilson's eyes that evening. My ability to hold my head up in the presence of many people was too often predicated upon the hopeful assumption of their partial amnesia. Concerning those I generally held in high regard, I hoped my personal social credit would hold out until I could free myself of all dependence upon them.

I wondered how I had gotten this far. How had these people, particularly the level-headed Mr. Wilson, granted me any credibility in the first place? I had taken some concepts that worked in one segment of the industry (the grain business) and projected them directly onto the playing field of another (cattle) and everyone bought into it. I had to admit that the confidence I had for my ideas, and the faith I had in their realistic application, had originated almost entirely in the credibility others had been so readily willing to place in them. I had supposed myself an authority, presented my supposition to others and, winning their concurrence, accepted it as evidence in support of my initial claim. I thought of that book Noel Hyman had recommended, written in 1841 by a Scottish journalist named Charles McKay, and recommended more recently by one of the speakers at a National Committee for Monetary Reform convention, *Extraordinary Popular Delusions and the Madness of Crowds.*

In fact, I had converted to my cause a few industry leaders, who had then helped me immensely in developing a broader following. Of course, their support for my ideas had corresponded with their own self-serving and wishful projections, a line of thought that provided instant relief from uncomfortable self-reproach. Very little business activity is based entirely in altruism, perhaps, I considered, even in the case of Daniel Wilson. It was all fleeting in any case, a delusion just as the book described.

On the recreational front, Dave, one of my buddies from the office, suggested we take up scuba diving. He had recently borrowed a few thousand dollars and turned it into a quarter million in a bull market in soybeans. He had since given up his customer service position in order to trade his own account full-time. I guessed he was planning for a more expansive future and I thought it was a great idea. We began taking lessons twice a week. Golfing season had begun as well, so Dave, Troy, and I spent a day each weekend drinking too much beer on the course and then partying afterwards.

Sarah worked in the industry and I met her at one of the trading seminars. The first thing I noticed was her soft voice and intelligent manner of speech. She wasn't glamorous or sexy by Hollywood standards, but her Eastern Mediterranean features were striking: large lively hazel eyes, modest naturally glossy lips surrounding a pliant mouth, faintly conspicuous nose, and a slightly bronzed complexion. Her lean athletic body and magnetic character foretold of self-discipline and zest for life. She impressed me as a generally beautiful person and I immediately had a desire to know her better. My interest in her was not sexual, however, and that avenue of thought was further curtailed by the fact that a male friend accompanied her. I assumed they were together.

We talked occasionally after that day, and went for lunch few times. I gradually became interested in spending more time with her and asked if she had a boyfriend. More specifically I wondered about the guy I met at the seminar. "No, that wasn't anything," she said. "Are you thinking we should get together?"

I told her I thought it might work out and she invited me over for dinner. She was a superb cook and served one of the most exciting meals I've eaten, a powerfully zesty endive salad and grilled lamb chops marinated in garlic, lemon, and oregano, Syrian she said. Because we had known each other for a while without a sexual component, Sarah was the first woman I'd actually respected as a person for some time, and our relationship was based on a kind of mature reciprocation.

She had considered it her place as a friend, when she suggested that I should get hold of my trading losses and take a serious stab at managing my life. I knew she was right and, for the first time, I caught a glimpse of the stupidity inherent in the idea that I was a special case that needed to advance quickly so I could live life fully. I was dealing with a smart observant lady who knew the ropes, and the bullshit had to end.

A few weeks later I invited my brother Barry, who is fifteen years my junior, to visit. Because he played and sang country music, I customized a tour for us. He flew to Chicago and we headed south toward New Orleans in a rented car, planning at the end of our travels to return by air. We were unhurried, sipping cans of beer and throwing the empties in the back seat, while we took time to appreciate the countryside. We took country roads that wound up and down and around forested hills and valleys in Kentucky, and saw sights that inspired memories of the film *Deliverance*. We were thankful to have sufficient gas when I easily discarded the notion of stopping at one little ramshackle corner store for cigarettes. The two local fellows lounging out front, country boys who came into focus as we drew nearer, stirred up visions of social incompatibility. Back on the interstate, we were soon in Nashville where we found a good hotel. The concierge was helpful in getting us tickets for the Grand Ole Opry and we felt especially fortunate, even after we discovered about half the seats were unoccupied. We saw a few of the great ones walk on the stage before our eyes: Hank Snow, 'The Singing Ranger,' and Roy Acuff, 'The King of Country Music.' Our shared appreciation was a genuinely satisfying brotherly experience, as in a smaller way was the eye-rolling moment we shared when two middle-aged ladies near us wondered too loudly why the entertainment wasn't more to their liking. Afterwards, we visited the Willie Nelson General Store and caught a glimpse of Johnny Cash's 'One Piece at a Time' car.

We resumed our journey south from Nashville, country music playing on the radio. Hank Williams Junior sang *The Ride*, a relatively gripping song, for a country tune, about the ghost of his father picking up a hitchhiker along the very stretch of road we were on. We drove down some secondary roads in Mississippi, staring in wonder at the rudimentary shacks that may well have been there a hundred and fifty years ago. In Natchez we toured a few magnificent antebellum homes and, in the evening, we went to a local club to sample a little southern blues. The authenticity of the setting, for which we had gained an appreciation earlier in the day, heightened and intensified the soulful effect of the music beyond any I'd experienced in the clubs of Chicago.

On to New Orleans we drove. Once there, we checked into the Riverside Hilton. I viewed the whole trip as a gift to the younger brother I hadn't been much of a role model for, nor had I been around to participate in his childhood. I believed that he must have yearned to know me a little better, the heroic figure he barely knew. I therefore willingly covered all the expenses. To this point in our trip, we had been restrained by an attitude of respectful inquiry because we'd explored so many sights and sounds that were new to us both. As well, despite copious daily beer consumption, I had been generally thoughtful and cautious, as one naturally is when finding his way in a new territory.

I'd been to New Orleans several times before and, once there, I became exhilarated by the idea of showing Barry around the unique old city. I developed a haughty propriety toward it, as though I was giving him a tour of something I owned. I slid from there into an insolent state of mind, flippant, cocky, brash, and defiant. Watching an effeminate waiter waltz between tables in a large, nearly empty bar, I was filled with a sneering scornfulness that bordered on loathing. As he slipped past our table, my puffed-up contempt turned flagrant and I committed an act that was at once that of a tyrant and a bully. With complete negligence regarding the safety of my brother and a headlong courting of personal disaster, I impulsively shifted my foot just far enough into the aisle in the dimly lighted room to catch his, as he glided by with a tray of empty glasses held aloft in practiced waiter-style. I was shocked at the outcome as he sprawled forward, tray and contents flying ahead of him, but held onto a composure behind which I attempted to deny playing a part in the calamitous scene.

He nevertheless complained to his co-workers that he had been tripped. As several of them directed hostile glances toward us and then began moving to close off our exit into the street, we headed for another door that opened into an empty alley. That was not necessarily a mistake but it soon proved futile as an avenue of escape. About six of them very quickly surrounded us and forced us physically against a brick wall. We were helplessly trapped and held there. We might have been punched, kneed, and badly beaten in retribution but they were mercifully satisfied with a terrified apology and, with no more than a vicious warning, left us there. It was still early evening, natural daylight illuminated the alley, and we walked back to the hotel to get ready for a nine o'clock show at Pete Fountain's Jazz Club.

Still feeling subdued by the events of the afternoon, I didn't drink much more that evening and the thrill of Fountain's clarinet peeling out Dixieland Jazz was less uplifting than it might have otherwise been. As we left the club and turned in for the night, I sincerely hoped that I carried the emotional strain of the ugly incident for both of us, and that Barry had freely enjoyed the evening, as he seemed to have done.

The next day we took a fascinating cruise through the brackish bayou with the owner of Cajun Swamp Tours. I enjoyed the day immensely, except in those moments when searing waves of guilty self-revulsion arose, replays of our narrow escape in the alley, drenching my neck and upper body in a clammy sweat. I wanted to escape that heavy shameful memory and comfortably look my brother in the eye again. I hoped he was pleased with the day's outing, free of the lingering dread I had experienced, and without harsh judgment of his hero.

We had reservations for dinner at prestigious Antoine's, but there was plenty of time for a stroll along Bourbon Street and a few much needed drinks to quell my unrest. Familiar with the restaurant's dress code I had lent Barry a sport-jacket. Even so, before we could be seated, we had to pick a tie from the selection they kept on hand. Once we were seated, I decided to start with Oysters Rockefeller and asked the waiter how they were prepared, my level of sophistication being such that I had experienced cases in which they were not up to my standards. "They are the original, sir," he exclaimed with an Italian accent, which implied to me that he didn't understand my question.

As for being the 'original,' I thought his claim a rather amusing, flippant, and bold application of that frequently abused assertion. Once more I asked, this time more carefully, how they were made, and once more he insisted they were the original. "What do you mean, the original?" I asked with growing contempt. Only then did he enter into a lengthy explanation of how, prior to 1900, John D. Rockefeller liked to take the train from New York to New Orleans, how he frequently dined at Antoine's and how, on one memorable occasion, he specified the manner in which he would like *his* oysters prepared.

"Oh, I see. Well, I will have them as you have always served them then," I finally capitulated, trying to salvage my worldliness with an appreciative grin.

We ordered drinks to pass the time, white wine with the starters, red wine with our beef and lamb dinner choices, and a round of Grand Marnier following dessert. I viewed dining as a form of entertainment and always approached an occasion of this sort as though the slightest moderation was entirely inappropriate. I was still trying to make up for my recklessness of the night before as well, and no amount of grandiose generosity was too much. I remember the waiter touring us up and down the many aisles in the basement where the restaurant's extensive collection of wines was shelved from floor to ceiling.

Beyond that event the evening remains a blur. I vaguely recall inviting two prostitutes back to our hotel room, but have no recollection of our interaction with them. Hungover and packing for the flight back to Chicago the next morning, part of me wished my brother would illuminate the mental blank spots, while another part hoped he remembered less than I did. Apparently nothing was missing from the room, but I didn't know how much money I had at the start of the evening, so I couldn't consider calculating the cost. I wondered to myself why I tended to hire hookers when I was too drunk to remember, probably too drunk to perform sexually as well. It didn't appeal to me at all under more sober conditions and it too often happened when I was responsible for others who trusted in my familiarity with a city. It was a dangerous activity and always deepened the already shameful after-effects of a drunken debauch, the details of which I could never clearly recall.

Back in Chicago, I introduced Barry to my girlfriend Sarah and she invited us over for one of her wonderful dinners, same delicious grilled lamb chops but this time she served a bracing salad of diced potatoes flavored with olive oil, lemon, lots of chopped green onions, and season salt, not for the dull palate. We went to the office the next day where he met several friends, including Noel Hyman of course, and we toured the Board of Trade floor. Sarah joined us for dinner at Gene and Georgette's, where I convinced Barry to order lobster along with a steak I knew he could not hope to finish once he had seen it. I believe he ate until it was too painful to continue, wanting to satisfy my convoluted notion of kindness.

When we got back to my place, he mentioned that some of the people he'd met seemed very intelligent, including Sarah and several of those I worked with. I proudly agreed of course. He observed that one fellow he'd met, a trader named Tim, may have done too many drugs. I knew there wasn't any doubt about that. In fact, Tim had recently attended his sister's wedding in Mexico and, in answer to my query, "How was Mexico?" he had replied with serious confusion in his voice and a skewed facial expression that matched, "The ground is really hard there."

But I responded to my brother too harshly that evening, with the assertion that Tim was a mathematical genius. I might more appropriately have laughed at the truth of his words and thereby flattered him for his astute observation and brotherly intimacy. Instead, my reaction had burst forth from a disagreeable mire of insecurity, where my priority was always to preserve an image of superiority.

The next day I took my young brother to the airport and, although I would have liked to say more regarding some of the things that bothered me, how much I loved him and how honored I had been with his visit, I said, "Thanks for coming. I hope your flight home is trouble-free." I wondered what he would share with the rest of the family, with my parents, and how he would describe his trip and the lifestyle of his senior sibling. Sarah said she really liked him and spoke, through her lovely smile, about the fun we had. I hoped she was right, but worried uselessly about the balance of good and bad, delight and depravity, and how Barry might judge my character. I didn't think I'd gotten to know him much better either, having expressed little curiosity about his life, his accomplishments, and his views of the world. He might have valued my personal interest.

Dave and I completed our scuba diving course, and nothing stood between my PADI open-water certificate and me but a medical examination. I liked old Doctor Ruben. He'd been a straight shooter with respect to my high blood pressure and now he was shooting straight again. "I shouldn't give you this. If you run out of air in a hundred feet of water, you don't have the lung capacity to make it to the surface." He paused, and then continued, "I will give it to you, only if you promise to give up smoking. Can you do that?"

I had smoked since age seventeen and I was thirty-three – sixteen continuous years – and my habit had grown to two packs of Marlborough cigarettes per day. Giving no thought to the magnitude of the moment, I said, "All right, I'll quit." He signed the required form and wished me luck. Halfway down the stairs that led from his office to the street I was confronted with the enormity of the decision I'd committed to and, at the same time, with a shameful aversion for betraying the good doctor. I did not doubt that he meant what he said, and I was certain as well that he believed me to possess sufficient integrity to mean what I said.

With almost no further deliberation on the matter, I arrived at a decision. I would walk the roughly twenty blocks home and I would stop in each of the many bars along the way and drink a shot of scotch and smoke two cigarettes. I had developed true abhorrence for the aftertaste of cigarettes and I was nearly nauseated by stale stinking ashtrays, especially in the morning. Thus, I had acquired a slender predisposition for the concept of not smoking. The theory behind my plan was that my mouth, so abused by the dry bitterness of the scotch and the filmy filth of the cigarette smoke, would taste so horrid in the morning that I would not want to smoke, ever again.

I don't remember much of the process, although I suppose I pondered being a non-smoker while nearly killing myself in the act. I awoke the next morning with the desired outcome, as far as my mouth was concerned. I walked into the living room and discovered a cigarette pack that had three or four left in it. It lay beside an ashtray with one disgusting half-smoked butt in it. I emptied the ashtray and wiped it out, then made some coffee. I found myself in a condition of mental limbo, afraid to move too quickly, waiting to see how bad the craving would get.

With no further struggle of any kind, I was suddenly a non-smoker. Some sort of psychic change had come over me and I simply didn't smoke anymore, and I felt very good about it, for hours, then for days and weeks. Never again, despite continued heavy alcohol consumption, wild partying, and the presence of other smokers, have I ever been tempted by the notion of inhaling smoke into my lungs. Prior to that day I could not have imagined an hour without it. In all the days thereafter, I reacted to the very idea with revulsion. I could only conclude that the mind is a peculiar phenomenon.

Soon after that Sarah attended a course in Miami. At her invitation I shared her hotel room. Dave came down as well and we spent a few days diving at Key Biscayne and Key Largo. John Pennekamp Coral Reef may not be world class, but I felt as though I had discovered another dimension, a compliment to flying in a sense. I developed a tremendous zeal for the sport and, though it was expensive, I easily cast aside all limits when thrilling new horizons beckoned.

Part III
Conquest and Euphoria

Chapter 15

That fall I found a five-acre property on the shore of Fox Lake, a little over an hour from downtown. The house was only a Quonset hut, not elaborate, but it offered a mind-expanding view over the property and onto the lake, a cozy wood burning stove, and was not in bad shape. I would have to replace the carpets but little else to make it comfortable. I was lured by the small garage, pleased with the lushness of the trees, the vast lawn area, and the promise of flowering plants when spring arrived. The land and the lake represented an earthy retreat to something genuine. In addition, I had reached a point where isolation appealed to me as a triumph over the scrutiny of others.

In the mood for a rural life, I bought a new four-wheel drive Mitsubishi pick-up. To meet the requirement for a down payment on the acreage I borrowed ten thousand dollars from Troy. I would pay that back over the next two months and we didn't bother with paper work. The level of casual trust among traders, such as we were, was significant. Ten thousand dollars wasn't much, I admit, and I'm sure Troy's ego was fed by looking at it with that perspective as well. But still, it felt good to be trusted, judged to be one for whom that was not an imposing sum. With constant concern for my exterior image, my stage character, I presented myself as an invincible big shot, while inside I was always surprised when granted the respect of my peers. The grasp this messy dichotomy had on my life was mind-numbing sometimes. Mushy internal doubt pushed at the seams of an external façade which, more and more, I feared might be torn away.

Sarah was an enthusiastic supporter of the idea from the beginning and, once I took possession, she spent weekends there to help with renovations. We had become a couple in most respects and I came to like her mother a good deal as well. We had gotten to know each other better when she joined Sarah and me in Florida. After Dave and I had done some diving and he departed, the three of us enjoyed a day touring the Everglades.

By the end of 1983 I had established a routine of sorts. I went to my place in the country on weekends, and sometimes during the week when I needed to drink myself into senseless oblivion because I was on the wrong side of a market and painfully losing money. Because it was an hour-long commute by train and then a ten-minute drive, however, on weekdays I often stayed at the Union League Club downtown or at Sarah's. I continued to play squash at the club as well, enjoying the classy old steam room and sipping on a Tom Collins after the game. During one of those sessions I teamed up with my squash-playing partner to import fine Spanish Rioja wines, at around sixty dollars per case of a dozen, for our personal consumption.

The various vintages of Rioja were young and immature, according to my friend, and would be much improved after being 'put down' for a few years, an investment for future enjoyment. I'm sure he eventually enjoyed the rewards of that scheme. My stock of fine wines was usually consumed within a few months, sometimes two bottles in a single and solitary evening, without its being put down. It was John Sargent who passed on the wisdom his socialite mother had apparently handed down to him: "Drinking too much isn't good for you. But, if you are going to drink, good quality liquor is always better." Like John, I found solace in the second part.

In the first quarter of 1984 I drank too much whiskey at a cattle feeders convention out west, joined clients for another weekend of extravagant debauchery at a convention of macroeconomic extremists in New Orleans, and met John Sargent in Quebec where we spent a night in Montreal and then relocated to the Mount Tremblant Resort for a few days of skiing, drinking, and rehashing the impending demise of the economic system. It isn't that I didn't enjoy the attributes and ambience of places I visited – I did – but my appreciation was diluted by the vaguely persistent conviction that I was yet to genuinely exist. I did not experience thankfulness, for example, because my mind was obsessed with avaricious designs for greater certainty. I feared that continuing abundance was not yet guaranteed, which, when decoded, meant that my very identity was not yet assured.

During that time, the clearing firm John Sargent worked with held a promotional grand opening for its renovated Chicago operations. As a result of some affiliation unknown to me, Henry Kissinger was there autographing a book he had just published, a copy of which I gratefully accepted. Not being a tall man and having a voice that is famously conciliatory, I was comfortable visiting with him on what seemed like equal terms for some fifteen minutes. Upon reflection, I saw the incident as exemplifying my general state of bewilderment. Rather than learn what I could of world affairs from a man of rather incredible experience, I proposed some of my own ideas, implicitly viewing his record with pompous contempt. I was privately dismayed at my arrogance and only grateful that I was not more overtly disrespectful. Socially, I smugly footnoted the occasion when I thought it advantageous to my image, with people other than John Sargent, that is, because he whole-heartedly shared my disdain for the establishment and had not even collected one of the books.

In late March, Dave and I spent a flawless week scuba diving and drinking the world's finest margaritas in the relaxed atmosphere of Cozumel, Mexico. He was an even-tempered, fun-loving man who did not dwell upon issues. We laughed a lot, joked about women and life, enjoyed casual days of diving locally off the beach, experienced an exhilarating sixty-foot drift-dive along stunning and bottomless Palancar Reef, and survived a precarious night-dive from a sixteen-foot aluminum boat that was far too dimly lit by a flickering twelve volt bulb that wobbled in its bracket at the stern.

As the week progressed, I marveled at Dave's exceptional capacity to be a good friend. He was a very good friend, simple as that. He didn't seem drawn down as a result of his losing battle with trading his own account and I was able to briefly forget similar woes. The excursion was entirely memorable, without a single cause for regret. It was an irrefutable example of the abundance in my life, impossible to ignore, and I believe it buoyed me up for a while and expanded the horizons of my perspective on being. Shortly after that, I signed up with Alliance Francaise for lessons in French. I had placed renewed value on character, external character rather than internal, broader rather than deeper, but self-improvement nevertheless and a source of fulfillment.

Yvonne, who was in the process of moving back to New York from Denver, stopped to visit and stayed at my place a few days. She had retained her warm joyful character and reluctantly accepted the new loner image I presented to her. It wasn't an entirely false image because I was very much a loner, though not always alone. It was obvious she considered my hovel in the country beneath the aspirations she once had for me, those she had also believed were mine, because Yvonne was a city girl who aspired to the finer things in life. I really cared for her, cared about her. But the novelty I craved in everything wasn't there and I couldn't change that. Part of me wanted to find a way back to the relationship we had once shared, but the path was grown over, the door of passion closed.

From time to time I had scanned, in the *Chicago Tribune*, the section devoted to the matching of romantic partners. On a whim, I formulated a description of myself: white, mid-thirties, financially independent, fun-loving, and wanting to share life with someone. I mailed it in. I never would have disclosed the action to anyone I knew because I thought it an act of desperation for desperate people, except in my case, that is, because I viewed it as research, investigation. My overall lack of sincerity, therefore, was another reason to keep the adventure completely clandestine.

I didn't give it much thought in the interim and was therefore quite astounded when a total of eight letters dribbled in. They had been submitted to the anonymous box number designated for responses and then forwarded to me by the newspaper. I was skeptical as I began to open the envelopes. But the letters were enthusiastic and contained some quite alluring phrases. Several contained photographs of not unattractive ladies, and I experienced a sense of popularity, even desirability. There was incredible variety, too. One was clearly a pretty Italian, half were moderately adorable blondes and brunettes, and one wrote that she was black, very attractive, and interested in meeting a white man. My mind reeled at the evidence of available abundance; my thoughts were not inspired by sexual greed as much as visions of romance. The feelings I developed while rereading the letters and studying the photos were not pornographic in nature, but rather those of kind regard and affection. Indeed, I felt privileged and a little overwhelmed, as though I had been placed in a position of trust over a precious collection of art. It still rather amazed me that these very eligible and presentable women had responded, that they had viewed the newspaper's service with that degree of trust. I worried that they may someday make themselves vulnerable to men with corrupted intentions.

I considered my own intentions, including Sarah, and I knew that I did not want to mess things up with her. I experienced a little guilt, but thought of how Sarah always made her own decisions and never seemed very dependent upon my attention. In fact, she was too independent sometimes. In any case, as excited as I was to think of making new female acquaintances, this would have to remain casual, tentative and completely covert.

Louise Giuliano's photograph was of a pretty girl with a sparkling smile and it included enough of her bust to reveal that it was ample. I called her, using the number she'd given, and we arranged to meet at a bar downtown. She was sexier than

I'd imagined and her breasts had been understated in the picture, which was justification enough for listening while she talked non-stop about herself for over an hour. I suppose I should have been getting to know her as a result, but it only narrowed my interest to the point where I knew I wanted to have sex with her and spend only as much social time as was necessary to accomplish that. We'd had several rounds of drinks and finally she disclosed her physical availability by saying, "You like my girls, don't you?" giving them a little shake and adding, "I see you peeking at them."

I said I did like them and she revealed in a short time that her preoccupation with sex, at the very least, equaled mine. We went to her place and had an enjoyable frolic, although not especially memorable. Afterwards, while we lay on her bed, she smoked cigarettes and talked some more. She chose to tell me about other relationships she'd had, one in particular she really enjoyed. It was with a young guy in his twenties and they did it three times in succession, she said. I said I'd love to see her again, but that I had to get home right then.

I'd made another appointment for two days later, with a lady who hadn't included a photo, and that session ended after a few drinks because I wasn't attracted in the least. Again, there was a lot of one-sided talking, during which I felt my life was being wasted. I waited for an amount of time I considered polite and said, as respectfully as I could, that I didn't think it would work out.

I talked for an hour on the phone with Judy Beth Anderson. The conversation was mature, upbeat, and established that she was a girl who respected herself, was seriously looking for someone to spend recreational time with, and was not only interested in sex. She lived with her father about ten miles from my place at Fox Lake. That was appealing, but it might complicate things if she were to become comfortable visiting me at home. I was quite sure spending time with her would be pleasant, however, and we agreed to meet in the town for dinner in two weeks.

Meanwhile, I had planned a trip to Seattle, to meet with a prospective client in the logging and lumber industry, and then on to Vancouver for a seminar. I arrived late in the evening, had dinner at the hotel, and went to my business meeting the next morning. Both the company president and his chief financial officer agreed that lumber futures had a place in their pricing and risk management efforts. We planned to follow up the meeting with regular telephone contact and I was satisfied that it had gone well enough.

As I took a shortcut across a broad un-groomed property that appeared to be in the process of reclamation following the dismantling of an old building, I noticed a rather skimpily clad girl watching me from the perimeter. Being always the opportunist, especially in response to subtle suggestion, I veered off the course that would have taken me directly to the parking lot of the hotel I was staying in. As I came closer she looked a little older than at first glance, at least not a minor, and when I said, "Hello," she surprised me with a boldness that only lacked practice. "Are you interested in a little company?"

Because I almost always was, I said, "That would probably be all right. You seem kind of new at this, how much?"

"Fifty dollars?" she suggested, with a note of uncertainty. If she had indicated any doubt about her intentions, I was prepared to walk away. But, despite her obvious rookie status, she seemed to be firmly decided upon the course she was following. Perhaps she needed the money; perhaps, I thought it more likely, she just wanted a walk on the wild side, as I often did. I supposed her motive wasn't any of my business and, although my part in it could hardly be construed as benevolence, I was convinced I wasn't causing any harm.

We passed the concierge and front desk without uncomfortable scrutiny and went up to my room. We began removing our clothes and I noted that she hadn't asked for the money upfront. Instead she said, "I have to wash you first." So we went into the bathroom where she ran warm water, soaped a facecloth, and washed my penis.

It seemed like a smart thing to do and it felt good, so I said, "Maybe I should wash you, too," to which she agreed, and I did.

She did not seem like a hardened hooker, coldly clinical and cynical, and I believe she did not mind her work, at least in that instance. We took our time and the whole event was as pleasant as it was satisfying. Afterwards, I asked her how she got started and why she did it. She said, "I like sex and I don't do it with just anyone. This is better than going with some drunk from the bar and I may as well get paid for it."

To be honest, I really liked her and her friendly no-bullshit attitude. I paid her sixty dollars and hoped things went well for her. I wondered if a woman could do that sort of thing and not be somehow corrupted by it. I wondered if I was corrupted by it, immediately identifying that as a very deep question and dismissing it as none of my present concern.

A cousin I'd spent a lot of time with when we were kids lived near Seattle and we got together to reminisce over dinner. Carolyn, a year or two older than me, was the one who pulled me off the quiet old mare we'd been riding and, because of my damaged face, delayed my entry into first grade. We laughed about that again. She had declared many years ago that she was a lesbian, and since then had been living openly with her girlfriend. I had no opinion on the matter; each to his own was my view. She was a real tomboy when we were kids, running across the prairie one day and catching two young foxes by their tails, things like that, and we enjoyed a few hours of nostalgia. You certainly don't know where life is going to take you when you throw off the shackles of convention and religion.

In Vancouver I spent some time taking in the beauty of the place between sessions at my three-day seminar. Someone mentioned the nude beach on the Pacific shore near the University of British Columbia, Wreck Beach I think they called it. I did some research into directions and checked it out, even joined the sparse crowd for some all-over sun tanning, without any social interaction. While there, it crossed my mind that I could have attended the same seminar in Chicago. But I liked to be in different places. I also observed that I drank far less when travelling alone in unfamiliar surroundings, away from familiar friends.

Novelty seemed as much a source of mental escape for me as alcohol. I was happy to wander in a sort of daze, between imagining myself living in the place I was visiting and imagining living in centuries past. Of course Vancouver, although visually alluring, is not generally mysterious in a cultural sense and has that distinctly North American dearth of ancient history. But I thought of something my mother said one time, maybe it was following my divorce from Jo-Anne: "When you were little and got a new toy for Christmas, or your birthday, you usually only played with it for a short time and then threw it off in the corner." She offered the statement as though it profoundly defined my character. I guess it did; whether it was women, location, or lifestyle, novelty was the only consistent desire in my life.

Soon spring arrived in Chicago and the lake at the end of my property inspired me to take up wind surfing. I bought the necessary equipment and set out to conquer the sport with a how-to booklet as a guide. To say it was challenging would be vastly understating the exasperating frustration, physical exhaustion, and cursing rages I experienced in the process. With grim determination I persisted, however, and before fall I was cruising around an island situated off my shoreline and out into the larger body of the lake where both wind and water were more formidable.

I had once possessed that kind of simple relentless determination, supported by brazen confidence, with respect to my career. But something had changed and my move out of the city seemed symptomatic of an underlying dwindling of my optimism and aspirations. There had been no shift in my objective of achieving financial independence, but I perceived fissures developing in my self-confidence. My state of mind regarding my business and finances was occasionally one of desperation; my work with prospective clients was forced and willful, too often driven by vague anxiety and neediness. A slate of firings had taken place at Holloway and Associates as well; I was safely apart from that turmoil with an independent contract, but maybe it was a hint that we had been living in a big bubble and things were starting to slip away. Eventually my edginess manifested itself in resentful feelings toward others in the office and I began to despise those who were experiencing more success than I was. Still, for the most part, all that suffered was my sense of wellbeing.

I forced myself to call prospective clients and I tried for the disciplined daily approach I had observed Noel Hyman practicing for years. Every afternoon, once the markets closed and he'd taken care of reporting to his existing customers, he began to flip through his Rolodex and dial the phone. It was a numbers game that kept lines of communication open, pried at potential clients' inertia, and eventually got him new business that was essential in offsetting the natural attrition of customers, a miserable norm in the industry. While he seemed healthily compelled by some basic instinct, I had no motivation but impending doom, and that was rarely sufficient to overcome my increasing dread of a salesman's biggest hurdle – rejection.

While in the city, I joined Dave and Troy in a summertime routine of golf and Cubs games at Wrigley Field; Sarah and I enjoyed dinners out and dinners at her place. We spent a few weekends away as well. While alone at my place in the country, I cut the grass, trimmed trees and hedges, worked at my windsurfing as though it were a new career, and spent more than a few evenings dining, drinking, and slamming away at bent-over Judy Beth Anderson from the newspaper classified section. I desperately needed a world apart from the markets, my clients, and the heaviness of keeping score.

With increasing frequency I left the office after work, propelled by a skulking need to vanish without social niceties, and went directly to the bar-car on the train. Except for rare occasions when I collided with another lonely heart for a night of blacked-out inseparability, I got into my truck and drove home in a blur only to continue drinking until wistful hallucinations of grandeur were followed by oblivion. Too often to go unnoticed, I phoned my assistant in the morning to report that I was sick, which had a pathetic ring to it, so I switched to boldly asserting that I was taking the day off. That at least left me with the appearance of control. Increasingly, I retreated to reading by the fire for whole days, historical novels mostly, because they relocated me with respect to time and geography. I went through a half dozen, including James Michener's *The Covenant* and *The Source*, followed by *Shogun*, *King Rat*, *Taipan*, and *Noble House* by James Clavell. Next I escaped into a dozen or more historic espionage thrillers by Frederick Forsyth, Robert Ludlum, and Ken Follett, and thence to a few classics I felt obliged to have read, such as Dante's *Inferno* and *War and Peace* by Leo Tolstoy. I began, but could not endure, Bertram Russell's autobiography.

Clients visited and I stayed in town overnight to party with them. Occasionally Sarah joined me, as she did one October evening when we took a client, who had become quite a good friend, and his wife out to a Greek restaurant on Halsted Street and from there to a Montreal Canadiens versus Chicago Blackhawks game. As things were, on the visible surface, I was proud of the image of success I projected. I might well have been internally grateful for it, too, had I not been possessed by an ever-present anxiety, some unidentifiable emptiness.

Chapter 16

On balance, 1984 had been a good year: my income had held around ten thousand per month; I'd paid Troy back his ten grand; I had enough set aside for managing taxes through an IRA contribution, and my bank account was more than flush. Although I suffered miserably with not being able to make money trading, I had not given gobs of it away. That permitted me to seize upon a vision of rough-country escapism, made manifest in a new 1985 four-wheel drive Chevy Blazer. Unlike the Mitsubishi, it offered a large enclosed rear compartment that could serve for overnight forays, vagabond style. The dream of riding off into the sunset had magnetism.

When the broker, whose New Year's party I had disrupted the previous year, invited me back for a pre-Christmas social evening, I was happy to escape the quaking pang of rejection his not doing so would have caused. His direct but polite entreaty that I control my drinking this time was that of a reasonable and caring person. When the time came I complied, stayed a respectable interval, wished him and his wife a Merry Christmas, and left believing I had partially redeemed myself. Thoughts that I might do well to clean up my act on a broader basis haunted me as I rode the train home.

By the time I arrived, my determination was such that I glanced at the remaining, unexplored responses to my ad in the paper and threw them into the fire I had just started in the comfy old stove. I spent the next day buying Christmas cards and writing notes to members of my family and long-time friends. I flew back to my parents' place for a family Christmas and returned to Chicago on New Year's Day. That evening I opened a bottle of Rioja Gran Reserva and reflected on my prospects for 1985.

I committed myself to playing squash, attending French classes, and I decided to find another dojo and take up karate again – activities that were a positive part of my life, kept me from drinking all the time, and seemed an investment in my physical health and sense of wellbeing. I'd renewed my membership to the Art Institute as well. A lady named Celia, who had left Holloway and Associates to finish her master's degree in music, and with whom I had only brief social contact at the annual party in Florida, informed the staff that she was giving a graduate soprano recital. That had an appealing ring of sophistication and I decided to attend. I was fascinated by her beautifully powerful voice. When I told her so after her performance, she was delighted to hear it and obviously happy that I had shown an interest. We talked long enough to discover that she lived in my old neighborhood and to decide we would meet for lunch one day at a restaurant we had separately enjoyed. We exchanged phone numbers.

Sarah had recently begun expressing disappointment with our relationship; more specifically she expressed disillusionment with me. Then, after an evening of drinking, I showed up at her place and she let me stay the night in her bed. I woke up and found myself lying alone in a cold soggy bed with the stench of urine in the air. Knowing her guest had pissed the bed long before I realized it, she was slumped in a chair and glowering at me with a mixture of anger and sad regret. I think drinking too much might have served as a pathetic excuse had it happened only once. But it happened again several weeks later and she informed me that I wouldn't be sleeping there anymore. Despite that, Sarah maintained contact with me and lovingly expressed hope that I would alter my course.

As disgusted as I was with this development at the time, I had perfected the art of suppressing bad news and degrading circumstances to a degree that such events, in my rationalizing mind, did not somehow pertain to the authentic me. When

Sarah told me she had decided to go to Egypt and take a cruise up the Nile, in order to connect with the culture of her ancestry, I asked if she would like me to join her. She was not wholly enthused and it was a few days later when she agreed we would probably enjoy doing it together. Because my friends, Bob and Karen Hawk, had raved about Aiya Napa, I wanted to add a few weeks in Cyprus to the trip. Bob had been especially thrilled with the topless beaches, upon which I didn't elaborate with Sarah. We booked an organized, double-occupancy, two-week excursion for the Egyptian portion. Sarah planned for a few days in Cyprus, because she felt she couldn't be away from work any longer, and I planned for two weeks.

The animosity I felt for former friends in the office poisoned my days. Because it stemmed from sources that were obscure, well beyond the petty judgments I passed on them each day, I could not stop it even though I would have liked to. The simple surface logic that said they were well-meaning people who had always been kind to me was powerless against the self-loathing I could only deal with by turning it outward.

Piling on increased self-disgust, one slushy wintery morning I was walking from the train station and decided to jaywalk through the stalled traffic. A man that I angered, when I judged him to have discourteously cut me off, by tapping on the rear of his little red sports car as I crossed behind it, jumped out and began punching at me. He didn't connect and I didn't fight back; instead I turtled with my hands over my head and face. The loose files I held flew out of my hand onto the sloppy sidewalk. Once he gave up the attack and returned to his car, I picked up the papers with my trading notes on them and headed sheepishly on my way, mortified that anyone I knew should have witnessed the humiliating incident, and the cowardice I displayed while being attacked. The upshot of suppressing an event of that nature was increased general ill will.

When Darcy Eckhart, Holloway's managing partner, called me into his office to ask a few questions about Troy's performance, specifically his usefulness in providing information from the trading floor and servicing my clients, I did not hesitate to undermine his credibility. I had abandoned him at a convention in Colorado so I could party with my friends, and I knew he had gossiped about that. I had also been irritated recently with his cavalier market comments and dubious insinuations that he had known beforehand what would happen, especially when it was contrary to my trading positions. Nonetheless, because he had been a close friend for nearly four years, I experienced a tinge of guilt. Obviously his co-workers, floor brokers who were senior partners, had been instrumental in commencing the action and Darcy was merely trying to find out how I would react to Troy being let go. It was a Friday and it turned out to be his last day.

I had left the office early and never again saw or spoke to a man with whom I had shared so much of life. Dave called to inform me that evening and I heard later that Troy returned to West Texas. It became more and more disturbing to reflect upon scraps of evidence that suggested an even broader agreement on his dispensability. To contemplate his leaving with the impression that his friends had betrayed him saddened me. The enmity I had harbored for my former friend was thus transformed into a shameful smudge that smoldered near the core of my existence.

When Judy Beth came over on Saturday my mood slowly shifted from glum to miserable; then it shifted to uncaring and belligerent. Despite the friendship and affection we had shared, and the fact that we had never been cross with one another, I cruelly dismissed her, just as Troy had been dismissed. Feeling completely alone, unable to read because of my whirling mind and prior alcohol consumption, I sought oblivion. Things seemed to be falling apart generally and it appeared I would go with them.

In the world of business, when someone is terminated like that, everyone is expected to carry on as though the terminated one had never existed. There is no discussion, except what is necessary for the reassignment of responsibilities and that is apt to be littered with nameless criticisms of how things were done. It's a technique for supporting the company's stance and reunifying the workforce. At the end of the first week without Troy, I muttered some encouragement to my assistant, advised my clients of my forthcoming absence, and left with Sarah for Egypt.

I was thrilled to be on my way to a truly exotic land; the phrase 'Voyage of Sinbad' was a touchstone for my fantasizing. I remembered my Aunt Dorothy asking me at age seven what I wanted to do when I grew up. "See the pyramids," I had answered, and I resolved to send her a postcard. Everything went smoothly with our connecting flight in Munich and I considered it a bonus when I caught on camera a nice image of the red tile roofs of that seemingly neat and clean city. As we travelled from the airport to our hotel in downtown Cairo, my eyes were glued to the views from the window of the bus, as though I could quench a deep visual thirst in the marvelously unfamiliar world.

On the morning of our first full day in the country, I found myself sitting atop a camel while it trudged slowly along a rock-strewn trail that climbed toward the great stone Sphinx and the world's most extraordinary monuments. Sarah sat astride her camel as they slogged onward directly ahead of me. I giggled inwardly each time I looked at her back, recalling the childlike glee in her eyes as she climbed into the crude saddle.

I marveled with incredulity at my surroundings – the bewildering human accomplishment implicit in all that was visible and the unfathomable antiquity that it represented. I had with me the 35mm Canon camera Barry, my brother, had given me as a Christmas gift. But I'd been reading some 'teach yourself photography' books, and I knew that midday sunlight was not the best for taking pictures. Free of that temptation, and leaving the camel behind, I simply wandered and gaped, immersed in a superbly nourishing presence of mind.

In the afternoon we visited The Egyptian Museum, which must have, by tonnage, one of the world's greatest gold hoards. But it is all in the form of glorious sculptures: larger than life-size likenesses of Pharaohs, their queens, attendants, and the ever-present lions. The facial features of the humans portrayed were God-like in their perfection, the eyes large and beautifully overstated, the bodies noble, lean, and lithe. The story of King Tutankhamen, who reigned 1332 to 1323 BCE, launched me into a quiet space of unknowing as I perused the facts: he ruled Egypt thirty-three hundred years ago; he was a pharaoh of the eighteenth dynasty, in a period of Egyptian history known as the New Kingdom. Grasping the time line was exhilarating for someone whose childhood community had only just marked its first centenary. With increasing fascination, I pondered his mask, a golden image framed by a fanning golden sunburst that exemplified his everlasting glory, which alone consisted of eleven kilograms of gold. Where did all the gold come from? What was the relative wealth in that ancient land? Who was the now obscure artisan that had designed and executed that magnum opus?

It was, however, the less ostentatious, remarkably well preserved, vividly painted, and curiously lifelike limestone sculptures of Prince Rahotep and his wife Nofret in her satin-white gown, from 2600 BCE and during the Fourth Dynasty, that were my favorites among the massive collection. With captivated bemusement I gazed into their startlingly convincing eyes. A profound sense of affiliation arose within me. I sought after the slightest thread of mutual and empathetic connection. With all his glittering importance, King Tut had not inspired a similar warmth and urge for rapport.

That evening, when I noticed an orange hue begin to permeate the desert sky, I became the photographer. Sarah and I quickly arranged a taxi, grabbed the camera, and returned to the pyramids. The Saharan backdrop was perfect; the mysteriously hazy Halloween-orange that cloaked the horizon gave way seamlessly to a grainy blond luminosity as it swept skyward. Just as we arrived at an ideal vantage point for photos, four horsemen appeared above the skyline in the south. Fantastically, with their white turbans and blustering galabeyas, the wind-blown tails and manes of their fiery Arabian mounts, they rode to the very foreground of the great pyramids. I went to work on the shutter button until they rode on, and couldn't wait to see the results once the film was developed. Sarah was still gazing with amazement in her eyes and I decided the biggest objection to taking photographs must be that, although one has the pictures for a long time, he cannot actually be present for the event. In any case, we were both ecstatic over our good fortune in witnessing what must have been an especially genuine and timeless Saharan scene.

The next morning we joined a bus tour of Cairo and its Nile Delta surroundings. There was no hope for disguising my tourist image: strangely dressed, conspicuous skin color, camera in hand, and gawking preoccupation with a foreign land. I would have preferred being an Egyptian for the day. Sarah, with her Levantine facial features, dark hair, and large dark eyes, could have passed rather well as a local woman if she were willing to dress in a full length black galabeya and cover her head, mouth, and nose. She quietly insisted, without judgment, she could never surrender to that traditional mold, despite its appearing so natural in the ladies we observed all around us.

We stopped at and entered an elaborately arched and domed mosque, its vast interior illuminated with dozens of small chandeliers and its expansive floor covered with hundreds of woven cotton mats, warm rusty reds and soft earthy greens. Men standing in semi-circular rows went through the prescribed motions for prayer, entering and leaving quietly and with deep respect. Later, we spent time wandering the alleys of a souk and watched while intensely intricate patterned silk rugs slowly materialized on hand operated looms. I decided I should have one to add to my collection, which still only consisted of a prayer rug I'd bought in Istanbul over three years ago while sharing my prize-cruise with Yvonne.

Out the window of the tour bus I watched a woman negotiate for a melon with a man who sat upon the seat of a four-wheeled cart loaded with them. A small, sleek, harnessed and blinkered Arab mare stood patiently between the shafts. The image of the horse and vendor making the laborious trip into the city from the farm area every day of their lives stirred within me the notion of enduring commitment. It reminded me of my agrarian beginnings and my parents' unwavering acceptance of their lot.

In the rural areas of the delta, fields cleared of dense semi-tropical forest covered more land than did palm peppered desert. But the arid climate was evident here and there: puffy clouds of dust flew from children's feet as they vied for possession of a soccer ball, and from the feet of a donkey that bore two radiantly clad giggling girls down the main street of a village, and from those of another that clip-clopped along under an enormous bundle of coarse Nile grass, as his driver conducted him from behind with a flimsy baton. Another donkey had the task of trudging round and round a water well, hitched to the end of a twenty-foot shaft that operated a pump at the center. Grazing nearby, upon the dry husks of a recently harvested cornfield, was a long-eared co-worker who would spell him off at the end of his shift. And another conductor, with baton gently rising and falling, played his part in perpetuating this symphony of a thousand years.

In the shade of date palms pendulously laden with ripening fruit, women in stunning cherry-red, sky-blue, and sunset-orange outfits ambled along the hard-packed or roughly paved roads. Sometimes alone, but more often in pairs and engaged in animated conversation, they appeared entirely unaware of the various goods and chattels that seemed balanced precariously on their heads. Near the river, a community of university students made an industry of reproducing on papyrus paper those intricate, brilliantly colored images that so exclusively symbolize glorious Egypt in the time of the Pharaohs. I had hardly imagined the existence of anything so remarkably genuine in appearance and quality, and I had no difficulty selecting three of them for what was becoming a collection of superb travel mementos. In fact, I longed to establish a tangible and indelible link with the glorious state of mind I had experienced over the last two days, a blissful suspension of my own inadequate reality.

On the morning of the third day, we and our luggage were loaded onto a comfortable Nile cruise boat and we settled into our cabin. I had no prior conception of life along the Nile and I was spellbound from morning until night as we glided past rudimentary villages, coarse and tenuous tracts of farm land, and the barren desert sands creeping relentlessly toward the shore line. Direct contact was often fended off by no more than a few sturdy palms whose roots drank directly from the current. Local people fished, swam, bathed, washed dishes, and brushed their teeth in the enormous river that had been a source of life itself for more than a dozen millennia. I was disappointed when we were informed that so much as putting our hands in the water may result in regrettable contact with parasitic tropical bacteria, to which the locals were obviously immune. I wanted to touch the Nile, but refrained.

The Nile touched me nonetheless. I was touched by the beauty and simplicity of the gleaming white-sailed feluccas that plied back and forth; the unhurried people I observed living in communities of mud huts; a father wending along a sandy path with his two adorable daughters at his side. The vibrant dresses worn by the prepubescent pair, in celebration of the month of Ramadan and in preparation for the Festival of Breaking Fast at its end, were in conspicuously cheery contrast with the parched landscape. I longed for the apparent simplicity. However, in place of a down-to-earth renunciation of material ambitions, typically a prerequisite to living happily within that simplicity, my vision included having a few million dollars in the bank first, a little something to fall back on. I would be content to practice minimalism once I had acquired enough to be happy. The visible evidence that people living on a few dollars per day were happier and more contented than most people I knew strongly suggested that happiness was not to be found in money. It did not interfere, however, with the vague notion that my higher aspirations placed my being above the sorry insignificance to which they were bound. Therefore, a large contributor to their happiness was simply not knowing what I knew. To accept one's circumstances and strive for happiness within them was a wonderfully consoling cliché for those who lacked the cleverness and grit to soar beyond.

After a few nights on the river, we arrived at Luxor and checked into a fabulous Oberoi Hotel, located on an island several hundred yards off shore. To get from the hotel into town and back, we had the choice of sculled or motorized water taxis. We rode tour buses to The Valley of Kings and The Valley of Queens, both of which are occupied by dozens of tombs and offer an unimaginable exploration of elaborate ancient burial rites. The dry air ensured remarkable preservation of intricate carvings and paintings along the walls of tunnels through the millennia. Centuries of pilfering buried treasure by marauding hordes had not vanquished the trove, and more recent discoveries remain intact as a vibrant link with the mysterious past. We rode perhaps two miles to Karnac Temple on a horse-drawn carriage with two double seats for four passengers and a single for the driver. The single chestnut mare was not large and trotted the whole distance at a good clip, the sun blazing directly overhead and the temperature at one hundred and ten degrees. When we arrived I deliberately walked round to the front of the horse and examined her chest and shoulders for perspiration. None, not breathing hard either, as she began to chew on the bit of coarse roughage placed on the ground in front of her. It resembled in dimension and apparent lack of palatability the marshy slough vegetation we referred to as cattails on the prairie. I supposed that trip would have killed the horses I'd known; if not on a single trip, they'd have died more slowly of malnutrition.

The extensive ranks of human-headed lions and lion-headed lions that faced the avenue leading to the main façade of the gigantic shrine were indeed magnificent and impressively symmetrical. But it was their very existence, the fact that someone had proposed their construction so many thousands of years ago, the scale of the project and the challenges of achieving such perfection, that I found so inconceivable. I believed we could not accurately imagine Egyptian society in the time of the pharaohs. Its sophistication in terms of scientific thought, discriminating aesthetics, and spiritual fabrication has been lost to us, and we are doomed to climb our own exasperating mountain only to discover, as they did, that it is no more than a complex illusion, clearly, as it had all come to an end. The physical skeleton of phenomenal greatness is all that remains, while all the particular feeling-thinking essence of the phenomenon has vanished.

I gradually developed a craving to immerse myself more thoroughly, to further sever my connections with the world I'd left behind in Chicago. I yearned for a formless and timeless state of mind, and began to separate myself from Sarah, to put in place a buffer that cooled the social interdependency we had enjoyed to that point. I didn't know how to civilly state my wishes, or have the courage to do so, especially when doing so risked the appearance of selfishness, or worse, foolishness. I know, when confronted with inter-personal hurdles like this, there were other fears, too, unnamed fears. The natural consequence of that predicament was to use manipulation, a resource formed of long habit. As well, I dragged into play a typically obstinate streak, all of it to satisfy my simple and honest wish to explore this male dominated society on my own. Neither had I gotten over Sarah's cool response to my bed-wetting, and the other reasons she had given for backing away a few months ago. Ego-motivated spite and bitterness justified my hurtful attitude. I went off and did what I wanted to do, but an aura of sadness followed me. It seemed I had so often been driven to make difficult choices that meant leaving behind circumstances of warmth, familiarity, and comfort, in order to answer a powerful inner cry for more curiosity and excitement, some compulsive notion that I must go on alone to explore the unknown.

Making the most of my solitude, I wandered the fascinating avenues of ancient Luxor. Women shopped at outdoor vegetable markets and filled baskets with fresh produce, while men only paused near those and browsed with more interest at other shops lining the broad litter-free main street. Everyone went about their business as I supposed they had done daily, for longer than anyone could imagine. My imagination sought to know the nature of 'being' which must accompany living agelessly, where and as your ancestors have always lived. While poking along a section that was primarily a clothing bazaar, with rainbow arrays of hanging galabeyas, the crisp hues vibrant in the bright sunshine of the open street, I began talking with a Nubian fellow who was roughly my age. He was a little taller than me, lean and lithe, and his ebony complexion was accentuated by the starched whiteness of his full-length galabeya, and by his teeth when he smiled. His English was fluent and his demeanor amiable, so I was pleased to accept his suggestion of a cup of tea at a small table in the shade. I have since observed that it is common, in countries we habitually refer to as less developed, to invite foreigners to visit because it provides an important source of insight into a larger world and, quite often, an opportunity to practice a second, third, or fourth language.

The temperature, even near the shore of the enormous river, was over forty degrees Celsius, well over one hundred degrees on the Fahrenheit scale. My new friend suggested I buy myself a galabeya, assuring me that I would be much cooler than I was in the light pants and shirt I wore. When we finished our tea, that's what I did and, at his further insistence, I purchased the seemingly popular cap and wrap-around headgear as well. "Just wet it before you put it on and it will keep you cool," he said. It was very effective. I felt like Lawrence of Arabia.

Before I returned to the Oberoi that afternoon, he invited me to come back across in the evening and he would take me to a men's tea and hookah tavern. I did that as well, and felt immensely privileged as he interpreted some of the conversation concerning local affairs and national politics. Most of the men were much fairer than he, merely sun-darkened Arabian in appearance, but there didn't seem to be any particular notice of one for the other, or of my singularly light complexion either, and I felt entirely at ease in that especially masculine enclave.

He told me of his plans for commercial farming in Sudan, his native country. When I shared that I had a familiarity with that industry, he began to explore a partnership idea that I found intriguing. The far-away originality of it was tempting. On the way back to the water-taxi landing area, he expressed his gratitude for meeting me and thanked me for the opportunity to practice his English. We stood and talked a little more as there was time remaining before the last taxi embarked. We shared a reluctance to terminate what had been a warm and mutually gratifying encounter. Then he made an offer that honored me greatly: he thought I should marry his sister. The man loved to laugh but he was never flippant and he meant what he said. She lived in a village adjacent to Luxor and he offered to arrange a meeting for the next day. I toyed with a romantic vision of myself running a farm business in the Sudan, married to a beautiful Sudanese lady, far away from the struggles of my present life. Had I not been scheduled to fly out the next morning, I might have experienced greater difficulty declining his offer. As it was, however, I believed our relationship had reached its practical upmost and I bid him a heartfelt farewell.

Many people I knew would judge the man negatively for trying to match his sister with someone whom he thought would be a good business connection. I considered the bias inherent in that attitude, as I observed the single oarsman pulling us across the rippling surface, tacking against the current, the bow pointing far to the left of the hotel lights. I wondered how I would tell my friends about the man walking through the bazaar with four wives in his entourage. I supposed he was in his sixties, the lady adjacent to him was a similar age, the next probably in her forties, the next perhaps thirty, and the last not more than twenty. There were a dozen children ranging from a few years in age to teenagers, with the distinct probability of another dozen who were older and absent. The family was out for a walk, my Nubian friend had told me, and the sight was not uncommon. If a man could afford to marry younger women and support an ever-larger family, he often did so. I observed that his first wife continued to hold a prominent position at his side, along with the man's undivided attention. The obvious cheerfulness and easy-going relationships between the wives themselves, and the quiet, well-mannered children, made me think the entire concept must have far-reaching implications.

I wasn't thinking that either the marriage proposal, or the family arrangement, was preferable to traditions more familiar to me; I wasn't thinking in terms of 'good and bad' or 'right and wrong' at all. I was examining my own state of mental conditioning, the fact that mental conditioning had happened to me. I refuted the too-easy proposition that one set of beliefs is more enlightened than another and simply explored the vast differences: the variation in accepted customs certainly, but more significantly the dissimilarity in mental conditioning that allowed the family in Luxor to live in apparently cheerful harmony, when so many others would react with angry vehemence at the notion of living in the same circumstances. "What unknowable forces preceded such dissimilar conditioning?" I wondered.

The flight to Abu Simbel, toward the south end of Lake Nasser and the colossi that were relocated to save them from deep submergence by construction of the Aswan Dam, was an almost mystical experience. We rarely lost sight of the fabled river while vast stretches of sand passed beneath our wings until we finally touched down at an airfield that been all but abandoned to the desert. I was thrilled, delighted to share it with Sarah despite her anxiety, and happy to have a window seat as we lifted off for the return flight to Cairo. The following day we would depart for Cyprus.

Chapter 17

Just before we landed at Larnaca airport, Sarah informed me that she had booked a room on the coast near there and was spending her last few days alone. I was sorry not to have treated her with greater kindness, and thankful for my freedom at the same time. I rented a car and drove to Ayia Napa, at the east end of the island, where I planned to stay for about ten days.

It was paradise, just as Bob and Karen had promised. The long picture-perfect beach stretched from a white rocky outcropping on one end to small rugged cliffs on the other, and the turquoise waters of the Mediterranean Sea lapped tranquilly at its gentle slope. I'd chosen a table in the open patio dining area of my pleasant beachfront lodgings and marveled at the setting as I savored a classic English breakfast of boiled eggs, kippers, and toast. As other guests trickled in, I realized they were almost exclusively Northern European, Scandinavian and British, and I was grateful for their hushed deportment. After eating I walked along the beach where only a few others were present that early in the day. Near the far end, I came to The Flying Fish dive shop, which was already open, and divers were busy with preparations for the first beach dive of the day. I talked to a suntanned young man with curly blonde hair, one of several instructors from Finland who operated the business. When I told him I was there for at least a week, he suggested signing up for lessons that would lead to an advanced PADI rating. I immediately decided in favor of the idea and it became the primary daily focus of my time there.

When I left the shop and walked back, about two hours later, the beach was much busier and I was challenged with managing my line-of-sight in a not-offensive manner. Females of all ages and physical design (I'm certain a disproportionate number were the most beautiful women I'd ever seen) were strolling along, sitting on deck chairs, and lying on the sand, with their breasts exposed. I was dazzled by repeated observation of individual beauty, with which I struggled for discretion, and the simultaneous observation of a phenomenon so beautifully free. Couples held hands, parents sought the choicest location on the beach, children tagged along, grandparents fussed over grandchildren, clusters of young men and assemblies of young women bantered amiably. I seemed to be entirely alone in noticing the toplessness.

Most days I engaged in two sessions of one or two dives each and was very soon enjoying an easygoing friendship with Aleksi, the fellow I had first met. The diving experience was otherworldly at times, and very instructive. Navigation, search and rescue, night diving, ditch and recovery of equipment, helping with groups of beginners, there was a heavenly ease about it that remains etched in my memory. The water was so clear and the visibility so exceptional we were able to look over the gunwale of a dive boat and see the outline of a sunken ship in a hundred feet of water. Wreck diving in the Mediterranean, Aleksi reminded me, has been made abundant by many millennia of maritime misfortune.

It was surprising to me that, by the third day, I too had become accustomed to the circumstance of topless women. I discovered that nice breasts and nice eyes had roughly the same appeal. It seemed odd that there may actually be more titillation in the almost uncovered than in the totally uncovered. I wondered why on earth women spent so much money buying as little material as possible to cover something, or to cover as little of something as possible, that is better left entirely uncovered. Perhaps, in the final analysis, maximizing titillation was the objective.

I have only a single regret concerning my stay in Aiya Napa. On my second to last day there Aleksi had three newcomers sign up for an introductory class and asked if I would assist him. He introduced me to Jackie, a pretty young lady from South Africa, and informed her that I would be her dive buddy while he concerned himself with the safety of the other two. We walked out from the shore and went below in about twenty feet of water. She occasionally reached for my reassuring hand as we swam around near the bottom, and I kept an eye on her until we used up most of our air and surfaced.

I thought little more of it. But she lingered around the dive shop and I finally asked her if she'd like to join me for a little cruise on one of the twin-hulled sail boats they rented at a kiosk further back along the beach. She agreed and off we went. She was travelling alone, she said, and her home was Cape Town. I barely got the small craft off shore before she removed a loose-fitting pullover by reaching down and, in one smooth motion, lifting it above her head. She thus revealed two facts: she wore nothing beneath it, and she was very pretty indeed. She proceeded to lie on her back on the white canvas deck that stretched between the hulls and appeared instantly relaxed.

I, in the meantime, was struggling to catch the wind in the sail and make way beyond a rocky outcropping that loomed ever larger as the gap narrowed. Finally I could see that, although we were nearly clear, I would need to make sure we didn't graze a bit of rock just below the surface. I put my foot out and applied enough force to push us free of it. The pain was instant and excruciating. I groaned inwardly in agony and tried to imagine what I had done. Because I'd seen them while diving, it came to me quickly. I had stepped on a sea urchin, and with considerable force. I tried to put the pain aside, got the boat sailing nicely, and sat back with the hope of giving my striking passenger my full attention. It was no use. I shared what had happened with her and said that I must go back and have it looked at. She was silent, rather disappointed I assumed. I didn't know her well enough to accuse her of being self-centered, but there was no indication of concern for my condition. I silently shared her apparent regret. It had been a poor end to an unusually promising adventure.

I asked the Greek doctor how many spines were in my heel. "Millions," he said. I asked him what I needed to do. "Just leave them alone. They will all fall out, no problem," he assured me. He gave me a tube of ointment to soothe the discomfort. The pain wasn't yelping sharp anymore and I could hobble along quite well, if I didn't put pressure on my right heel. I was leaving soon to drive across the island in any case.

The next morning I went down to say farewell at the dive shop and Aleksi told me my advanced certification card would be issued and sent to my address in Chicago. I walked up to a hotel on the main street that ran past the resort area and talked once more to an artist I'd met there. He painted acrylics and, in one especially, he had captured quintessential Cyprus. I arranged to stay in touch, leaving open the option to purchase it later. On the way back to my room, I thought about the three superb bottles of local white wine I'd enjoyed over the whole time I was there, and how little I naturally drank when so pleasantly distracted otherwise. I signed out, packed my things in the car and, as though I was banishing myself from utopia, stuck to my firm resolve to explore more of the island's enchantment.

I drove to Nicosia, the capital city, beautiful except for the wall that divided it and the whole small country in half. I watched the U.N. peacekeeping soldiers patrolling for a while and experienced sadness as I thought of my artist friend's story of being forced to give up family owned property and relocate to the south because he was Greek instead of Turkish. People have lived upon this ancient land for thousands of years. How had it come to that?

I left the city and drove westward, toward the Troodos Mountains. In just a few hours I was cruising along a very high road, enjoying a breathless view of softly rolling peaks as they stretched to the western horizon. All the hues of a pastel rainbow hung in the hazy sky and tinted the soft woolen clouds that lay interwoven among the hills. In the midst of a slow curve I paused to greet a contented looking elderly man who tended a large herd of goats. Using hand gestures and pointing at my camera, I asked if I could take his picture, to which he acquiesced. The man was probably seventy-five, with a harshly weathered face, full white mustache, and eyes that conveyed something like gentle condescension. I thought he must see me as foreign in all conceivable ways. I wanted to tell him about the many days I had spent riding alone on the vast prairie as a boy, and of herding cattle through the uninhabitable sand hills. I found myself hoping that he somehow sensed I knew him better, that I placed more value on his solitary days than he may have assumed.

As the road wound its way down, departing the arid uplands to enter a verdant valley that held in its fold a very pretty town with a hundred red tile roofs covering as many small chalky white houses trimmed in Mediterranean blue, my acquaintance with a humbler life, as it was surely meant to be, seemed fully restored. A graceful white church stood out modestly in the center of the town, while the residences stepped up the slopes among the trees on either side of the valley. The whole effect was breathtaking and I knew I must stay there a while. I found a bed and breakfast establishment and my lovely motherly hostess turned out to be the pleasantest lady I'd ever met. Her English was only slightly better than my Greek. She showed me to my room and managed to convey that dinner would be ready in two hours, and to suggest that I have a nap. I didn't know what it was going to cost and I didn't realize that all my meals would be included. I was the only guest that evening and I have felt ever since that my presence was genuinely appreciated. I was hungry and tired and, according to her nature, she seemed fulfilled completely with providing for those needs.

The old-fashioned window in my room was made up of small panes separated by metal strips and it swung open upon wrought iron hinges. It opened upon a stunning view over the center of town and down the valley. Grapevines ran along the top and down one side and sweet green grapes hung in abundance at my fingertips.

Then she called, in words that I didn't understand but with a message that was unmistakable. I went down the stairs to the dining room where a single place setting awaited me. She poured some coffee and left, soon returning with the first course: orzo soup with a zesty lemon flavor. Some minutes later she returned again, this time with a self-satisfied smile that gave her away. "Kleftiko," she announced, assured by long experience that her roasted lamb would be unforgettable. Lemon roast potatoes appropriately accompanied the large portion of meat and she served me a little feta cheese salad on the side. As I sat undisturbed in that cozy home, taking pleasure in each morsel of mouthwatering food, enhanced still further by the authenticity of its creator, a small realignment occurred somewhere deep in my psyche. It occurred to me that no amount of alcohol or sexual exhilaration could ever be a substitute for the precious nature of that moment.

The next morning, just as I finished enjoying a dainty but abundant continental breakfast and coffee, a friend of hers stopped by, a fellow whose English was quite fluent. He suggested I should drive to the next small town and visit a museum there. He drew me a little map and told me the proprietor was a professor who had worked many years in London. Upon retirement he'd returned and had since amassed a wonderful display of Cypriot artifacts, some very ancient.

I arrived in the early afternoon and found myself immersed in a day I could hardly have imagined. The proprietor was delightful, as was his wife, and they were just sitting down to a little repast with three young Australians whom they'd hired to do some casual labor around the place. They insisted I join them and meet those other travelers. All in their early twenties, two men and a woman, they were university students on a yearlong journey around the world, something more common among their fellow countrymen than most others, I have the impression. After a pleasant hour they went back to their yard work and my tour began.

His collection was extensive indeed. It included, along with much more, countless pieces of red clay earthenware, including cookware, bread baking ovens, various sized water jugs, and even children's toys. Of the last two, he insisted I pick out examples and take them with me. I objected on the basis that they were precious pieces, to which he responded with a sweep of his hand, "But I have too many." I asked how old some of them were. "Perhaps a thousand years, maybe more," he said, as he indicated the rough calcified whiteness on the surface of a round one-gallon jug with handle and spout. Roughly a foot tall and ten inches in diameter, it was an impeccable specimen and I considered how I would pack it on the plane. I accepted his offer and I believe I honored him in doing so.

I thought I would leave then, but he and his wife announced their wish to take us all out to a local restaurant for mezes, a traditional Greek style of eating that consists of roughly thirty bite size courses served unhurriedly over many superbly convivial hours. The wine flowed copiously and I overindulged in that aspect. Nevertheless, I remember him offering to lead the way back to my lodgings, then kindly doing so, and the fact that our farewells all round were wholly heartfelt. The next morning I strolled awhile through the peaceful town, embraced my dear hostess to express my overflowing gratitude, and drove on to the ancient Temple of Aphrodite at Paphos, on the western-most shore.

The extensive array of ruins, much of it submerged just offshore, is considered by some to be the site of mysterious Atlantis. It is a great diving attraction but time was running out. Even the part that isn't submerged was a lot to explore and, by the time I left, my heel with its million spines was slowing me down. After driving a few miles and thinking about it, thinking how much I wanted a meaningful remembrance of this enchanted island nation, I decided to phone the artist in Aiya Napa and ask him if he would deliver the painting I liked to Larnaca before my flight left the following evening. He would send it in a taxi, he said, and instructed me to give the eight hundred dollars to the driver.

That night I stayed in a small hotel in another quaint little village. On a morning walk along a dirt road near the outskirts of the town, I came to residences from which people emerged into their routine days. I stopped in front of a yard where a woman tended a fire that burned robustly in one of the fascinating clay bread ovens I'd observed so often. I wanted a closer look but didn't want to impose or frighten her. She looked at me and smiled, then called out toward the house, a name I presumed. A very little girl, perhaps five years old, came out first and her ten or twelve-year-old sister followed her. The older girl said, "Hello, my mother is wondering if we can help you." Her English was flawless and I complimented her before telling her that I was interested in the oven and the bread making process. She passed my request on to her mother who smiled a bigger smile.

"We will put the bread in soon," the daughter said.

I asked if I could take their picture together near the oven and they were pleased to pose for me: mother stood behind the two girls while their brother, who was between the girls in age, stood to their left, nearer to grandma who wasn't about to leave her chair at the side of the house. Smoke curled away from the flaming tree branches that would heat the oven. They stood stark still, except for the younger girl shrugging her shoulders with excitement, and my heart melted so that I had to wipe a tear away to see clearly through the lens. I was seized by a forlorn vision of them carrying on with their lives, in the small corner of the planet that was their world, while I would leave them and continue on with mine, so far away. I desperately hoped that I would return soon and not lose touch with them, show them the photograph perhaps and get to know them better. I spoke further with the young lady, about her school and family and other things. Finally the bread went in. It would be an hour, she said, and invited me to return and taste it. I thanked her and explained that I had to catch a flight soon, but that I was so happy to have met them. As they waved goodbye, I thought the goodwill they bestowed upon me, through their generous smiles, far exceeded the depth of our short acquaintance. They were not bound by the kind of conditioned reserve that wants a hint of reciprocation, as it tentatively dispenses its generosity.

Perhaps I was ready for change, to be reawakened to a new perspective. I certainly had acquired a different state of mind over the last several weeks. I arrived at the airport, dropped the rental car with time to spare, met the taxi driver, and bought the framed painting which was at least as satisfying as I had remembered. I had the pieces I'd purchased in Egypt as well, the prayer rug and the papyrus motifs, and managed to get them all on the plane, along with my earthenware water jug. I settled in for the long flight home, really not wanting to be there and longing for more of those easy days at Aiya Napa. My heart was saddened with longing for the simplicity I had perceived in scenes along the Nile and the unpretentious gentleness so often demonstrated by the Greek people of Cyprus.

With sincere gratitude to Sarah for the fabulous experience and to mollify the guilt-ridden consequences of my detached and unfriendly behavior, I prepared and forwarded a copy of the pictures I'd taken along the way. She called to express her appreciation and compliment me on their quality, without the slightest hint of bitterness. That is the sort of sweet mature lady she was. But we were a couple no more.

My soprano friend and former office acquaintance, Celia, and I got together on a few casual occasions, and one night after a nice dinner and a few bottles of wine we rather easily and naturally decided to sleep together. At the same time, out at Fox Lake, I met a lady realtor in a local pub one night and we began a casual sexual liaison. But I wasn't looking for a continuous relationship, and I let both of these situations slide while I went out west to visit clients and attend an anniversary celebration in the rural neighborhood I still referred to as home.

I had gone to a single-room country school located three miles from the farm for my first eight years of formal education. I was one of eighteen students in eight grades and one of several that still commuted on horseback, traversing three miles of solitude that was fragmented only occasionally by sounds of nature, some shrill and some barely audible above the muffled clip-clopping of unshod hooves on the dirt road. In operation from 1910 to 1962, my father had been a student there and my mother taught there for two years before I was born.

Although it was situated on flat prairie, at least partially visible for the whole way there, the school was named Hillsborough. This year being 1985, farm families who had lived within a few miles of each other all their lives were getting together, and many of those who had moved away were returning, to celebrate seventy-five years of existence as a community. Many elder members of the families were only a generation away from being original settlers on the land. My parents on both sides were in that category. The historical record was short, but included dramatic changes in technology and lifestyle, if not in quality of life, as many old-timers still contended with fond regard for the 'good old days.' Horses had been the only source of transport and lugging power back then; party-line telephone service arrived in the forties; electricity didn't arrive until the fifties; nor, therefore, did running water. As far back as memory permitted, I'd been surrounded by firsthand reminders of life when it was remarkably rudimentary. I had my own distinct recollections of hauling water by hand, butchering our own meat, and long cattle drives through the sand-hills on horseback. I recalled vividly the solitary hours I spent riding and hunting, all the dry, dusty, windy prairie days and the back breaking physical effort that was required to survive.

Therefore, to the extent that I was able to circumvent the high-flying image I'd formed of myself, the image to which others so generously subscribed or condescended, as the case may be, I was able to connect with my earthy beginnings. I'd grown up close to the ground, with the fundamental nature of life and death near at hand. Although I had envied the few who were obviously better off financially than we were, I knew that a lot of money wasn't a necessary ingredient for survival, or even for the enjoyment of daily life. Despite my long held opinion that their lives were limited, mundane, and going nowhere, I knew the people I'd grown up with were generally honest, down-to-earth folks who knew instinctively what it meant to be a neighbor. I also knew that they couldn't have imagined my lifestyle, much of which had been entirely beyond their moral code and cultural confines, almost all of it far removed from their conscious aspirations. I felt certain I could never have stayed there and lived the way they lived. At the same time, I knew that the path I'd been following was tenuous at best, and approaching its end.

The ground beneath me was unstable and two incidents involving my brother Dennis brought that instability to the surface. Six years younger than I, chronologically exactly between Barry and me, it seemed my need to impress him far exceeded rational thought. Dwight, the tough and courageous young man who had intervened on my behalf against our ninth grade literature teacher, Mr. Benson, was attending the reunion. Wild and reckless in his youth, he became an angry and worrisome rogue after graduating high school. Eventually, to everyone's relief, he left to join the navy and had not been back for those many years. Although his acknowledgment of me had been amiable enough, his remarks about a long-ago encounter with my sister behind the barn were tasteless, if not out of character. My suggestion to my obviously indignant brother, that I could probably take him out with the karate I'd been studying, was no less than delusional egotistical bullshit. He could easily have killed me if he decided to and I expect Dennis, who'd been a pretty good scrapper in his own right, knew it.

Later in the day, news surfaced that the very large ranch next to our farm was coming up for sale. I turned to Dennis and seriously suggested we should buy it. He was quite interested, as well as implicitly convinced that I must have the kind of money that would support such a statement. A little way into the conversation I had to indirectly admit that I didn't have it, by suggesting that we talk to an uncle who had some money. My brother immediately dismissed the plan as unrealistic, sensibly stating that having too many family members involved in such an adventure would be a recipe for disaster.

I let that indiscretion go as quickly as I had the former, hoping self-consciously that my back-to-back hollow proclamations of personal prowess had gone undetected by my brother. Crude crosscurrents of thought continued to work on my mind. Those two distorted contentions seemed to have arisen in conjunction with a deep longing for identity, the foundation of which lay buried within the fabric of my origins. Those thoughts collided with the certainty that I could never again comfortably immerse myself in that community.

I wasn't back in Chicago very long when I received a phone call from the CEO of Beckert & Co., the nationwide firm I had worked for in Denver five years ago. He wanted to talk about a position there and invited me to meet him in New York the following week at company expense. We met at the firm's headquarters in One World Trade Center, talked with the CEO of the company's commodity trading subsidiary, and they offered me a job as Vice President in charge of their futures trading division. The salary was very good, the perks more than satisfactory and, along with an eventual position on the board of directors for the subsidiary, I would be given no-cost financing to take down a block of company stock. It would be a large shift and I said I would think about it. In fact, I saw immediately that it was an opportunity to simultaneously escape the customer business I had become so weary of and an exhilarating foray into something new: corporate management.

I knew I was inclined toward rejection of everything the job represented; I knew how much I longed to abandon the financial industry in its entirety because of the lack of fulfillment it had brought me. I saw the enormous inconsistency between these truths and the attitude my prospective employers would be expecting; yet, I knew also that I could not turn it down. An irresistible and overriding attraction lay beneath the contradictions. I perceived within the position, in an as yet completely undefined way, a last-ditch opportunity for banking enough money to break away in the style I had always envisioned. A week later I called and said I would take the job.

I'd given myself two months in which I would plan and execute an exit from my current customer business, inform the partners at Holloway and Associates, and arrange to sell my place in Fox Lake. I agreed to make another trip to New York in the meantime, to familiarize myself with corporate structure, the state of the commodity futures department, and the executive committee I would soon be a part of. Although I expected most of my clients to transfer their accounts to other brokers with a western or mid-western presence, I decided I would take my current assistant with me to service customers that chose to continue the relationship. I foresaw a shift of my own emphasis away from agricultural futures markets, toward the financial industry where currency and interest rate futures, options, swaps, and other derivatives presented larger opportunities.

One Friday I came home to find an enticing note in my mailbox, unsigned. It expressed regret that we hadn't seen each other in too long a time and invited me to call and arrange for a romantic evening. I would only discover its actual source many weeks later in a conversation with the lady realtor with whom, incidentally, I had listed my acreage for sale. For the time being, however, I guessed it must have come from Celia and I called her. We planned to meet the next week and had an exquisite evening. I began to envision her as the ideal executive wife, cultured, refined, from a good family in the east. I invited her to join me for my business trip to New York and arranged for us to enjoy a weekend in Manhattan.

Celia was ten years younger than me, pretty in a very presentable fashion, and wholly undecided in her plans for the future. Her rather complex personality was, at the same time, sophisticated and down-to-earth. She partook easily in the finer things of life while implicitly dismissing materialism as not fundamentally important within the context of her youthful idealism, all of which was entirely consistent with the manner in which we became engaged to be married. It happened spontaneously, during a very expensive dinner at a French restaurant in Midtown. Her acceptance of my proposal had me riding high on a tide of airy romanticism as we celebrated with champagne afterwards, and I remained aloft for our blissful lovemaking that evening and sensual cuddling through the night. Nor was it diminished the following morning as we picked out an engagement ring consistent with her quixotic character, not an expensive diamond but rather a large and beautiful sapphire. As we travelled together back to Chicago, I responded with enthusiastic acceptance to Celia's suggestion that we visit her parents and several of her siblings the next weekend in Connecticut. In fact, I was thrilled to be standing at the brink of a revolutionary change in lifestyle.

Although the rationale I offered for my change in employment occasionally rang hollow in my own ears, and I had sometimes to amplify my words to overcome that effect, I announced my parting to the partners at Holloway with pride, asserting that I was moving up. I approached my closer friends, Noel and Dave, similarly, mainly to discourage critical personal feedback. I had no intention of sharing my awkward private reasoning. With clients I pronounced the switch with gratitude for their loyalty in the past and regret that I could not have refused the opportunity. Regarding my engagement to Celia I felt that, for the time being, I would rather keep it under wraps. Our relationship had not been a longstanding one, and I hoped that time and the geographic change would render it a more credible image. I had no desire to arouse the notion that I had not given these rather sweeping changes enough thought, to leave behind me an impression of willy-nilly haphazardness.

Inwardly, it felt like a narrow and fortuitous escape, as though the earth were crumbling right behind me. I believed, rather than grasping at the next rung of a ladder, I was in the process of leaping cross-wise to another ladder altogether, and not a moment too soon. That sentiment applied equally to the financial opportunity and the respectable marriage.

One lovely fall day under a clear indigo sky, Celia and I spent the afternoon walking from the Art Institute through downtown, across the Chicago River, along Michigan Avenue, onto the beach, and north to Lincoln Park. I took photographs along the way, trying to capture memories of a city I had truly admired and enjoyed. On my last day at the office, they threw a generous farewell party after the markets closed. Dave gave me an original watercolor painting of the Chicago Board of Trade building, the view that had swelled my ego on countless mornings while I made my way to work in a taxi. Proceeding down LaSalle Street, toward its intersection with Jackson Boulevard, the landmark Mecca of futures trading had loomed with prominence at the end of a canyon defined by bank headquarters and other corporate edifices. A chapter in my life was closing and I was somewhat saddened by the notion that I had not always made the most of a dream come true.

Chapter 18

Once I got settled into a temporary apartment in New York, and into my new office, I began to travel to branch offices and examine the skeleton of the department that it was my job to stir to life. The company's presence in the business had shrunken to the point of embarrassment and, except for a few good producers scattered across the country, there was not much to work with. Few branch managers saw the futures business as a priority and I did not immediately see how I could make a difference.

I hadn't been back in New York for long when I got a call from Yvonne. I knew she had returned from Denver but I hadn't called her yet, because of the guilt I still felt over taking her virginity, the remorse over dumping her as a partner, the regret associated with losing passionate feelings toward her, and now, my decision to marry someone else which would finally extinguish her hopes and any possibility I had of further compensating for my wrongs. She'd gotten my number from Bob Hawk and wanted to tell me about the welcome party she was throwing in my honor. She suggested a Saturday evening two weeks hence, for which I had no other plans. I saw no avenue of retreat and thanked her enthusiastically for her thoughtful and generous intentions. Feeling miserable as I hung up the phone, I continued to wilt under the weight of a gloomy impasse, wishing for a painless escape.

With a sense of urgency regarding my perceived need to do something significant in my new position, I decided to pursue the development of a derivatives operation from head office and advertised on the street for trading capability and sales help. I had in mind that foreign short-term interest-bearing instruments could be combined with currency swaps to substantially enhance the cash management practices and returns for large to very large corporations. The margins were small and the calculations intricate, but the money involved was regularly in the billions. I was fortunate indeed, as I soon hired a young mathematical whiz and a flamboyant middle-aged man who moved easily among the top echelon of the business world.

My carousing and alcohol consumption had been greatly subdued by this new preoccupation. But still, as happened upon the occasion of a former drinking acquaintance showing up in town, I had a runaway or two. I couldn't seem to go out for a social evening without the risk of drinking to excess and causing some regrettable outcome. We went bar hopping after dinner and, perhaps because Bob was a big man who I thought would protect me, I became quite mouthy with a bouncer at a men's club. But my friend's size seemed to be offset by his desire to avoid trouble and the next thing I knew blood was pouring through my fingers as I held my hand over my nose. I complained that it was broken and expected some sympathy. Instead he said quite flatly, "I think you'll be all right if you go straight home. You were pretty obnoxious, you know. I'm going back to my hotel." I did go home, washed away the blood, had another drink, and went to sleep, only to awaken once more in an abysmal sweating state of embarrassment and regret. Gnawing dread that there had been chance witnesses, that the damage was not contained, lingered into the next week and I remained alert for clues at the office.

The party Yvonne threw was first class in every respect. Present, without exception, were the friends we'd shared during our time together in New York eight years before. After a few drinks, I was able to overlook the reality of my undisclosed matrimonial intentions and join in the revelry of bygone days. Bob and Karen Hawk were there and not a word of their visit to Chicago was spoken, as though Cynthia, and Bob's unwelcome tactics on the beach, had never happened.

234

After a few hours, however, although the drinks flowed liberally from the start, it became evident that much of the old momentum was absent. The party thinned out rapidly and ended before midnight. Yvonne and I were alone.

With my worldview confined to a foggy capsule, the result of too much alcohol, I submitted to an immediate emotional impulse: I loved her and wanted to stay with her. We had a few more drinks and went to bed together. The conversation turned to a discussion of our individual lives since we'd been a couple, including her sexual encounters which, it seemed to me, she spoke of vengefully as though she meant them to be hurtful, as indeed they were. But I pressed her for more of the same. Perhaps she expected me to see that she had done things that were out of character for her, in response to my unfaithful behavior. It became a very sad affair and I started to cry; we both did. But I was still irritated with her promiscuity, and it seemed a good time to tell her about my upcoming marriage, motivated by retaliation. Amidst slobbering tears I lamented, "I have decided to go on without you and build the life I've denied myself. I love you but we can't go back there. I had to do it." I think she was heartbroken, once again, and felt betrayed because I hadn't told her before she arranged the party. I'm sure I said I was sorry, but I'm not sure what happened after that.

Very early on, in the development of my business idea, I interpreted the response of prospective clients as quite positive and concluded that the business potential was enormous. I withheld that perspective from the CEO, however, to maintain a bargaining advantage while I proposed that I needed to form a profit-center to attract and hold good people. Because the outcome seemed remote, he immediately assigned the company's interest in the negotiations to his first vice president, essentially a yes-man with little understanding of the business I referred to. Consequently, I found little resistance to my demands for a structure that would result in huge returns to this new profit-center, and to me personally, if my plans succeeded. The arrangement would be very profitable for the firm as well; I simply did not want to be debating the size of my reward after the fact.

I spent the next few months with my head down, fiercely committed to this new venture. Because of introductions I gained through the CEO of Beckert, the parent company, I found myself in the offices of chairmen and CEOs at many of the nation's leading businesses, including airlines, railroads, banks, department store chains, and so on.

I spent Christmas at Celia's parents' beautiful home in Connecticut and we decided on a wedding date in February, as near as was practical to Valentine's Day. I returned to New York, went to work through the balance of the holiday season, advised my friends of the wedding plans, invited some of them to be there for the momentous event, and asked Bob Hawk to be my best man. I felt certain that I had turned a corner in my life.

When Celia visited for a weekend, I picked her up in a Jaguar Vanden Plas that a dealership let me test drive for a few days. We both liked it a lot, but decided instead to spend the thirty-six thousand dollars on furnishing the large suite we'd rented. We were married on schedule and I became a member of a reasonably wealthy, long established New England family. My mother and younger sister travelled to the East for the wedding and, while I did my best to make them comfortable otherwise, I may have been oppressive with respect to my significant advance up the social ladder. Back in New York we settled into married life, enjoying theatre and musical performances and building friendships as a couple, primarily with the friends I'd known since my first stint in the city. Celia proved to be a wonderfully creative cook and we spent many pleasant evenings at home together, over sumptuous dinners in our luxurious flat. I was kept busy with work and frequent cocktail gatherings in the boardroom afterwards. Celia arranged for auditions and was soon engaged in the music scene with her polished soprano voice.

We had a few rough spots, however, because my anger was easily aroused. I didn't think her association with a gay company of musicians was good for my reputation in the business world and convinced her to drop an opportunity on that basis. On another occasion, one in which I had drunk far too much to be reasonable, I judged that she had been particularly curt with a friend of mine. In a rage, I cuffed the back of her head, twice, with my open hand. Then I went to bed and passed out.

In the morning she was in bed beside me, but didn't stir when I got up with a bad hangover. It was only seven o'clock, but I'd planned to meet Bob Hawk early because we were driving up to his cottage to spend the day windsurfing. Being the first and only time I ever struck a woman, I suffered a severely shameful reaction. I began to worry about her being physically okay and I came face to face with how much I really cared for her. The shame turned to wretched fear that what I had done was irreversible, and I could not wait to hold her and to apologize. It was still too early to call her, but my suffering kept mounting. It was eight o'clock when I got to Bob's and I put on a smile while we loaded things in his car. At nine o'clock, with an hour of travel time remaining and unable to take it any longer, I asked him to pull into the next service station. Her voice, as she answered the phone, was as sweet a sound as I have ever heard. My words were heartfelt as I said, "Honey I feel absolutely horrid about last night and I want you to know how much I love you. You do not deserve to be treated that way. I had no right to do that and I am so sorry."

Between short sobbing catches, she graciously offered her forgiveness. "I know you didn't mean it. Thank you for calling. I'm all right now and I hope you have a good day with Bob."

I did my best to enjoy the day, remembering that Celia had an interview in the afternoon anyway, and I held off drinking too much so I could continue my amends when I returned.

A few weeks later, my brother Barry phoned and told me about a connection he'd made with an outfitter who took people on horse-packing trips in the Rocky Mountains. He wondered if Celia and I had an interest in joining him and his new friend for a week on horseback in the wilderness. Celia had not ridden a horse before, but she possessed an indomitable spirit that was perpetually open to something new. I thought perhaps that was why so many very good women, such as she undoubtedly was, were attracted to men who often lived outside social norms and were not narrowly confined by sensible timidity, such as I could probably be described. In any event, the decision took hardly any time and, after we informed Barry that it was a 'yes,' we began shopping for the gear we would need to spend our days comfortably in the high country, where the weather could vary wildly any time of year and our accommodations would be rudimentary at best.

My brother was right. The week we spent out there was captivating. Clusters of tiny pastel alpine flowers hugged the earth and twinkled up at us as the horses plodded steadily higher, beyond the tree line and over high mountain passes, where the vistas were often in excess of one's capacity to behold. Gurgling aquamarine glacial streams slowly increased in volume as they descended thousands of feet and swelled into raging rapids. Farther down, as the slope of the terrain leveled, they were transformed into broad, placidly gleaming currents that surrounded small, unspoiled islands where no man had set foot. For a week, we slept in tents with the full awareness of being in grizzly bear country; we ate meals cooked over open fires and caught cutthroat trout from the shale shores of icy alpine lakes; huddled together in the warm glow of a crackling fire and gazing in the direction of the setting sun, we felt the empty chill of infinity descend upon us as the silent darkness of night crept ever nearer at our backs; we travelled along craggy granite ridges and followed goat trails across barren and precipitous slopes that forced me to turn my life over to a belief that our sure-footed equine friends were in no way suicidal. I was awed each day by the strength, stability, and endurance of the trail animals.

I was completely enchanted by this intimate experience of the back country, by the freedom inherent in living out-of-doors and going off to bed under an umbrella of starlight, with only a thin canvas wall between me and the occasionally stirring wilderness night. We lived out of pack-boxes and drank from alpine streams. I found delight in photographing far-off peaks with glacial backdrops, flowers ablaze in alpine meadows and, using a telephoto lens with a close-up filter, mushroom clusters and primordial fungi in the shady dampness under giant spruce trees. More than two thousand miles from my executive job in New York, I considered it a unique, once-in-a-lifetime window into a special world, one in which I could only dream of playing a meaningful part. I had never before been so completely removed from our mundane manmade environment, the conditions I believed we all lived under as an unquestioned matter of course.

My consciousness of that freedom was thoroughly uplifting, while the associated physical discomfort and inconvenience were a challenge. Celia struggled near tears at times, with the arduous nature of the trek and its apparent dangers, but made it through in stellar form, often with Barry's caring support. I was often preoccupied with my own aches and pains, not having spent much time in the saddle for many years. Instead of compassion toward my wife, therefore, I too easily adopted the callous sink-or-swim attitude I'd learned from my father. Although I had placed my brother in an awkward position, by complaining on several occasions about the food we were served and the livestock we relied upon for transport, I assured him throughout, and again at the end, that it truly was the trip of lifetime. When I expressed my hope that I had not been too unreasonable, he responded with his characteristically easygoing ability to see the best in everything and to harbor no regret.

I returned with an expanded awareness of my options, and with a subtle change in my commitment to life in the world of finance. My days in New York were completely opposite to the mountain conditions which had brought with them a great release from daily attachment to material progress and organizational maneuvering. Nevertheless, I relished some aspects of my city position. I dressed with pride each day in one of the six suits I'd purchased on the advice of an esteemed businessman's tailor, along with the fitted shirts, silk ties and underwear, and, in winter, a woolen overcoat with silk scarf and kid leather gloves. It had cost seven thousand dollars to appropriately upgrade my wardrobe and I considered it money well spent.

I especially appreciated my open-ended expense account, and the pricy, prestigious yacht club membership the company had paid for because it would bolster my image and the potential for higher-level business networking. My highly paid executive secretary, Serena, was impressively proficient in the art of buffering communications on my behalf, and organizing my schedule of meetings and lunch dates. She was constantly engaged in industrial espionage as well, which I found at least as entertaining as I found it useful. Typically, sometime after lunch, she asked me if I'd like a coffee; then, cup and saucer in hand, she came into my office, asked me if I had a minute, discreetly closed the door behind her, sat prettily on one of the elegant straight-backed chairs, and delivered the scuttlebutt she had gleaned from casual intra-office gossip and spending her lunch hour with other executive secretaries.

The business venture came together a bit slower than I had forecast, to which the chairman and the rest of the subsidiary board of directors responded with undisguised impatience. I remained discretely excited, however, because, despite the absence of immediate results, the apparent magnitude of the endeavor continued to grow. Working against a three-year contract and not yearning for quick results, I was looking ahead to an eventual explosion of activity and the benefits that would accrue to me through my contrived, and by then longstanding, agreement for profit sharing. I had no doubt that it would come together prior to the end of the term of my employment, still two years hence. The team I felt so positive about was small, but had proved surprisingly effective.

Celia and I discussed taking a honeymoon vacation and decided we should plan it for the end of the year when business activity would be near a standstill. At that time we could be gone a few weeks and a second extended absence of the newest board member would be less conspicuous. With concerns of that nature, I always thought it best to be boldly assertive, after plans had been made, rather than engage in a frustrating upfront discussion. I left the arrangements to Celia and in mid-December we left for the Far East for three weeks.

Other than the punishing, guilt-inflicting rage I fell into upon our arrival at the Kowloon Hilton, because a bottle of her contact lens solution leaked in our luggage and stained a six hundred dollar alpaca wool navy blazer, Celia and I had a generally harmonious and fascinating adventure. I had a vision of Hong Kong from reading *Tai-Pan*: glorious merchantmen appearing on the horizon under full sail, laying at anchor to take on exotic cargo, or slowly taking their leave upon an agreeable breeze; the mansions of wealthy traders majestically facing the open sea from Victoria Peak; millions of industrious Chinese in the bustling streets, each determined to secure a piece of the action. Although the crucible in which my vision had originated was a century and a half past, I was not at all disheartened as I discovered little had changed, in essence, except ignorable bits of technology.

It was immediately evident that the fantastic cities of Kowloon and Hong Kong were built upon opposing shores of a deep and expansive harbor which remained, for the continent of Asia and the immensely resourceful nation of China, a vibrant gateway to worlds beyond. Along the wharves, a multi-colored parade of giant cranes arched skyward from heavy barges awaiting cargo to offload. Vessels of all shapes and sizes, including thousands of flat bottomed sampans and batten-sailed junks that had plied the same channels since the second century CE, dotted the water in every direction as far as the eye could reach. The sea had always prevailed. It was in the air and present in every scene as a backdrop, making it impossible to overlook the vital historical partnership.

At nearly every glance, Hong Kong was not less than spectacular. Its streets were a plethora of jumbled gaudy signage, fabulously abundant outdoor meat, fish, fruit and vegetable markets, and an impossible cluttering of laundry clad balconies overhead. And no scene was more spectacular than that of a couple of colossal floating restaurants. To celebrate the end of our first full day, we chose Jumbo, rather than its competitor Sea Palace, and boarded the launch which promptly delivered us across an expanse of glimmering emerald sea. Although anchored upon the open water, its massiveness seemed as stable and solidly situated as a part of the earth itself. The eight-course meal was a culinary extravaganza and, because the sun had set while we dined, the return trip had us looking back in wonder as the lavishly illumined three-story establishment slowly receded to manageable dimensions and its reflection upon the water added to the mesmerizing effect.

I quickly fell into the comfortable seclusion of travelling, and thought little of the career I'd stepped away from. As we rode the century-old tram to 'The Peak' the following day and gazed at black kites soaring aloft on a persistent breeze, I experienced a sad yearning to have been present in mysterious times gone by. At once, I saw the folly of my longing: I knew that hardship and monotony accompanied all ages, and that the limited (only slightly better than bovine) capacity of human foresight was responsible for distant pastures always looking greener. I began to examine my notion of reality. My eyes drank in the whole magnificent sight of Victoria Harbor, with Kowloon to the north bathed in the midday sun, and I realized I had never known what was real and what was not. I could never decide, believe, or commit to anything with the firm resolve of 'this is it.'

It was easier to believe in the authenticity of a foreign setting, as in the case of bamboo scaffolding stretching flimsily upward for forty stories on the exteriors of new high-rise buildings, just as it had no doubt done a hundred years ago at four-story construction sites. I had the same impression as I mingled with the generally well-dressed millions who surged along the bustling streets beneath the Christmas lights and the colorful clutter of commercial signs, nearly all in Cantonese. It wasn't difficult to imagine a parallel, if more rudimentary, scene a century or two earlier.

Because there was a reciprocal arrangement with the club I had joined in New York, we sat and enjoyed a few drinks at the Royal Hong Kong Yacht Club at Causeway Bay. On the left, moored along piers and anchored further out, was a vast array of leisure vessels ranging from modest to gargantuan. On the right, as conspicuous if less distinguished, was a floating village of some consequence. On the left, people with money puttered here and there, coiling halyards and fidgeting with instruments. On the right, those with fewer options available to them, the boat-people, fished off the back of their residences and carried essential supplies along plank walkways that connected each home with the shore by a system of continuous bridging from one boat to another. Neither population looked happier than the other, or less determined as they went about their affairs.

I instinctively felt the floating village was the more 'real' and naturally scoffed at the emptiness surrounding the wealthy and their distractions. Perhaps that had to do with my always-fully-employed farm upbringing. I knew of recreational endeavors as well, and how seriously I engaged in them, windsurfing, for example, and flying, and diving. But that was the point: I didn't seriously view my engagement in life as the real thing. I also scoffed at those who chose mundane vocations like farming, ranching, running a small business, or working at the same job for thirty years, even if it led to continuous advancement within a corporation or institution. Consequently, I looked to the past and to places far away, geographically and culturally, for the genuineness I felt was lacking in my own present circumstances, despite the broad range of options available to me.

In the hotel room I discovered a book that kindled my interest, *The Teaching of Buddha*, placed there by the Buddhist Promoting Foundation, which had been set up by a wealthy Japanese businessman for the purpose of spreading Buddha's message, very much parallel with Gideon Bibles in the west. I began reading and soon associated my personal desire to step aside of it all with the story of the wealthy and privileged Prince

Siddhartha who separated himself from family and fortune in order to wander in search of enlightenment. His decision was probably more complex because his father, King Gautama of the Shakya clansmen, had been overjoyed to have a successor. His motives were nobler as well: the young prince felt a deep need to go in search of spiritual answers, while I craved only to be free of society and responsibility. The first few pages related a series of events that took place twenty-five hundred years ago and attracted me as I would have been attracted to a historical novel. Because his yearning for answers was prompted by his observation of human struggles and suffering, however, I found myself identifying with his premise and became interested in his discoveries. It was our desires, the book said, that were the foundation of our suffering. I understood it to say, our desires originated in illusion and the misunderstanding of reality. References to the impermanent nature of everything captivated me and I sensed that some profound insight had only just escaped my comprehension. When we checked out I took the book with me, feeling a little guilt, instead of gratitude, because I hadn't grasped the intent of the people who placed it there.

We left Hong Kong by train and, after crossing into China, we rolled along in the open countryside. People were working in the fields, mostly flooded rice paddies, I guessed, while water buffalo stood lazily, awaiting their next task. 'Old Canton' resonated in my mind with the mystery of antiquity. As I watched through the train window, however, Guangzhou, as it is now known, seemed much like Hong Kong. Its shiny newness and vibrant commercial activity were inconsistent with vague notions I had of a backward China. We went straight to the airport and boarded an Air China jet for Beijing.

My expectations of China were fully satisfied as we landed in the capital city, disembarked down a temporary mobile stairway into the chilly open air, walked a hundred yards to get inside, and then stood waiting for our luggage in a very Spartan and unheated terminal. Through a grimy window I watched an older-model three to five ton truck crossing the tarmac and pulling up under a wing of the aircraft in which we'd just arrived. It had a very catchy baby blue cab and was hauling a tank that completely filled the fire engine red box. A man then climbed on top of the tank, while another grabbed the hose and placed the nozzle in the wing, and began hand-pumping jet fuel.

The Beijing segment of our trip was organized and, following an unexplained delay, we were soon herded onto a bus and heading toward our hotel. The city was generally low-rise, one, two, or three stories high. The wide, largely vacant streets were lined on both sides with an excess of undeveloped space. It reminded me of prairie cities I'd visited in the sixties and seventies, where older, more central neighborhoods had experienced a thinning of their populations as people departed for the suburbs. Everywhere, it seemed, activity was minimal. But the hotel staff were friendly and helpful, our room clean and comfortable.

The next day we visited the Forbidden City with its formidable classic Mandarin architecture and wonderfully grotesque sculptures. I gaped in amazement as thousands of white robed devotees glided through a Tai Chi routine in enormous Tiananmen Square. After a refreshing day of outdoor tourism, we were taken as a group to a large sparsely decorated restaurant, with an even sparser population of other guests, and served an unforgettable meal of Peking duck. That evening we visited a three-story shopping mall of some consequence, primarily designed to attract and serve foreigners, and purchased a few items of clothing to match the increasingly wintry weather that was forecast. Silk scarves were a bargain, red full-length silk underwear cost a few dollars, a couple of woolen toques and two pairs of woolen gloves completed our requirements, all for less than ten dollars.

On our second day we were to tour the Great Wall, but it had snowed an inch or two during the night and the driver did not want to risk the forty-five mile trip on a slippery road. I decided that being in China and not seeing the Great Wall was unacceptable and, judging the amount of snow that had fallen to be quite insignificant, I tried to arrange a private trip. I asked a man who worked at the hotel and spoke English if he knew of anyone with a four-wheel drive vehicle that would go out there. I said I would pay one hundred dollars. "Oh no," he said with some surprise at my suggestion. "No one will do that, it is not allowed. Only government can arrange tours in China." That, I supposed, was a quintessential brush with the communist system. It left me fuming with revulsion, the very idea that having and being willing to spend the money was not, in and of itself, sufficient to arrange events according to my will. But there was no hope in pursuing the issue further and we opted instead for a thirty-mile tour to the Ming Tombs.

The most notable impression I had in the whole day was that of a young man, visible at some distance from the road as we passed by on the bus, trudging across a flat and barren snow-covered farm field. A rifle, probably .22 caliber, rested casually on his forearm, and he represented for me a mirror image of my teenage years, when I spent so many solitary hours under similar circumstances in search of a jackrabbit to feed whatever Border Collie we had at the time. But I experienced none of my usual recurring romantic desire to live, or to have lived, in this harsh environment, perhaps because it was so much like the one in which I had grown up. All along the country roadside, I witnessed familiar sights: cattle roamed the snowy fields, stopping to eat from intermittent piles of fodder; small horses pawed the snow away and nibbled at the green shoots beneath it; leafless poplar trees probed their gnarled fingers into a pristine azure sky; and people skated in the frosty air on frozen sloughs, cleared of snow for that purpose alone.

In populated areas, however, distinguishing characteristics were more evident: most people went about on foot or on bicycles, even in the snow, while freight moved on horse-drawn wagons and unusually large tricycles; men and women alike wore comparatively drab woolen clothing and round fur hats which, judging from one cheerful rosy-cheeked Mongolian face, provided ample defense against the cold.

Following a thought-provoking inspection of the Ming Tombs we climbed aboard the bus and, to keep us occupied on the return journey, our guide proudly delivered his rendition of John Denver's *Country Road*. I thought it a courageous and well-practiced performance. As I watched and listened, however, I felt that a part of him was crying out. I experienced a feeling of loss on his behalf, dispossession perhaps, or the preclusion of physical and mental access to a wider world. Everywhere we went, I had the sense that less of life was spontaneous there, that most everything was done by government edict, and I sensed a stifling lid had been placed on free expression. That impression persisted as we toured a fascinating, if drab and dimly-lit, silk factory in the afternoon, then an outsized tourist distribution center for artifacts, including stunning silk tapestries and row upon row of handsome red fox pelts.

Having returned to the hotel, I continued to ponder my observations and I expressed to Celia my hypothesis that much of Asia had long seemed content with myriad forms of authoritarian government. Otherwise they might have stumbled upon some version of the democratic process that originated with the Greeks and had evolved to varying degrees in European based cultures. Celia, however, showed no interest in my political science considerations. Instead she had drawn open the heavy drapes to expose a common area outside our window, where a large snowman had been constructed. He smiled at us through his charcoal eyes. Under his huge rice-paddy-style straw hat he sported a carrot for a nose. His red cape puffed out and away, reaching to the ground from his beefy neck, and a bright ornamental Chinese fan rested on his broad chest. It was Christmas Day and we were moved by our hosts' open-handed gesture.

Back in Guangzhou we stayed at The Garden, part of the luxurious Mandarin chain and in posh and glitzy contrast with our no-frills Beijing accommodations. From its utilitarian plainness at street level to the grotesque majesty of the buildings that housed its officialdom, the capital had surely belonged to another country. Perhaps the difference was inspired by the Cantonese themselves; perhaps the southern latitude helped, but another world greeted us while we walked out in the early morning. Thousands upon thousands of bicycles converged in a two-wheeled rush hour. Sound and activity flooded into the city's streets and the open-air fish market bustled with a raucous vibrancy that might have roused the army in Beijing.

Although completely foreign on the surface, we felt somehow safely immersed in familiarity. We didn't know what we ate at a friendly out-of-the-way café, where not a word of English was exchanged, but we never doubted the good intentions of our hosts. We'd collected a coarse and heavy dragon-festooned jade carving in Beijing and were delighted to find the general contrast further exemplified in the smooth delicate lines and subtle shades of the jade carvings we found in the south. We bought a lovely elegant piece, and a beautiful hand-painted scroll with a pair of orange-robed monks nearly lost from view in the shade of a peaceful waterfall.

My respect for Celia as an exceptionally versatile travelling partner, who displayed extraordinary enthusiasm throughout, grew by the day. That she had done a remarkable job of arranging itineraries and accommodations was incontestable. I really liked my wife, adored her in fact, and I could have freely declared it to anyone, without hesitation. I happily considered the artifacts we purchased along the way as an investment in our future together.

"Tomorrow morning," she reminded me, "we take the eight o'clock train back to Hong Kong and catch our 2:15 flight to Chiang Mai, Thailand."

Chapter 19

In the north of Thailand, not far from the Burmese border, we were introduced to the 'hill people' and to life in and around a smaller Thai city. In every instance it was obvious beyond subtlety that tourism had impacted the people and the economy of the area for some time. A quaint and rudimentary society had retained its links with the past while bolstering those aspects that had especially fascinating appeal to people visiting from the western hemisphere. They had successfully converted their culture into a salable product.

With the exception of several children who wore black colorfully braided ceremonial attire for our benefit, the people of the village we visited in the hill-country were dressed in everything from loose traditional clothing to slacks and sport shirts. The wrinkly-faced lady who operated the dark and dingy opium tent wore a shawl that covered her head while her unkempt local patrons lounged slovenly on grubby cushions. She offered us a draw on her smoldering pipe, which my friend Bob Hawk had held forth upon as very good value, but we respectfully declined. Our guide explained that, although the national government discouraged opium production, growing poppies was still popular in the hills, as was the recreational smoking of opium. We strolled on, passing small cultivated patches of large velvety reddish-pink and white blossoms, among which some of the round green pods had already formed, and heard how many of the teenage girls became pregnant from playing with teenage boys. Perhaps that happened while their parents were preoccupied in the opium tent, but it was of little consequence because older men, who had some material means and several wives already, were quite willing to marry them and absorb them into their families. The shanties that were their homes blended with the jungle. Vendors offered us hand-carved wooden bells and apparently genuine wooden crossbows, along with trinkets of less practical value.

We toured Wat Phrathat doi Sutep, with its impressive dragon-banistered three-hundred and nine step staircase, and observed saffron-robed monks with shaved heads practicing their devotion at the foot of a giant gold-colored statue of Buddha positioned in the center of an elaborate shrine. Walking along a neat hillside collage of thatched roof market stalls and watching them, suppliant with alms bowls in hand, we learned of the spiritual reciprocity that was unfolding before us: dozens of monks provided the people a daily opportunity for merit-generating charity, while they themselves humbly and graciously accepted the offerings of food as given.

We travelled along a jungle road until we arrived at a place on a riverbank where red-smocked handlers bathed a half-dozen elephants after they had ostensibly spent the day towing teak wood from the dank tropical forest. I observed, as they stacked the enormous logs with their trunks, that the wood did not look freshly harvested, having been greyed and worn smooth from countless previous stackings; nor was the trail into the jungle disheveled by the evidence of recent industry. Although staged, it nevertheless provided a window into the past and a demonstration of the brute strength of an elephant.

In the evening we were taken to a dinner theater venue and entertained by several troops of graceful and stunningly attractive female dancers, with the natural beauty, modesty, and loveliness that is peculiar to the women of Thailand. The meal was delicious, too, except for the pork intestine stuffed with stomach contents, the texture of which I found disagreeable. I regretted asking what I had been eating.

The next day, we went on a representative tour to see the city's craftsmen and skilled manufacturers. Silver arrived in Thailand, we were told, in the form of coins smuggled through

Burma from India, because the silver content was worth more than the monetary value of the coins themselves. It was a peculiarity created by inflationist policies and isolationist practices, not unlike the depression era devaluation of fiat money in the United States and subsequent prohibition of its convertibility into gold. Partially prompted by that footnote of pecuniary folly, I bought a silver bowl of elegant, if somewhat busy, hand-wrought detail, and a large spoon whose handle terminated with the architectural flare of a Thai temple roof.

At a storefront featuring elegant handcrafted silk umbrellas, Celia purchased one with vibrantly embroidered long-life birds perched upon the pink flowered branches of a cherry tree, the background a satin sapphire sky. Inside, the silk factory was light, warm, clean, and spacious, working conditions in sharp contrast with those we'd observed in China. Millions of cocoons awaited bleaching, then soaking in small heated wok-shaped bowls, the processes that preceded unwinding the arduous work of silkworms and isolating thin fibers that could then be strung upon spools and eventually woven into fabric. The entire operation was authentic with genuine purpose. There is little surprise, I thought unhappily, that polyester has assumed a position of prominence in societies cheapened by impatience. Our world is distanced from nature and craftsmanship as a result.

The teak and rosewood furniture manufactures caught my attention above all others, the sweet fragrance of the freshly hewn wood, and the remarkable craftsmanship of the workers as they chiseled the raw material into intricate panels. I went to work with a designer and we created plans for a teakwood dry bar with six full-length vertical panels that folded out to eight feet wide. Each panel was to include flowered cherry branches with a varying but satisfying mix of long-life and happiness birds. The piece, consisting entirely of one-inch lumber, would weigh over four hundred pounds and cost an amazingly reasonable nine hundred dollars. It would take three months to complete the work and an estimated month for it to arrive in New York by ocean freight for an additional cost of eight hundred dollars. I gave the man a check, wrote down our address for him and, with big smiles all around, we shook hands on the deal.

Shortly after we checked into our hotel in Bangkok, a neatly dressed man with a smile and manner that exuded amiable credibility suggested we hire a boat and spend a day cruising the canals that were the primary thoroughfares of the city, Venice of the East, some said. Of course that was a perspective which incorporated a western bias. More accurately, I conjectured, Venice may be termed Bangkok of the West.

It was a fascinating day on the water. The seats were luxurious and a canopy ran the full length of the sleek high-prow vessel, which had capacity for a dozen, although there were only the two of us, our guide, and his skipper on board. Neighborhoods of vastly varying economies fronted the waterways: luxurious chalets of the wealthy extended out and over the water with large patios ornately foliaged and furnished for entertaining; middle income folks occupied apartment buildings and small thatched-roof houses with backyards that were fenced at the water's edge; lower incomes seemed to predominate, however, people who lived at the water's very edge and made their livelihoods upon it. Clothes hung on lines over ramshackle decks that also served as piers. People brushed their teeth and bathed as though there was no separation between their living quarters and the canals. Moored before them were the small flat bottom boats they used to ply their segment of a floating commercial network each day, with produce for sale, or food prepared to serve others whose working hours were also spent afloat.

In the broad main channels, huge wooden rice barges wallowed and lolled toward quays at the urging of small tugboats. Beyond the fringes of the city, we travelled channels so narrow that jungle undergrowth whisked our faces and I worried that our thirty-foot long boat might be grounded despite its flat bottom and shallow draft. The small gasoline engine being mounted fast on a shaft which extended twelve feet aft, at the far end of which was the propeller, was thus explained. The whole assembly swiveled for steering purposes and for depth management. It allowed the driver to react directly to all circumstances. It was a noteworthy example of singularly appropriate technology. Out in the country, when the jungle parted, we passed rice paddies and other farming operations. We squeezed aside as we met farmers on their daily journeys into town with fresh produce. I marveled at the inclusiveness of the tour. More than most other aspects of a foreign land, I always wanted to know what the countryside held in store, both nature and agriculture. Touring it by watercourse was novel indeed, and wholly satisfying.

Back in the city we followed the Chao Phraya River for a look at some of Bangkok's countless Buddhist temples. Wat Arun, its splendidly ornate prang soaring seventy meters skyward, dominated the view. But it was only one among a medley of striking structures constructed with veneration for the Buddha and his message. After six delightful hours, which included a tasty lunch purchased from a floating vendor and consumed under conditions of captivating tranquility, we slowly approached the embankment where our boat tour reached its conclusion. We were pleased to stroll for a while.

Bangkok's wats, as the Buddhist temples are referred to, are a magnificent testimony to man's capacity for creativity and sacrifice in the glorification of a spiritual concept. While they may be modest in scale when compared to the Vatican, for example, they far exceeded anything I had ever seen with respect to ornamental detail. The surfaces of the prangs, as the towering spires are called, were lavishly adorned from top to bottom with crystal-petal pastel flowers, while scimitar-like blades extended skyward at the ends of red-tiled roofs. There was both magic and mystery in it all and my interest in the Buddha and his obvious influence was increasingly stimulated.

Despite the tremendous reverence and veneration exemplified in the many glorious edifices, however, it was the ubiquitously observable happiness of the Thai people that spoke loudest. A young lady, with a child holding on tightly behind her, buzzed along a busy street on a moped. Very pretty in her brightly colored summery outfit she seemed unusually relaxed, beaming in our direction with a friendly smile as she passed. More than a few, while going about the activities of their day, had waved to us during our tour of the canals and river earlier. There was a humble pleasantness about Bangkok and the welcoming countenance of her inhabitants that prompted me to contemplate the causes and conditions of such desirable circumstances. The pacific aura that wafted around the temples was perhaps real after all, and rather generally influential. In the book *The Teaching of Buddha*, I had been exploring the Dharma, the Buddha's message. It had spoken of all the suffering that is common among humanity, and of the great knowing compassion of Buddha. Something unusual and unexplainable was going on, I sensed only subtly, and a gentle mood washed over me.

We flew south to the resort area of Phuket and checked into a bungalow, rented to us by a fellow Bob and Karen Hawk had met while visiting there from Saudi Arabia. He had cast off the materialism of the West and opted for a simpler life, with a Thai wife, by the Andaman Sea, where little cups hung from the tapped trunks of rubber trees and ramshackle houses pushed back tropical vegetation, or were precariously perched above the shoreline on wobbly stilts. But hawkers beat the beaches much like they do at the Pacific resorts of Mexico, and it was evident that decades of tourism had created a culture that had little other raison d'être. It was an agreeable setting, though, with a dreamy seaside ambience.

As if to prove that heavenly surroundings were an inadequate cradle for peace and harmony, I sank into a frustrated and unhappy morass. It had to do with going scuba diving for a day and I suppose my predicament stemmed from codependence, meaning that it had its origins in my inability to sort things out and express myself with integrity, while believing that others could and would do the same.

"Do you want to go diving?" I asked Celia who had, with my encouragement, passed her introductory course at the end of last summer.

Looking up at the scuba shop's advertisement, she replied, "I don't think so. I don't feel confident enough."

I felt a stubborn need to convince her, because I wanted to go, because I had formed a vision of us doing it together, and because the idea of going off and leaving her alone for the day seemed shamefully selfish. "You would be all right, you'd enjoy it," I urged her.

Her voice assumed an edge as she insisted, "No, you go and enjoy yourself. I'd be more comfortable sitting on the beach and reading for the day."

How simple it would have been to take her advice. But it wasn't within my confused thinking to simply separate our individual preferences and walk away without a burden of guilt. What would her father and brothers have to say, if they could see her sitting alone on the beach while I selfishly pursued my interests? I could not let it go at that, so I sat down near her and applied a model for communication I'd learned from my father during my childhood and adolescence. I picked away with discursive innuendo and sarcasm, just beyond the perimeter of the real issue, with the warped objective of transferring my guilt to her, and thereby inducing in her a capitulation. Instead of changing her mind, Celia became upset with my irritating antagonism. I gave up, stormed away toward the dive shop, and spent the day feeling horrid about the disharmony and pain I had caused. Obviously, the price was much higher than straightforward honesty would have exacted, but that kind of maturity seemed tragically unavailable to me.

On the evening prior to our return to New York, we held hands and walked along the beach in a gentle tropical breeze. We visited with two very brown little boys who each carried a heavy pineapple and, although we weren't buying, they smiled handsomely as I took their photograph. We strolled until the sun created a fiery orange backdrop that transformed the surface of the sea into a sheet of copper and turned a half-dozen long high-prow fishing boats into slender black silhouettes. We had many wonderful photographs and a few thousand dollars in artifacts by which to remember a grand holiday. The rough spots were swept away without further mention.

It was early January 1987 when we returned, and I delivered glowing reports to anyone interested, ranging from philosophical overviews to detailed travel logs, according to their capacity to endure. Drawn to my attention by the flippant comments of a board member, my recent absences from work suddenly loomed large. To compensate for a sense of truancy, I turned my focus toward achieving immediate results. Even more important, a large insurance company was acquiring the old brokerage firm, with a takeover bid that was friendly to no one but Beckert's chairman of the board, the largest stockholder and a man in his late sixties. A few subordinate heads had already been sent rolling, as well as that of the CEO of the subsidiary. I felt secure enough with my contract and business plan, but the company man who arrived on the scene to act as new temporary CEO made it clear in a brief interview that immediate results were paramount to them.

We opened several more large accounts in short order and my team was ecstatic. Some very long-standing employees of several other departments were let go, and Serena, my faithful secretary, began to display incessant anxiety. We continued to do our best and I kept the new boss up-to-date with our promising progress. Those reports seemed to be well received but it was a nervous time for everyone. Other department heads began disappearing more frequently and one day, right after I returned from lunch with a prospective client, Serena opened my door to announce with fear in her voice that I was wanted in the CEO's office.

He, with his right-hand henchman present for the interview, offered to pay out in full the one and a half years remaining on my contract and to pay a seventy percent markup for the block of stock I had taken up when I arrived. I signed the agreement they offered me and was given the balance of the day to clear my personal belongings out of my office. Serena helped with that, sniffling with grief much of the time. I met briefly with the members of our little group and suggested they carry on with the plan because they were each very effective at their part in it.

I may have been hasty in accepting their offer and probably could have pressed for increased compensation in court. I had viewed the venture as little more than a toss of the dice from the beginning, however, a mere postponement of my longed-for final escape from the industry. The two checks were sizable, and disappointment over the termination of my business plan was easily transformed into a cloud with a silver lining. I had no regret. Even as I left the building for the last time, I was anticipating an open road of unrestrained spontaneity.

Chapter 20

Celia and I talked a lot over the next few days and reached a decision to buy a small camper trailer to pull behind my Chevy Blazer. We planned to explore some parts of North America neither of us had seen before. We got free of the lease on our luxurious apartment and put our belongings in storage, except those we would need for a much simpler life style. We headed north and, with my determination to place a good amount of distance between my unsatisfying past and me, we were travelling through Maine toward the border with New Brunswick before we finally slowed our pace. In early May the parks and other camping areas were still nearly empty of visitors and we often had our choice of campsites with spectacular views and serene privacy, such as we had at Fundy National Park on the Bay of Fundy.

Among other choices for reading material, I brought along *The Teaching of Buddha* I'd snatched from the hotel in Kowloon a year and a half ago. I had looked at it a few times since and decided to make a more serious effort to understand the contents and to examine the benefits of meditation. In the cool quiet of forest settings, I would carefully select a seat of dry deadfall and commence the deliberate stilling of my busy mind. Before long I discovered that I could meditate longer, and to seemingly greater effect, if I took a couple of bottles of beer with me. Despite my overall failure at achieving any spiritual progress, it was an important surrender to the very idea of another dimension in the human experience.

We travelled onward, through Moncton, New Brunswick, crossing Confederation Bridge to Charlottetown, Prince

Edward Island where Canada became a country in 1867. North of there we stopped to see the home of *Anne of Green Gables* and wandered along the red sand-dune beaches of the quiet and exquisitely picturesque little Island.

We returned to New Brunswick, then drove on to Nova Scotia and looped around the largely uninhabited and breathtaking Cabot Trail of Cape Breton. The cerulean sea lapped at the pebbled shore in rich contrast with the green tinge of new spring grass and dark, sparsely scattered spruce and pine bluffs that nature had painted haphazardly upon the harsh rocky landscape. Still on Cape Breton Island, the fortress built by France's King Louis XV at Louisbourg caught us in its historical grip and we camped near there for a few days. One of the largest European forts in North America, construction began around 1720 and took more than twenty years. By 1758, however, it was permanently in the hands of the British and remains an icon to a pivotal period in the history of Canada.

I was repeatedly captivated by charming harbor scenes where idle lobster traps were piled by the hundreds along the piers and brightly painted fishing boats bobbed alongside on bowlines. The background was invariably a quaint village in which a lustrous array of fisherman's cottages rose upwards beyond the water and blended into natural and peaceful hillsides. Celia was a pleasant companion, always in easy agreement with my next whim for sightseeing, amenable to eating here and there in restaurants, and wonderfully creative with respect to the meals we cooked for ourselves out-of-doors.

The next leg of our journey took us across a one hundred and twenty mile stretch of iceberg strewn ocean, from Sydney, Nova Scotia to Port aux Basque, Newfoundland. As the icebreaker ferry approached it, the barren shoreline that is home to this community tugged at all my desires for a remote existence. It has been a white European outpost since distant whalers, after whom it was named, first visited in centuries gone by. In fact, irrefutable evidence indicates there were Viking settlements on the island in the preceding millennium.

Newfoundland is a harsh and beautiful place, the barren expanses of its interior confined by a brutally rugged coastline that seems to have exactly the personality required to greet the ferocious North Atlantic. We had left the trailer in Sydney so we could more easily drive across the island, following the Trans-Canada Highway for six hundred scenic miles, to its end at Saint John's, or its beginning. A Newfoundlander told us it is both the beginning and the end, that the highway merely loops west forty-eight hundred and fifty miles to Victoria, British Columbia and returns again. Saint John's, a long serving old port with an incredibly welcoming and defensible harbor, has turned its face to the world across the sea since Sir Humphrey Gilbert claimed the land for England in 1583. The first such colonization in the name of the British Empire, with the rest of the continent at its back, it has endured centuries of international squabbling, falling several times to the Dutch and French, reclaimed each time and further fortified by the British. Then in 1949, it finally voluntarily let go of its colonial status, if retaining a fierce loyalty to the crown, and become the capital city in the tenth province of Canada.

We stayed in a pleasant bed and breakfast, made our way up to Signal Hill in the blustery morning for a view out to sea, and stopped for lunch in a cozy English pub near Water Street. The lady behind the bar, in front of which we sat and enjoyed a pint of beer with our fish and chips, was an animated personification of local character. She listened to a crackling short-wave radio to keep up with goings-on at the harbor. Incredibly good fortune for us, she overheard and identified ocean-going tugboat operators preparing themselves for the salvage of a troubled vessel, currently listing badly some hundred miles to the southeast.

"It is the law of the sea," she said. "If a ship has been abandoned by the crew, which this one has, our men will race to the location to salvage what they can, hopefully save the whole vessel. The first tug to get a line on it will set up a company with the others, because he can't handle it alone. He will get the biggest share as manager, though, so there'll be a race to get to it. It's quite a show. You had better get up there and watch them leave. Hurry up, take care of the bill when you get back."

We left immediately and headed back up to Signal Hill. The wind was still brisk in our faces and we had a narrow view of the violent sea that raged beyond the quiet inner harbor below us. The engines roared as the tugs forged their way into a battle with the sea. Beyond the broad opening they smashed into fuming white-capped breakers that appeared to be forty or fifty feet from peak to trough, an invitation to destruction, it appeared to me. Perhaps a dozen of them entered the fray with seemingly breakneck abandon. In that moment, I believed I must be observing cold, calculating courage, and I admired the unknown and mostly unseen men for it. But I did not know enough of the nature of the challenge to give up the idea that it was a form of insanity. There had to be a death defying attraction beyond the potential for profit, perhaps something intrinsic to their sea-obsessed lives.

It was not like the risks taken by those in my business, where money alone was the focus, and the biggest physical risk was spilling a drink on one's tie. This endeavor, I thought, must be more in the nature of a dangerous sport, like bull-riding or gator-wrestling. The fact that it is in every way a team sport, however, and that a large prize is to be shared, must make it one of the very best.

A man standing next to me, next to the glistening canons that had fortified the harbor centuries ago, shared that a freighter bound from Rotterdam to New York and loaded with iron ore had begun taking on water in the storm. Responding to its mayday call, helicopters had already lifted the crew to safety. It was, therefore, a legally abandoned ship and fair game for the Newfoundland salvage operators. There was little more to do but go back down to the cozy pub, thank our hostess for the once-in-a-lifetime tipoff, and await further reports. Gratitude welled in my chest, accompanied by a sense of having glimpsed the character bred into these men by the severe and desolate landscape, and the cruel cold deep that surrounds the island. I reacted with nauseous aversion to the notion of being aboard one of those screaming sea-tossed tugboats, but I recognized it as fear born of something unfamiliar, and not quelled by inborn predisposition. An observer, merely entranced by the spectacle, I would never get past being a foreigner in their company.

As we drove back over the long road to Port Aux Basque the time passed easily because we had much to reflect upon and the geography remained mysteriously magnetic. I was grateful for Celia's presence and enjoyed sharing the adventure with her. I knew the photographs I'd taken would meet with her enthusiastic approval and she would want to have a few framed. The partnership she generously offered me was always genuine and free of demands for reciprocation. We hadn't discussed plans for the future either. The circumstances of my life, both our lives, were mirrored in the open road. Free of the past and free of the future, we lived each day where it found us.

By afternoon the following day, we were camped near Halifax, Nova Scotia, at Peggy's Cove, a model representation of the idyllic maritime village. Everything about it was picture perfect: lobster traps stacked on the pier, small fishing trawlers gleaming with fresh coats of paint, rudimentary fish-cleaning shacks, and quaint wooden houses dotting a rocky coastline. Character was everywhere in abundance, a paradise for photographic content and composition.

We returned to our camp after a cursory tour, made a meal of freshly caught prawns, and were liberally imbibing a local wine, when I realized the sun was setting, that it would set directly across the water from the most scenic aspect of the cove. We jumped in the Blazer and arrived in time. Despite being a little tipsy from the wine, I managed to compose the finest shot of the whole trip as the sky blazed with rich salmon-hued oranges and soft golden yellows, all mirrored in the smooth-as-glass little harbor and framed by the velvety black outlines of boats and waterfront buildings. A pier jutted out; a few masts and yardarms pointed up and down symmetrically, and a single gull was caught motionless just off center. While doubtlessly less exotic, the quality of the photograph exceeded my previous best, the sunset shot of the Arabs on horseback near the base of the great pyramid at Giza. Celia would no doubt have it framed, a gratifying thought.

Back at our campsite, I relaxed with another glass of wine. All that we possessed was visible from my plastic chair near the fire. I could hardly have been happier with life, I realized as we finally retired to the small camper for the night. We were both smitten by the carefree lifestyle we'd adopted and equally free of any social or cultural pressure to conform. I had essentially retired from paid employment at age thirty-seven, with a wife that was twenty-seven. It wasn't the unfolding of a plan; I had merely abandoned all serious concerns for the future.

We travelled on to the arresting little town of Lunenburg, where illustrious replicas of the triple-mast 'HMS Bounty' and the schooner 'Bluenose' were built. From there we travelled a leisurely route back through New Brunswick and into Quebec. Millions of snow geese, proceeding north on their annual migration, swarmed for miles along the Saint Lawrence River and painted the surrounding farmland glistening white in their pursuit of nourishment. In Quebec City we wandered across the Plains of Abraham and absorbed the particulars of another pivotal episode in the geopolitical development of North America, the inevitable dominance of the territory by Great Britain.

I wondered how different life might have been, if French were the language of the continent, for example, if British parliamentary procedure, the English legal system, English literature, business practices and cultural customs had not been our dominant common heritage. It is wonderful to have a large French community in Canada, Spanish communities in the U.S., and all the other ethnic groups across the two countries. Our rich multicultural circumstance is unique in the world and has been sustainable, with the degree of harmony we all enjoy, solely as a consequence of the social equanimity that has been the foundation stone of these nations' inherited character.

Getting along is not always easy, and it is work that never ends, but we can be grateful for our inherited willingness to seek accord, to listen calmly to the voices of minorities, and try to do the right thing. Integral to any society's humanitarian triumph, however, must be the reasonable expectation that minorities will, in their appeals for fair-mindedness, give full respect to the common good and yield to the notion of equality, as well as claim it.

Celia didn't have much interest in my dissertation on that topic, preferring, it seemed, to simply 'smell the roses' as we strolled along the picturesque cobblestone streets of the old French city. I turned my attention to the rough-hewn oak doors of hoary religious sanctuaries, the rows of splendid three-story stone houses that had once been homes for wealthy merchants and ship-owners, the imposing old Chateau Frontenac with its sprawling citadel exterior and pyramided aquamarine copper roof. Panoramic scenes of the voluminous St. Lawrence River wending its way to the Atlantic Ocean provided a frequent reminder that, although Quebec City is an inland port, its history is a reflection of forces that stirred in the world at large.

When we returned to New York, we spent some time with a rural realtor, looking at places in the verdant rolling farm country of the Mohawk River Valley. I thought I would like to try writing and that a quiet rural setting would be conducive to that effort. We found a wonderful old two-story stone house on two hundred acres and the price seemed to represent extraordinarily good value. After deliberating over it briefly, we decided to call the search off for the time being and spend the next month or two travelling west across the plains and beyond to the mountains. We had been married for more than a year and Celia had not yet visited the farm in Montana or met many members of my family.

We spent nearly a week getting there, and the next week socializing and touring the neighborhood, before my brother Barry decided to join us on another leg west. It was slightly cramped, but the trailer was designed to sleep four if necessary and we were in an exceptionally carefree state of mind. When

Barry suggested that I follow up on a lead he had for a summer job, packing and guiding on horseback in the Rockies, I had no resistance to the idea. We drove to the small resort community where Mr. Alex Webber's well-established outfitting business was based. I caught up with him at his office and learned the operation consisted of several hundred saddle horses, dozens of pack mules, and about twenty-five guides, packers, and wranglers. He told me he had a day riding operation for which he needed a manager. Thirty horses and four young cowboys would be my responsibility and I could start right away at eleven hundred dollars per month. That was roughly a tenth of the salary I'd received at my previous post. Rather than a vehicle allowance, I was able to pick out a comfortable saddle and put it on any horse of my choosing, as they arrived fresh, fit, and sometimes a little rank, from the winter range where they had roamed undisturbed since the fall. I signed on.

The Elkhorn trailhead was at the lower end of a mountain gorge that rambled lazily at first and then climbed steeply upward, while the creek in its bosom carved a path through the rock and spruce trees on its way down, roaring rapids alternating with clear placid pools. The scent of spruce and pine wafted on crisp mountain breezes and the scent of horses became remarkably ordinary. Besides managing the little business, I often opted to guide guests on the full day ride we offered. We took lunch with us on a pack animal and, at midday at the far end of the trail, we built a fire, made a pot of coffee, and lounged away an hour in an alpine meadow before returning. Bear encounters were not uncommon and required patience while the burly omnivores decided what would happen next. Elk and deer moved off into deeper forest, and spruce grouse fluttered noisily and ungracefully into low boughs.

Celia got a job as a clerk at a wine store, entirely appropriate because she reveled in the knowledge she acquired and I enjoyed the benefits of the discounts she received. We cooked countless dinners on the small barbeque and sat together over a second bottle of wine as the air chilled sharply with the rapid onset of a mountain sundown. From time-to-time we joined some of the crew for a pub night and Celia set aside the skillful range of her marvelous soprano voice to impress everyone with excellent renderings of Patsy Cline songs. But those occasions were rare because I went down to the barns to feed horses at five-thirty each morning.

I gained some proficiency at shoeing and packing horses. I learned something of mountain navigation and secured a backcountry guide license. I quickly lost about twenty pounds of flab, which helped me get on a horse once again with a supple bounce, rather than a strained lurch that was entirely dependent upon the animal's patience. As the weeks passed, I put ten pounds back on, the weight now re-assigned to my legs and trunk in the form of muscle and sinew. I felt like fifteen years had been shed along with the roll around my waist. Each chilly dawn brought with it a vigorous desire to get moving. The sweet fragrance of the river valley rose on a cool breeze and my chest swelled with new vitality. My former lifestyle flickered ever more dimly in the receding past.

Celia left for ten days in mid-summer to fly back east and visit her family. I went to work every day and partied with the boys some nights. But I went back to our camp alone and got to bed quite early. More than a week had passed before a solitary girl in her mid-twenties, an average looking brunette in obvious good physical condition, firm and muscular for a girl, came by the corrals before noon one day. She said she was a member of a state police force and was travelling with her mother on a two-week vacation. We had a friendly chat and she said she might return for a horseback ride later.

Mountain weather was so unpredictable that we wore the same outfit every day: felt cowboy hat, boots, jeans, long sleeve shirt, and down vest. I kept a Storm Rider jacket nearby and an Australian oilskin raincoat tied behind the saddle when riding. Certainly the evenings could cool down quickly, but cold rainsqualls and even snow flurries could drift through without warning. Constantly dealing with horses required suitable clothing in any case.

That day, the afternoon sun was unusually hot and I had removed my heavy hat and was showering my head with cool water from a hose when she returned. I accepted her offer of help and she sprayed water down my neck and back as I leaned over. I reacted by grabbing the hose and cooling her off as well. We tussled a bit, which melted barriers, and she hung around for the last few hours of the day. Assuring me she would pay me a visit at the camp that evening, she wandered off looking far more girlish than she had earlier, and far less cop-like. I thought little more of it while the boys and I rode four horses and trailed another twenty-five back along the river to the stables for the night. We unsaddled and fed them, and I went home, stopping to buy a case of beer to have something on hand should a social occasion warrant it.

I had a shower and shave as well. In the hour after I finished a steak, I drank a few of the beers. About eight she drove up and I offered her one. She said she didn't want to drink anything and said she had told her mother she was visiting a friend for the evening and may not be back until morning. She was quite matter-of-fact about it really, as women can be if they know a man finds them attractive. I preferred it that way because, if it is the man's role to be in pursuit, there is a lot more finesse required, even though the conclusion is never in doubt. So we climbed into the bed in the trailer and kicked off a frolicking good physical encounter. Her matter-of-factness softened quickly and the delight she displayed was that of a connoisseur. Her breasts were not large, but firm and attractive. Her body was conditioned, velvety smooth, and her passion became heated until she writhed with enthusiasm. We spend the entire night in a heated cycle: vigorous sensual pleasure followed by deep sleep, followed by still more, and then more. I was surprised at how easily and repeatedly aroused I became with her. Of course Celia had been absent over a week, but the improvement in my physical condition, the hardness of my entire body, was a source of fresh vitality.

In the morning I made coffee while she washed up at the shower house. When she returned, she smiled and said, "I'm a little sore, you know."

I said, "That was really something. Thanks for coming over." We held each other a moment and said, "Be happy," or "Take care," or something. Then she drove off to meet her mother and I went to feed the horses. It had been a perfectly satisfying encounter. Too bad I had to betray Celia. I hadn't done that before and I promised myself I wouldn't do it again. I wouldn't have done it that time, if things hadn't been handed to me as if by forces beyond my control. Then I realized I needed to wash the sheets before Celia returned and make sure there was no other evidence.

Because getting to the backcountry was number one on everyone's wish list, Celia and I took a couple of horses, compliments of Mr. Webber, and rode seven miles to one of the operation's stationary camps for a weekend. The food and lodging was complimentary as well, and we were grateful for the opportunity to get away, as frequently travelled as the trail was.

When asked, a week later, if I would like to trail a half-dozen fresh saddle horses fifteen miles into a remote wilderness area and lead a few others that were getting a bit tired back out to a rendezvous point along a notoriously rugged mountain range, I could hardly believe my good fortune. "Why don't you and your wife pick two good saddle horses from the bunch and enjoy yourselves for a few days. Stop in at the high-country lodge for a couple nights. I'll get word to the cook to take care of you," Alex Webber said.

The weather was perfect, the animals cooperative, and our moods happily anticipated a glorious trek as we left the truck and trailer behind and headed up the trail from the staging area. Three hours later the horses clambered up a steep, stony switchback until we came out above the tree line at eight thousand feet. For the next four hours, we trudged silently across the barren tundra ecology of the true alpine, a world few get to fully experience. Pikas chirped from the shale rubble of minor avalanches, speckled ptarmigan scurried before us into the short scrub, eagles soared aloft on powerful updrafts, and a pair of sure-footed mountain goats monitored our progress from high upon a death-defying ledge. Having crossed over the gentle crest of the pass, a gradual slope eventually delivered us onto a trail that switch-backed steeply down for three thousand vertical feet through thick forest. We finally broke out of the forest's cool shade, crossed a shallow river where the rapids gleamed blindingly in the late afternoon sun, and came to a halt before a large log chalet in a perfectly pastoral setting. The cook appeared under the gigantic moose antlers that hung above the door and said, "Come on in. Supper's on and the boys will be right out to look after your horses."

We stayed a day to rest up. We rode down the valley in the morning, sat by the clear rippling stream in the afternoon, and quenched our thirst with its icy purity. The three meals a day were abundant and exquisite. Snoozing in the shade of a giant spruce was deeply restorative. On the second morning, we rode away on different saddle horses, trailing three others. The horse I was riding, a young cowboy told me, was his favorite but needed a rest after two months of slogging along high-country trails. I said I'd take care of the old boy.

We had to climb back out of the valley, surmount a less challenging pass, and follow a trail along another creek that fed into a river five miles on. The day was sunny and calm and became a bit stifling by early afternoon. Horse flies pestered the animals to the point of their preoccupation. We shed some outer clothes to let the air flow round our perspiring bodies. My old horse tired and slowed his pace to a crawl. Tapping my boots into his sides had no effect, nor did lashing the ends of the reins across his rump. Something like despondency had him in its grip. No physical impairment was evident, he wasn't lame, and no benefit could be realized by poking along and extending the journey. I was becoming irritated, swearing angrily at the beast. Because I rode so many different horses and often only discovered a bothersome character flaw out on a trail somewhere, I carried a pair of comparatively innocuous bronc-riding spurs in my saddlebag. I stopped and strapped them on, feeling rage close to the surface.

Celia's courage had been much more impressive than I admitted or acknowledged. An equestrian rookie, she had faced her fears with remarkable self-control and refrained from complaints of physical discomfort, which had to have been traumatic at times, in one of the most challenging environments imaginable. Doubtless, some of her strength found its origin in the trust she placed in me and the assumption that I must know what I was doing.

It was too late to take that line of reasoning into consideration once my rage began to overwhelm my mental faculties, however, as overwhelm them it did in short order. I do not know how long I was engaged in a furiously indignant battle with that dumb animal, to almost no avail. I don't know how ridiculous it must have appeared in her eyes, or how fearful she might have become while wishing that it would end. I know that driving the spurs into that horse's sides had a nearly imperceptible effect on his pace and, as a consequence, I fell further and further into a vulgar spitting rage. I justified and rationalized my anger to her. I tried to calm down and preserve the enchanting image of the two previous days. Repeatedly, however, I succumbed to the welling-up of another crazed fit of wrath. Finally, in a state of exasperated mental fatigue, I let the hopeless hated beast trundle at his slothful pace to the finish, with only an occasional spurring to remind him of my incensed discontent.

It seems unfortunate that although I remain intellectually aware of the glorious freedom we felt, the romantic vision of us lolling alongside the high-mountain stream, and the transcendent nature of a window upon the cosmos as viewed from an alpine pass, the segment of the adventure most readily and tangibly available to me is the insanity that manifested itself because circumstances were contrary to my will.

Only a few weeks later, as the short mountain summer yielded to the cool days of fall, and feathery larch trees began to highlight the slopes with yellow and orange pastels, we prepared to end our brief stay in paradise. Alex Webber offered me a head guide position for the next summer, with a raise to fifteen hundred per month. I was hooked on the simple liberty of mountain life and more than willing to take on more of the most physically strenuous work I'd ever engaged in, but Celia and I decided we had best remain flexible.

Chapter 21

In early September Celia and I found a place to park the trailer for the winter and made a fast trip back to New York. The farmhouse in the Mohawk Valley we had liked so much, when real estate shopping in the spring, had sold. We discovered the new owners wanted to rent it and moved in, removing our belongings from storage. Even as we were in the middle of that process, we made plans to travel overseas. I was drawn to the brisk Atlantic climate of the English Channel and we secured a cottage across the river from a historic fishing village named Fowey in Cornwall. I had become determined, regardless of the notion's whimsical nature, to pursue a career in writing, and the prospect of success would be much enhanced by remote seclusion in an inspiring location.

Celia was of course amenable to the idea and, once we arrived, began immediately to take invigorating daily walks along the coast. When I walked with her, we enjoyed the maritime views from our perch high above the wind tossed ocean. There were days when the harbor below was shrouded in mist and freighters drifted by wraithlike in the haze. The lights of the town across the water were refracted into spherical rainbows and the drone of foghorns hung on the air. On clear days, the water turned sky-blue and the winter sun lit the rocky coast like a soft floodlight. The course foliage appeared rusty-green and dozens of small fishing vessels came into view well up the mouth of the broad, unhurried old river. Looking inland, thousands of downy-white sheep dotted verdant hillside paddocks and medieval church towers lanced the horizon. The rudimentary trail dipped and rose sharply as it hugged the precipice. It ensured a good physical workout just as the fresh sea air ensured the enjoyment of hot chocolate by the fire when we returned.

We enjoyed grocery-shopping trips into the village, extracting insights from the superbly cantankerous old skipper while crossing the River Fowey on his sturdy little ferry. Celia was ready and willing to work with any ingredients I had a whim to explore in our search for local culinary adventure. Other days we went for drives on the narrow, winding, and hilly country roads. Timeless hedges blocked a driver's vision on both sides, and 'quick' seemed the only response applicable to oncoming traffic: quick on the brakes first, and then quick to agree on a plan for mutual passage. We marveled at striking examples of Tudor architecture and exterior design. We snooped around ancient graveyards behind ancient churches, where the moss and leaves had tried for a thousand years to conceal severely weathered headstones with names that had grown faint and dates that stretched back over unfathomable generations. I savored the antiquity, drank in the crisp fresh air, and dreamed of living so long ago. But I had to start writing in earnest if I were to accomplish anything.

I decided on a novel concerning the colonization of North America and the migration of people from the British Isles. I reflected on the fact that almost two weeks had passed, taken up by exploration, the ferry rides on foggy mornings to get into town, the antique book store, other intriguing shops, and the walks along the coast. The colored-glass door at the front of the old inn proclaimed the courage of those men of Fowey Haven who joined Sir Francis Drake in 1588 to confront the Spanish Armada. Fascinating, but I needed to be serious about a career.

I quickly discovered that re-inventing myself was not going to be as seamless as I had envisioned and I became frustrated. I began to find it difficult to be without a productive occupation, a job description. Quite often the first questions asked, following introductions between new acquaintances, have to do with livelihood. Our society makes it difficult to be without a job description because that is very much our identity. It's that important. I was consequently crashing headlong toward an identity crisis, which would be far less a crisis if I were alone, I concluded.

Despite her unconditional support, as well as the concrete encouragement I had received from members of her family, I began to react to Celia's presence as though she were a reflection of my imminent failure, the cause perhaps. I could not get past it and I became more and more miserable and less tolerant. I became critical and blaming. Finally she offered to return home and leave me alone, an offer I accepted, and soon felt heartrending sadness over. I was hardly able to contain my tears, or speak through the constriction in my throat, as I drove her to catch the train that would deliver her to Heathrow and thousands of miles away from me. I wanted to ask her to change her mind and stay. But I wanted to be left alone; I needed to be alone, because I didn't know how to share my frustration and grief with another human being. All my life, I had chosen to go it alone and the pain of casting away proffered love was not unfamiliar.

I returned to the empty dwelling, which reflected an even greater emptiness within. I had to steel myself against remorse and carry on, but I was suddenly painfully restless in a place that had recently represented a dream come true. I came to terms with the rental agency and vacated the pretty cottage that sat high above the coastline, looking out upon the infinite steel-grey sea. I checked into a room at the old inn, an inn through whose lead-framed window panes the Spanish Armada may have been sighted on the horizon four centuries earlier.

Relentless internal agitation forced me onward after staying two more days in tranquil Fowey. I made my way to Bristol where I determined to celebrate my freedom. In consequence, I overindulged in a frenzied feed of fish and chips, followed by too many pints of warm beer. I spent a night and the succeeding day in a nauseous physical state that was exacerbated by recurring mental nausea that arose each time I reflected upon the callous dismissal of my faithful and loving wife.

I made my way from there to London and called upon Moira, my former workmate and Noel Hyman's assistant. She had returned to her native England in the interim and was now married. Celia and I had stopped in to visit them briefly when we first arrived in England a few weeks prior; now I had to explain how she suddenly decided to go home to be with her family for Christmas. Because her husband was busy with work, Moira and I had the next day to enjoy together and decided to make our way to Greenwich.

We had a fabulously memorable day in which we viewed the extensive collection of marvelous British maritime painters and other artists at Queen's House, perused intricate models of illustrious sailing ships and the Lord Nelson collection at the Maritime Museum, had lunch, and then strolled up to the observatory, pausing at the first meridian where, I reflected, "time begins." For the whole day our conversation was relaxed and agreeable. Although I had not turned to her with gut-level honesty, I felt empathetically consoled regarding my circumstances and I came away feeling less fear, less compelled to be something I was not, as nebulous as that self-imposed demand had been.

My long-time friend and her new husband had been gracious hosts, but an overwhelming need for solitude drove me to move on. Before I left them I made plans to rent an apartment at Torremolinos, on the southern coast of Spain. I was very much in the mood for a warmer climate and the Mediterranean shore seemed as good a location for ignoring Christmas as any. I could not dredge up any practical enthusiasm for writing, as romantic as historic Andalusia is, with its face turned toward the timeless sea. But I did become more determined regarding the idea of meditation, and, reviving the slender spiritual threads that had found their origin in the Buddhist volume from Hong Kong, I committed to an hour each day of trying to focus on my breath and still my mind.

I found it very difficult to sit still, thoughts raced through my mind, and I could not help watching the clock grind slowly to the end of the hour. When finished I walked up the street to a tavern and rewarded myself by with a pulse accelerating café con leche. I arrived a little earlier than usual one day and noticed a dozen local men leaving the tavern, commercial fishermen I discovered by asking the bartender. They stopped by every morning for café con leche and brandy, before leaving in their modest fishing trawlers for a day on the water. Their routine immediately appealed to me as a civilized beginning to the day. I decided that I could combine it with my meditation, since that was presently my most work-like daily endeavor. I thus began to take a café con leche with a shot of local brandy on the side and, while sipping at the mellowing combination, I tried to enter a space of mental passivity and serenity. I soon learned that an additional shot of brandy further prompted the desired effect. I limited myself to two because I did not want to appear a sot, despite my desire for more of the sense of comfort I found in it.

I suddenly developed a craving for tobacco as well, especially after I arrived back at my apartment from the spiritual sessions in the tavern. My craving was not for cigarettes, but for chewing tobacco, Copenhagen specifically, as I had been taking that into my system – chewing, that is – while working with the cowboys in the mountains. I had even bought a few cans of my own, quite sure that I could never become addicted to such a filthy, repulsive habit. I had given it up and forgotten about it when we returned to the east, where it was not easy to find in any case. An addiction, though, can give rise to the most cunning mental processes, ending in the manipulation of one's own mind, and the manipulation of those who may represent a source of supply.

I thought of Celia. It would be nice to have her join me in Torremolinos. We could tour Gibraltar and cross over to Morocco for a few weeks and, by the way, she could bring me a few cans of Copenhagen. When I called her, she was happy to hear from me, if somewhat taken aback and hesitant with respect to my proposal that she fly back across the Atlantic to meet me. Once she agreed, I requested, incidentally, that she buy a few cans of Copenhagen and bring them with her. I don't think she identified my obsessed desire for tobacco, given the innocent desire most people have to be loved and her characteristic propensity for shining a positive light on events without rigorous analysis. That is hardly surprising, since I myself did not possess the degree of honesty necessary to identify my manipulative thinking as the product of a cunning and powerful addictive nature.

By the time Celia arranged her flight and advised me of her arrival ten days hence, I had decided to board one of Europe's generally luxurious tour buses and head west for a few days in Portugal. I met a Moroccan man about my age on the bus and we went exploring together. He'd been to Portugal before and was familiar with Algarve, the southern-most part of the country. Having travelled extensively, he was able to converse with insight on a wide range of current and historical geopolitical topics including much concerning North America. Subscribing to Muslim principles and practices, he didn't drink alcohol and I consequently did not over-indulge in his presence. He suggested stopping in Faro, a small coastal city, which turned out to be an excellent decision. It was exceedingly peaceful and genteel – quaint, tidy, and picturesque.

Modest whitewashed private residences blended with graceful alabaster-white public buildings. Cobblestone side streets were swept clean, and pleasingly patterned tiled colonnades and plazas were kept immaculate. Imposing Carmo Church provided a point of reference while we wandered along the quiet harbor-front and visited other highlights. The hotel at which we shared a room was comfortable and very reasonable, as were the several restaurants we visited. When I left on the third day, to return to Torremolinos, it was with some reluctance and I privately committed to a longer stay in the future. I was grateful to have met my travelling friend as well, but we had exhausted our interest in each other and it was time to say goodbye.

Celia was flying to Madrid, then catching a short commuter flight to Malaga where I promised to meet her. I had travelled by bus once before, to the ancient city the Moors had conquered. The mark of Islam was frequently prominent there, especially in the ruins which had not received much restorative attention. Perhaps they had not been given much importance in this staunchly Catholic nation with pride in its own traditions. I'd gone to a bull fight there, too, not because I expected to find it entertaining, but because I thought I 'ought' to go and determine for myself what the attraction was, just once, since it was readily available.

I had watched with some interest as the matador taunted the bull with his red cape and deftly dodged a few of the animal's frustrated charges. I was dismayed with humanity's capacity for cruelty when the picadors systematically stuck small barbed spears in the brute's neck muscles to irritatingly hang there with the purpose of making a better show by increasing his rage. Men on horseback used longer bladed spears to chop at his neck muscle and weaken him, I was informed, which would reduce the intrepid bullfighter's risk as he came in close for a daring finale, a segment of the performance I found disturbing in the days that followed. At last the groggy animal, which seemed rather small as a male bovine specimen, grew less inclined to play the game. Perhaps it recognized the overwhelming and lopsided odds. Having had little chance to demonstrate his prowess and faced with the necessity of doing something on a heroic scale before his ferocious opponent lay down in front of him, the matador stuck his rapier between its shoulder blades and into its heart. As the crowd stood and cheered raucously in appreciation of the foregoing spectacle, a colorful victory parade was made of dragging the dead creature from the ring by three or four men on horseback. I felt that I came away with reduced bewilderment regarding accounts of the bloody Spanish Inquisition and increased comprehension regarding atrocities carried out in colonial Mexico and South America.

Parting with that diversion, I had discovered a market area in the old seaside town and bought a delicious assortment of seafood items with which to make a bouillabaisse. It turned out very well and I decided that is how I would welcome Celia to Spain: take her to the market where we could choose the ingredients for our celebration dinner. She would not find the bullfight attractive; nor did I wish to take her on a walk among the ruins where abundant garbage had lain for years and where too frequent human defecation had not weathered long enough to give up its revolting stench.

Our greeting at the airport was as planned and we were sincerely happy to hold each other and kiss deeply. I found Celia physically very attractive and I sincerely adored her personality. She was a good wife and loved me unreservedly, never seeing the need to present me with a list of my past transgressions. We went off to the market and then caught the bus back to Torremolinos. I had already purchased an ample supply of wine from a small well-stocked corner store just down the street, the proprietor of which I had visited many times. He was friendlier than most men I had met in Spain and seemed keenly interested in my activities, as though he would have me enjoy his country to the fullest. Just the day before, I had told him of my wife's visit and my plans for her happy arrival. He had enthusiastically explored his stock with me in an effort to choose a half dozen bottles of fitting vintages and bouquets.

I had plenty of garlic, lemon, tomato sauce, and so on, and Celia loved to cook. I opened some wine and that added still more to the radiance of the moment. The hours passed joyfully. We ate and drank to our uninhibited satisfaction. The French doors that led to the balcony were open and the smell of the sea wafted romantically into our third-floor apartment on a tepid breeze. In the late afternoon we retired to the bedroom and let our spirited reunion find its physical expression in a frenzied session of sensuality, after which we fell into a deep and inebriated slumber in each other's arms.

When we awoke some hours later, the sun had gone down and the breeze coming through the open doors had gotten stronger and cooler. As I walked into the main part of the apartment I noticed my wallet lying as though it had been flung onto the wicker couch. It was emptied of cash. Further checking around revealed that other valuables, including my wedding ring, had been taken. I realized my Visa card was gone. Fortunately our passports and Celia's purse containing some cash and a credit card had been in the bedroom, apparently beyond the thief's comfort zone. We shared the feelings of invasion and regret that accompany an incident of that nature. I expressed anger and Celia was the first to see that nothing either irreplaceable or immediately essential was missing.

Taking the only action necessary to mitigate further cost, I went down to the corner store to use the telephone to prevent the use of my Visa card by reporting it stolen. I was temporarily mystified by the cool reception I received from the formerly friendly proprietor. He seemed hardly to know me and was unwilling to engage in conversation, as though his previous good command of the English language had been taken from him. He was bewildered with my claim that I had been robbed. I let it go, concluding immediately that he had been an accomplice, and used the telephone for my intended purpose. Afterwards, I asked where the police station was and found he could not understand my questioning.

The next day we made our way to a local precinct headquarters. Although skeptical about achieving any specific results, we thought that reporting the event was the right thing to do in the interest of general social good. The duty officer greeted us in English. But once again, I noticed a sudden decline in a man's command of that foreign language when the subject turned to theft. After a frustrating few minutes we left feeling somewhat abandoned by the principles of common decency. I indignantly condemned the country and its people for protecting one of their staple homegrown industries, along with their obvious attitude that foreigners were fair game, and we began making plans to depart for Gibraltar.

I smiled inwardly to think of the irritation suffered by Spain, with respect to Gibraltar being a British possession and military base. The tall, surreal steel-wire fence at the border; the wary exclusion of Spanish citizens from a geographically undeniable part of the Iberian Peninsula; the sea-abutted tarmac of the Royal Air Force base, which stretched across a vast vacant interim space and terminated at the outskirts of a very, very English town, nestled alongside the formidable Rock; all those aspects I found outrageously satisfying as I nurtured my resentment toward the thieving Spaniards.

We visited the elaborate network of caves that served as an air-raid-proof military hospital in World War II, and gaped with perplexity at the monkey population, while keeping a safe distance from the spoiled and aggressive beasts. We walked back and forth past the shops on the short main thoroughfare, observed with delight the Britishness of the place, and rested our weary feet while we enjoyed high tea. Options for entertainment seemed limited, however, and, having verified the solidity of The Rock of Gibraltar, we booked ourselves on a ferry to Tangier, on the northern coast of Morocco.

By comparison, even with Spain, we found ourselves in a challenging foreign environment. We were immediately accosted by hucksters and assertive would-be guides. We wandered too aimlessly into the fringe of Tangier's old medina quarter, the maze of narrow meandering unnamed streets found at the center of many North African and Eastern Mediterranean cities. The area had developed haphazardly from as far back as the days of Carthaginian colonization in the fifth century B.C.E. and had been deliberately designed to deter, frustrate, or trap invaders. We were fortunate to turn back before we became utterly disoriented and desperately dependent upon opportunistic assistance. Back along the main road, which fronted the sea, we located a tourist assistance office and arranged to take the train to Casablanca, a little over three hours south following the Atlantic coast.

Casablanca impressed me as Morocco's least Moroccan city. Its appearance was instantly more expansive, with substantial European flare along its broad open boulevards. Perhaps because it faced the Atlantic, it had succumbed to new-world influence that featured tall modern office buildings and airy palm tree shaded leisure areas. Local people seemed less inclined to pressure visitors and that is why Hassan was able to make our acquaintance.

A young Moroccan man whose command of the English language was still quite elementary, he was neatly dressed, clean cut, and patiently genteel. We sat with him awhile and talked about his country. We found that, although he was not formally educated beyond high school, English was his fifth language, after Arabic, Berber, German, and French. We told him we planned to go to Marrakesh next and he suggested taking the train, which he would help us arrange. He didn't want money and was pleased to spend the time for no other reasons than to learn of the world and practice his English. It was not the first time I had heard that potentially deceptive refrain, but a weightier degree of authenticity accompanied Hassan's words and demeanor. He said his family lived near Marrakesh. He then suggested a good hotel in the medina and promised to meet us there the following day. I remained on alert, having recently experienced solid reinforcement for my skeptical predisposition, but could see no potential harm in his claims and proposed actions.

We arrived late in the evening, checked in, and decided to retire for the night. In the morning, when we walked out the front door of our more than adequate accommodations and into the sweeping expanse of the main square, I slowly turned round and round, my eyes clutching at the shifting vistas before me. I felt suspended at the edge of a mysterious revised reality. Baroque turrets and spires pushed skyward above an untidy sandstone metropolis for as far as the eye could see. The area immediately in front of us was uncommonly alive with an array of busy souks and other more mystifying human interaction, all of which receded and elusively vanished into the narrow alleyways that perforated the far perimeters. Hassan appeared from nowhere and welcomed us with his naturally good-humored smile. From the first day, discussions between us were always respectfully directed to me. Although he was most attentive to Celia's comfort when formulating plans for us, he never referred enquiries to her directly, always through me with second-person reference to Miss Celia. He maintained that discretion even when he sought after her wellbeing or for her views on a suggestion. More and more we came to trust him.

On the first day, we dutifully followed him as we wandered into a hopelessly disorienting maze of streets, some no wider than a meter, where merchants flogged everything from hookah pipes to animal feed from small crowded kiosks on either side. Berber carpets were a common sight and my interest in them grew with each stall we passed. Enquiries were met with immediate fervor, of course, and it was difficult to break off each exchange and move along. I knew that Hassan was torn between protecting his new relationship with us and collecting a commission of some kind from any commerce he originated among his network of associates. That's how it works. But he was careful not to join in negotiations or to reflect the slightest partiality.

Finally we entered into a serious bartering session concerning two exquisite Berber specimens. The carpet dealer, with his intimidatingly abrupt, opaque-eyed, poker-faced manner, was asking five hundred dollars each. With the few words of English he admitted having in his repertoire, because the potential for confusion is always a useful wildcard, we struggled exasperatingly for clarity regarding price level. In the end, we were pleased with our purchase of two splendid timeworn hand-woven rugs, each measuring four feet by eight feet, for a total of six hundred dollars.

Hassan said they had been previously in use on the floors of nomadic Bedouin tents and, since they were obviously not unused, that tidbit was easily believable. The stitching was much courser than I had observed in good quality silk rugs, because these were made of heavy cotton, but with a taut weave and intricate design nevertheless. The mix of shades portrayed an elegance befitting pragmatic modesty, rather than bold opulence. Still dwelling on aspects of the transaction, I reflected that, as a result of many centuries of accumulated experience, these traders were not only astute negotiators, but adept at heading off negotiations altogether. Being intimidatingly isolated and disoriented within the maze of the bazaar, and completely dependent upon our friend Hassan for our successful exit, had weighed further upon my bargaining fortitude. I might have done even better on the price, but Celia said she really liked the carpets and I expected she had no thoughts at all regarding the monetary aspect, so I happily dismissed further reflection on the matter.

On the walk back to the hotel, Hassan suggested we rent a car the next day and visit his parents at their farm outside of town. Because of my immediate hesitation at the thought of engaging in business of a contractual nature, and actually driving a car in Morocco, we delayed, promising we would discuss his generous offer and give him an answer in the morning. With that, and his helpful suggestion for dining that evening, we parted for the day. After a fine meal, we felt confident in taking an evening stroll through the bustling throng of residents, tourists, performers, and hucksters.

I usually resisted any sort of solicitation, especially in circumstances so alien. But what he said, and the way he said it, led me to engage a middle age Moroccan man that looked like thousands of other middle age men in traditional attire. His wrinkled face and parched hands, both dark and severely weathered, were offset by a white cotton headdress and full-length galabeya. Some of those outfits had the appearance of being freshly washed, crisp and clean, while others had become soiled with sweat and dust. The latter described the garments of the man who attracted my attention with the words, "Give me five dollars and I'll give you ten back."

"Wait," I said. "If I give you five dollars, you'll give me ten back?"

He confirmed that those were his words and, when I handed him a five-dollar bill, he followed through with his promise to double my money by giving me a ten. "Now give me ten and I'll give you twenty," he promised. I tipped a little further toward his amiable style, sharing more easily in a grinning exchange.

Wondering when and how the inevitable hoax was going to surface, I confirmed his words once more and, once more, the transaction unfolded according to our mutual understanding. With his twenty-dollar bill securely in my hand and quite certain that my suggestion would be badly received, I thanked him and hinted at walking away. He became quite insistent while his half dozen cohorts, who had until then remained essentially invisible at the periphery, drew closer. The effect was intimidating and my mind became absorbed with formulating an exit strategy.

"Now give me twenty," he said, implying that the game would continue. I decided that one more turn would give me the time I needed to plan our disentanglement and handed him the twenty. When I held out my hand in expectation of receiving forty dollars back, he said that he had not promised to give me anything back that time. As I began my indignant rebuttal, he and his pals dispersed so quickly it seemed they had not been there. I'm sure he had been standing in front of a small table of sorts, but it had vanished as quickly as they had, probably a collapsible prop in a scam that has been performed for centuries, perhaps by many generations of the same family. I flew into a yelling, swearing rage, feeling fully justified as a victim. But no one seemed to care. I sought in vain to catch a glimpse of the perpetrators and hoped in vain to attract the police or other help. Celia took my arm and we left the area, hoping to meld into the multitude.

It wasn't the money. I'd given him a total of thirty-five dollars and he had given me thirty, so the outlay had not gotten beyond the original five dollars. But I felt as though I had been cheated by more than the petty extent to which I had. My pride had taken a blow and Celia had observed it. Alone and anonymous I would have been angry and resentful, but less inclined to suffer as an outraged victim who continued to verbally annihilate his antagonist. I had been outmaneuvered by dishonesty, not outsmarted, a term I refuted as entirely inappropriate for describing the childishly unsophisticated deceit. I continued to feel offended and remained bitter, until my opinion of the country and its people sank so low that it impaired my ability to enjoy being there.

The next day I told Hassan about it and he was not surprised. He told us we had to be careful, that people in Morocco considered foreigners easy prey and many lived off their gullibility. Something about his acceptance of those facts, and his matter-of-fact advice, was enlightening and I gained some insight into an important matter regarding cultural perception. I assumed that sportsman-like uprightness was a universal virtue that I could rely on, even as a substitute for awareness. I began to see that, for some people, gaining an advantage was considered a greater virtue, simple blatant manipulation being one among many arrows in such a man's quiver. Their supposition was that of a dog-eat-dog world, perhaps accurately describing conditions in segments of all cultures and, therefore, only more prevalent in some on a relative basis, perhaps just more openly admitted. *Caveat emptor* is generally good advice no matter the product, the culture, or the assumed benevolence of the vendor. I thought of the scams perpetrated upon uninformed victims in the investment business, the covert undertakings of politicians seeking power, and the money governments directed toward patching up faulty schemes, all in the affluent west, the self-proclaimed model of virtue where corrupt individuals are often cushioned against direct condemnation and prosecution by the institutionalized character of their criminal behavior, sly and brazen nonetheless, melting into anonymity as quickly as possible when the swindle has run its course.

Sometimes I thought that money honesty, held to be a prime virtue during my prairie upbringing and one of the few I had taken away with me, was actually a foolish and regrettable obstruction to becoming rich. It had been a source of personal pride, however, and any remaining claim I had to character and morality depended upon it. I only worried vaguely that I had already rendered the quality quite imaginary through my dealings with former business partners and the firms that had employed me.

Celia and I discussed the idea of renting a car and decided that Hassan's proposal was an adventure we could not turn down. The next day we allowed him to guide us through the rental process and found ourselves driving through the Moroccan countryside, with him and his very attractive girlfriend. She was obviously a liberated Moroccan lady. Her long black hair flowed over her shoulders in striking contrast with the iridescent yellow of her outfit, which, conceding to custom and adding to her exotic appeal at the same time, was more of a traditional swaddling wrap than a dress.

Hassan's parents lived on a small farm, with a donkey, goats, and sheep, and their house was situated near the gravelly bank of a clear and lively little brook. His father received us pleasantly enough, while his mother displayed her delight without reserve and couldn't do enough to make us feel comfortable and welcome. We sat on cushions on a large blanket spread out by the stream. She served us tea from a silver teapot and homemade bread that we were meant to dip in a silver bowl containing their own sweet, fresh olive oil, all placed with care on a large and ornate silver tray. Hassan said the matching set was his parents' wedding gift, a family essential because visitors were so important. I felt quite overwhelmed with a deep appreciation for their kindness and with the sense that I was part of an event that could be neither fabricated nor replicated. Hassan, knowing already of my fascination with terracotta, had his mother show me the cookware she used for preparing couscous. It was comprised of a comparatively heavy reddish-clay pot for boiling water and a container that fit nicely on top of it. The latter held the bagged couscous so that it could be steamed through the five small holes in the bowl's bottom. It was a work of art, stylish in its shape and design, and decorated with soft earth-toned bands around its outside.

As I held up it for inspection and rotated it a few times with admiration, Hassan's mother spoke to him. He translated, "My mother wants you to have that bowl."

"Oh no, I couldn't," I replied with heartfelt gratitude for her offer.

"She will be disappointed if you don't take it," he said. I looked at her and could see in her generous eyes that she would be.

"How will I thank her?" I asked.

"You have honored my parents with your visit." Hassan smiled sincerely. His mother nodded with acquiescence and delight in her eyes.

The world according to their awareness seemed so untainted and basic, especially when compared to mine, but in relation to Moroccan city life as well. Just as I had, Hassan had chosen to break with his rural heritage. He seemed to have maintained the connection, though, and to have retained greater respect for his roots and parents, an uncomfortable contrast with the contempt I harbored in that regard.

I came away from that pleasant afternoon encounter much convinced that a shallow judgment and generalization of Moroccans, based on one bitter encounter, would have been deeply flawed. When Hassan suggested we rent the car for a week and drive a few hundred kilometers south to visit some friends of his, English teachers he said, we wasted little time accepting his proposal. I would have to book hotel rooms along the way in my name, he informed me, as he and his lady friend were not supposed to travel outside their home state without a permit, a seemingly unreasonable government edict that I was willing to ignore if he was.

Our destination was Ouarzezate, known as 'the door to the desert' Hassan told us, on the other side of the Atlas Mountains. Along the way we stopped at a busy market, bought fresh lamb, and cooked it over an open fire near a set of rapids on a small river. We made tea with the water from the swift flowing stream and enjoyed complete solitude for several hours. The hotels we stayed at were of marginal quality, but reasonably priced at two or three dollars per room. Invariably, there was evidence of telephone service that had been installed during French colonial occupation and was now inoperable. Electrical services, with similar origins, were hazardously out of date and no one had bothered to change bulbs that had burned out. It was much to Celia's credit that she never hesitated or complained with respect to the crude and unpolished nature of these days. Instead she was thrilled with the novelty of it. For me, the whole adventure seemed a delightful respite from the sanitized lives to which we were accustomed. Our route was generally south, over miles and miles of twisting deserted road, the rough surface usually a dusty mix of dirt and gravel. We passed through a predominantly dry and rocky landscape except for the lushness near streams that snaked through valley bottoms. Where thin natural ground cover did exist in the upper reaches, it was common to observe prepubescent boys and girls attending their families' sheep or goat herds while they grazed over jagged mountain terrain that wouldn't have supported cattle.

The day we arrived, true to his word, Hassan introduced us to a half dozen people from England, all of whom were teaching at a college nearby. They were vibrant and instantly likeable, quite obviously delighted to have visitors and to see Hassan again. We met them again the next day for an afternoon picnic on the bank of a placid rock quarry. We shared a fabulous lunch in the still warm air under a cloudless sky. We drank a lot of wine with our meal and kept on drinking wine as we basked in the heat and took cooling dips in the tepid pond.

My memory is this: In one moment Celia and I floated luxuriously in an inflatable raft and sipped our wine, looking back across the crystal clear pool of water to its granite shores, upon which our new acquaintances were happily reposed. In the next moment, it seems, I was suffering from constipation and searching for a secluded place in which to make an attempt at some relief. I failed at both and returned to the car. I had acquired a severe and stifling headache as well, which sometimes happened when I drank too much alcohol over an extended period during the day. I fell into a miserable and angry state of mind. When Celia approached me to ask what the matter was, her presence became a catalyst for my self-pity and I flew into a belligerent and crazed response. Drunker than I realized, I pushed her away. Hassan came over and attempted to restrain me. He suggested I not be mean to Miss Celia, that she was trying to help me. For entirely unexplainable reasons, however, when she came closer again I kicked out wildly toward her shins.

My recall of the day from that point forward is a blur. Although I know we put the episode behind us (me, by suppressing its actuality and hoping others hadn't noticed), my memories of the return trip to Marrakesh are limited to its factual occurrence. A few days later we said goodbye to Hassan. He had tears in his eyes as he folded the hundred-dollar bill I gave him to express our heartfelt gratitude. It probably was a significant amount of money for him, but I don't believe it was the source of his emotion. He had mentioned several times the possibility of emigrating and he had often shown a particularly warm regard for us. The explanation lay within some mix of those two factors. The warmth I tried to convey while grasping both his hands in mine, and the wish I expressed that we might meet again, were profoundly sincere.

Celia and I started on the last adventure of our visit to North Africa: we rode local buses back to Tangier, stopping at points of interest along the way, such as the foul but fascinating hide tanning factory at Fez. In an area the size of half a city block, briny ponds, putrid vats, and tiered stone surfaces were fully engaged with the soaking, salting, and curing of hides from every animal I had seen in the country. Men and boys in shorts and without gloves, skipping along barefoot on the slimy surfaces, busied themselves with dragging, folding, and spreading the revolting raw material as it proceeded through its transformation into the fine leathers we'd observed in markets. I'd visited a hide plant once near home, because I wanted several deer hides tanned, and it is a smelly business that doesn't even lend itself to sanitization through production-line technology, similar to the killing floor of a meat packing plant. Those workers wore rubberized hand and footwear, however, even hip waders and masks. I contemplated a realization that Europe and North America have only benefitted from advances in technology and concerted efforts to clean up production processes, especially with respect to working conditions, in the last one hundred years or so. Visiting countries that have yet to do so can be a fascinating, often quite short, step back in time. Rather than make a harsh judgment on the basis of social backwardness, I saw that we were separated by no more than a few generations of affluence, not by degrees of sophistication, but by an aversion to things unpleasant, a luxury we have been able to afford.

Part IV
Desperation and Hope

Chapter 22

We returned home to our country residence, the old farmhouse where we had as yet spent almost no time. Spring was not long in coming and I filled my idleness with the purchase of a horse and saddle, three yearling steers to graze some of the grass, and a new Ford Ranger truck to haul the asparagus crop to town. I had agreed to harvest the eleven-acre patch after the former owner's son promised to lend me the necessary equipment for spraying pesticides, cultivating between the rows, and transporting three migrant workers up and down the field each day to harvest the crop. For forty days, they cut up to four hundred pounds of asparagus daily. At the same time, we consumed as much fresh asparagus as we wanted, sopping with heavenly hollandaise sauce that Celia made from scratch with each serving.

Celia planted a huge garden and we got a dog from the humane society, a German Shepherd-Collie cross that had one floppy ear. She had been abused as a pup and was a bit untrusting at first, and she howled through the night because we kept her outside in a small shed, but she eventually found herself at home. I named her Perro and only beat her once for digging in Celia's garden. She caught on very quickly, as though she'd do her best to please, and I admired her athletic strength and animal nature when she caught a full-grown groundhog by the scruff of the neck and shook it to death.

I bought a rider-mower to keep the grass down in the extensive yard and I cleaned out the old shop, sweeping the dusty floor as though we had purchased the place. I listened to Celia's beautiful soprano voice through the open kitchen window as she expressed her contented glee at being married and pregnant. She said it had happened one night when we had gone to bed a bit tipsy and fallen into in a bout of romping good romance. I was happy with the situation. Celia had demonstrated her willingness to follow me anywhere and accept any course of distraction or lifestyle I chose for us. I smiled from a place deep inside as her casual rendition of an Italian aria drifted across the yard, and laughed heartily to myself when Perro joined in with a prolonged wolfish howl.

In mid-June I received word from Alex Webber. He offered me the head guide position for his weeklong trail rides. Except for guiding the longer and individually customized trips, that was the prestige job of the outfit. I knew the country was spectacular. The offer was a real ego-booster and it represented a once-in-a-lifetime opportunity to learn about packing horses and navigating the wild unmarked mountainous terrain. A few days later, with no verbal objection from Celia, but in conflict with the anxiety she simply could not hide, I phoned and accepted the offer. I could not overcome the tugging at my heart as I packed and prepared to leave, and tears streamed down my cheeks as I waved goodbye to Celia and Perro. I thus drove out of our yard and began the two thousand mile journey west.

The brief interlude I'd enjoyed that spring was undoubtedly the happiest I'd ever been as an adult. But I simply could not overlook the prospect of a new adventure. On the surface there was an element of grim integrity. As I had explained to Celia and convinced myself, I felt obliged to accept the man's generous and complimentary offer. But the stirring deep within me, the appeal to my wandering wild side, represented a lure I could not have resisted even if I had stopped to examine it. Celia was sad and anxious about spending the summer pregnant and alone. My tears flowed profusely because it felt like another heartbreaking 'Y' in the road. Once more I was leaving behind the comfort and security I'd shared with a loving partner, so I could partake of adventure offered by the open road. I sobbed openly for miles and miles, but pressed on until the attachment weakened and I could justify my actions from the detached viewpoint of a larger perspective, one in which everything assumed less importance when weighed against a life of spontaneity and the freedom to respond to impulse.

Sometime during my four days on the road, which included a brief stop to visit family and to pick up the holiday trailer which would be my home between pack trips, Mr. Webber decided that I would be head guide for his three and four day trips, the ones that stopped over at the lodge Celia and I had visited the year before. I was disappointed with the shift in plans and not happy about spending the summer with old Luke, the fretful and cantankerous cook that reigned over the camp. I was nearly horrified when he informed me that Audrey, a crass and ornery female I'd met the previous year, was to be head packer for the operation. But I was a long way from home and in a poor position to argue with a man who had already stated his reasons with an appeal for my understanding and cooperation. Besides, I was especially delighted with the news that Barry, my youngest brother, who had also signed on for the summer, would be joining me as assistant guide.

The job came completely devoid of all unnecessary trappings and, from time to time, without warning, put you in touch with the perimeter of life itself. We cowboys, the guides who assumed responsibility for getting guests into camp safely and the packers who took care of transporting necessary supplies and guests' duffle, took the brunt of challenges. Unruly horses and shifty weather, clients' personalities and lack of preparedness, those topped the list. But the demands of trail life were sometimes severe for everyone. On several occasions, at an elevation of eight thousand feet crossing Krummholtz Pass, people wanted to turn back or find a short cut. They gasped in disbelief at their physical distress after sitting on a horse for six hours. Occasionally a high mountain storm arose, blasting sleet in their faces and thrusting spear-points of cold wind through their light summer clothes. At that point the warning that their clothes might not be sufficient could finally be understood. Questions arose: "Can we turn back?" or "Is there a short cut?" I snugged down my broad-brimmed black Akubra hat and drew the stiff oilskin collar round the back of my neck. They would survive; they might never forget, but they'd never tire of telling the story either. One pair of fellows became completely disillusioned with their dream vacation, concluding their discomfort was simply unacceptable at the end of a day on the trail, and paid several thousand dollars to be lifted out of the remote camp by helicopter. I stood nearby on that pretty mountain day, wondering if they had misunderstood, missed the point perhaps. Without the slightest sympathy, prompted only by a plea for broader awareness and appreciation of this heavenly realm, I genuinely wished they could have got it.

It plainly isn't available to everyone, I concluded. Conditions surrounding my beginnings were rudimentary and physically engaging, with nature always close at hand. Soreness, thirst, stinging insects, a little trickle of blood, real men ignored such trifling irritations and went about their day. Yes indeed, I was quite at home again, on horseback among these giant primordial hills. Solitary and arduous, I believed my existence had more meaning than it had done for a very long time.

Many of the days I spent in the rugged backcountry were truly exquisite. Vistas on either side of the treeless trail winding across the alpine tundra of Krummholtz Pass filled my mind like a pleasant dream. We saw snow-white mountain goats peering down from a thousand feet above, but could rarely spot the noisy pikas that whistled from craggy outcroppings ten feet away. Once settled at the same camp for a few nights, we'd take relaxed rides out for the day. After lunch near the silvery rapids of a mountain stream, I'd stretch out in the shade of a spruce, pull the big Akubra hat over my face, and doze so soundly that I floundered in a void of what, where, and when upon awakening.

My brother and I had some good times with old Luke, the cook, and ornery Audrey, the lady wrangler. But they seemed increasingly bitter about the arrangement and, one afternoon not long into the season, they challenged us in a way that compelled Barry to take ten pack animals and ride ten miles out to a supply depot, load supplies, including fifty pound bags of horse feed, four to a horse, and return with it all intact the same day. It was a daunting task for a novice, and my brother had far less experience packing than I did by this point. Although we had not divulged that fact to them, our adversaries seemed to have guessed it. The odds were stacked brutally against him completing the job without a 'wreck,' as a broad assortment of messes and disasters are referred to in the trade. We were worried, but cornered. There was no way out that wouldn't undermine all respect for us and serve as humiliating fodder for the balance of the season back at the barns where everybody gathered and nattered.

Thankful that we were unaccompanied while working in the chilled morning air, I fervently related every aspect of packing I could think of. As we brushed and saddled the pack string and his saddle horse, we continued discussing both basket hitches and barrel hitches because he would have a wide range of cargo to load. I had him practice a few diamond hitches and we talked about how he might load the ten horses and then string them together without a wreck. I pointed to the pile of discarded stones that had served to adjust previous loads and to save them from rolling under the horses' bellies, all the while suppressing the urge to voice my apprehension. But he was a brave fellow and, after he'd had a good breakfast, he climbed aboard and I handed him the lead shank of the number one packhorse. He disappeared into the heavy bush that concealed a long bend in the trail, then the last pack animal vanished. The interminable waiting had begun.

Taking them out for a day ride, I led the camp's guests to one of my favorite spots. The horse trail we followed ended in a heavily treed box canyon. After dismounting and securing the animals, we were able to scramble on foot about a thousand feet further, mostly vertical, up a rocky and only barely detectable path. The trees grew shorter quickly and all but disappeared at the crest, where suddenly we burst into an untouched alpine world of brilliant and perky wild flowers. Clusters of tiny pink blossoms hugged the mossy surface, solitary innocent white ones stood a few inches taller, patches of tiny pastel blue forget-me-nots dotted the landscape, and ever-present Indian paintbrushes turned blood red at this higher altitude. The meadow ran ahead of us a hundred yards further, before ending at the pristine shore of an icy blue glacial lake. The perfectly calm and sunny day left that silent paradise as completely flawless as any French Impressionist was ever able to imagine and portray.

As we stopped at the edge of the little lake, however, my thoughts were far away with my younger brother. I saw in a moment of precious clarity that the conscious enjoyment of pretty circumstances did not depend nearly as much upon the weather and absence of pests as it depended upon the serenity of one's mind. Nature's gloriously untainted creation, as it appeared that day, was no more than a distant backdrop to my agitated state of mind, my distracting thoughts, and the disproportionate level of anxiety they created.

The concern I had for the success of my brother's packing job served as a catalyst in opening a Pandora's Box of regretful misdemeanors, incidents pertaining to the concept of 'a caring and responsible older brother' and, following the cerebral spider web from there, other could-haves and should-haves that were family related. The guests became boring and their questions were an intrusion on my gloomy preoccupation. A veil of remorse thoroughly dulled the tranquil image before me. My desire to return to camp, where I could wait out his return in solitude, alone with the impending doom that found its roots in the magnification of my unresolved and unforgiven past, obliterated the blissful ambience that I might have savored with happy gratitude.

I knew I was in a special place, by all measures enormously privileged. I contemplated the fact that I wasn't there in a deeply conscious way, from the Buddhist perspective I had read about, not capable of seeing purely 'as it is' without distraction. It is curious that we imagine our surroundings can provide circumstances in which we will experience a happy mind. Reality is, in fact, quite the opposite. Full appreciation of beautiful surroundings is dependent entirely upon a happy mind, a mind that can be present, undistracted and entirely aware.

After a few hours, in which we ate lunch and lounged around, we clambered down the slope again, mounted up, and let the horses set their own instinctively accelerated pace back to camp and a daily ration of cubed green alfalfa. A cloud of anxiety hovered over me for the duration, while my half dozen charges seemed blissfully subdued by the mystic effect of the day's outing, depending of course on the invisible state of their minds and the absence of underlying turmoil. Help with unsaddling and feeding the horses arrived promptly in the person of Audrey, but unspoken divergent attitudes regarding the young packer's return rendered it unappreciated. There was still no sign of him at five-thirty and I trudged up to the lodge for supper.

"Your brother not back yet?" Ornery old Luke barely disguised his glee.

I participated unenthusiastically in some idle chitchat with guests and, as soon as it seemed polite, put on my hat and strode out in the direction of the corrals. Beyond the outside rails, the still empty trailhead gaped menacingly from the dark hole in the bush. Cold dark shadows crept across the valley floor, quickly closing ranks, and a chill swept up from the creek. As the sun dropped behind the callous jagged heights of the Sundance Range, I reflected anxiously on the fact that dusk in a mountain valley was an abbreviated affair. One of the saddle horses needed its front shoes reset and I decided that monotonous task would be a merciful distraction.

Horses' shod hooves cause a muffled series of crunching thuds on well-worn but gravelly mountain trails, and sometimes a foot thumping a solid tree root is audible. With a whole string of horses very heavily laden, even though they go about their long day of trudging in a dismal silence, there is a subdued rumble. It is felt as much as heard – sensed, perhaps. Maybe it was wishful thinking, too, again. I listened intently, wanting and doubting in the same hesitant breath.

Then the big Belgian-cross gelding's head came into view, and then a man's face appeared and revealed the biggest smile I ever hope to see. I watched with mounting gratification as his neatly packed string trailed out of the bush behind him. My smile grew; tears welled in my happy eyes. "Holy cow. He did it!"

That was not the end of the controversy, however. In fact, it may only have increased the adversarial determination of the lady wrangler, who thought she should have been head guide. Audrey had been in the service of the outfit for half a dozen years compared to my one. The cook harped about the unusual circumstances of my brother and me working together, an arrangement that smelled of favoritism, he insinuated. So they set out to undermine our circumstances and interfere wherever possible with the fun we were obviously having. There were two factors operating in their favor: first, they were both endowed with zealous aptitudes for gossip and applied their talents liberally whenever back in town; second, Barry and I loved to push the envelope during our day rides, providing guests with lasting memories of high passes and seemingly treacherous ledges, then partying with them in the evenings, sometimes drinking more than we should have. Dinnertime tales of our brazen and heroic handling of a grizzly bear encounter stirred a cynical if not sinister response from Luke, who sensed encroachment on the hoary mountain-man image he cultivated. As a consequence, we spent as little time as possible over meals at the lodge, in the immediate presence of too much negativity, and had as much fun as we wished while performing our duties as we felt appropriate, without regard for public opinion. We hoped that Alex Webber was above being influenced by the meddling chatter of our antagonists and we were willing to accept the consequences if he wasn't.

The day ride across Big Horn Pass to Ptarmigan Summit was much longer than most, but we loved the magnificent scenery and the impression the sturdy animals' enduring performance made on our guests. As loose shale tumbled away from the horses' feet, ladies especially leaned inward toward the steep upward slope of the mountain, in an attempt to deal with their fear of the all too obvious abyss on the downside. Sometimes there were tears, but we assured them that we had never met a suicidal horse, the truth of which I am not certain, and that their actions were if anything a source of imbalance for their hard working mounts. Frequently, as we lounged around after lunch in the shadow of the Sawbuck Mountain Range, with the snow covered peak of Mount Ashby glistening in the sun, the question arose, "Do we have to go back the same way?"

The answer was yes, and there wasn't any way to convey our complete confidence in the relative safety of the adventure. It was similar to expressing the logical notion that there is no risk on a giant roller coaster. We had a heartfelt desire to leave guests with an imprint of the country we had come to love more with each passing week, and we were as thrilled as they were, with their excited recollections and the gratitude they expressed when they were safely back at the lodge. Sadly, their comments during dinner were not met with happy enthusiasm by the disparaging cook and packer. They were reluctant listeners at best, and conspired later to carry back to the boss exaggerations of the risks we took and the extra work to which we subjected the livestock. We carried on in spite of the gathering clouds.

The job had a surprising spin-off, the result of wearing rustic cowboy gear, being in fantastic physical condition, having expertise well beyond that of our clients, and assuming command in a rugged, remote, and romantic environment. Nearly every trip had one or more unattached women on it and they invariably made their desires obvious in the afternoons around the corrals and in the evenings beside campfires. In response, my own habitually unrestrained desires were easily aroused. The confluence of this mutual attraction was too obvious, no doubt, even though any culmination of desires had to be postponed until we got back to town at the end of the trips.

At the camp Barry and I shared a tent, which tempered temptation, and not much happened at the conclusion of trips in these early weeks either, because we shared the trailer on our weekly night off. I thought it inappropriate for my younger brother to witness me cheating on his sister-in-law, whom he liked very much. Still, long evenings of gay drinking around the fire, or partying in the lodge long after old Luke had retried to his tent, often led to affectionate displays, and the phenomenon merely exacerbated the animosity of our wet-blanket rivals. It provided more fodder for their case and, while we were harvesting the rewards of our circumstances, they were busy gossiping about it.

Their efforts to undermine our enjoyment eventually paid off. On one turnaround in town, Mr. Webber met with me to announce that he was putting Barry on other duty. Worse yet, he was making Audrey my guiding partner and bringing on a new fellow to do the packing. Barry and I accepted his decision and continued to perform our duties as reassigned, meeting in town once week. But I determined then and there that I had been treated with less respect by the outfit than I deserved. I severed any remaining ideas of future service with Alex Webber, whose allegiance was obviously with my adversaries, and opened the gate to making the most of a summer without my wife.

The next week out I agreed to accompany two men, for whom I felt a masculine out-of-doors connection, and the well-behaved teenage son of one of them, on a day ride to the alpine lake at the end of the canyon. Having emphasized the rigors of the climb at the end of the canyon as a deterrent, I was not surprised when the half-dozen others of the group decided to take an easier ride with Audrey. I was surprised and dismayed when Rebecca, a lady in her early thirties from Chicago, expressed a desire to come with us. Despite further skepticism and warning with respect to the physical challenge, I could not thwart her wishes. As it turned out she was pleasant enough, vocally reserved in fact, which left plenty of space for our manly interaction on the ride out and the hike to the crest. As we lounged on the soft tundra foliage before the shore of the icy blue glacial lake, the men loosened their shirts, unbuttoning them to let the light breeze circulate, offsetting the warm rays of the noonday sun. "Does anyone mind if I loosen my shirt?" the lady asked as she casually exposed enough of her chest to hint at an ample and bra-less bosom. No one minded, it seemed. For me, new interest in the girl was aroused. Her kinky shoulder-length hair suddenly seemed more pleasing, and I noticed her eyes for the first time, soft green and animated as they rotated slowly in my direction.

The men said they'd like to hike around the lake, if they could, before we had lunch. The lady said she would like to stay put and asked delicately if I would stay with her. I agreed, regretting that I wouldn't share the hiking experience with my new friends. But a choice hardly seemed to exist. As soon as they were over a small rise, she removed her shirt completely and smiled. I was enjoying her presence; her rather elongated breasts were punctuated with two-inch circles in the tone of dark chocolate, and I was happily comfortable with not curbing her freedom to do as she pleased. We sat ten feet apart, talking intermittently and enjoying a nearly perfect interlude in that alpine heaven. As though she decided she must crack the facade of innocence in order to shift us to a different stratum of intercourse, she said she needed to pee, stood, pulled her pants down without increasing the distance between us, and squatted. As her stream trickled into the alpine tundra, the notion of 'rut' leapt into my mind and a delicious lewdness consumed me.

The passive, hygienic, and innocent ambience of our surroundings gave way to a new reality, one of primal instinct. I smiled with unreserved enthusiasm as she stood again, leaving her jeans around her ankles and looking straight at me with an impish grin. Stirred by seemingly wild and risqué circumstances, and my own nearly painful physical arousal, I stood, unbuckled my pants, dislodged myself from my underwear, and faced her, naked to my knees. She removed her pants and panties entirely. Without further exchange and completely naked now, she gathered her clothes and approached me. She used them to build a little bed for herself on the lush turf. I offered her my shirt for additional padding. Content, she laid on her back with her legs invitingly open. I never did completely remove my pants or take off my boots. It was what she had in mind, I supposed. From which moment forward I know not, but I considered the whole episode perfectly appropriate.

A few days later we were back and partying in town, tourists and cowboys alike. Rebecca stayed close by and I felt assured of another encounter. That idea didn't rate as high as drinking, however, and by the time I turned my interests to her, she said it was too bad, "sad," she said, that I had drunk so much and that she was not interested as a result. She was leaving the next morning, she told me, and I was returning to the camp.

I called Celia before leaving. She missed me, she pleaded, and wanted to visit. We made plans for two weeks hence. I would meet her at the airport and we'd drive home to the farm to spend a week with my parents. It tugged at my heart to hear her anxiety and her longing. I had to steel myself against surges of guilt, with the rationalization that I would never become attached in any of these encounters and undermine my marriage.

The next four-day excursion included three New York based flight attendants, one of whom worked as a model as well. Victoria was her name and she loved spending time around the corrals while I saddled horses in the morning, and again when I unsaddled and fed them after a day's ride. She adored horses, she said, and had always wanted one of her own. She was exceptionally beautiful, entirely unblemished, with classic Caucasian features: perfectly formed nose and brow separating her twinkling blue-green eyes, natural sandy-blonde hair that set off the healthy shade of her smooth cheeks. She wore almost no make-up, because she didn't need to. Her lips were full and natural. She was simply enchanting and I began to expect her presence. I found myself missing her until she showed up.

Victoria told me she had only recently separated from her airline-pilot husband, because he repeatedly cheated on her. That was the primary reason for this exotic trip west, to assuage the lingering pain of that sad experience. I didn't wear a wedding ring, because it had been stolen during the break-in at Torremolinos, and I never voluntarily disclosed that I was married, especially when a pronouncement of that sort would impair the flow of electricity I enjoyed so much. Audrey and Luke, however, made a point of informing guests that I had a lovely wife, whom they'd met, and that we were expecting a child. I viewed their behavior as needless subversive activity. I had no intention, in any case, of denying my situation. If confronted with it, I merely downplayed the significance of my conjugal commitment. I convinced myself that truth and morality had little importance in an environment so wholly supportive of primitive urges.

When we trailed single-file out of the camp for the day, and again when we returned, I arranged as subtly as possible the positioning of her horse directly behind mine, and Victoria promptly cooperated. We could then continue talking, or rather, share an intimate nearness, which included prolonged periods of enchanted silence. Victoria and I stayed up later than the others one night, drinking quite a bit, infatuated with each other. Consequently, I slept in the next day, which resulted in Luke grumpily lighting the fire in the lodge's huge cook-stove, a serious offence, he made it known, since he liked to stroll into a warm room and enjoy his coffee first thing.

When we got back to town, Victoria and I wanted desperately to spend a little more time together. At Victoria's request, one of her girlfriends agreed to accompany us. Sensible, I thought, as we went to the trailer, drank some wine and, after a few short hours, kissed goodbye very briefly, the first and only kiss we had indulged in, as much as the urge had been there all along. I looked upon the encounter as a treasure of unblemished romance, two ships signaling each other in the night. Sadly, suffering from my customary regret that I could not live more lives than one, I did not expect that we would meet again. The spheres encompassing our two existences were worlds apart.

Greta from Germany joined us on the next round. She turned out to be an experienced rider, very athletic, with a pleasant manner and a free spirit. She sat straight in the saddle, relaxed, natural, and in complete control of her horse. Her very large breasts wobbled freely beneath her shirt and I suspected that compliance with American prudence was all that kept them under wraps. I liked Greta and enjoyed spending time with her, but my mind was too often on Victoria and I had no other desire. I told her of my married life as though it was a relief to share it openly with someone whose presence I enjoyed, even self-satisfying to feel the morality of my openness. She stayed late as we kept the fire burning in front of my tent one night. Strangely, another much plainer girl came along at one point. She sat with us awhile and, when Greta went to relieve herself, she proceeded to dissuade me from doing anything immoral, possibly motivated by her own righteousness, possibly at the instigation of my co-workers. In any case, she stayed long enough to ensure the moral outcome she had in mind for me that evening. I was meeting Celia in a few days anyway, which left me mostly grateful.

Back in town the party was on and Greta joined us. Not long into the evening, she whispered that she would like to spend some time alone with me. We left for the trailer and, after a mesmerizing session of fondling her gigantic breasts, we got into bed together. I desperately wanted to save my sexual energy for my wife and therefore refrained from ejaculating even though we abandoned ourselves to erotic playfulness for some time, impassioned petting, rolling on top of each other, and lying still with me inside her from time to time for as long as I could control myself. It was therefore with simultaneous regret and relief that I responded to Barry's knocking at the door and his reminder, voiced from outside, "We have to leave for Denver early in the morning and I want to get some sleep." It was a reasonable request because we shared the camper, so

Greta and I dressed quickly and our acquaintance ended in a fleeting farewell.

As Barry drove my Blazer toward the airport the next morning, I felt uncomfortable sitting in the passenger seat across from him. The juxtaposition of my actions the previous evening and the rapidly approaching prospect of greeting my lovely and pregnant wife, whom he had always been pleased to treat as his sister, tugged at my core. What kind of image did he have of me? He would be forced to suppress the truth of my behavior, just as I would. Could he shift from accepting his older brother as a partying, carousing cowboy one day and admire him for his marriage to a charming and devoted wife the next, a responsible father to be?

I could reflect upon images of myself in those two scenarios quite comfortably, even more comfortably when permitted to do so under conditions of anonymity. I had practiced the art during adolescence, while riding home on the school bus. Staring blankly out the window, I had cringed with shame at being bullied by older boys in front of girls, or occasional belittling in front of my class by my literature teacher. A cold shudder would rock the core of my existence and, in defense, I had to induce into my mind the hypothesis that no one had noted my humiliation. I had to look beyond the recent past and the ugly present, to envision a day when I might be reconciled and recompensed with a life that was in line with my belief that I didn't deserve such injustice, that I was actually destined to rise far above these intolerable and degrading circumstances. It was this distant hope and vision that permitted me on succeeding days to interact as an equal with friends and to ask a girl to dance at the community hall on Friday night, terrified as I was of her refusal. So, I had been well trained at accepting varying images of myself. I could disconnect and reconnect, more or less effortlessly. Still, I feared that Barry might think less of me. He might conclude that I lacked the dignity he would have preferred in an older brother. On the other hand, perhaps he liked my free spirit and adaptability, as I did when I thought about it.

Celia looked overwhelmed with relief when she saw us waiting at the arrivals gate. My heart went out in response, my enthusiasm honest as well, because I seriously liked my wife very much. I liked being married to her. I continued to worry a little about Barry's view of my duplicity, and his position of forced complicity, as we collected her bags and proceeded to the parking lot. When we got to the farm my parents were happy to see us of course. They were delighted with the prospect of a grandchild. Suddenly that other world was far away and references to it were kept purposely brief.

The five days at the farm flew pleasantly by and there was too little time before we headed back to the mountains. Celia and I talked about getting a place out west in the fall. It was completely my idea, but she readily gave me the go-ahead to do some real estate research when my summer guiding job ended. She did emphasize that she was often lonely and would be happy when we were together again. I knew in that moment I didn't want to part with her and wished the summer were at an end, although I refrained from expressing that sentiment and merely assured her that it wouldn't seem long.

There was an envelope addressed to me, to be picked up at the office, the man who would drive us to the trailhead informed me the next morning. He drove us round that way so I could pick it up. It was a rather stirring note of fondness from Victoria, as well as a very stirring set of photo-images that she used for modeling auditions. Sitting in the truck with other members of the crew, I withheld any reaction and quickly tucked the envelope in my duffle bag. I was impatient for the moment when I could review the contents in private.

The note informed me that she had arranged to work a flight to Denver, including a two-day layover, and would come out to see me when I was next in town if I wanted her to. I spent the whole week oscillating between a euphoric daze and a state of anxiety, the latter because I had no contact with the outside world and feared she may interpret my delayed response as a lack of interest. Finally, however, the end of the week arrived and I was handed a message she had left at the office, with a

Denver hotel phone number on it. I called immediately. She wasn't at all disturbed because the lady who received her call had explained my schedule. She was ready to leave immediately, with her flight attendant friend. They had a room reserved in the resort town for the night. I had little more than enough time to shave and shower after a week in the bush, drop off my laundry at the cleaners, and meet them for dinner.

After we ate dinner with her friend and visited over a few snifters of Grand Marnier, Victoria and I went for a stroll along the bank of the river that meandered through the town, holding hands at first, and then kissing passionately at intervals, back and forth over a mile of groomed pathway for two hours with a complete absence of regard for our whereabouts. Addressing her concerns, I explained that I didn't think my marriage was inconsistent with a fleeting relationship between her and I, an innocent sharing of time together, given how naturally drawn we were to each other. We discussed how we might spend more time with each other before I headed back in a few weeks to resume my station of spouse and father-to-be. I suggested, because I was faced with a two or three-day drive that could be extended to five or six, she might join me for all or part of it. I had that flexibility because I was stopping to look for property in any case. She was quite certain she could arrange flights to accommodate our wishes. Later we met her friend for coffee, as previously planned. "My chaperone," Victoria called her. "Because I'm not sure I could trust myself alone with you for very long," she sighed with a blameless vulnerability that sent my senses reeling. I accompanied them to their hotel, stopping only briefly before kissing my enchanting darling goodbye in the hallway.

Chapter 23

Barry left the outfit a week before I did, rather disgruntled with his lot as it had turned out, and headed back to the farm. I got in touch with a realtor and began to look at farms and small ranches in the foothills. I picked the right fellow because, after a half-day of driving around, he said, "It's a little further out than you wanted, but I know of a place that is exactly right for you and the seller is highly motivated."

We drove north for an hour with a panoramic view of the Rockies sixty miles away to our left. About ten minutes before we turned west toward our destination, we drove past an eighty acre clearing in the primarily treed landscape, a grassy meadow surrounded by a mix of virgin pine and spruce forest. A quarter of the space contained a crystal clear pond, the irregular meandering shape of which defined the lowlands. Its calm gleaming surface reflected the images of a dozen Black Angus cows and calves as they grazed lazily in the soft glow of an afternoon sun. Undulating foothills rose up and beyond the pastoral scene, to the majestic eastern slopes, their peaks a series of jagged spires set eternally against a cloudless sky.

The scene affected me dramatically, permeating the same cavern of undefined longing that my proximity to Victoria seemed to fill. My eyes turned back to the road with the hope, and a silent appeal to the universe, that the property we were going to look at would have some of the same constituents. In minutes we entered a long driveway that was lined with tall mature spruce on both sides. On the opposite side of a two-acre yard stood a large hip-roof barn and extensive corrals with cattle handling facilities. As we turned to the left, a twenty-five hundred square foot house came into view. Beyond the house, across fifty yards of lawn, the northeast perimeter was defined by dense woods that occupied the adjacent property. Once inside, I could see that the rooms were expansive. Three of them had wood-burning fireplaces and the windows were large, including French doors that opened onto a full-length deck. The basement floor was fully above ground in the front and opened onto the lawn with its own French doors, making the house somewhat of a two-story, with nearly five thousand feet of living space. Pausing on the deck, the realtor permitted me a silent moment to gaze southward over the lush valley where a small river looped into the east side of the one hundred and sixty acre parcel. Except for the tall pine and spruce grove that was contained by the river's loop, the small ranch was cleared of forest and a gentle breeze chased undulating waves across the knee high grass that blanketed the pastures for more than a half-mile to the south-west corner.

I controlled my excitement. The vendors, who had been present much of time, were absent just then and I asked the agent what he knew of their circumstances. "I believe they have taken possession of another farm and are actually in a bit of a bind," he said. I knew the real estate market had experienced quite a setback recently, as a result of high interest rates. I knew that mortgage money was still expensive, keeping pressure on things.

"The house is much larger than I wanted to buy," I said. "That's why they're asking two hundred and thirty thousand. If it was an eighteen-hundred square foot bungalow, which is what I had in mind, this place would go for one-eighty."

He didn't reply, astutely.

"Let's write up an offer," I said. "One hundred and eighty thousand dollars, cash, no conditions. Leave it open for five days and tell them I'm leaving tomorrow for New York, driving and not available, so they'll have to take it or leave it."

I called Celia and described the dream home I was hoping to obtain for us. She was delighted, of course, and said she couldn't wait for me to get home. The next day, after arranging to meet Victoria in Minneapolis on my second day of travelling, I started east. We had discussed travelling back on the north side of the Great Lakes, through Ontario, Canada. After meeting her at the airport, we headed north toward the border, beginning an adventure that I anticipated would be several heavenly days, terminated by a permanent farewell and resolute resumption of our previous lives.

It was heavenly indeed, from the beginning. Nestled between the bucket seats in the Blazer's large interior was a bulky, hard plastic covered compartment, quite smooth except for the coffee cup placements that were pre-formed in its lower forward edge. A lot of the time while we were driving, Victoria perched herself upon that less comfortable space and slouched against me. I never doubted that the continuous ecstasy I experienced was mutual. A large insect smacked and smeared the windshield. I asked her, "What is the last thing that goes through a bug's mind when it hits the windshield?" She smiled at me playfully, her eyes gleaming with inquisitiveness. "Its asshole," I ventured, concurrent with apprehension that it may be in bad taste. To my relief, she immediately burst with laughter, and we giggled with intermittent spontaneity for the next hundred miles.

We stopped at roadside viewpoints that offered panoramas of unfathomable Lake Superior and the rugged granite hills that led away from its northern shore. We held each other, kissed, and marveled at the beauty in and around us. We stopped in late afternoon and arranged to spend our third night in a quaint cottage nestled against the cerulean grandeur of Lake Heron. Following another dreamy, wine-enriched dining experience, we strolled arm-in-arm along the shoreline until we came to a very long pier. In that moment it seemed somehow appropriate that I permit our separation, as though I were preparing to let her go. I stood at the foot of the pier while she ventured out upon it, across the calm water in the breathless evening air, until she was silhouetted at the far end by the backdrop of the setting sun and its crimson reflection on the water. The dark unembellished outline of her form suddenly appeared forlorn.

Nearly staggering with melancholy at the idea of abandoning her in a few days, I rounded a corner in my mind and my heart sank with the implications. How could I, for my own sake, logically turn away from a life of bliss of this magnitude? How could I ever be happy again in the good and right, but so relatively mundane, circumstances of my marriage?

We had not engaged in sexual intercourse to that point, because she told me she was not on the pill. We had slept together every night and done nearly everything but copulate, but her reservation and my respect for her decision had been sufficient. Heady romance and the thrill of our deepening love had been enough to that point. The awful decision I had to make weighed heavily, however, and I felt a need for reassurance that my commitment to her was not misplaced, for increased evidence of a co-commitment. Later, after we had gone to bed and were reveling in a passionate embrace, I rolled on top of her and pleadingly whispered my desire to be inside her. "All right, but be careful," she acquiesced. I eased my throbbing rigidity into a super-heated luxuriance that threatened to consume all my senses. More importantly, I felt that she had surrendered to my possessing her at some vital core level of her being. That's why it was a little disconcerting when she threatened, rather unlovingly given the circumstances, "If you come in me you're dead meat." I had been seeking a panacea for my emotional vulnerability and the brashness of her remark had not helped.

Had she just presented a side of her personality that ran contrary to the unblemished image I held? Or was it merely a symptom of the fear she had about becoming pregnant? I put it down to the latter and thought the better of her for having that kind of common sense and self-respect, although she might have been more sensitive and affectionate with her choice of words. It was hardly something I wanted to worry about during our remaining time together. Late in the afternoon, two days later, I dropped her at a train station outside the city and continued on alone. I had one hundred and fifty miles to go: rapturous day-dreaming about my blissful future in one moment, and in the next, nausea to the point of vomiting over the abhorrent task immediately in front of me. I had called Celia from the hotel that morning and said I would arrive later in the day. We had spoken only briefly, but she said she would have dinner ready.

Finally, having slowed to a crawl much sooner than I needed to, I turned into our yard. Perro came bounding down the driveway. Celia opened the door and ran toward the truck with her arms open to receive me. I was emotional enough, but for reasons I was thankful were not apparent. I hugged my dear wife with all the love I wished I could give her 'for as long as we both shall live.' I frolicked with Perro and listened while Celia expressed her happiness that I was home. I looked at her full figure and asked how she had been feeling. "Very well, just tired sometimes," she smiled. Then her eyes sparkled. "Come and see my garden." Green cucumbers and large yellow squash peeked between a cover of grainy broad-leafed foliage; bright red tomatoes clung to vines suspended upon a bamboo trellis; row upon weed-free row of potatoes, beets, turnips, and carrots thrived just beyond a swath of pumpkins whose deep orange glowed in the afternoon sun. I smiled and marveled at her truly excellent success. Reminded once more of how creative and resourceful she was I expressed my genuine admiration, while my heart quaked, torn asunder with guilt and nearly unbearable sorrow.

"I have a bottle of champagne on ice," she said as we turned toward the old farmhouse. In the living room, she had strung a large decorative welcome home sign from the ceiling. She handed me a small box with a ribbon around it. It contained an identical replacement for my stolen wedding ring. I opened the Dom Perignon and filled the tall crystal glasses we'd received as a wedding gift. To preserve my emotional and even physical stability, feeling very nearly panic-stricken in that moment, I consciously decided to block from my mind the irreconcilable contradiction of my circumstances. Instead of being immobilized by dread, my head and torso felt mercifully cloaked in an infinitely more tolerable numbness.

"Have you heard about Rob Simpson?" Celia asked.

"No, what?" I asked, as my mind flashed back to our shared history of loutish partying and sexual marauding in Chicago. I thought of his hilarious claim to be on a straight gin diet, and roaring along Lake Shore Drive with *Wellington's Victory March* vibrating through the armrests of his Jaguar.

"He shot himself at his mansion in Nantucket," she said reluctantly, with obvious deep concern. Perhaps she thought Rob and I had been friends on more meaningful terms than had been the reality.

I was shocked nevertheless, and uneasy as I reflected that, despite all those nights of debauchery, he had a wife and teenage daughter at home. Wanting to side-step the possible significance of those details, I exclaimed, "Shot himself? Jeez, he had it made: two big houses, partner in the firm, successful trader." Variations on the image of Rob Simpson's final, hopeless moments passed before my eyes intermittently all evening. Each time, I had to shore up the shaky rationalization that my case was not like his, and I had to assure myself that I would not succumb to a similar pitiful demise, no matter what.

We finished the champagne. We had wine with the beautiful leg of lamb she had prepared, a favorite of mine. Celia drank very little, out of concern for her pregnancy. But I could hardly get enough, without seeming more gluttonous than usual. As the evening drew on, I dwelt fearfully upon her probable expectation of making love. Around eight-thirty, I insisted that I wanted a little time alone; perhaps I would take Perro for a drive. I was certain of my objective before I left home. I drove into the small town five miles away and stopped at a payphone booth to call Victoria.

"I love you and miss you so much," she said. "How is everything going?"

"Oh, fine," I said with reassuring boldness. "I love you, too." I felt uplifted, briefly.

Before I got home, I was swamped again by the vileness of my situation and the sadness of having to give up one of two nearly perfect worlds. I put my arm around Perro who sat beside me on the truck seat. She licked my face where a tear had trickled down. I drank a bit more when I got back. At last, Celia announced that she was exhausted and was going upstairs to get ready for bed. I followed shortly and crawled in beside her.

As I held her and told her it felt good to be with her again, the natural and strong affection I felt was truly genuine. Kissing her passionately was more difficult and required a mechanical persistence. Finally I fell asleep in her arms.

She had arisen before me in the morning and I could smell the coffee when I awoke. As I swung my feet out of the bed and onto the floor, I brushed aside a fresh onslaught of disturbing thoughts regarding my predicament. I put on my housecoat, went downstairs, and selected a chair at the kitchen table, while Celia poured me a cup of coffee. She sat down directly across the table and looked at me with an expression that contained a disconcerting mix of hesitancy and certainty. I had no time to dwell on possible explanations before she asked calmly, "Have you been unfaithful to me?"

It immediately seemed to me that mere unfaithfulness would have been a gift to both of us, relative to the whole truth, and I slowly opted for the opportunity to claim honesty as a remaining virtue. Hoping to ease her pain, however, I wanted to downplay the weightiness of my admission. "Yes, I have," I said with regret in my voice. "Why do you ask?"

"Because you called me Victoria several times during the night," she murmured on the verge of tears, but with determination and the strength of a woman who is certain of her rights. Then she got up and went into the bathroom. In that moment, I was no longer a life partner with whom she could share her tears.

I went outside, stroking my hand along Perro's back as she accompanied me down the walkway. My gut was in knots over Celia's pained reaction to my betrayal, as though a deep irreparable sadness had entered her life. I also realized that we would never experience the wonderfully reassuring bond of being husband and wife again. At the same time, I experienced the notion of progress. The door had inadvertently been opened and a first step in my grim ordeal had been taken, mercifully easier in that it had happened without my conscious initiation. Celia had mentioned last night that she'd agreed to sing at a friend's wedding in Chicago next weekend. When she asked if I would accompany her, I had withheld any definite response. Now it would be easier to decline.

My mind turned to the process of rationalizing and justifying my decision. Either Celia or Victoria was going to suffer, one or the other, whatever I decided to do. Why should it be Victoria when the greater amount of happiness would result through my choosing to leave Celia and be with her? It would be better for Celia in the long run because I no longer felt affection toward her, my physical desires had been diverted, and she would be forever subjected to a cold mechanical relationship. It seemed that my meeting Victoria was a kind of destiny, a gift of blissful union that was well beyond the rather ordinary relationship Celia and I had shared. We may not have been meant for each other after all. On and on I ruminated, unwilling to admit that I was leaving Celia and running off with Victoria because I wanted to, simple as that.

It was a completely self-centered, self-willed disregard for everything beyond my own impassioned desires. I gave almost no consideration to the pain and disappointment it would cause her family, especially her mother and father who had always treated me with the highest regard. Nor did I think of my own mother and father with whom we had so recently celebrated the prospect of another grandchild. I did not contemplate the destruction of precious relationships that had grown up as a direct result of our marriage: mine with Celia's father and brothers, hers with Barry and my mother, our friends who had supported and honored us during and following our wedding. No amount of mental juggling could have subdued the guilt-ridden turbulence arising from these realities, if I had allowed myself to look at them directly. I had to marginalize that sort of close examination in defense of my sanity.

It was deep within my nature to be drawn relentlessly toward a new, more exotic, and seemingly superior experience. I could not say no to an opportunity that promised those rewards. Thoughts of dutifully trudging the path I had previously chosen, for the sake of others involved, were accompanied immediately by the deepest conviction that it would involve relinquishing something essential to my being. I assigned little importance to the concepts of tradition, compliance, loyalty, and commitment. I had no notion of maintaining dignity and respectability as sources of inner strength. I held those who governed their lives by mundane social norms in total contempt. It was a kind of supreme arrogance that was essential in my desperate drive to overcome a sorry self-insufficiency through limitless clamoring. Therein were both the reason and the capacity to behave as I did. When the promise of fulfilling my dreams appeared, I abandoned all else for its sake. Deep inside, my very life depended upon it.

Celia assumed, correctly and tearfully, that I would not accompany her to the wedding. Because I would be free, I phoned Victoria that night and arranged to spend the weekend with her. Friday afternoon the realtor called to say the sellers had accepted my offer. That was a cause for celebration, which began as soon as Victoria arrived at the farmhouse. The relief of being with her again, having essentially made a decision with respect to my marriage, was so elevating that I got very drunk. At some point Victoria announced that she was back on the pill, but I don't recall taking advantage of the fact.

I suffered with a throbbing headache the next day, the kind that blended itself with excruciating tension in my neck, but I managed to carry on, motivated by the general good fortune of my circumstances. Briefly exacerbating my hungover remorse was a touch of guilt over us sleeping in the house that Celia and I shared, in the guest bedroom mercifully, but in which the queen-size bed had belonged to Celia before we were married and would again soon. I was on edge even more with concern that our rural neighbors, who had been especially caring and supportive of Celia in my absence, and who had a habit of casually dropping in, could do so at any moment.

In that crazed state, I came up the idea of astounding Victoria with the explosive power of a .308 caliber Browning lever-action rifle I had. In an insane moment that would sting my mind with shame for years to come, I decided that it would be enormously impressive to watch pumpkins explode when hit with the one hundred and eighty grain bullets. We selected two large pumpkins from Celia's garden and drove to the back of the two hundred acre property. They merely sluggishly split open when hit, not resembling in the least the head-exploding images I'd seen in a film about the Jackal, which I had imagined replicating as an enhancement to my masculine stature. Victoria kindly voiced her amazement at the noise in any case.

In the afternoon, we loaded some camping gear in her little Toyota truck, along with our two dogs, hers being a pampered purebred Norwegian elkhound, and drove to a nearby lake where I proceeded to get roaring drunk again. I remember the too large dogs frolicking in the small tent, something entirely contrary to my lifelong 'pets belong outside' principles, but one must capitulate in the face of cuteness, especially when clinging with desperation. I awoke hungover once more, we packed things up, and Victoria returned home.

When Celia came home from the wedding, I suggested we should separate for a while. I would move out west alone. After several gut-wrenching questions, which I responded to with a cold certainty that I did not feel inside, she accepted the proposal without further dispute. Characteristically, Celia chose to deal with emotional disturbances inwardly. Her reactions and responses were, as a consequence, always measured and dignified. The maintenance of a stiff upper lip, by a person who is presently being made the object of dishonor and deceit, makes the task easier for a perpetrator, in the moment at least. She called her sister's husband, who had a business from which he could borrow a truck and with whom she had a brotherly relationship. He would convey her things back to Connecticut and move her into a small house they knew was available for rent.

I phoned Barry and told him I had purchased the farm and could use his help to move. I didn't tell him of my impending separation. He did his research, decided to travel by train, and called back to say he would arrive in three days. Meanwhile I spent a considerable amount of time finalizing the real estate transaction: sending and receiving faxes, transferring money, and arranging for physical possession upon my arrival. I arranged to sell the horse and the cattle I had purchased before I'd left in the spring, to a local scavenger and dealer in anything, a horse thief in a class well beneath that of anyone in a Morocco bazaar. I was thankful, nonetheless, because I was in a hurry and did not have the energy to shop for a few dollars more. My last ride on the horse was a wild, exasperating three-hour chase through tall grass, swamp, and tangled undergrowth. The three head of steers did not want to come out, separating from each other to elude capture and doubling back at every opportunity. The horse had no experience with cattle, absolutely no instinct regarding the task at hand, and had to be dragged viciously into every turn and spurred forward in every attempt to contain the small herd and keep it moving with some cohesion, usually too late. After I finally got them in and loaded in his ramshackle trailer, the bargain hunter demonstrated his complete lack of insight by saying, "That horse is quite impressive." He followed that with, "You are an accomplished rider." I felt the whole thing was an embarrassment and the only redeeming feature of the afternoon was that it had not been witnessed by anyone who knew the difference.

Celia and I began packing our belongings, separating the things she had brought with her, and many of the wedding gifts, from the majority of our possessions which we agreed belonged to me. Celia had little attachment to the large expensive furniture we had purchased together two years earlier, and the house I had yet to furnish was huge. The point is, we went about it mechanically, for the most part.

I steeled myself during the moments I sensed she was sobbing quietly. I tried to say things that distanced us from the task at hand. I wanted to ask her more about the events of the summer; the neighbors she said had been so kind to her; the cattle getting out of the fence; and the local fair that she had participated in and eagerly described as so quaint and colorful. But I had to be careful of my tears welling up as well, and the intermittent longing to hold her and tell her it was all a mistake and to invite her to join me in starting over again. I know she would have, because she had an enormous capacity for maturity and forgiveness.

If one is sufficiently bold in asserting his position, no matter how ludicrous it might appear, most decent people will not engage him with cross-examination. I told Victoria that my wife and I were parting ways amicably, that she would move to Connecticut and have my baby there, and that it was fine with her. Victoria was content to accept that and join me immediately in a new relationship, as though the other had never existed. After I joyfully met Barry at the train station and we had been driving for a half-hour, I decided it was prudent to divulge my changed marital circumstances before he walked into the house and greeted his sister-in-law. I suppose, because I presented the facts without emotion, as though they had no greater implication than the act of trading one horse for another, he demonstrated little reaction. When we arrived, he greeted Celia warmly with a brotherly hug. I was glad of that. Casual conversation between us was somewhat strained and less cheerful than normal, because of the sad and inconvenient course of events unfolding in our midst, but not a word was spoken in that regard. The ugly truth was delicately circumvented.

On the second evening he was there, Barry and I drove to a pub in a town not far away. I had arranged to meet Victoria there so I could introduce her to my brother. I think he demonstrated some distaste for my decisions during that encounter. The warmth he might have offered her just wasn't there and, although I initially interpreted his reaction as bashfulness in the face of her striking appearance, I thought later that he may have needed more time to shift his allegiance, to get past the fact that he felt a brotherly affection for Celia and genuinely cared about her. On the drive back, we talked very little and I sensed that he longed sadly for a different unfolding of circumstances. If so, he never expressed that sentiment. Maybe the fact that only two and a half years had elapsed since our wedding served to diminished the significance of our separation and soften its impact, I hoped.

Chapter 24

The day finally came when Celia's bother-in-law arrived with his truck. Over the course of a few hours, we dutifully loaded her things and said goodbye. On the next day we finished packing my belongings in a rented U-Haul moving van, which Barry drove. We filled a two-horse trailer with outdoor items as well, which I pulled behind the Blazer. Perro sat on the seat beside Barry and they became good friends over the next four days on the road. To help divert wasted and painful reflection on the past, I placed a picture of Victoria on the dash and immersed myself in a cross-country adventure with Barry. During the days on the road, we stopped at scenic lakeside spots along the way and brought out the Webber barbeque for unhurried feasts. We found motel rooms and stopped in good time at night, leaving ourselves time to relax over a beer.

On the last day, we stopped briefly to pick up the keys from my realtor. My excitement mounted as we approached the new ranch. The mental image I retained of it was nothing short of stunning and I hungered desperately for validation. Barry had not seen it yet. It was with nearly childish glee that I anticipated his reaction.

He liked the place a lot and decided to live with me for a while. We went to work buying two hundred calves to utilize the small feed yard for the winter and give him something to do. Barry's connection with the man who had guided us on that first tour of the mountains, three years previous, led to the idea of putting together a guiding outfit of our own. Our friend was no longer using his base camp, which he had a permit for, and we arranged to lease it from him. I remembered the long plateau of higher ground that looked out between the larch and spruce trees over a vast, grassy montane clearing with a creek meandering lazily in its midst.

In mid-November, I drove into Denver and met for lunch with Sherry Mason, the young lady who had been my assistant and lover some ten years previous. She was working for another commodity trading firm, had gotten married, and had two sons. It was nice, some of the old electricity was still there, and she said she always thought we might have an affair someday. I took it as a compliment but was not overly excited with the idea, realizing that my feelings for her had become more sisterly. She said the firm she worked for was trying to develop more business with cattle feeders and suggested I give her manager, Daniel Fox, a call to discuss possibilities. I was enticed by the implication that I had personal capital yet to be exploited, from my reputation as the local boy who had gone off to Chicago and New York, obviously accomplishing great things and accumulating valuable and worldly experience.

I called Daniel, a man I had barely heard of with respect to the business, and arranged to meet at his office. He seemed a quiet unassuming gentleman, and he easily agreed upon a three-month interim contract with an upfront fifteen thousand dollar retainer, predicated entirely on my record in the ten previous years. Sherry was delighted that we would work in the same office again and I assumed the cocky air of a man assured of proving his worth in a short time.

I planned a general blitz on the industry and began to make a few calls to some former contacts. Only after several deadpan responses was my memory jolted by reality. It had never been easy, and I had little of my former stamina for such activity. Besides that, it was a ninety-minute drive into the city. But I intended to play the game, showing up at the office several days a week and putting in enough time to demonstrate my commitment. My appearances soon dwindled in number, however, and, by the time the three months were up, I had not recruited a single new customer. Being preoccupied with the new priorities in my life, I simply let the arrangement drop without apology or explanation. Mr. Daniel Fox proved his stature as a gentleman by not raising a fuss over it or saying anything that might have embarrassed Sherry Mason.

Without realizing it I had crossed a last barrier of respectability, and it seemed to put a seal on the lowering of my standards. Consistent with that, I had developed a habit of drinking myself into oblivion at one of the seediest old hotel bars in the city. My long-time drinking friend from university days, Peter Kane, who had coincidentally moved back to the west as well, also made himself at home there. He associated with a group of his co-workers from a government building nearby and they frequently gathered at the bar for a liquid lunch, most of them not returning to work in the afternoons, which made them predictable companions. The switch in my preference for venues, from swank lounges and piano bars serving single-malt scotch, to pitchers of beer served on small, round, ratty terrycloth covered tables, I construed arrogantly as scoffing at pompous glitz, rather than recognizing the degeneration of conditions in which I felt I belonged.

Out on the ranch, I bolstered my self-confidence with playing another role. Time flew by with the excitement of buying fifteen horses and outfitting ourselves with riding saddles and pack saddles and all the other tack that we'd need to take guests on week-long mountain adventures. Victoria arranged to spend as much time as she could at the ranch and accompanied us as we attended horse and tack auctions, and planned in other ways to fulfill our vision of a wilderness camp and guiding operation.

On a sunny winter day in mid-December, just as I was preparing to leave the house for the barnyard and an inspection of my livestock inventory, the phone rang. It was Celia's mother. "Hello, Richard," she said. "I am calling to let you know that you are a father, that you have a beautiful daughter, and that both she and Celia are doing fine. Celia wanted you to know that she will be given the name Elizabeth Anne, as you and she had decided together."

I felt a powerful tug at my heart, and a nearly overwhelming submersion in guilt, and a desperate longing to be there for my wife, to share in this event. I was aware of the graciousness in my mother-in-law's voice and words, and felt drawn back into the family that had been so kind and welcoming. Of course, I could not express those sentiments. I consequently responded with a burst of loud enthusiasm and gratitude that was couched in the glib, but unvoiced, allusion that my absence was not in the least extraordinary. I hoped this lady for whom I had always had great respect would see it that way as well. My first response following the call was to relate the news to my brother. Almost simultaneously I began planning to visit my wife and baby. Just as quickly I became embroiled in the complexity of my emotional attachments.

My emotional dependency on Victoria's loyalty and commitment was almost crippling at times. Each time she left, my mind was fraught with anxiety about her return. Before each visit, I arrived early at the airport and fretted over her continued devotion until I could hold her in my arms again. I became easily jealous at any reference she made to other men, but tried very hard to hide it. When drinking, I was especially vulnerable to revealing that weakness. I found my only solace in observing that she often demonstrated a similarly inordinate degree of insecurity. My security sprang from her insecurity, but I worried that I may push her beyond the limit by announcing a trip to visit my wife and daughter. I decided upon visiting Victoria first for a few days, to ensure her of my devotion and explain that I had to do the right thing by going to see my newborn daughter. I planned a trip east and juggled my itinerary to fit hers, waiting until I arrived to explain the second leg. Staring out the window of the plane, it occurred to me that my life had acquired a tentative aspect, that apprehension prevailed where there had once been brazen confidence and a sense of being in control.

Victoria was only mildly disconcerted at my announcement. It was the turbulent state of my own emotions that led to my unreasonable state of mind and the quarrel we had during our last few hours together. It was our first, and the heaviness of it swamped me with lethargy for the remaining days of my trip. My visit with Celia and my daughter, despite the warm affection and overflowing goodwill I felt toward them, was subject to an undercurrent of anxiety about my future with Victoria, a sense of urgency about steering our precarious ship of romance back into a safe and calm harbor before it capsized. Nevertheless, I developed a strong attachment to my little girl. When I said goodbye, after holding Elizabeth a great deal over the three days I was there, and gazing into her eyes as she stared unknowingly but trustingly back into mine, I knew a large part of my heart forever belonged to her.

Back out west again, Victoria and I resumed our intoxicating togetherness and, with Barry's enormous enthusiasm, the three of us planned and worked toward a summer in the mountains. Early in the new year of nineteen eighty-nine, Victoria announced that she had been granted a transfer to Denver as her base with the airline. Two weeks later, Celia announced that she and Elizabeth were moving out west as well, because she had developed an attraction for the Rockies during our visits, and because she wanted our daughter to know her father. In early spring, they moved to the small resort town in the mountains where Celia and I had spent the summer two years earlier. Celia became immediately supportive of my newest adventure by putting together a range of menu suggestions for the camp. I travelled out to see her and Elizabeth, and she visited the ranch one weekend, which coincided with my parents being there. Occasions such as that had to be arranged around Victoria's comings and goings, which was currently less difficult because she was unusually busy, stockpiling her time off for our summer adventure.

Most of the time, Barry and I were left alone to enjoy casual days of practice packing and riding horses at the ranch, getting to know our neighbors at local community events, visiting our favorite saloon in the evenings, and reaching out for ideas and support for our new venture. We became quite well acquainted with a number of men who had years of experience with horses, packing, and mountain adventuring. Typical of their willingness to help us with advice and other more concrete contributions was Winston Holmes, a local cattleman, horse enthusiast, and trucker of nearly anything that needed moving from one place to another. Holmes' image from a distance was notably rectangular, his height of five feet eight inches being about twice his width, dimensions that described the whole length of his body, except for his head, which, when combined with his exceptionally stout neck, formed a smaller rectangle of the similar proportions which rested squarely upon the larger one. Closer up, his alert, light blue eyes and a mouth that seemed forever on the verge of laughter drew attention from his remarkable shape and left one anticipating a predictably cheerful and amusing opening line. That Winston got things done was soon apparent, as was his delight in the novel employment of a range of equipment for hauling things.

In mid-June, when we guessed the snow had finally melted in the valley that cradled our high-country camp, and the rivers that raged with the spring thaw had become fordable again, we arranged with Mr. Holmes for the trucking of our livestock and the enormous quantity of gear we would pack in on horses once there, and left for the mountains. Fortified by stony obstinacy, I hardened my heart as Perro howled at being tied up and left behind when we drove out of the yard. I had arranged with the neighbor kids to feed her and give her some attention while we were gone, but deep in my chest I suffered the pain of her abandonment. My knowledge that a dog could be a real handicap 'out there' if not experienced and disciplined was reinforced by stories of them running back to their owners when chased by bears they had inadvertently roused. As well, having a dog in close quarters while working with horses could invite a stray kick from time to time, and its unintended connection with a human. I knew that Perro was easily trainable, but I did not wish to appear soft and sentimental to my brother either, on the threshold of an undertaking that required rugged fortitude. I hoped she would get lots of attention from the kids and not miss me too much for too long.

We arrived at a clearing we used for our staging camp and unloaded everything. We had brought the Blazer and camper, as well as Victoria's small truck which she had donated to our use for the summer. The next day we began early to pack our entire camp on ten horses. The vehicles would remain behind as we trekked into the road-less wilderness. A half-dozen canvas wall tents for sleeping quarters and a larger kitchen tent with an asbestos stovepipe hole in the roof, groceries and cooking utensils, outdoor gear including Swede saw, axe, shovel, and extra rope, Yukon stove, and much more were carefully balanced and secured with basket or barrel hitches, covered with tarps and battened down with diamond hitches.

One of the horses, a sleek agile-looking Appaloosa, freshly loaded and tied to a tree, began bucking his pack off. He snapped the lead shank that had held him and proceeded to buck deliberately and efficiently until his load was scattered across a hundred feet of brush at the edge of the clearing, and the rigging that had secured his pack saddle was torn away and kicked free of his hind legs. When his back was completely bare, he stopped, shook himself refreshingly, and began grazing, as though it was all in a day's work. He had broken the packsaddle, which left us one short, and we were puzzled and perturbed at the somewhat ominous beginning. But we quietly gathered things up, picked another horse, and repacked the load. Only some weeks later did we gain further insight into the episode, when a visiting friend of Barry's pointed to the nearly invisible traces of spurs being repeatedly applied to the Appaloosa's shoulders, a professional bucking horse. "You gotta love horse traders," he smiled.

The trip into our base camp began almost immediately with the fording of a significant river, sometimes forcing shorter horses to swim a few strokes as their back-ends were sucked downstream by the powerful current. It consisted, subsequent to that, of a breathtaking six-hour ride through a verdant valley with mountains arching skyward on either side. Our first trip was more arduous than we expected future trips to be, because stretches of the main trail were still boggy from a heavier than normal seasonal runoff. We were forced to seek higher ground, often resorting to elk trails along steep, heavily treed, and rocky slopes. Because of those detours and a few repacking jobs that were at least partially a consequence of the rougher terrain, it took nine hours in all. Horses and riders alike were exhausted. But we were finally there in the midst of a dream come true.

It was a week before we had any guests arriving and we took five days of it to set up tents, cut wood, and familiarize the horses with hobbles so they could graze in the thousand acre meadow adjacent to the camp. Hobbles kept them from ranging too far and made catching them easier. We explored the immediate area as well, on foot and horseback, including the two connected alpine lakes that began about a half mile from the camp and offered cutthroat trout in such abundance that we could plan on lunch with certainty, taking a frying pan and butter with us. It was a piece of heaven.

It was a rugged frontiersman experience as well. Frosty mornings gave way to soothing heat from the sun by midday, but necessitated the wearing of a down-filled vest and heavy Storm Rider jacket upon emerging from the tent at the break of day. Casual work around camp permitted sneakers and lighter clothes, but most of the time we wore sturdy riding boots, heavier long-sleeved shirts, and blue jeans. Hefty jack knives hung conveniently from broad western belts, ready for quick alterations of equipment or the emergencies that could pop up when working with horses. Each time we went out on the trail, we donned heavy leather chaps and tied full-length oilskin raingear behind our saddles. Barry carried a twelve-gauge pump gun loaded with slugs. In my scabbard, with its stock at easy access just above my left knee, was a Winchester, model 94, 30-30, known for its sloppy but non-jamming lever action. Barry's choice of weapons was much harder hitting at close range than mine, and I determined to heed his words, "If you ever have to shoot a bear with that, keep shooting."

With our base camp ready to receive clients, we rode back down the valley to our staging camp, travelling much lighter on the return, unsaddled the horses, fed them with oats and hay bales we'd hauled in, and drove into town for refreshing showers and a sit-down restaurant meal. The next day we would pick up our first guests, seven Australian agriculture exchange students.

From the beginning, they demonstrated a devil-may-care attitude and were an ideal group to start off with. All of them had horseback riding experience and had worked with livestock on farms. They laughed and joked as we secured groceries and their duffle on the packhorses, and several helped with the saddling of their own horses, something we would not have permitted in the absence of their obvious competence. I only needed to prompt them to suck up the back cinches tighter than they could have imagined, to shift some of the strain from the horses' girths during steep climbs and, perhaps even more important, during sharp or sustained descents. It was not uncommon to see horses with severe chafing of their girths, sometimes swollen, bleeding, and out of commission, because of too much strain on a front cinch.

When the ten of us and our five pack animals set out, it was already noon on a glorious day and we trailed along jovially. Around two hours into the trip, we caught a glimpse of two riders coming toward us with a pack animal of their own. As the distance between us grew shorter, we decided to veer off the trail a few hundred feet to let them pass without interference, especially with our pack string. It was after they had passed that we noticed one member of our group was missing. Almost simultaneously, our heads turned collectively toward a racket further out in the bush. A single horse raced parallel to us, at a full gallop, with no evidence of a rider, leaping over clumps of brush and looking very much like a runaway. We watched in amazement as Gerry's hand appeared above the horse's back and pointed toward us in a mock pistol shooting display. Having been crouched behind the horse, supporting himself on one stirrup until then, he eased back into the saddle without apparent struggle, as his mount continued its flight underneath him. "Bloody rodeo clown," one of his friends scoffed, providing us with some insight.

"What on earth can you say to that?" I chuckled to Barry as he grinned from ear to ear.

It set the tone for the week. They loved the food and raved about the chocolate cake Victoria had mixed up and Barry cooked in the Yukon stove, a surprise celebration of my fortieth birthday. They fished, hiked on their own in the bush, and built themselves a cricket pitch with a trimmed tree branch for a bat and a roll of masking tape for a ball.

A new acquaintance and his wife, who lived a few miles from the ranch, had loaned us a decent looking dun colored gelding, "to put some miles on," they requested. He had bucked both of them off over the course of the previous year and actually fractured some of their bones in the process. And that was after some expensive training, they said. 'Gift Horse,' we named him. He was as gentle as could be, easy to catch, and stood quietly while we packed him. He was well-behaved on the trail and carried his heavy load with poise. On a day trip out of the camp, I decided to ride him. I reasoned that he'd put a few days of work in by then and was less likely to act up.

We'd been out about five hours and all had gone well. Then one of the girls near the back hollered out to announce that she had dropped her hat. We could see it laying on the trail a hundred feet behind her. It was on a part of the trail that crossed a steep shale incline for about a mile, so we told her to wait and I would go back and get it. Gift objected to turning around, and then refused to go back past the other horses. It wasn't optional, I informed him with a kick in the sides and a light snap of the reins across his rump. He reared up a bit, then again, and again, to the point where he could have gone over backwards on the uneven terrain. A few solid jabs with my spurs brought that dangerous activity to a halt. But in the next moment he began bucking headlong down the steep slope. It is easier to ride a bucking horse on a downslope in loose shale because he can't put much lift into it, but it certainly undermined our claim from a year ago that no horse was suicidal. The drawback was that, despite there being little threat of falling off, there was virtually no way to stop him. Leaning well back in the saddle to accommodate the treacherous gradient deprived me of significant leverage on his head. I considered that I might have to bale off.

We were several hundred feet down the mountain, and still going, when I came up with a solution. Fifty feet ahead, and just off to the right of our course, was a very large spruce tree on the otherwise naked slope. I thought that would probably stop him, and began to haul his head directly toward it. Moments later, still aboard a panting but stationary mount with his nose lodged against the tree trunk, I looked back up the hill, beyond the four feet of branches that were sticking out behind me, to see my companions sitting in silence and wondering what would happen next. Luckily, the heavy chaps, denim Storm Rider jacket, and tough Akubra hat had protected me from the abrasive bark and needles of the spruce boughs.

"Come on, Gift," I threatened through gritted teeth. "Let's see how well you can buck going uphill." Adrenaline pumped as I pulled him backward with firmness and quickly spun his head upward to face the others. I knew what a horse could do and the sharp incline was less than prohibitively steep. It was my turn now, and I used the spurs on him, then again, and again, to ensure a momentum that would not cease until we crested the trail once more. He scrambled and lunged and rocks flew, as I leaned well forward over the horn, but it was an easy ride. When I looked up to the sound of the Aussies' cheers, I saw that they were scoring the ride with open hands thrown in the air, fingers spread wide. "That's a ten, mate, if I ever saw one," Gerry drawled with a delighted grin, amidst other raucous declarations from his cohorts. Gift was soaking wet with sweat, but quite back to his gentlemanly self. I was more exhilarated than I thought possible and struggled to maintain a composed nonchalance.

Back in town at the end of the week, we partied with our new friends and said goodbye to them the next morning.

Victoria went back to work. Barry and I met the five people we would be entertaining for the next week. They were not as eager and exuberant as the first guests had been, but a pleasant enough group who needed more help and supervision than the last. They were passively interested in all aspects of the process of getting to camp and always grateful for the meals we prepared. Barry, being an excellent outdoor cook in any case, developed surprising skill with the heavy cast iron grill we frequently placed over the open fire.

Along with the good food, two other trends were developing in our camp. Barry had played guitar and sung in a country music band during his late teens and early twenties, and he was more than willing to share his talents while we sat around the campfire on chilly mountain evenings, much to the enjoyment of guests and myself. He knew I loved a song called *Night Rider's Lament*, a ballad concerning a letter a young cowboy received from back home and his older pal's response to it, and he sang it beautifully. The refrain, the words of which he altered to fit our circumstances, went like this:

"Why do you ride for no money
And why do you pack for short pay
You ain't getting' nowhere
And you're losin' your share
Boy, you must've gone crazy out there.
Ah but they've never seen the northern lights
They've never seen a hawk on the wing
They've never seen spring hit the great divide
And they've never heard ol' camp cookie sing.
He said now
Why don't they ride for their money
Tell me why don't they pack for short pay
They ain't getting' nowhere
And they're losin' their share
Son, they all must be crazy down there."

I felt great affection for my brother and I delighted in the truth expressed by the words. Sometimes my eyes watered with joy and gratitude.

The other developing trend was soon evidenced by metallic grey circles on the bottoms of our pack boxes, made by the cans of beer I insisted on hauling in. I repeatedly made certain of other more compact sources of alcohol as well, because it took a lot of beer to satisfy the demand over six days, particularly with the Aussies, for example. Because I contemplated shortages with considerable anxiety, I usually put a bottle or two of Crown Royal aside as a private supply.

Just as the demand for booze was unpredictable, so was the effect it would have on me by the end of the night. It had been that way for years and had caused all sorts of regrettable outcomes, but I had not stopped. On the third night with our second group of guests, Barry began playing his guitar around dark. Everyone huddled comfortably around the fire except me, because I felt restless and wanted a little space. I moved well back of the others, into the shadows nearer the edge of the bank that dropped off about fifty feet to the meadow below the camp. I had been sipping a bit of whiskey in the afternoon and evening, as well as sharing a few casual beers with the others. I didn't think I had drunk a lot and it caught me by surprise when I found myself wavering on my feet. Suddenly I tipped backwards and tumbled part way down the cliff, through thick undergrowth, until I came to a halt against a short but sturdy pine tree. I grabbed the tree in an attempt to get to my feet, pain throbbing around the lacerations in my face. As I reconsidered, deciding to sit a moment and think my position through, my hand came away from the trunk gooey with sap. The sound of Barry's guitar and voice continued uninterrupted and gave me hope that no one had noticed my disappearance or suspected my humiliating circumstances.

I could not face returning to the fire, so I determined to make my way further along the incline and climb back up some hundred feet away in the vicinity of my tent. I stumbled forward on the steep and slippery terrain, obstructed by tree trunks and lashed by tangled undergrowth, everything shrouded in darkness. I feared twisting an ankle or being jabbed in the eye, but I eventually pulled myself into the clearing near my tent, crawled inside, and passed out.

I awoke in my clothes the next morning and appeared at the cook tent where Barry was already busy with breakfast. After wishing him a good morning, I turned away and went to check on the horses. Nothing was said about the night before, but I cringed at the potential embarrassment of the incident for the rest of week. I also worried over the deterioration in my sense of balance.

During the pleasant sunny afternoon of that day, after we had caught a half-dozen cutthroat trout and were enjoying a lunch cooked over a wood fire on the shore of the lake, I found myself suffering from some unidentifiable insecurity and longing for affirmation of Victoria's devotion. Chatter among our happy visitors, which Barry seemed to enjoy wholeheartedly and participated in with enthusiasm, served me as no more than a buffer against outright panic. We would not get back to town for another three days.

Chapter 25

I desperately hoped Victoria and company would be there when we got back to the hotel in town. She was expected to show up with three of her flight attendant co-workers and my long-time friend, Bob Hawk. An inveterate opportunist, Bob had jumped at the chance for a mountain adventure immediately after I informed him about the other guests. It had taken him no time to envision the prospects. Sometime around last Christmas, I had heard that he and Karen had 'split the sheets' – puzzling, I thought, because they had always had such an easy going, partying, dope-smoking, share and share alike, laissez-faire marriage.

They were not at the hotel when we arrived, but I began immediately to anticipate her arrival in time for dinner and I went to clean up. A good friend of Barry's was joining us for the next week as well, and he was there to greet us. While the three of us ate dinner together, I revised my hopes once more, now anxiously expecting them in time to have a few drinks in the evening, during which, finally, all my excruciating anxiety about Victoria's loyalty would be relieved. I had a few drinks over dinner, but tried to hold off until they arrived. Finally around seven, after Barry, his friend, and I had finished our dinner and had a few more drinks, I could take it no longer. I called to make sure they had at least departed on the four-hour drive. Victoria answered and assured me they were having a very good time at her place in Denver. They'd eaten a steak dinner, were well into partying mode, and would leave first thing in the morning. I swallowed my disappointment and stifled the indignation I felt welling up. I envisioned Bob having convinced them to participate in one of his freewheeling sexual excursions. Suffering a miserable state of abandonment, I got very drunk.

The next morning I awoke to muffled conversation between Barry and his friend. We had shared a room with two double beds and Barry had slept on a cot. I was lying on my left side and my left hip felt cold. With horrified anticipation I reached down to feel the sheets with my right hand. I had wet the bed and it seemed impossible that the smell of urine hadn't drifted into the nostrils of my roommates. I could only hope not, and forced a cheerful, "Good morning," to them. I pulled the bedclothes tightly around me to contain the evidence while I shared in the mutual chatter of waking up. I determined to stay where I was until they left for breakfast, which took another agonizing half hour. After I got out of the bed, I made sure my embarrassing situation was hidden as much as possible, since we would be returning to the room to get our things. I showered and went down to join them.

The three of us left for the staging camp to feed and water the horses, and began saddling up in preparation for the day's ride in. When Victoria and our guests finally arrived, we sorted their duffle into balanced loads and packed up. I remained in a foul mood and objected unnecessarily to the bulk and weight of some of their belongings. I persisted for the balance of the day, managing a resentful and punishing snubbing of Victoria, feigned enthusiasm for seeing Bob again, and heart-winning joviality with Victoria's attractive friends. I had a headache and, when we got into camp, I began to drink again.

Victoria said she wanted to talk, which I thought would be about my attitude. Instead she pleaded, "Your friend Bob has been pursuing my friends to the point of embarrassment. He seems to expect them to be easily available. It has made them quite uncomfortable at times."

Even as we talked I could overhear him presenting them with the idea of skinny-dipping in the lake. I considered that it would be difficult to say anything to Bob and felt a little putout that her friends considered themselves too good for mine. I tried to be reasonable and said, "I will think about it. Meanwhile they are adults who have almost certainly been around some, and should be able to look after themselves."

After dinner and a bit of drinking, well before everyone else tired of the campfire and Barry's music, Victoria and I went to our tent where my general animosity and her annoying concerns fueled an argument. I reached for the Crown Royal to top off my already advanced inebriation. By the time the others retired, I was drunk and using foul language that was not contained by the canvas walls of the tent. I determined by the mix of voices that Barry had been invited to the girls' tent, perhaps for the protection they felt they needed, and that Bob must have gone to his own alone. Too drunk to grasp reality, I continued on with my loud obnoxious reproach, stubbornly, stupidly and vindictively denying Victoria's begging for my return to sanity, until Barry shouted out, "That's enough. Keep it down."

Fortunately, that was a low point, and the remorse I suffered the next day was enough to change my attitude to one of careful good behavior. On the third night it snowed a few inches and we awoke in a mountain wonderland. Victoria and I walked a mile to catch the horses in the morning and fell in love again with each other and our shared dream. We caught two with the halters we'd taken along for the purpose, climbed on, and rode them bareback into camp at an easy lope.

At the end of that trip, Bob, Victoria, and I left for the ranch, the flight attendants returned to work, and one of the girls from the previous group was going out to spend the week with Barry, as we had no paying guests booked. Because the grazing was better, they trailed the horses back into our basecamp. I knew my brother was looking forward to a few quiet and restful days.

As we neared home at the end of the four-hour drive, I could hardly contain the anxiety I felt regarding Perro's wellbeing, and I made up my mind not to leave her again. When we drove into the yard, my eyes searched the area where I had left her. She wasn't there. I hoped the neighbors had her at their place and, as soon as we unloaded a few things, I drove over to inquire. The children's father greeted me at the door with his usual friendly smile, but soon began to relate his best guess at the events surrounding the dog's disappearance. "She often howled," he said, "even though the kids spent time with her. We had checked on her in the morning, about ten days ago, but that day there was a large gathering of people at the property next door. She became especially distressed when there were people nearby and we think someone probably came over and turned her loose. We were gone all day and found her missing when we returned. We think they must have taken her with them."

"I'm sure the kids did their best and I don't want you to feel responsible in any way," I said. I turned away feeling heartbroken at the loss and bitterly remorseful about abandoning her as I had. Perro seemed like the last tangible connection I had with my marriage, and the happiness I had known with Celia. As I drove slowly back to the ranch house, I leaned over the steering wheel and moaned aloud, "I love you, Perro, and I hope you are happy wherever you are." I hoped she had gone with someone who would care for her. I simultaneously feared, for a moment, that the neighbor's story was a fabrication to spare me some sadder and more heartrending truth.

As I entered the house, Victoria turned toward me, asking what had happened. She was visibly concerned and her words were heavy with sadness and sympathy. Rather than accept her compassion and seek solace in it, I only replied irritably that someone had stolen the dog. I kept my despair to myself, rejecting the soothing warmth of connecting with another human being, because I could not allow anyone to come that close. It seemed appropriate that my sorrow be preserved in its purest, most searing form as an enduring punishment for my desertion of Perro, my loyal, innocent, and trusting companion, and my desertion of Celia, too. I remained in a surly mood for the duration of our time together, and immediately after my long-time friend Bob Hawk left, I regretted not having a more lighthearted visit with him. He had come a long way to see me and he had no reason to pass this way again.

In any case, my remorse in that regard was not enough to alter my miserable attitude toward Victoria and I found myself complaining, with demeaning nit-picking obstinacy, that her dog made a habit of urinating on the wheels of my Blazer. She said nothing in reply and a few hours later I saw her through the kitchen window, on her knees washing the tires. Observing her humiliation made me sad, and I regretted my abusive whining, but I said nothing more to her about it. The next morning, she drove out of the yard to catch a flight to somewhere, and I headed back to the mountains.

Barry and his friend, Nancy, looked like wet rags when they rode into the clearing and up to the corrals at the staging area on Friday afternoon. Quite uncharacteristically, he complained of a terribly cool, rainy, and snowy week in the high country and a treacherous trail on his way out. He was quite down, as though he had been given the dirty end of a stick, so I offered to take care of the horses and they went into town to clean up and relax until the following day. I could sense his urgency to get under a hot shower and I knew very well how good it would feel. I don't think the guilt I felt over his circumstances was justified, but I was burdened with it anyway, in addition to my other regrets.

We packed up and left the staging area for the base camp on Sunday. Five guests had paid for the six-day adventure. The pleasant group included a couple from San Francisco and three young adults who were good friends, two males and the sister of one of them. On the first day in, we went for a day ride into the high country beyond the lakes south of the camp. Our course wound upward, back and forth across the rocky bed of a small creek that tumbled down from its origins high above the tree line. As we followed it higher, we were often forced to climb well up the sides of the gorge and work our way around granite outcroppings, thickets of stunted spruce and clumps of wiry dwarf willow, to avoid the sheer walls and chasms that frequently blocked our passage nearer the bottommost levels.

The ravine gradually gave up its rugged steepness, the confining sides fanned outward, and the streambed turned a lush mossy green. Ahead was the year-round realm of the ptarmigan, the marmot, and the mountain goat: a vast sloping plain of tundra, where summer was brief and winters harsh, where a chill howling wind could blow in a snow squall without warning any time of year. I wondered to myself, at such transition points, if our guests knew how fortunate they were to be entering the alpine, if they knew how few people ever experienced the magnificence of the high country. That day the temperature hovered around seventy degrees. The sky was a radiant sapphire dome that met the horizon well below our viewpoint. The noonday sun breathed warmth and vibrant life into tiny brilliantly hued flowers that dotted the landscape.

Barry pointed to our two o'clock. "There are some rams sunning themselves beneath that rock ledge about seven hundred yards out, looks like a few good ones in the bunch." I took my binoculars out of the saddlebag and confirmed his guess.

"I wonder if we could hike around this side" – he pointed to our eleven o'clock – "and get above them, then come down with that overhang blocking their line of sight and get a good look at them." Everyone was enthused with the idea, even after we explained that it would probably take three or four hours. Trekking around mountains often involves distances that are unimaginable when one first sets out. We rode the horses back about a half mile, and tied them to the first trees that were sturdy enough. Unless we wanted to walk back down the rough two-hour stretch we had covered so far, it was imperative they be tightly secured with a short lead, nose high to preclude attempts at grazing, and with separation that ensured no entanglements. It was going to be a long wait and they would be fidgety before we returned.

We loosened the front cinches a bit and hung our chaps and spurs on the saddles. We decided to risk a few hours without rain gear, to lighten our loads because of the substantial climb ahead of us. After an hour, the view opened upon a breathtaking and infinite panorama of peaks dotted with glistening white glaciers beneath a clear blue sky. The down side of the mountain abruptly disappeared just beyond our position, leaving the impression of a sheer vertical drop with thousands of feet between us and the forested subalpine below. Another hour passed before we began a slow descent, as quietly as possible, toward the outcropping. From the changed perspective we could not even be certain it was the same location and we would not know if the rams had moved on until we were much closer. We worked our way down, emphasizing the importance of careful silence to our guests, who, until this point in their lives, had rarely had cause for it. There was an updraft wafting in our favor but it was variable. I knew the bighorn sheep's senses of hearing and smell were so highly developed and fine-tuned it often seemed they were alarmed by some sixth sense when a predator entered their immense open range.

We were very close. Barry and I signaled to each other that, once they discovered us, they would run up the mountain, their habitual avenue of escape. We inched closer, to within a hundred and fifty feet of the ledge. Then a smaller ram suddenly appeared to our left where none had stood a second before. We froze. But his large, all-encompassing eye, a glistening orb with electronic sensitivity, had captured a glimpse of danger and he took a few nervous steps parallel with the slope, enough to signal the small herd. In seconds they were frantically surging from directly beneath us and turning uphill, their mammoth heads propelled forward by compact but powerful bodies. There were seven in total and we agreed that at least two had full three hundred and sixty degree curls in their horns. They moved almost effortlessly, higher and higher in their practiced escape, loose shale rattling away from their scampering hooves, until their powdery white rear-ends disappeared completely in a landscape which seemed to preclude that possibility.

The remaining descent to the trees where we'd tied the horses was effortless. Our single pack animal for the day, a mule we had named Fitzsimmons, had been relieved of her two panniers earlier and now we ravenously unpacked our lunch from them. As we ate we shared in the aftermath of a fulfilling and fascinating mountain adventure, a rarity indeed. On the way down, as he and I rode along side-by-side and slightly ahead of the guests, Barry informed me that he was baffled by the married fellow's comment, "I'm surprised we don't see more wildlife."

Unlike me, Barry hadn't spent much time away from this primal reality, its fragile and tentative existence and its inhabitants' uncanny instinct for invisibility. The comment bewildered him and he interpreted it as a lack of gratitude for our efforts and for the good timing we'd experienced with the rams. I wanted to help him understand, without admitting that I had once lost that intimacy with nature myself. I said, "It is curious that people envision wild animals placing themselves on display, just wandering around casually in an environment where life and death are often only separated by seconds. Growing up and living in the city, they could not possibly know. It is only sad that they cannot fully appreciate the exceptional nature of today as it was."

"Speaking of wildlife," he said, "I didn't tell you about the bear in the staging camp last week." I turned my head toward him with interest as he continued, "I heard something outside the camper around midnight. It was a warm night so I'd left the door open, except for the screen door. I sat up enough to see the door and realized a bear was sniffing through the screen, his nose right on it. While I was thinking of reaching for my gun, he backed away, went around behind, and climbed the tree we'd backed it up against. From there, he jumped on the roof and peered through the vent, like he'd been there before. I hollered and he climbed down and left." Then he grinned boyishly through an otherwise cool veneer. "You'll thank me for not trying to shoot him through the roof of your trailer."

I returned the grin, thanked him for his self-restraint, and suggested we'd best report it to the wardens at the forestry office. "I've done that," he said, "and they promised they'd bring out a trap."

When we returned to the staging camp from our week in bush, we discovered a three hundred gallon tank with a heavy spring-loaded door that stood open at the front and, eight feet beyond the door, inside at the far end, some scraps of beaver carcass hanging on a hook and stinking to high heaven. Because we decided they needed to be fed more frequently, it was my turn to spend the night in the camper, feed and water the horses in the morning, and leave for town by midday.

BANG! The sound ruptured the dead silence and reverberated in the clearing, around midnight. It lingered, echoing back from the thick forest, as I sat up and swung my legs out of bed. I reached for the flashlight and pulled on my pants and shirt. I put a chew of Copenhagen in my lip and levered a bullet into the chamber of the 30-30, then let the hammer down carefully. As soon as I stepped out in the cool air, I could hear the rasping, angry breathing of the captive. Rifle in my right hand, with the hammer pulled back again, and flashlight in my left, I inched toward the big metal cage. From twenty feet back, I squatted and shined the light inside. A grizzly, on the small side, sat hunched against the far end, snorting and slobbering in a fit of rage.

I think, because of my recurring acquaintance with aloneness, I had come to have no fear of my own death or demise. I had felt abandoned myself, and I had felt the searing culpability that follows abandoning others. The combined effect had created a void where confidence of enjoying the future might have resided. I easily opted for living intensely, with reckless abandon. It was not a selfless, mature, and healthy absence of fear, not the phenomenon known as courage, like a soldier who is willing to die for his country. It was more like self-abandonment, combined with a crazed desire to experience life at its rawest and most brutish base. I think, subconsciously, I invited a violent clash with nature, dared it to try me.

That's why, alone in a dark mountain valley with a trapped grizzly, I felt excited but not rattled, intensely interested and open to nameless risk. I was truly pleased with my solitude. I gradually moved forward until I squatted on the ground within inches of the door. A long rumbling growl accompanied each of his exhaled breaths, as I spoke to the bear playfully, "You've got yourself in mess now, haven't you?" In a moment of absent-mindedness I reached out to support myself, to rest my hand on the metal bars through which I was observing his several hundred pounds of wrath. Caution and common sense prevailed in the instant that followed and I adjusted my feet instead. In the same moment, with the speed of light, long piercing claws protruded two inches beyond the bars and an ugly snotty slobbering nose and mouth snorted a death wish between them. His pig-eyes seemed to water with the fury of disappointment. My hand would have been punctured, perhaps even seized, had I not altered my initial impulse.

The unhappy prisoner snarled and wheezed continuously through the night, while I had a decent enough sleep, all things considered. Once in town, I told Barry first and then we contacted the ranger who had left his number with the trap. Later in the day, we headed back to the hills with our troop for the week, three hometown friends of Barry's whom we had been happy to have join us as non-paying guests. As we arrived, the ranger was hooking onto the big tank that still contained the grizzly.

"I don't think this is the end of your bear trouble. I think it's a black bear that's been climbing onto the trailer and breaking into your stores," he said.

"Does that mean you'll be bringing the trap back?" I asked.

"Hell no, we got bear problems in towns and no more traps. You guys *want* to be in the bush with the bears, those people don't. They're everywhere this year, black and grizzly. All the rain we've had has slowed berry development and they're panicking over getting enough to eat before they hibernate. You'll have to take care of things yourselves."

"What do you suggest we do, I mean, if he continues to wreck things around here?" Barry asked.

"Shoot the son-of-a-bitch, I guess," he smirked and got in his truck. "Take care, fellas," he said as he glanced back through the open window. The suspension that supported the very effective contraption, and linked its frame to the axles, squeaked repeatedly as it obediently followed his truck and disappeared with its cargo into the initial bend of the narrow trail.

The first night we were in camp was a social affair and the drinking started right away. I didn't notice, however, that the others were sipping their drinks slowly and generally enjoying conversation. It often happened that my approach was more determined, more gluttonous I suppose. Barry decided to say something before it was too late, or before someone else did. "They didn't bring a lot of booze, you know, and the rate you're going, you'll drink it all up on them."

With all the excitement over the bears, I had forgotten to replenish my supply while in town. Fortunately, I planned to ride out midweek and meet Victoria, then we'd ride back in together. I anxiously hoped she would remember to bring more whiskey with her.

Although it only took about four hours to ride down the valley to the staging area, where Victoria would not be arriving for at least another six hours, I couldn't wait any longer. Socializing without a drink or two was becoming more uncomfortable and I craved only to sit in solitude on my favorite horse, a bay gelding I had named Samson. For the first few miles, the vastness of the mountain wilderness provided a sort of cosmic interlude. The single saddle horse I was trailing out for Victoria followed easily and Samson was a master at setting his pace to accommodate a whole pack string. And yet, as I went along without a single mishap, my mind was tormented. To ease my restlessness a bit, I stopped to drink from a little brook, put in a fresh chew, and walked for a while. I looked forward to seeing Victoria, but with the objective of satisfying a sorry dependency as much as greeting someone I loved. Despair had become a subtle backdrop to every other state of mind I tried to enjoy. Just before we came to the last river crossing between us and the camp, I tossed the reins over Samson's neck and swung myself back into the saddle. I noted the ease with which I did it, all in one seamless motion. I remembered the good feeling it had given me two years ago, when Celia and I had first engaged in mountain life. My boots dragged in the water and cooled my feet as we forded our way toward the clearing on the far bank.

I saw a flash of movement through the open flap of the wall tent where we stored a few non-food supplies. We always left it open to preserve the tent because large omnivorous intruders could slash a canvas wall open with no effort at all and barge in through their own entrance. As soon as the mid-size black scoundrel realized he was no longer alone, he scurried out of the tent, lumbered around to the back of it, and disappeared into the bush at the north perimeter. The horses gazed upon the scene without alarm, as I did, until I urged Samson on toward the corral where I dismounted and hitched them both to the top rail. As I unbuckled my chaps and tossed them across the saddle, I noted the Winchester in the scabbard which hung at Samson's left side. Not expecting another visitor, I left it there and walked over to the supply tent to get a few flakes of hay from a square bale. A can of WD-40 lay empty at the entrance, punctured by sharp claws and sucked dry by a rubbery slithering mouth. "Pigs!" I expressed my irritation over the damage and disorder the bear had left behind.

My arms full of hay, I started back toward the horses. To my astonishment, the bear had circled the clearing and was coming back in at the south end, to my one o'clock. The horses were a hundred feet away at my ten o'clock, and so was the rifle. Ambling casually, not intimidated in the least by human presence, the invader headed straight for the tent again. He obviously felt right at home and viewed me as the trespasser. I recalled the advice of people who had survived direct encounters: "Talk to them."

"Maybe you better fuck off, bear," I uttered repeatedly in a calm ordinary voice, intending that the calmness of all involved should prevail. I hoped he understood, but I felt assured he wasn't going to alter his course, except perhaps to become more aggressive toward me. In the same instant, my mind was on gripping the trusty 30-30 and levering a bullet into the chamber. My heart pounded in my chest and ears, as I side-stepped in an arc that preserved as much distance between us as possible, but which ultimately led me back to the horses whose stances had now assumed some rigidity. Their ears pointed briskly in the same direction as their curious but not yet startled eyes. I kept my eyes on the bear and hoped the equine instinct for flight didn't result in snapped lead shanks and a panicked retreat, which would leave me particularly vulnerable. As long as they hung around, the bear would not likely consider approaching the larger animals. As I drew closer, I talked to them, too.

When I dropped the hay just out of his reach, Samson returned a low rumbling murmur through his nose and shifted his glance toward me. It takes a lot of excitement to dislodge food from the top of a horse's priority list. Finally there, I brushed his right shoulder with my hand and promised, "That's right, old buddy, all's well."

Slowly, while keeping an eye on the advancing culprit, I reached across the back of my loyal pony and with relief grasped the wooden stock. With mounting excitement, I stepped a half-dozen paces away from the horses, working the slack lever action evenly and noiselessly to slip ammunition into place and cock the firing pin. The bear had reached the tent just then and stopped, looking in my direction to assess his risk before helping himself to more of our belongings.

The thunderous explosion cleaved the utter stillness of the valley and barked back from the rocky slopes at the perimeter. I levered another shell into position, noting the likely effectiveness of my first shot. In the same instant, I adjusted my gaze to observe that the horses had only jerked their heads and stirred their feet a bit. A black hulk lay motionless, save

351

the sorry repetitive kicking of one hind leg, testament to a life that dwindled with the expiring nervous system. It didn't appear warranted but, with Barry's warning fresh in my mind, I took careful aim and squeezed the trigger. Death did not respond. I felt briefly that I had tarnished the perfection of the moment with that expression of doubt.

I brushed the hay under the horses' noses with my foot and extended their leads so they could reach it. I walked over to the carcass and noted the sheen of the healthy black coat. I noted the blood that had trickled from just left of his right eye, stone dead on the first shot. Maybe I shouldn't have tried a headshot, but I had. The second bullet had gone through his neck and lodged in the tin wall of a spare Yukon stove we hadn't hauled into the base camp. I looked at the cans of food he had pried open and sucked clean. I picked up a can of tuna that had deep creases in its top where nail-hard claws and powerful incisors had remained frustrated.

I heard men's voices. It was illegal to shoot a bear without a hunting license, which I couldn't have gotten at that time of year in any case. I quickly unfolded a plastic tarpaulin and spread it over the evidence. Then I walked over to the camper and deposited the rifle behind it, because I had not unlocked the door yet. I made a show of strolling calmly toward the horses, just as the men exited the bush. "You hear a couple shots?" one man asked.

"No, I didn't," I said, demonstrating little interest in the question as I reached with measured pretense to adjust a cinch.

"Must have come from back the other way," the same man concluded as they turned hesitantly to retrace their steps.

"Maybe," I said, still unbelieving that anyone had been in the vicinity.

Just as soon as they had disappeared, I walked back to the trailer, anxious to inspect the mayhem I had glimpsed on my preoccupied pass a few minutes earlier. The side window frame had been pried free and lay twisted on the ground, the glass shattered. The screen, which had represented the only remaining obstacle, had presented no resistance to swiping, tearing claws. In the interior, under the window, was the table surrounded on three sides by a cushioned seat that could be transformed into another bed. The foam cushions were missing completely, clenched, pulled out through the open window and dragged away. The smell of food that had been cooked in the trailer, bacon for example, may have been the attraction. He never managed to get bodily inside, fortunately, because the window opening was too high off the ground, and the hole in the roof, where the vent had been ripped from its hinges, was too small. "Bastard, you got yours," I muttered vindictively.

Just then Victoria drove in and I began to scheme at divulging the tale with the greatest possible impact. I led her over to the tarp and pulled it back. She hardly seemed surprised and enquired rather calmly as to the details. Disappointed in her reaction, but still pleased with the event, and looking forward to sharing it with Barry, I spread the tarp over my prize again, tied her few things behind her saddle, and we started back.

Barry, when I announced the news, seemed almost indignant. "Isn't that something," he retorted. "I spent good money on a guide a few years back to kill a bear, and you managed to shoot one under natural conditions."

I sensed that both of them harbored resentful feelings toward my rather heroic adventure. I wondered if a backdrop of irresponsibility, too many drunken embarrassments, and the leadership role I insisted upon, but didn't deserve, were behind their subdued, perhaps even obstinate, responses.

His next comment was only slightly friendlier. "Too bad you didn't skin the bear and salvage the hide; must have been in top condition in advance of winter."

"Yes, I suppose I should have," I responded, not wanting to admit that I really did not know how to do it.

The day after the bear incident, Victoria and I stayed in camp while Barry took his friends for a ride. We went for a walk, during which I decided we should have a sexual romp on a mossy hillside, without any romantic preliminaries. Victoria looked a little bewildered as I became physical with her and began removing her clothes, but she didn't resist. Soon after we had lain down, I became horrified with the realization that I could not get an erection because my motive had almost certainly been domination and a display of prowess. The next minute, she was lying on her back and laughing, which I took as an insult. I said I didn't think it was funny and pulled my pants up. Nothing more was said about it, but I believed the humiliation I suffered was a kind of evening up for the dog-peeing-on-the-tires incident that had occurred during our brief stay at the ranch a few weeks ago.

When we got back to the staging camp three days later, the carcass had started to smell. I wanted to report it as soon as we got into town and I called the ranger. "Oh, for Christ's sake," he blurted back on the line, as though he wished I hadn't told him. Settling down, he continued, "Well, I can't do anything with it. Just drag it back in the bush with a horse or the truck. Get it out of sight and then watch out for the damn grizzlies. They'll smell it from miles away." When we returned the following day we did as he suggested and, although the carcass almost completely disappeared over the next week, we encountered no more bears in that area.

Having no guests for the week, Barry, Victoria, and I trailed half-a-dozen horses into the base camp, where they could take advantage of the better grazing conditions. These six had been losing weight on the watery mountain grass and they still had plenty of work to do, especially packing the camp out. Barry rode his horse back out the next day to tend to the horses we left at the staging camp, while Victoria and I stayed on with the rest. During these days alone with her, my efforts shifted unexplainably toward demonstrating my courage. Mid-morning of the second day, I spotted a large boar grizzly passing through the trees about fifty yards above the camp. I called Victoria and pointed him out to her. While she was aghast at the proximity of the beast, I immediately suggested we run ahead of him to get a picture. She didn't think that was smart, but I insisted she carry the camera and I would carry the gun. Secretly, I hoped we would not succeed in getting close to him. It was dangerous to play around with a large animal like that, stupid really, and the small rifle was not an effective defense. I couldn't let Victoria know that fear had gripped me, but that's why I didn't hurry after him and gave up rather easily.

That afternoon I got quite drunk. We'd decided to have a nap in the tent, but moments later the horses came bounding into camp with their hobbles on and bells ringing, as they did occasionally, hoping to get some oats. I got up to have a look at them and caught hold of the Appaloosa, the professional bucking bronc, which we had not used all summer and permitted to follow along as he pleased because of his destructive prior training. He never caused any trouble, quite a gentleman when he wasn't saddled. In fact, one of Barry's friends, who had some experience as a bronc rider, rode him on several occasions while he was in camp, always without a saddle to avoid entanglement if the horse blew up, but he never did. Otherwise we had left him alone, planning on his immediate disposal when we returned in fall. But the horse was truly an athletic specimen and made you want to ride him. I had drunk just enough to feel all-powerful and decided to throw a bridle on him and climb on. His step was quick, lithe, and powerful. I called to Victoria to come and see. As she poked her head out of the tent she exclaimed, "Please get off him. I don't want you to get hurt while we're here alone." Once again, I didn't heed the caution she expressed, but I didn't push my luck to an extreme either. His manner was pleasant, whether you were on the ground or on his back, and he responded to neck reining with immediacy. I rode him back and forth at a walk, never more, and finally slid off. As my feet hit the ground I was swamped with panicky relief, as though I had just escaped a shark attack. I pretended an attitude of self-satisfied triumph that I didn't feel. I continued to drink the rest of the day and don't remember going to bed.

Chapter 26

The following morning, we threw the saddles on the horses and headed down the valley, six of them tied 'nose to tail' behind Samson. Actually, they were not tied nose to tail, as some outfitters literally strung packhorses together, because we thought it abusive for a pokey member of a string to be putting painful strain on the tail of the horse ahead of him. We tied the lead shanks to a loop of lighter rope that attached to the forks at the back of the pack saddle on the horse directly ahead, spreading the force of pulling back, if there was any, between the leader's girth and the back cinch. Sometimes there were brutal yanks from behind and our method resulted in snapped loops, which were quite easily repaired, rather than the excruciating loss of hair, skin, and bone from a horse's tail.

There had been some heavy rain showers during the previous three days and it had rained nearly all night. That meant we'd be slogging along some wet trails, and some of the creeks we needed to cross would be swollen into rivers with unpredictable bottoms. Roughly two hours into the trip we came upon such a creek: the roiling surge had swelled to about eighty feet across, overflowing its banks and bending the brush and small trees along its edge to almost horizontal. The gently sloping entry to the ford was about fifty feet wide, and the exit on the opposite bank was just as wide. But danger existed on the down-river extreme of the exit, the outer limit of opportunity to gain a dry footing once across. The bank rose abruptly and the water rushed alongside at a depth of six feet, precluding any prospect of climbing out. Stories of riders and horses being swept away by raging mountain watersheds flashed through my mind. A man and his horse had both died in the spring, only a hundred miles to the north.

Nonetheless, in a single moment of negligence, I allowed Samson to enter the water nearer the downside of the ford, meaning that we had less room to maneuver against the current, less chance of arriving on the other side in a position to safely get out again. We were irrevocably committed to the crossing before I realized what I had done. I turned my saddle horse's nose upstream, as much as I could without hampering his ability to make way at the same time. But I had no control over the pack string, which began to swing further downstream behind me. My attempt to drag them back from the brink, by leaning over in the saddle and heaving on the lead animal's halter shank, was only dragging Samson with them. The force of the water was overpowering us. At more than five feet deep, the horses' feet were unable to gain sufficient traction. It became obvious that we would not make it. I realized how helpless they would be, tied together as they were. I envisioned the shorter horses being sucked under and eventually pulling the others with them. Well, I decided before it was too late, there was no point going down with them. I let the rope slip from my hand and focused my anxious reliance on the steady powerful exertion beneath me. The stocky bay stretched his nose forward just above the surface and waded slowly, persistently, toward the opposite shore. He finally lumbered free.

Victoria was holding back tightly on the reins of her impatient and fidgeting dapple-grey, his instinctive fear of being abandoned by the rest of the herd mounting each minute. She hadn't let him enter the river yet and I called across, "You may as well let him go, just be sure to enter on the high side to give him room." I could tell she was fighting her own fear and I watched anxiously. She knew from experience that you could not look down into the water, that you must keep your eyes focused above and beyond it, to avoid the mesmerizing effect that can draw you right off your horse. The grey slogged ahead calmly and steadily, and she was soon beside me without mishap. Meanwhile, the six members of the string were lodged together like large lengths of driftwood against the vertical bank. They stood motionless, essentially weightless, but holding their ground beneath some overhanging willows, while the swirling water threatened to dislodge them. Their noses appeared to float horizontally upon the surface. They had no chance of climbing out from where they stood and their eyes reflected terror. Their instinct for flight from danger was brutally thwarted by the fact that I had tied them together. They seemed to sense they couldn't move independently, but they had no power of reason that would permit them to work together. I simply could not abandon them, loyal servants every one, each with his own amusing peculiarities, and our only mule, Fitzsimmons, whose big sad eyes seemed to plead with me.

I couldn't reach them from the bank because of the thick vegetation and the possibility of slipping into the water beneath them. I would certainly need to avoid any sudden, uncalculated moves. "I'll have to cut them loose from one another," I said, still not knowing how I would go about it.

"Oh, God, you can't go in there," Victoria pleaded, having been warned that you can be kicked to death by a horse that is flailing with its feet in deep water.

"Fitzsimmons is the closest and least likely to panic," I said to convince myself. "I'll climb on her back and try to reach the others from there."

I noted the fear in Victoria's eyes as I checked to see that my knife was in its leather sheath on my hip. I removed my chaps and waded in, letting myself be carried along the bank for ten feet down stream. I felt the heat from the mule's warm work-hardened body as I swam onto her back and sat upright between the forks of the packsaddle. Because they were travelling empty, I had folded the tarpaulins we normally used to cover loads and tied them between the forks. That provided padding for what would have otherwise been an extremely uncomfortable seat. The only lead I could reach from there belonged to the horse tied behind her. I pulled out the jackknife and opened its four-inch razor-sharp blade. Trusting everyone to remain calm, I turned my upper body enough to reach and hold the rope with my left hand. I cautiously turned a little more and severed it with the knife I held in my right hand, then carefully folded the blade again and tucked the knife back into its sheath to ensure it wasn't dropped in the water while I maneuvered toward the next objective.

I patted Fitzsimmons on the neck and promised I'd return if she would wait. A tall spooky-eyed Appaloosa we had named Moose was the horse whose lead I had cut first. He stood parallel to the mule, facing the other way. Putting his disturbingly peculiar visage out of my mind and placing my trust in his normally docile character, I crawled onto his back, talking to him all the while. I knew I would be able to reach another lead from that new position. Once I had straddled him and turned to look, I realized I could reach two leads from there if everyone held their positions. But the one I went for first wasn't the horse tied to him, which was a small wall-eyed pinto who usually had a bad attitude. I had to lean over the pinto, whose ears flicked back at my touch – not surprising. He stood still, though, and I managed to get the knife out again and into position, grasp the lead of the other horse, and cut it. It seems that animals sense when they are being helped, and often do their very best to overcome powerful instincts for fight or flight. Their movements were only slight, but seemed much more pronounced to me because of my precarious perches. My back got a terrible kink in it from the awkward position I'd had to assume, but I wrenched myself upright on Moose's back again. With similar cautious maneuvering I crawled along and severed the leads of the two horses at the end of the string, but left the blade open to expedite the separate operations because the cold water was starting to numb my legs. Having separated all but one, the pinto, I made my way back to Moose and swung my legs around until I sat backwards on him. From there I could go to work on the last remaining link in the chain. The little wall-eyed pinto was on the verge of bolting as I leaned forward to face him, the knife in my hand. I knew there was nothing to be gained by conversing with the devilish little fellow, so I simply trusted that speed was my only companion and went to work on his lead shank. The wickedly sharp blade cut through the heavy cord easily. Much relieved, I folded shut and stowed the knife.

From my backward-sitting position on Moose, I crawled across and onto the mule's back again, facing forward. Mules are very intelligent, experience had shown me, and they are more rational than a horse. "Fitzsimmons, we are going to turn upstream," I said, "and walk along, hugging the bank, until we are out of here." Her oversize ears flicked independently, expressing confusion. I nudged her forward and pulled on her lead to establish an upstream heading. I think she had better traction with me on her back, because she made immediate headway. It was tough slogging, but she inched forward. It seemed she realized that she had a way out. I hoped the others would follow but didn't look back. Finally I felt her tough little feet biting firmer ground and we started to rise above the water line. She trudged up the gravelly slope and stopped on dry ground. I slid off and fell to the ground next to her, because my numb feet and weary legs had failed to support me. I sat there, contented, laughing with relief and disbelief, as Victoria rushed toward me with tears in her eyes and the other horses cleared the creek.

"You deserve a medal," she said. "You just showed me again the reason I love you so much."

It was the real thing. I knew it. Along with gritty determination, agility, and skill, my effort to save the horses was an authentic demonstration of selfless courage. Victoria could be proud of a man who acted that way. I had it in me. That's why I loved mountain life, working with horses, and why I was so thankful to have left the hollowness of the business world far behind me. Too bad I couldn't have waited, though, and let nature take its course, instead of making an ass of myself and demonstrating quite the opposite with the incidents of the previous two days in camp.

Back in town, we met with Barry. Nancy, who had been in the picture more and more frequently as the summer progressed, was with him. Barry informed us that the couple we had booked for the next week had left a message at the hotel saying they couldn't make it. That was to be our last paying trip. Suddenly we were finished for the season. Barry, especially, was anxious to get back to the ranch for the fall, because he had been gone all summer, and because he planned to do some hunting. I think his priorities had shifted toward Nancy as well. She was leaving the following day, which left the three of us to head back in and close things down.

I found myself struggling with increasing insecurity and paranoia. I began to see the whole venture as a fantasy that had largely failed to materialize, a delusional squandering of money, too, because it had cost much more than we'd collected from paying guests. It had not improved relations with my brother either, and certainly not with Victoria. I could barely contain my own resentful state of mind at times. I was more vigilant with Barry, but I realized I had been mean and disrespectful to Victoria. I'd tried to impress her with daring and fearlessness, but never did I simply offer her loving kindness. It seemed I could not, as much as I wanted to and often developed the best of intensions in her absence.

As we dismantled the camp, preparing to load it on the trail-weary pack animals and haul it all down the valley again, there was an air of melancholy that everyone did their best to overcome. Ordinary sadness, accompanying the termination of a much-anticipated event, was a large part of it for Victoria and Barry, I hoped. For me, the greater ingredient was grief over parting with a dream, for which I had been physically present, but too often mentally distracted, preoccupied with anxiety and remorse. We spoke in terms of returning next summer, but I felt that none of us believed in our hearts that we would. We were only being kind to one another by avoiding the complex and prickly truth. We even stashed a few of the heavier and more cumbersome belongings, including the Yukon stove, under a tarp, beneath the boughs of a large spruce. It would be there, even when we didn't return, as an expression of the happy vision we had shared.

On the ride out, there wasn't much chatter. As the horses plodded over the familiar trail, I wondered what my brother was thinking. To placate Victoria, hoping to expunge the lingering effects of past errors and omissions, I made occasional observations of the valley's splendor and tried to resuscitate our shared fondness for special moments.

All the horses carried heavy packs, some well over two hundred pounds, and the trail was soggy and challenging. Just before the last crossing, Gift Horse stopped, wavered on his feet, and crumpled to the ground. A cursory inspection indicated that he wasn't going to die on the spot. He was simply exhausted and wasn't going to get up with the pack on his back. It appeared as though we'd put all the miles on him that his bruised and spiteful owners could have wished for. We loosened the diamond hitch and pulled the tarp away so we could untie the basket ropes that secured the panniers. The safety knots that we always put in the cinches made it possible to remove his saddle, even though he was still lying down. He didn't even get up as we left with his pals and crossed the river. Once we unloaded the others, we forded the river again, taking the tough little wall-eyed pinto with us. Gift Horse had gotten to his feet in our absence, but stood motionless with his head hanging down while we packed his burden on the pinto. After a nudge to get him moving, Gift joined us as we made our final crossing. Our boots dragged through the water and the little packhorse swung downstream, the pack buoying him up enough that his feet barely gripped the riverbed.

Sometimes I thought we should pause and spend more time just taking it in. But I usually led the way in going from one job to the next. I found it uncomfortable to pause and smell the roses for too long. I couldn't look my brother or Victoria in the eyes, sustain a friendly smile, and converse in a relaxed manner. I became restless, even disoriented, and needed the distraction of apparently purposeful activity, or the emotional buttressing I experienced almost immediately with a few drinks.

We patched up the bear-damaged camper trailer with pieces of plastic and duct tape so Barry could sleep there, while Victoria and I set up a small tent for ourselves. Winston Holmes, driving the truck that would transport our horses home again, arrived in the morning soon after we'd enjoyed a bacon, eggs, and pancake breakfast with plenty of our last camp coffee for a while. We went to work loading gear in Victoria's truck, hooking the trailer to the Blazer and, finally, loading the horses into the fifty-foot semi-trailer Winston had backed up to the only ledge we could find nearby. They still had to step across a gap and jump up about two feet, but the completely bushed beasts seemed to know they were about to get some time off and cooperated fully.

I was alone, driving the Blazer with the trailer behind it, my mind wavering between relief that we were on our way home, amazement at countless aspects of the summer, and occasional waves of regret for some of my actions. Ten minutes after we had pulled onto the main highway I was still lost in my thoughts, not paying attention, when I entered a gradual down-sloping curve that would go on for a mile and a half. The bumper hitch trailer swayed slightly, which had a noticeable impact on the short wheelbase Blazer. I was going sixty miles per hour and, as soon as I touched the pedal, I realized the electric brakes on the trailer were not working. I tried as gently as possible to bring the truck and trailer into line with each other and the road again. I flicked the manual brake switch back and forth, trying to restore the trailer brakes. There was nothing there!

Meanwhile, the trailer swung too far in the opposite direction, further aggravating the sway on the Blazer, an outcome that was almost certain to accelerate without some drag on the trailer. Had I been going uphill, the problem would have been resolved quite naturally. As it was, I was gaining speed and, in only two more alternating attempts at trying to steer toward a solution, it became obvious that I was headed for a very serious wreck, the kind you didn't walk away from. I didn't dare apply the brakes for fear the whole outfit would simply jackknife and slide out of control, off the edge of the road and down a precipitous shale slope on one side or into the jagged dynamite-blasted rock wall on the other. I could hear the truck tires squeal with each pass and I was sure the inside wheels were leaving the pavement. The swings became increasingly wide and violent, to the left, then right, again and again with no apparent end. Completely gripped with terror, I must have reacted with something like instinct, because I had no prior experience with these circumstances. With very careful timing, watching for the exact moment in the rearview mirror, I began slamming on the truck brakes as hard as I could, just as the trailer arrived directly behind on its wild swerving path toward destruction. I aimed for that brief second when the two were exactly in line. I couldn't determine that it was working at first, but it seemed to retard the increase in speed at least, and it was something versus nothing.

Several more times, I steered it back from the brink and stood on the brakes as the camper passed directly behind. It was working! The speed became manageable and the swings were reduced, until I was finally certain I had regained control. The whole episode probably lasted less than two minutes, but my fingers and hands were cramped and numb from gripping the wheel. They shook uncontrollably as I struggled to put a chew of Copenhagen in my lip. My whole body was shaking. Five miles later, the entrance to the first service station east of the mountains came into view. With the residual effects of panic still raging, I was desperately impatient to set my feet on solid ground.

The truck with the horses turned in behind me. Winston Holmes and his son got out with looks of disbelief on their faces, a mixture of vicarious fright and deep concern. Over coffee they confirmed the wheels had been leaving the road, so much so that they could see daylight under those belonging to the trailer. "We were sure you were headed for a wreck," the professional driver said with relief in his voice. "I've never seen anything like it. There didn't seem to be any way you'd ever get out of it."

I was very uncomfortable getting back in the Blazer, but I had no choice. For the rest of the four-hour trip I relived the dread of what could have happened, afraid that my life was getting more precarious every day. I felt very alone and vulnerable. And yet, once we arrived home and I related the tale to my brother in Holmes' presence, with his ongoing confirmation of the treacherous circumstances, I assumed an attitude of skillful superiority. Later, I wanted to approach Barry and tell him how the fear had gripped me, and how I had been rescued by some incredible force that must have been outside my limited self. But I didn't do it. Nor did I speak to my loving partner about it, because I thought the whole episode hinted at my deficiency.

Victoria went back to work while Barry and I settled into life on the ranch. We decided to run cows on the pasture next spring and proceeded to accumulate a herd that would calve in late spring, more in line with the nature of things. Barry had his own ideas and I was willing to defer to his judgment on that subject. I decided to write the exam for a real estate license and pursue the marketing of ranch and rural acreage properties. So many had unparalleled pastoral appeal in the largely untouched foothill countryside.

More and more I resented Victoria's job. It separated us, which always left a gaping void in my life, and the nature of her work filled me with anxiety because she was staying overnight in hotels, dining out, and probably partying with airline pilots. Feelings of jealousy gripped me when she related her activities and, even though the content of her words was harmlessly innocent, fear and loathing at the thought of her betrayal consumed me. In late October she announced that she was bringing her sister out to see the farm. I knew she would bring her dog as well and, for some time, I had even resented him for coming between us. He represented an alternative source of comfort and companionship that reduced her dependence upon me.

My state of mind was grim and resentful as I worked with the tractor and loader, cleaning corrals while I awaited their arrival. My purpose was to demonstrate the seriousness of the cattle operation and forestall as much as possible any frivolity they had brought with them. When they got out of the car and walked toward me, I barely looked up, ostensibly preoccupied with my vital work. I eventually shut the tractor down however and, with a minimum of social grace, welcomed her sister. At the same time I withheld any display of affection for Victoria and scowled as I glanced at her dog hopping around in a state of excited idiocy.

We had drinks and an elaborate barbeque steak dinner, with copious quantities of wine. Barry and Nancy, who had informed us that evening of their intention to be married, retreated to his private abode in the basement soon after that. I don't know how much Victoria and her sister drank that evening, but my recollection is of my receding progressively further into a dark and ever-narrowing tunnel. In an explosive moment of drunken and constricted reasoning, my anger became focused on Victoria and her dog. Manifesting the anger I harbored generally, my indignation soared to the point of insanity. I walked a few steps to the entrance and returned with the 30-30 rifle which had been leaning in the corner by the door. I rashly insisted that I would shoot her dog if he ever became a problem around the ranch. She challenged me saying, "You would not dare do anything to my dog." I threateningly worked the lever action, which she knew would load a bullet in the chamber, and started for the door as though I would take up her challenge that very moment. Having made my point, however, I went no further with it.

Even as I turned around, I felt an irresistible need to urinate. I put the gun down and went to the bathroom. By the time I returned, I was amazed to discover they had vanished from the house. I went outside. Victoria's little truck was gone. The dog was gone. They had obviously been waiting for an opportunity and jumped on it. Victoria had been the victim of my crazed drunkenness before and I had always been able to assuage her

366

fears. But, even as I staggered into my bedroom and passed out, I was concerned about her sister convincing her that I was crazy and, with tonight's episode, even dangerous.

When I came to in the morning, I lay very still and began to search within my hazy mind, peering back into the tunnel, seeking some orderly arrangement of the facts. I would need to let it lie for a day or two, unless I heard from Victoria sooner, which I prayed I would, if only to relieve the horrible fear of her leaving me. I would explain that there had not been any ammunition in the rifle, that I would never harm her dog. Drunkenness was a good excuse for acting out of character. When her sister had gone home, I'd have a chance of restoring things to normal. With those thoughts and ongoing attempts to rationalize my behavior, as well as the hope that the events of the night had gone unnoticed by my brother, I drove over to Winston Holmes' farm where Barry and his fiancée were busy stacking small square hay bales on a trailer. Holmes, with whom we had now become quite friendly, was gathering the small stacks of bales in the field and loading them onto the trailer with his tractor. Working with him was always more like a social event, and I was pleased with the distraction of helping out for the next three hours, joining in the banter as though nothing was amiss. Not a word was mentioned regarding the events of the previous evening.

Barry and Nancy hauled the load of bales back to the farm and I returned alone, going to the house to gain a bit of much needed privacy. Hangover aside, I felt very unstable, as though I would burst apart with dread and remorse. Waves of sadness washed over me, and guilt arising with memories of Victoria's persistently generous affection brought me close to tears. I longed to hold her and express my love and gratitude, to make everything right again.

Since we had returned from the mountains, Victoria had been parking an MGB convertible in the garage at the farm. She had been leaving a lot of possessions there, including clothes and riding gear, dog bowl, and bathroom items. The most frequently used entrance to the house went through the garage and, as I stepped inside, my heart sank into my stomach with a combination of disbelief and desperation. Her little car was gone. In the house, the entrance closet was emptied of her riding boots and hat. In the bedroom, her clothes had vanished. The bathroom was cleared of her things, toothbrush, make-up case, and hairbrush. I walked back to the garage. Yes, even the dog bowl was gone. I was devastated and immediately realized the reconstruction period was likely to be much longer than I had initially feared. She didn't call and, two days later when I called, her roommate said she wasn't there.

The next weekend I was scheduled to attend a training program for new realtors. I would be staying at a hotel in the city and would have a good excuse to casually drop by and see Victoria. Friday night, however, several of the attendees continued to party after the others had turned in. One was a moderately attractive girl who showed an increasing interest in remaining close to me as the night progressed. She and I got very drunk and decided to jump in the pool, long after it had officially closed. We were soon asked politely to get out. Then we decided to order another drink in her room. I spent the night there, passed out on her bed, still in my clothes in the morning. The next day during breaks, we discussed the great time we had, but I decided that I would remain loyal to Victoria. In fact, a week later when Victoria finally agreed to meet for coffee, I employed that passed up opportunity as a pressure tactic. I implored her to make up her mind about us and thereby either earn my continued loyalty or set me free to take up a new love life. The proposal brought tears to her eyes. She stood up shaking her head sorrowfully and walked out of the restaurant. I immediately regretted taking that approach. I had made a huge mistake because of my anger toward her, and I feared it would be much more difficult to arrange another meeting.

I left there and joined my drinking buddies from the government office. Once comfortably settled in the dingy bar, I began to swill enough beer to forget my misfortunes. Fat old Mary, by far our favorite waitress, would hold her tray above her head with one hand and threaten to grab a guy by the crotch with the other. "Check your bag?" she'd blurt out to a round of howling guffaws and shrill whistling applause. I felt utterly at home drinking and laughing with Peter Kane, the longest standing drinking buddy I had in the world. I'd always connected well with another long-time friend of his as well, Allen Lonsdale. He had the greatest sense of humor and we'd often laughed ourselves silly over some lewd joke or another. At some point I noticed he wasn't there that day and asked Peter where he was.

"You haven't heard?" he said with disbelief. "A few weeks ago, he ran a hose from the car exhaust pipe, through the window, and sat there with the motor running – killed himself. He left a suicide note for his wife, apologizing that he just couldn't go on anymore."

"Jeez!" I was stunned. "On purpose! Allen always seemed like the happiest guy around." I knew he'd had a little sex on the side and loved to drink just like the rest of us, but I couldn't see how that would lead to killing yourself. I'd always thought we were similar in many ways, Peter had even said so, but I guessed perhaps we weren't. "That's bewildering as hell," I said, and Peter agreed.

I believe it was midnight when I left to drive the two hours back to the ranch. But I must have parked on the side of the highway and passed out shortly afterwards. Just as the sun broke the horizon, I woke up sitting behind the steering wheel and facing an unfamiliar highway sign. In a miserable and groggy state, I determined that I had somehow been going the wrong way, that I was actually three hours from home and needed to turn around.

Chapter 27

It was the last week of November when two of Barry's best friends, former members of the band he had played with, visited the ranch and stayed for a few days. Friday night, we four men and Barry's fiancée jumped in the Blazer and headed for the saloon for a bit of partying. On the way home, after refusing to relinquish the wheel to my sensible and sober brother, I entered a curve which had become slippery with a continuing light snowfall. At sixty miles an hour the truck began to slide toward the outside edge of the road. I could not bring it back and only managed to send it into a skid that resulted in approaching the ditch at ninety degrees, back wheels first. When we finally stopped rolling, after flipping three times sideways and once end-over-end, and came to a rest with the vehicle lying on its passenger side, I was still in the driver's seat. Barry and Nancy were moaning in response to a few scrapes and trying to scramble to an upright position. His two friends were no longer present. I climbed out through the broken windshield, while the other two were able to escape through the broken window at the back of the Blazer's large interior. It was pitch black, with light snow still falling, and everything seemed deathly quiet. We found one of the other men sitting up, about thirty feet back. He said he thought he had been thrown out through a side window, declared that he was all right except for some pain in his leg, but did not know where his friend was. Then we heard someone groaning in the dark. We found the second fellow still lying in the snow some twenty feet away. He insisted he was probably OK, but said his back hurt quite a lot. I could just make out a cut on his forehead and a trickle of blood that ran along his eyebrow and down his left cheek.

Although it was a secondary road, used only by local rural traffic and seldom at midnight, only a few minutes elapsed before headlights approached from the same direction we had. It was a neighbor lady on her way home in a roomy Chevy Suburban and she invited us to get in, with the warning that we had better not be seen by the police if we'd been drinking. While we were on our way to the ranch, where she so kindly dropped us off, I began to assess the events of the evening. I realized how fortunate we were that no one was seriously injured, even killed. Being given a ride before the police found us was another incredible stroke of good fortune. When we arrived and were free to have a more open discussion, I saw that Barry was upset with me. But he was much kinder than I would have been, while his friends only played down the potentially fatal circumstances that had been their lot. We all agreed that the truck was a write-off and that I should wait until morning to report the accident. Nonetheless, I was encouraged to drink coffee in an effort to dilute the effects of the booze, in the event the police made a discovery, traced the ownership, and came to the door that night. They didn't, and a few subdued laughs helped keep my spirits up until we all retired. I was the only one who had not suffered a scratch or didn't feel some bruising or pain somewhere.

I couldn't go to sleep, repeatedly shifting my position to shrug off the horror that still engulfed me. My carefully guarded but tenuous sense of good fortune was too often swamped by visions of my brother and his friends dead, or their lives ruined by severe injury. Fear and self-loathing in the form of a cold sweat washed over me in waves that caused me to shudder. Finally I drifted off for a few hours, but I woke up too early with the hideous burden still upon me. None of the others were up yet, as I made coffee and cringed again and again at cerebral reruns of the awful realities that might have been. Barry was the first to join me. There was no laughter exchanged between us that morning, not even a smile, and he did not say anything that would lessen my discomfort.

I phoned the police, who went to inspect the scene of the accident and then stopped by the house. They agreed the roads had been treacherous and said they would submit a report that attributed the mishap to weather conditions. The fact that my insurance policy would cover the costs was a minor boost, but hardly sufficient as I slogged through the long hours of that most gloomy day. For the first time in my life, I considered my alcohol consumption as a source of trouble and decided to curb my drinking. From now on, no more than two bottles of beer per day, I promised myself sternly and severely.

But my resolution didn't stick, and I found myself back at the dingy bar with Peter Kane and his overindulging companions in less than a week. I pushed through the lethargy that enveloped me and worked at the real estate business, right through the Christmas period, to establish a good inventory of property listings. I was also quite surprised to be on speaking terms with Victoria again, finally, after a dozen attempts to contact her. Somehow, I convinced her to go skiing for a weekend. While we were together and enjoying each other's company on the ski hill, we decided to sign up for a holiday in Costa Rica in early January.

It may have been grasping at something that no longer existed, but we both enjoyed a truly wonderful time. From our luxurious resort bungalow, a package deal which included fabulous meals, we ventured out on scuba diving excursions in the Pacific Ocean, rode horses along the beach, and hiked arm-in-arm through verdant rain forest valleys that were graced with crystal clear streams and showering waterfalls. We rented a Land Rover and toured the beautiful rolling countryside which soon led to the mountainous interior. We ascended to the continental divide and traversed some of Costa Rica's high country, travelling over all but impassable roads to enjoy breathtaking views. Brahma cattle, grazing year-round on lush waist-tall grasses, carried more weight than I thought possible for that breed, which explained the lean but deliciously tender beef we'd been eating.

For the entire week, neither of us made any reference to the future. We confined our focus to the present, as though that was all we had, which probably explained the insatiable sexual desire we had for each other. It was only on the return flight that the subject of the future came up and Victoria divulged that she would not be rejoining me at the ranch again, ever. I took it as a stubborn and punishing affront and obstinately informed her that Nancy had now become 'the lady of the house' in any case. I would regret that remark for months to come, believing that kindness and patience might have given Victoria the space she needed to change her mind. I had always loved her more when it was too late. I returned to my routine with a heavy and anguished heart, while reruns of a thousand regrettable events tortured my mind every day.

I visited Celia and my daughter from time to time and achieved some solid results with real estate sales. By April the cows began calving and Barry was fully occupied on the ranch. The horses were still at large on the winter range further back in the foothills. I had achieved no success at controlling my alcohol intake, but my behavior had been decidedly more subdued since the accident, especially in the presence of Barry and his betrothed, who had moved in with him permanently by this time.

Management at the real estate brokerage firm I worked for scheduled another sales convention in downtown Denver and I signed up for it. After the Thursday evening course overview session, a large number of us agreed to meet in the bar for a nightcap. A very pretty lady, petite and blonde with sparkling blue-green eyes, selected a seat by herself and I immediately asked if I could join her. She smiled nicely and invited me with an open hand to take the seat across form her. Her name was Carolyn, she said.

When the waitress came to take our orders, she said, "I'd like a Seven Up and orange juice."

I wavered a moment, struck by her no alcohol choice, but finally said, "Oh, bring me a Budweiser."

"Did I detect some hesitation when you ordered your beer?" she asked. Surprised with her insight, I waited in silence as she continued, "Have you been thinking of quitting drinking?"

"As a matter of fact I have. Cutting back at least," I admitted. "You don't drink?" I asked.

"No, I've been sober for five years," she said.

The word sober meant very little to me. I simply concluded with disappointment that we weren't likely to end up partying. I wondered briefly how people who didn't drink ever got around to jumping into bed together and sought no further exchange on the topic. When she finished her drink, she stood to leave and said it had been very nice to meet me. Her response to a remark I made about meeting for lunch the following day was encouraging. I finished a second beer, went to my room to peruse the instructional material that had been distributed during our introduction to the weekend, and fell asleep early.

She really was a cute little thing, I reaffirmed as soon as she entered the conference room in the morning and joined acquaintances at another table, which meant I had to wait for coffee break to pursue my objective of getting to know her better. As we gathered around the large urns and a generous display of pastries, I inched in her direction as subtly as possible and finally got close enough to wish her a good morning.

With now-or-never determination, I said, "So, are you interested in getting together for lunch?"

"Sure," she replied. "Let's meet at noon."

As soon as we were excused for the lunch hour, more assured of our shared interest by her coffee break acquiescence, I walked straight toward her and asked if she had a favorite restaurant in the immediate vicinity.

"I have been thinking," she said. "Why don't we just grab a sandwich at the deli down the street and go to a meeting?"

"A meeting?" I replied with honest confusion. "We have been in meetings all morning."

"You mentioned that you had thought of quitting drinking, so I thought you might want to try an A.A. meeting. You know, Alcoholics Anonymous."

The thought had never passed through my mind. I really did not know what A.A. was. I'd only ever heard the joke about the difference between drunks and alcoholics: "Drunks don't have to go to all those meetings," was the punch line. I hadn't considered either label appealing at the time and barely laughed, wishing to avoid the subject altogether. But now I was cornered. If I wished to maintain the integrity of my own words with respect to drinking less, and spend more time in the company of a very lovely lady, I would have to go to a meeting of Alcoholics Anonymous. So I agreed and off we went to do as she suggested.

The large hollow-sounding room was furnished with ten standard eight-foot plywood folding tables, placed end-to-end to form a square of twenty-four feet per side, and the flimsy stacking chairs that surrounded that arrangement. A small, drab cream-colored cabinet stood in one corner and twenty-five additional chairs of the same style were unevenly distributed against the whitewashed walls that formed the room's perimeter. The concrete floor was tiled and the light framed chairs made a loud squawking sound when dragged out and pulled back again as people took their seats. They sauntered in one-by-one, some smiling and greeting acquaintances with a hug, while others remained silent, kept their distance, and looked quite glum. The walls were bare except for a bulletin board, with a disheveled collection of documents tacked upon it, and two long scrolls that hung side-by-side behind the man who I assumed was going to conduct the meeting, because he had a red binder in front of him that probably contained instructions or the agenda.

Some of the people looked like they worked in offices and were spending their lunch hour at the meeting. Like Carolyn and me, those men wore suits and ties and the ladies wore attractive dresses or jackets over nice blouses and skirts. Others of the group came in jeans, while others wore sweat pants and loose pullovers. I guessed that some of the latter clothes had not been freshly washed, and I thought that one man might have slept in the soiled and wrinkled outfit he still wore. On a cue that escaped me, the chairman pushed his chair back with a squawk and everyone else did the same. We stood up and responded to his request to take a moment of silence and "think of the still suffering alcoholic." I was still wondering who that was when he asked if there were any newcomers, and Carolyn prompted me to introduce myself.

Little did I suspect that the meeting would consequently concern itself with newcomers and that many of the comments would be directed towards me, "the most important person in the room," a few of them said. From that point on, I remember only three important aspects of my attendance at the Parkside meeting, as Carolyn later referred to it.

First, the very large fellow sitting next to me began to speak by saying, "Hi, my name is Al and I'm an alcoholic." He proceeded to talk about his drinking life and the sorry depressing direction it had taken until he found A.A. Sometimes he turned his head and upper body a little and spoke directly to me, openly and almost personally, as though he and I were alone in the room. He talked about the confusion and pain he had suffered and, once I discarded the ridiculous suspicion that he had somehow been informed of my personal case, I felt a close connection with the man. I felt that I was sitting next to the first person who ever understood what my life had been like, and what had been going on inside.

The second memory I have is that of reading the scrolls that hung on the wall, "The Twelve Steps" and "The Twelve Traditions," and reflecting on the words in Steps Four and Five. They seemed to recommend a close look at one's past in an attempt to determine what had gone wrong. More importantly, however, I perceived within that recommendation the opportunity to wipe the slate clean and start over again. That was the message that formed in my mind, clear and bold, as though it was actually written there and highlighted in flashing neon, "A chance to wipe the slate clean and start over again."

Third, as I thanked Carolyn for an interesting lunch hour, she picked up a small booklet and handed it to me, saying, "Here is a list of meetings in the city. I'm busy tonight, but you will find a number of them at various times and may want to attend another."

I thought often of that lunch hour throughout the afternoon at the conference, and I did not go for a drink when it was over for the day. Instead, I went to another meeting at 7:00 p.m. and, although I don't remember anything as significant as the effects of the first, I recall staying to talk with a small group of men afterward and purchasing a copy of the Big Book at their recommendation. I learned that was A.A. members' pet name for the book *Alcoholics Anonymous*, and after I returned to the hotel, I spent the balance of the evening reading it. I fell asleep with the book open across my chest and only set it aside at some point later in the night.

I awoke the following day, on Saturday morning, with the conference scheduled to conclude at noon, feeling that I had not slept so well in a very long time. I remembered reading a section called "The Doctor's Opinion" in which it said that alcoholics had an allergy to alcohol that often condemned them to drink in excess, once they had begun, and that they had almost no control over it, and no defense against the all too frequently disparaging results. Although I could not previously have described it as such, I knew immediately that it was my experience, over and over again. There was so much more the book had to say that pertained precisely to my case, and I was quite thoroughly convinced I must be an *alcoholic*. I did not resist the idea, being instead quite relieved to have found a body of thought that made so much sense. Many of the people I'd seen in the two meetings had impressed me as well dressed, well spoken, intelligent, openly honest, and very friendly. I saw no reason for not joining their numbers, as much as I could not envision sharing the association with my family and friends, including Barry. I thought it might appear that I was heading off on another crackpot tangent. When the conference was over, I asked Carolyn if she was going to the Parkside noon meeting again. She thought it was a good idea and, when the meeting ended, she convinced me to purchase a copy of the book *Twelve Steps and Twelve Traditions* for further reading. We exchanged telephone numbers and said goodbye with a friendly hug. It was a matter of profound and revolutionary significance that, as I drove home, my thoughts were focused on the fresh and promising new path to which I had just been introduced and not on my newest female acquaintance.

Part V
A Path with Heart

Chapter 28

It was mid-April, still early spring in the foothills. Brisk breezes bore an icy chill down from the mountains where snow lingered above the tree line. It was perfect weather for sitting in front of a wood fire and reading, which I did a great deal of in the following weeks. I developed an insatiable appetite for A.A. literature, and other illuminating material, reading many pieces more than once in my heightened search for new insight. I eagerly sensed there might be a whole new way of looking at things.

There were a few local A.A. meetings and I attended those. As I listened to members share their experiences, I became more and more determined to find relief from the agitated and anxious state of mind that had held me captive for so long. I also imagined that reports of a change in my character, along with my abstinence from alcohol, would convince Victoria to become a part of my life again. In spite of my continued desperate clinging to that hope, with no indication of a change in her attitude, my suffering gradually became less intense as though I had a sounder footing from which to face the world and my future in it. Following one of the local meetings, I had a good discussion with a man twenty years my senior, a gruff, tough old rancher who had introduced himself during the meeting as Will, announcing at the same time that he was an alcoholic. He was a large man, his hands a good six inches across, beefy and strong from ranch work and playing with horses, and he didn't smile that often. But he laughed easily and he seemed to say a great deal, using very few words. He said he ran cattle back in the hills west of my place and that he'd stop by some day.

Over the next month, Will stopped at my place to talk at least once each week. We mostly discussed the weather, bear or moose sightings, and calving cows. But before he left, he always said, "I just wanted to see how you were doing," and I noted an uncommon hint of sincerity in his voice.

One day, I told him that I had not settled on a definition of "a power greater than myself," a seemingly open-ended concept that was frequently mentioned in A.A. literature, and that I didn't have much use for the idea of a God.

He said, "Don't worry about that. It says in the book, you can use the group as your higher power and that's good enough. Just start thinking and acting as though there might be something bigger than you."

I worried less, but I did not let go of the issue entirely. In the chapter called "The Doctor's Opinion," the doctor referred to a psychic change several times, and I wondered if that was what I needed. It seemed more palatable than anything that sounded like 'religion,' a term that caused me to bristle with antagonism.

The real estate business, in which I had attained a solid foundation of listings, started to pay off in actual sales and I became so busy that I hired an assistant, a strikingly attractive and bright local lady who was a real help, and with whom I maintained a work-only relationship. She was married and that helped douse my lustful thoughts, but I think her physical attractiveness inadvertently acted as a catalyst in a far more important development.

Thinking and acting as Will had instructed, I uttered very sincerely to nothing in particular, "Higher Power, if I am to work these Twelve Steps and stay away from booze, I will have to be relieved of my obsession with women and sex." I had my striking new employee in mind as I said it, as well as Victoria and my new A.A. friend, Carolyn, who had driven out to the ranch for a few visits. Direct consequence or not, I soon realized that I had acquired a refreshing new disinterest concerning sexual relations. My compulsive and obsessive preoccupation seemed to have been suspended. I remembered my experience with cigarette smoking, more than seven years ago, and I realized with satisfaction that I had not wanted to smoke again, following the earnest bidding of my honest old doctor and the course of action I had taken as a result. Of course, after a three-year interval without nicotine, I had quickly become hopelessly addicted to chewing snuff, and remained so. But I retained a stern revulsion toward inhaling smoke into my lungs. I considered, also, that I might not wish to be permanently without any interest in sex, and then decided to be grateful for the reprieve and face that concern later.

Bouts of anger readily burst out in the form of rage at minor irritations, but I no longer suffered from constant anxiety. In other moments, 'crazy' best described the activity in my mind, as thoughts exploded volcanically and raced pell-mell without a trace of rationale behind them. But I found temporary relief in reading and attending meetings. I was sleeping soundly through the nights and usually awoke to face something like a friendlier world. Driving down the road one day, I experienced a vivid image of myself sitting serenely in a canoe, as it drifted aimlessly on a placid pond. Warm sunshine and peaceful quiet surrounded me. Looking over my shoulder I observed a dark wall of thick, tangled, and thorny forest, through which I had just hacked my way amidst the presence of biting insects, poisonous snakes, and countless dangers that lurked behind every tree – the first forty years of my life.

I started working through the Twelve Steps, which had held so much promise from the day I had first glimpsed them at the Parkside meeting. My goal was to expedite my recovery and gain some stability in my emotional life. After that, I would go to work straightening out my financial wellbeing, and seeking a romantic relationship. I did a lot of writing, looking at my past within the format of Step Four, which suggested a personal moral inventory. A new A.A. friend answered my query about doing Step Five, admitting everything to another person. He suggested I call a nearby Franciscan Monastery, because they were known to have done many such interviews with recovering alcoholics. I accepted his guidance and found myself driving through the park-like grounds of the monastery on the appointed day. I was certain that I had completed one of the most challenging parts of the A.A. program, and I looked forward to the accolades I was likely to receive for having done so well in only two months. In a small office with a gentle breeze wafting through a tall open window, I took a seat as directed. On the opposite side of the large oak desk that separated us sat a chubby redheaded Franciscan Friar. I read what I had written of my resentments, fears, and sex problems, as the Big Book had instructed, and I answered the few questions he asked for the sake of clarity.

He was kind with his response. "You will probably want to do some more work after you have been around a while, take a deeper look at all aspects of your previous thinking and behavior, perhaps. Meanwhile, you have a good grasp of the problem and the work you have done will benefit you, help keep you sober. If you don't mind me being blunt, I think what you have done is a very good Step One, admitting that alcohol was a problem for you and that much of your life was unmanageable."

I was disappointed, primarily because I had been impatient to get Victoria back and had been looking forward to presenting her with a much-improved version of my personality. I thought about a suggestion Will had made, which I had remained privately unwilling to accept, that I put the Victoria issue on the shelf, along with my attitude toward religion.

I had heard him say at meetings, more than once, "It takes about five years around here just to get your brains out of hock." I wondered if he didn't publicly repeat his bristly insights for my benefit, rather than address me directly. "I've never seen anyone too dumb to get this program, but I've seen a few who were too smart." That was another one he liked to toss on the table, ostensibly for general consumption, but which caused me unexpected discomfort.

I suddenly saw that my recent efforts had been rather academic in nature, and quite shallow. A phrase from a chapter called "How It Works," read at the beginning of every A.A. meeting I'd attended, popped into my mind with increased relevance: "...if they have the capacity to be honest." I began to wonder if I had that capacity, and it bothered me that I probably did not, not yet at least. But I relaxed my pace a bit and became content with reading, taking a closer look at things, and going to meetings so I could talk to, and learn from, others. My newfound willingness to consult, listen, and follow instructions was no less than a personal transformation in itself.

I spent more time with Celia and Elizabeth, my former wife and my daughter, and the three of us drove out to visit my parents and to attend the wedding of one of the men who survived being thrown out when I wrecked my Blazer six months ago. The five-hour drive offered us a chance to talk. Because of Celia's solid and mature personality, I was never uncomfortable being with her, even though she was occasionally quite direct with her comments. She told me that she had nearly given up on her objective of Elizabeth knowing her father, because she had been no longer convinced that I was a constructive influence. She told me she was very happy I had found a way to quit drinking. I thanked her again for her generous gift of moving west, so Elizabeth and I could be closer, and for her tolerance of my previous life.

She asked me whether I thought we could ever get back together, and we discussed that topic for many miles. I was a little uncomfortable, not wanting to say anything that could be construed as too encouraging, because I really did not know. I feared that I would have no enthusiasm for the physical aspect of a relationship with her. I wondered, privately, why I rejected the idea of mixing sexual intercourse with open and candid friendship, as though a close and mature relationship effectively anesthetized my desire for physical passion.

My parents were happy to see us, as always, and we had a very good time over the four days. When I dropped her and Elizabeth off at the end of the return trip, Celia gave me a book she had bought for me, *The Art of Happiness* by the Dalai Lama. She had remembered my interest in Buddhism, stretching back to our honeymoon in Hong Kong and the book I'd discovered in our hotel room. Celia had always been a devout Catholic with an incredibly open mind. I knew that, but I was nonetheless touched deeply by her impartial generosity, and her genuine concern for my recovery.

A neighbor, who operated a custom fencing business to supplement his ranching income, stopped in one day to say he had a client who had asked him if he knew anyone who could take on a privately guided mountain trip in the Canadian Rockies. "They are pretty well-off, two married couples," he said. "Have their own horses, would provide all the food and do the cooking themselves."

It seemed like a grand opportunity to do some exotic mountain riding without the drudgery of kitchen duty. I called my brother Dennis, because Barry was busy with the cows and his fiancée, and asked if he would like to help out. He jumped on it without delay. Next, I phoned Mr. Glen Ford, the name the neighbor had given me as a contact. I'd heard he was a very high-level banking executive. His holiday companion, Mr. James Edwards, we discovered was the wealthy owner of a mining company. They wished to cover roughly one hundred and twenty miles over an eight-day period, most of it in the backcountry of Canada's vast Banff National Park. He requested that we provide our two saddle horses, enough pack animals, the necessary tack, and the camping gear. During the trip, we were to take responsibility for all the packing and provide navigation skills. He had already secured topographical maps and would take care of all permits for crossing the border, entering the park, and grazing fourteen horses for eight days.

I said I would work out a price, probably a thousand dollars per day plus the cost of trucking the horses a thousand miles to the trail head, having the trucker wait for a week and then meet us at the other end for the return trip, perhaps another eight thousand dollars. As though he were agreeing to meet a friend for lunch, Mr. Ford said, "That sounds alright."

While gaining some familiarity with the Twelve Steps of recovery, I had taken a closer look at my relationship with Celia and its demise. My conscience was bothering me and it seemed a matter of urgency that I let her know of my honest regret and the respect I had for her. That she had been so generous and caring with respect to my relationship with my daughter added to my sense of moral obligation. Hardly completely selfless, perhaps I was anxious about her continued commitment as well. Consequently I prepared and mailed her a letter prior to our departure:

Dear Celia,

This letter may be surprising to you (not so much the content, but that I have written it). There are some things I wanted to say:

As a result of the A.A. program, I have discovered some things about myself. In essence, I have come to realize I'd rather be more like you sometimes and less like myself. No matter what plans we had or things we did, I always found some way to undermine our happiness. I have had great difficulty saying what I mean in a sociably acceptable way (for whatever reason) most of my life. I have concluded that it was a combination of resentments, self-pity, fear of rejection, and childish emotional insecurity. I used anger and guilt as tools which just confused you and clouded the issues. More recently, I have had to hide from my own guilt.

We supposed, during a previous discussion, that our marriage was a mistake, a mismatch of personalities. But, I was largely to blame for rushing us into it in the first place, when I did not possess the understanding, tolerance, and love of mankind to make a marriage work with anyone. It must have been heartbreaking for you to live with someone like me. You must have been deeply hurt by our relationship and its demise. I can only say that I was in no position to judge you. I hope you have cast aside the criticism and abuse and are happy living as you feel you should.

I have something else to say: I want you to know that my admiration for you is without bounds when it comes to the way you have handled our separation and divorce. Celia, you have demonstrated no anger or hatred, something I could never have done. Where you might have despised me, you've shown tolerance and have tried to understand. Where you could have shut me out, you have chosen to move here for Elizabeth's sake and to maintain your friendship with my mother. Such selfless thinking and action is a tribute to your Faith, and a true measure of the kind of person you are.

Thank you, for being you and for being there to raise our child. With the help of A.A., I hope I will be able to contribute positively to both of your lives in the future. My main source of happiness, for now, is the progress I'm making toward being the kind of person I really want to be.

With admiration and respect, Rick.

The prospective trucker, our good neighbor, Mr. Winston Holmes, was delighted with the challenge when I presented it. He went to work immediately, fitting his fifty-foot trailer with a ramp that slid out of sight at the back end, and hooks to hang steel fence panels along the sides, which together would provide a portable loading chute, adaptable to all conditions. Other preparations came together with equally creative forethought, and in late July we arrived at an outpost called Mountain Aire Lodge along the Panther River just before it entered the larger Red Deer River. We stopped there for an early supper and to get directions for the remaining five miles into our staging area. It would be the last commercial establishment we would see for over a week, in fact, the last manmade structure larger than either of two small, presently uninhabited ranger's cabins of crude, chinked-log construction for the whole one hundred and twenty miles.

We unloaded the horses, along with trusty Fitzsimmons, the mule, and our large quantity of gear, and prepared to camp along the Red Deer that night. Following the last rumblings of Winston's old diesel growling its way back along the shale road toward civilization, a weighty eternal silence settled all around us. We led the horses down to the river for a drink, fed them some of the Timothy hay bales we'd hauled in, set up the tents, ate a late supper, and crawled in for our first night in the wilderness. I had a profound sense of being home. In the few minutes before sleep carried all my thoughts away, I felt thankful for being free of liquor, clear headed, and much less likely to embarrass myself or anyone else.

I heard a fire crackling in the morning and crawled out to find Mr. Edwards placing the large enamel coffee pot directly upon the blazing wood, just as I had done the night before. "Am I doing this right?" he smiled.

"Looks like you've got it," I said, and thought, "This guy is all right. It's going to be a fine week working with him."

Mr. and Mrs. Edwards put together a breakfast of pancakes, bacon, and eggs, while Dennis and I brushed the girths of the mule and our seven horses and saddled them. Mr. and Mrs. Ford cleaned up afterwards. The guests took down the tents and helped organize the duffle into balanced loads, while Dennis and I packed up the six beasts of burden. It all took just under three hours. Having insisted beforehand that we not be delayed once the pack string was ready to move out, I looked to confirm that everyone had saddled their horses and was prepared to mount up.

I was riding a new horse that I had named Merlin, a stout, liver-chestnut Morgan with a white blaze running the length of his nose, a dark-tawny mane, and the character of a gentleman. I had put a few miles on him in preparation and knew that he learned quickly, but he had never been to the mountains before. I'd given my former favorite, Samson, to Victoria in a last ditch effort to regain her affection, which had failed.

After a perfectly smooth transition from stationary camp to trudging mountain caravan, we ambled west along an easy trail that followed the north bank of Red Deer River. A barely noticeable climb led us in three hours to pass through a mammoth natural portal, with thousands of feet of sheer mountain slope on either side, and past a small sign that announced our entry into Banff National Park. After four more hours on the trail, we came to a setting that seemed very likely to be the camping and grazing area that was our objective for the night. I sat my horse, who was working out even better than I had hoped, and waited. I milled the pack string slowly around the clearing, to avoid entanglement and to keep them occupied, while Mr. Ford took his time deciding on a specific location for our camp. I knew the delay was risky, because the pack animals would be irritable after a long hot trip and would expect to be relieved of their burdens. I held off saying anything to the man, and held off still longer, because of the newness of our relationship, and then it happened.

A quiet little bay gelding, that was notorious for falling asleep with his nose resting on a corral rail, suddenly turned the clearing to mayhem. He went ballistic, bucking violently, shaking his pack until the boxes were mostly freed of the lash rope and slung near the ground, where he began stepping in them and pulling the basket ropes away from the saddle. At one point the air was filled with the mist of Grand Marnier, because his shod hoof had landed upon the plastic bottle it had been decanted into for safety. It had burst like a balloon. Even then, with the packsaddle lying broken in a tangled mess and his back completely bare, he was not done. Nor had he stopped bucking when he disappeared back down the trail we'd come in on. "We have to unload now or there is going to be more of this," I said, displaying some irritation.

We tied up the remaining horses and unpacked them. I left the others to pick up the debris and set up the camp, while I rode back down the trail to see if the little bay had stopped running. At three miles, his gait slowed, the distance between hoof prints a little less, and I gained some hope. At four and half miles, something must have spooked him because they opened up again, and his pace was still brisk at six miles. Merlin had travelled twelve miles in, retraced his steps six miles, and faced another six in returning to the camp, if we turned around at that point. He also had seven days of hard work ahead of him. I patted my gloved hand on his sweaty neck and said, "That's enough, old boy, lets head back." Not a quitter, he loped easily into camp.

The next morning Merlin's head hung low. He stood tethered to a lash rope we'd strung between two spruce trees, still sound asleep. I went over and hugged his big nose and said, "You had better spend some time eating, my good buddy. There's a long day ahead." I untied him, placed the hobbles on his front feet, released the ringer in the bell about his neck, and watched him take carefully measured baby steps as he grazed his way into the meadow.

The operation was working smoothly otherwise, and we piled a few more pounds on each of the five remaining pack animals. Each day the total load was automatically reduced a little, primarily because of food consumption, and the Grand Marnier was gone.

From our first camp, near the confluence of Divide Creek and the Red Deer River, we headed north following that creek to its beginnings near the high point of a pass that separates two watersheds. Traversing the subalpine crest, we soon started back down toward the Clearwater River, along one of its tributaries, Peter's Creek. The whole day was spent in the bush and the rocky, often disappearing trail was a challenge to man and beast. The runaway incident lurked at the edge of my consciousness like a bad omen, manifesting as impatience and the desire to get this day behind us without another mishap. I looked forward to the third day, when we would begin our trek into the true alpine, and I anticipated that event as though it contained within it the promise of a safe haven.

Finally, much later in day two, we crossed the broad swiftly flowing river, which, despite its intimidating breadth, didn't exceed more than four feet in depth, and found a campsite near Malloch Creek. I was pleased with the pleasant conditions surrounding our bivouac for that night and the delicious meal the guests had prepared, and I felt satisfied that the guest members of our team were quite capable of taking care of themselves and their horses. Except for a general anxiety over the responsibility I had assumed, I had no concerns beyond that of spending a good week with Dennis.

My brother was a stranger to me, more so in some ways than the four guests whom I had never met before. Over the years we'd had our altercations, usually because of my careless speech or immature behavior, and I felt uneasy. I still wondered about his opinion of me. At night, when we finally crawled into the tent and into our sleeping bags, I felt that I would like to say more than "have a good night," but I didn't, because I wasn't comfortable with breaching the emotional wall that seemed to ensure a safe distance.

The next day, as we prepared to saddle up, I noticed that Glen Ford's little Arab gelding had a hairless patch where the cinch had rubbed his girth. Arabs are tough animals but thin-skinned. There had been too much torque, twisting and rubbing, carrying a heavy load over continuously ascending and descending trails.

"You need to tighten your back cinch to take the strain off the front cinch, or your horse will not make it," I said with the certainty I felt.

A half hour later, when he had the saddle in place, I said, "Tighten the back cinch."

"I have tightened it a bit, but he doesn't like it," Mr. Ford explained.

I walked to the side of the horse, took a firm grip of the back cinch strap and tugged it ruthlessly tight, until the skin on the horse's belly was slightly wrinkled under the leather. The horse pranced a little, kicking and crow-hopping on the spot.

By the time I said, "You can't sore a horse on the belly; he will learn to like it," the horse was nearly still again. I was still resenting Mr. Ford's delay at the first camp sight, the busted equipment and lost horse, but those feelings were largely appeased by this lesson in the intricacies of mountain horsemanship.

We rode west along the Clearwater River, crossing it back and forth occasionally, and climbing gradually all day into prettier and prettier country. We trailed along quickly on the spongy earth near Martin Lake, and stopped to watch a large bull-moose standing knee deep in the crystal clear water, his nose searching out and foraging on lush submerged vegetation. A pair of bald eagles screeched as they glided upon an updraft two thousand feet overhead, and the barren rugged slopes before us soared toward the sky and threatened a bleak impasse.

Ninety minutes later, when the trees had turned to dwarfs huddled together in tight little groves, and the miniature flowers that adorned the alpine meadow began to flourish, we came upon the Devon Lakes. They represented a gateway to the enormous expanse of Clearwater Pass. The area before us appeared as a paradise, far removed from any trace of humanity, except for the narrow horse trail that wound its way across the tundra to the horizon. Patches of toffee-colored shale blended intermittently with fingers of fall-tinted, knee-high scrub that reached down and across our path from the broad fields of blood-red turf that adorned the slopes. The high altitude grandeur glistened under the vertical rays of the warm midsummer sun, while our eyes were drawn back inevitably to the mesmerizing powder blue of the small glacial lakes in its midst.

We rode steadily on, finally establishing our camp at a lower elevation among the scattered spruce and pine trees that bordered the subalpine adolescence of the Siffleur River. We planned to spend two nights there, allowing one day for relaxed exploration of the hypnotic landscape. My brother and our four guests were visibly moved by the scenery and the setting we'd chosen for the camp. At first, expressions of lighthearted contentment were punctuated with beaming smiles. Then I noticed how waves of serenity veiled their faces, as one by one they gazed in solitude, far into the distance, upon an eternal wonder. I felt fortunate to be among a group of people who were so obviously comprehending and unreservedly thankful to be in this magical realm, a realm that I so cherished myself that I was usually dubious about others fully appreciating it. I warmed to their presence generally, and I reveled in my observation that Dennis had become speechless. I had not been to this place before either and, indeed, I believed it by far the grandest I had ever beheld.

I had a great need to share it with people such as were presently in my company, and not have it deprecated by shallow or pretended reverence. From that perspective, I felt fulfilled and became free to enjoy my own reflections upon it. Although outwardly sullen when occupied with tasks, an aspect of my character that would be a long time softening, I think I conveyed sufficient warmth and positive regard as well. But I had deliberately set myself apart, too, while establishing a leadership position during the first few days, and I supposed that my brother felt compelled to join me behind that partition. From that perspective I felt we may have been somewhat deprived of the natural exuberance exhibited by our guests.

The following day was one of spectacular touring, viewing, and shared amazement. It was capped off with an incomparable feast of steaks, specially prepared over a wood fire by Mr. James Edwards, and the revelry of a unified group of fellow wanderers. On the next day, we followed the ever diminishing Siffleur River for three hours, climbing only gradually along the verdant trough of alpine valley, until we reached that most peculiar point: where a once mighty river vanishes into its beginning and is, at the same time, forever reborn. For an hour on either side of midday, a herd of ninety-eight elk cows and calves moved parallel with our course, far above us upon the grassy slopes that hemmed us in. The high altitude and persistent breezes assured the animals of some reprieve from biting insects, made fiercer in the urgency born of fleeting summers.

I rode Merlin in the lead. The reins hung loose most of the day, while the mule trailed tirelessly behind, her lead nearly always slack. The endurance and unyielding pace of my new saddle horse, as we gained elevation hour after waterless hour, were interspersed with his brief self-directed halts, during which he breathed deeply three or four times, sighed, and trudged on of his own accord. I smiled with admiration for the big-hearted pony that carried me, approving of his clever adaptability and submission to the task. Fitzsimmons's humble march under a heavy pack was equally unperturbed. Her long ears flicked independently as though she were lost in private reflection.

"This is what it takes," I thought, as I reacted with stern resignation toward my aching right hip, tired butt, and throbbing knees.

By mid-afternoon we were climbing more steeply, toward the pinnacle of Pipestone Pass, between an impregnable thousand-foot wall of smoothly eroded limestone on our right, and gigantic shards of granite on our left. The moonscape that surrounded our small procession in all directions was so vast, bleak, and imposing, that I sensed the lot of us must appear as no more than ants to seven regal elk that stared inquisitively from their perch high upon a ridge. Aloft and aloof, their massive antlers appeared wraithlike against the wispy cirrus clouds that streaked the pastel sky.

Some people I had listened to in the meeting rooms of Alcoholics Anonymous insisted they found their Higher Power in nature. Surely, I thought, if there is a God of the Universe, He must have set aside this special slice of creation for His personal solitude. Right here, there must necessarily be the least separation between human existence and whatever exists that is Divine, and I tried for a sense of connection.

Just then a ruckus sounded behind me. I looked back, over the packs of the three horses trailing behind Fitzsimmons, just in time to see Dennis bash the little pinto packhorse in the head with his fist. He had begun acting up again, balking and bucking, just as he had two days ago when he had threatened to disrupt the entire pack string. That's why he was being trailed alone. My first thought was, "Horse heads are like steel and you could hurt yourself punching them, a lot more than you could hurt the horse." Dennis shook his hand in pain and cursed.

"That Goddamn knot-head. You should have a stick or something, don't hurt yourself," I said.

"It's too late," he moaned. The swelling in his wrist that night would substantiate his claim, as would the X-ray a week later, which indicated three fractured bones in his hand.

A half-mile after we crested the pass and commenced a gradual descent, the Pipestone River emerged from the damp mossy surface as a twinkling, gurgling little trickle. Unceasing was my fascination with the inevitable disappearance of one steadily diminishing stream into its spongy origins, only to be followed by the exquisite, pristine, and waterlogged commencement of another so soon after crossing a divide. I reflected upon the phenomena as a metaphor for the notions of impermanence and constant regeneration. I thought of the Japanese Buddhist term 'shunyata' used in my Buddhist book to describe a condition of infinite emptiness and radiant openness. The essence of all things was to fade away and arise anew.

We took the right tine of a fork in the trail and descended along a small tributary until it joined Mosquito Creek. For the next two nights we camped at Fish Lake where an abundance of cutthroat trout provided us with appetizers on more than one occasion. Mrs. Ford strummed her guitar (which we had strapped across the top of a fully loaded horse each day) and sang in a Carly Simon voice, while the backdrop for her evening performances was a blazing light show along the ridge, as the crimson sunset ran its course and gave way to star-studded darkness. In the mornings, I served my ailing brother a cup of hot coffee while he pampered himself with a few more minutes in the sleeping bag. He never complained about his swollen limb and worked as steadily as ever at all aspects of our arduous adventure.

As we rode out of the bush for the last time, to find Winston Holmes waiting with his truck, I fell into melancholy reflection upon a truly wonderful journey. Nobody wanted it to end, each one had stated clearly. But it had, and we began the long trek home. I believed the others would go home and be forever happy with their memories. But it was not enough for me and I longed to be back up there, high in the Pipestone Pass. I felt, in that moment, there was no promise of lasting contentment for me in the society of man, or in the pursuit of fulfillment in the material world.

Chapter 29

August was a good month on the ranch with my brother, Barry. His fiancée was away for most of it, which gave us some time to ride together, enjoy the foothills, and discuss the cattle operation. We laughed about the runaway horse, which I had since sold to a man in Alberta. I had phoned the Mountain Aire Lodge, once we got to the end of the trail, and asked them to be on the alert for a small bay gelding that was last seen heading in their direction, along the Red Deer River. The eventual purchaser had in turn called me to report finding him in the bush, catching him and taking him home. We never knew what got the little fellow going, but I had every hope that his new owner would be happy with him.

Barry didn't know what he was going to do with his future. He said he would like to get into the cattle business himself, but had no financial resources of his own. I thought about it awhile, thinking I could not operate the ranch on my own, and finally suggested that we look for some arrangement to get him started with a few cows. After talking to the bank, it seemed the only way of getting him some money to buy cattle was to put his name on the land-title for the ranch. We did that and set up the financing to buy him one hundred cows, nearly as many as I had. I felt good about helping Barry out, part of an ongoing amend for past neglect of my little brother.

We had a few visitors at the ranch. My long-time friends, Peter and Cindy Kane, drove up from Denver for a weekend. It was quite different, a little uncomfortable, spending time with my oldest drinking buddy and not drinking. But they had gone through considerable marital stress over Peter's irresponsible behavior since I'd last seen him, and he had cut back as a consequence in any case. We went to bed much earlier, which Cindy approved of whole-heartedly.

My little family, Celia and Elizabeth, visited and stayed for a weekend, too. I adored my little girl, who would turn two years old in December, and I took her for her first horseback ride.

I hadn't been looking forward to Nancy's return, for no specific reason really except that she seemed jealous of my relationship with Barry. She didn't seem pleased when Carolyn, my A.A. friend, visited either. Carolyn had stayed overnight a few times, but we kept sex out of the equation, primarily because of my newly acquired lack of interest in all but spiritual matters.

I don't think Nancy liked the new arrangement between Barry and me regarding the cattle either because, I suspected, she had designs on eventually getting him to a place of their own. And I know she was revolted by the sudden appearance one day of the receptionist from the real estate office. That young lady and I had carried on a flirtatious acquaintance, inspired by the electricity that just naturally arises between two people sometimes. However, our flirtations had always been confined to the office because she was married. So I was surprised when she had called an hour earlier to announce that she was on her way out to the ranch that afternoon.

It was immediately evident that she hadn't planned on hiking, or even touring the barnyard and horse paddock. She wore a nice skirt, low-cut top, and shoes with heels. I hadn't seen her for over a month and she looked thinner than I remembered, wore too much make-up, and seemed distraught. Before long she told me, with tears in her eyes, of her husband's infidelity. She said she thought of me as a friend and just wanted to spend some time with me. I held her in a friendly hug while waves of confusion passed through my mind. I could see that she felt dejected and I responded with feelings of empathy because we had always been jovial friends. At the same time, I considered her behavior somewhat pathetic, which led to a feeling of irritation.

She pressed her body against mine and nestled her pelvis against my thigh. I pressed my hand into her lower back, and felt her pubic area against my leg. As we led each other toward the bedroom, I became increasingly physically aroused, but I was not propelled into a state of eroticism, that lustful zone I had always previously craved. Instead, I fought to subdue the awareness that I was betraying my record of abstinence. Still not inclined to pass up an opportunity, I countered that obstacle by convincing myself that I was helping a lady in distress, and could not reasonably deny her want. I thought that whatever Higher Power had granted me the reprieve was not likely to see this small slip as much of a dent in my overall record.

We undressed independently and fell together on the bed. I thought she was physically attractive, despite her body looking and feeling somewhat emaciated, no doubt a consequence of the grief she had been dealing with. I had always viewed her as prim and pretty, probably quite timid in spite of her twinkling playfulness. I was therefore further aroused by the hunger she exhibited, her frantic craving for a distraction from sad reality, although I still did not become passionately involved. Our sexual engagement was brutally brief and without warmth. Afterwards, I wondered anxiously if we hadn't harmed our former friendliness, and I felt sorry that I couldn't have been more affectionate for her sake. She left a short time later and the whole episode seemed to have a great emptiness about it. I considered that I did not yet possess a decision framework that would limit my short-term reactions and keep them within the boundaries of the longer-term vision I had for myself.

There was only one man regularly attending the A.A. group closest to my home, because it had run into internal problems between members and largely dissolved. He opened the door to the little church basement each week, made some coffee, and waited out the hour, usually alone. That's why he was very happy when I came along. Only a month later, however, he announced that he had taken a night job as a security guard. He handed me the keys, saying that I would have to take over, that it was vital to keep the door open for the next newcomer who needed the meeting. I nearly objected on the basis that I was new and a very busy man, but I didn't, and I began to open the door each week, make coffee, and read A.A. literature for an hour before I locked up and went home. The meeting room became a haven for me, and the weekly commitment became an unwavering priority. I travelled to a few other meetings in the district, always announcing the unhappy state of my local meeting – my 'home group' as I began to think of it.

In mid-August, a couple from a town nearby attended the meeting. It had always been known as a 'step meeting' and we read the section on Step One from the book *Twelve Steps and Twelve Traditions.* Then we discussed the contents for the balance of the hour. They began to come every week and a few weeks later they showed up with another fellow, a tall man who had displayed an air of authority when he asked abruptly, "Who is the GSR of this group?"

"What's that?" I asked, feeling that I should probably have known.

"General Service Representative," he said. "There has to be one."

"Well, I'm the only member," I said, thinking with that information he would probably drop the inquisition.

"Well then, you must be it," he concluded without hesitation. "There is a district meeting this Saturday at two o'clock. You had better be there so your group is represented."

Old Will had said repeatedly, "If you are thinking right, you'll be acting right."

I had no acquaintance with that relationship, and no more than a very foggy comprehension of his meaning, though I soon discovered that the very design of Alcoholics Anonymous led people like me in the right direction, often without their being conscious of it. One had only to be open to guidance, which itself was an unusual state of mind for me. But there were two important factors, two crucial ingredients, behind my openness and willingness. First, I had been horribly lost and disillusioned with the wreckage of my life, as exemplified by the crashed Blazer and the near death of people close to me, and the shattering loss of my relationship with Victoria. I was ready to give up and cling to anything that promised an alternative. It wasn't working and I was desperate for a way out.

The second component had to do with the people I met in A.A. and the relationships I started forming with some of them. They had experienced variations of the same wreckage, which lent a tone of authenticity, a solid believability, to everything they said. In the presence of Will, and a half dozen other men, I felt like a child receiving loving mentorship from his parents, perhaps his grandparents or his elders, as I may have received from my grandfather but did not remember. I was often warmly comforted while talking with them and, although their suggestions were almost always brief, direct, even curt, the clearly apparent absence of self-serving motives dissolved the obstinacy with which I had long responded to good advice. In short, I had arrived at a state of unconditional surrender and I trusted them.

"Just ask yourself if you are doing the right thing," Will had advised me.

I went to the district meeting because it seemed the right thing to do. Then I attended the much larger area assembly on a weekend in September, because they said it was the right thing to do. As a consequence, I found myself feeling more and more a part of something important, something with a reach beyond my narrow world. I saw that it had significance in the world at large, and in the whole large world. I was buoyed by a sense of connection and I reflected with gratitude upon this first slender link with 'thinking right and acting right.'

Returning from yet another uneventful district meeting and lost in my thoughts, I had the sudden realization: this activity was not generating any income, would not result in personal recognition (being of no value on a resume, for example) and yet, it required my time and some expenditure of money. In the next moment, I realized that was the wonder of it, its spiritual nature. I was travelling with two men who had also been representing their groups that day, and they had probably said something that brought about my realization. I returned to the present and focused on my new friends. 'Hillbilly' was the label that best described Roger's mustachioed image and defiant deportment, the wayward son of a big-game guide, while Dawson was only different in that his hillbilly demeanor blended seamlessly with a ponytail punctuated intellectual bent. They had made each other's acquaintance long before sobering up in A.A., growing up in the same community and drinking in the same bars. With this newly discovered common ground, however, they had quickly become close friends. As I tuned in again, they were saying how fortunate we were to have this time together on the road, like a "travelling meeting," they concurred with surprising joyfulness, as though it was a very special gift. And I came to believe right then, with clarity and certainty, it was a special gift. We were three men who had been unlikely to develop close friendships in the uninterrupted sequences of our lives. But it seemed we had grasped a common bond which ran deep, and which shifted other aspects of our individual circumstances to the periphery.

Victoria was still often on my mind and, although I clung less desperately to the idea of getting her back, I called her from time to time. She had consistently resisted our getting together, until one day she invited me to join her and her flight attendant girlfriends for Texas two-step lessons at a saloon in the city. I didn't like the idea of meeting her amidst a crowd of city 'wannabes' dressed in their slick cowboy outfits and wearing boots that had never seen a barnyard, but I wanted to spend time with her. So the following Tuesday night I drove into Denver and signed up for dance lessons.

I was a little surprised when I found myself quite interested in the lesson and I was delighted to spend time with Victoria again, by far the most striking female in the saloon. I was thrilled with the physical contact of dancing with her, and I squeezed her waist a little tighter when she thanked me for being her partner. "Because many of the men seemed to be after more than just dancing," she added.

I suppressed the immediate surge of jealousy her last comment brought about and I wondered if she was really that naïve. Or, had she actually vindictively planned to disturb me with the remark? Focused on the basics of the two-step, I let it go and enjoyed the rest of the two-hour lesson. At the end of the lesson, when everyone ordered another round of drinks, I decided to leave. I thanked Victoria for the dancing, said it was good to see her again and parted, thinking that I could easily overdo it by staying too long, and hoping that the brief encounter might convince her of my casual regard for the whole affair and thereby induce in her a renewed state of desire. Lessons were twice a week and I met with her five times in succession, for dancing only, and left each time when the practice was over. She told me that she wanted us to be friends and nothing more. It seemed that wasn't going to change and I decided I could no longer tolerate the longing I felt while driving home, and worse, the images of her spending the night with one of the dudes that were so obviously available. I was disappointed when Victoria wasn't at all upset with my announcement that I would no longer meet her there. At least I had learned the basics of the Texas two-step and I began anticipating the upcoming local rodeo dance, as a kind of spiteful consolation for her cold disregard.

Chapter 30

During the months that followed the mountain trip with Dennis and our four clients, I worked diligently at a more in-depth review of my life to date as prescribed by the Fourth Step. This time I scoured my past and made an exhaustive list of the people and institutions I had resented, examining my feelings of anger right back to my childhood. I searched each instance to identify any fears that might have lurked in the shadows of the resentments. I prepared an outline of my 'romantic history' (the heading I placed at the top of the page), omitting the less socially acceptable aspects of my past sex-life because I did not want to risk misplacing the notes and having the details discovered by my brother, Barry, for example. Except for those details, I had been quite ruthlessly honest and it was a weighty piece of work that I carried under my arm as I went to talk about it with the Monk at the Monastery, Step Five, as it was referred to in A.A.

I had been somewhat detached while preparing for the event in the privacy of my home, but it was very unnerving to sit there and admit those unpalatable truths to another human being. The Franciscan sat quietly with a neutral expression, listening patiently for nearly two hours, while I revealed many of the ominous details of my inner existence for the first time ever. Finally, I breathed a sigh to punctuate the last page.

With no emotional reaction, he said sincerely, "This time, you have done a lot of good work. Thank you for trusting me to hear it."

He asked a few questions for clarity and probed briefly in several areas to bring more of my deeper feelings to the surface.

He obviously viewed my recovery as a work-in-progress and turned the discussion to Steps Six and Seven, advising me that they represented monumental advances in thinking about life, and that I should read and reread the essays on them, to gain some awareness of the freedom they implied.

I thanked him for listening and took to heart his parting words, "Make sure you take the time to enjoy the results of your work."

I spent an hour sitting on a bench, secluded by a half-dozen tall and fragrant spruce trees, breathing the cool fall air and gazing across the expansive manicured lawns, toward a treed hillside along the foreground of which ran the three-foot high fieldstone wall that represented the boundary of the Monastery's grounds. For the first time in my life, I consciously experienced a sensation of compassion and, with that, a sense of forgiveness founded upon a platform of unknowing. I could see that I had not deliberately intended any of the hurt and disappointment, of which I had been the unfortunate perpetrator. Although I knew it did not relieve me of responsibility for my actions, I saw that I must at least forgive myself. I took from my pocket a pen and small notebook and wrote:

I wronged people not from a personal perspective, not intentionally targeting individuals to receive the brunt of my anger and self-pity, for I often wanted to love those persons, to care for them and have them love me. My actions and my thinking were completely self-centered, driven entirely by fear within me, by my enormous insecurities.

As the instructions for completing Step Five had clearly stated, I had discovered something of the "exact nature of my wrongs."

I drove into the city because I had a few errands to attend to downtown. After parking the truck near the city core, I began walking along a busy downtown sidewalk. As I approached them, it seemed that people's faces became vivid reflections of their lives. I could see in them the trials and frustrations I had just shared regarding my own life. As I experienced the sensation of compassion, compassion for others this time, I began to look joyfully into people's eyes as I met them. They remained strangers to me in name only, and I marveled as I recalled references to "the brotherhood of man." Once more I took out my pen and notebook and wrote:

Awareness of my own past problems, resulting from defective psychological machinery; and being aware that I still have limitations, some known and others still undiscovered; and knowing how wrong thinking stood in the way of my own happiness, I can at least forgive one and all for any wrongs I might perceive as having been done to me.

I was awestruck by the notion that we are all in this together. It was a lofty plane upon which I had landed that afternoon. I thought those insightful moments must be spiritual experiences or, as I'd heard others referring to them, epiphanies. I could hardly wait to report the experience to Will, which I did that night after an A.A. meeting.

"I'm glad to hear you completed those steps, very important," he said. "Of course, a nice feeling doesn't often have much permanence about it. The disappointing reality of these brief insights into a better way of thinking, no matter how appealing they are at the time, is that they are not always sufficient to alter patterns of thought and behavior that have become deeply entrenched during all those undisciplined years of drinking."

That was an unusual number of words for Will at one time. I caught the gist of them, but it was a little hard for me to believe, at the expense of my euphoric state, that I would ever repeat some of the ridiculous things I'd done in the past.

Sitting alone that evening, I came to some conclusions regarding a Higher Power as well. Because of my continuing abhorrence for organized religion, I deliberately tried to maintain a non-denominational and unaffiliated position, as I entered my generic ideas in the notebook:

God: I have faith that God is in charge of the future. His will for me is good and His purpose is filled with kindness, understanding, and love. I know, without Him, my life is unmanageable. I know I must turn everything over to God: my will, my life, and the future. I believe, if I do what is right each day, the future will unfold according to God's will, and God's will is what is best for me. Turning everything over to God is humbly admitting that I do not have control over other people as well. I must live and let live. I will become helpful and useful by doing God's will, because people will trust me more and I will be a channel of God's compassion and love.

I was in a state of bliss by this point. At the same time, I knew that sharing any of these thoughts with old Will would only invite a puncturing of my balloon.

The first hard evidence of the functioning of my new arrangement with God arose when Barry and I purchased hunting licenses for mule-deer, whitetail deer, elk, and moose and made plans to do some hunting. Nancy did not seem pleased with the prospect, but how could a woman object to the idea of two brothers hunting together with the goal of supplementing the meat supply? I was finding her more and more irritating and often only barely contained my comments, for the sake of my relationship with my brother.

On the first day out, as we drove along the road adjacent to one of Will's pastures, a nice mule deer buck crossed in front of us, four well-developed points on either side. He disappeared into a narrow section of forest that stood between the road and an adjacent cutline. We drove on, and stopped a hundred yards up the road. I quietly got out of the truck and sneaked into the bush while Barry drove a little further, hoping to distract the wary animal's attention. I moved cautiously ahead over three inches of newly fallen snow that muffled any sound. Peering out the other side of the trees I couldn't see anything, but I stopped behind sufficient cover and waited. In no more than a minute, I spotted the large antlers protruding above the small poplars at the perimeter. He was taking a last precautionary glance before moving into the clearing a hundred yards from my position.

I had levered a bullet in to the chamber of my Browning .308 rifle earlier, and now I slowly cocked the hammer. My heart pounded in my chest until it seemed to cause a constriction in my throat. It seemed the big buck must be able to hear it in the intense silence. I watched through the scope as he stepped gingerly forward and came into position, completely free of the last trees, the crosshairs specifically targeting him mid-girth two inches behind his front leg. The explosion of the ammunition and the recoil of the rifle were obscured by the intensity of my focus on the target. When the deer immediately lunged forward, appearing to accelerate as though not hit, I automatically levered the rifle, aimed, and fired again, this time at a moving target. In the same instant, his legs folded and he sprawled forward in the snow. I walked directly to where he lay and took advantage of a few minutes of solitude before Barry came along the cutline with the truck. I noticed the spray of blood across the snow, stretching back far enough to inform me that he had been well hit with the first shot. I had a moment to admire the beauty of the animal and to be alone with the inevitable mix of triumph and remorse. I regretted taking the second shot, expecting that it had either missed or made a mess of stomach and intestines, or possibly destroyed some useful meat. I kicked the snow off the limbs of a small pine tree and leaned the rifle against a branch. Making quite sure that he was dead, I took out my skinning knife and cut his throat, although I doubted there was much blood left to drain.

While eviscerating the carcass, Barry held up the remains of the fragmented heart and said with a smile and obvious satisfaction, "Good shot." Only when we had completed that portion of the work did Barry take a look inside and relieve my uncertainty regarding shot number two. He pointed to two holes, where the bullets had entered the ribcage, with little more than an inch between them. "Very good shooting," he said.

"Holy cow," I exhaled. Then I looked at the beautifully machined, scope-mounted, lever-action rifle, and silently thought, "High power, no, Higher Power." The accuracy involved was beyond my unassisted skill. The thrill was more intense than I had experienced with the first deer I had shot at age seventeen. It felt more natural. Rather than boyish insecurity and bewilderment, I felt as though it had all been perfectly right, sort of primordially right. I felt a revitalized connection with some mysterious masculine archetype, as though I had only just then moved through some shadowy passage from boy to man.

I wondered if Barry sensed how profound my experience had been. I didn't dare to discuss it with him because I thought that it probably should have happened to me thirty years ago. I expected that it probably had happened long ago for him, but that he wouldn't have been able to define it, the process of growing up being a rather normal event for most people. In any case, I doubted that he would be comfortable with me talking about it.

In mid-November, four months after our mountain adventure together, I received a phone call from Mrs. Ford with an invitation to meet with her, her husband, and the Edwards couple at a local saloon for a reunion and review of the pictures they had taken. I was thrilled with the idea and agreed to meet them for burgers and drinks three days later on a Saturday evening.

After we gave the waitress our orders for drinks, mine a club soda and lime, Glen asked, "You don't drink alcohol?"

I thought of my abstinence during the trip, as well as Dennis's, but they must have interpreted it as an exception due to the job we were doing. Anyway, not wanting to get into a discussion about it, I said, "I did at one time, but decided I'd had enough."

It didn't bother me that they were drinking beer and other alcohol drinks, and I thoroughly enjoyed looking at the pictures. Mrs. Ford had enlarged several very good shots of Dennis and me, and had put together a small album, as a further expression of their gratitude for our efforts. It had obviously been everything they'd dreamed of. For more than an hour, while we ate and looked at the photographs again, I listened to their memories and their glowing compliments regarding our contribution. I felt happy and comfortable in their company.

At some point, the conversation drifted to other travel experiences they'd had, and it continued on from there, more and more on the same topic. In an attempt to include me, James Edwards asked, "Have you done much travelling, Rick?"

Still hiding behind my identity as a life-long mountain-man, because I had never informed them otherwise, I replied rather dryly, "I've been to Las Vegas once."

"Oh," they seemed to utter collectively, while immediately resuming reviews of their own vast travel portfolios. I grew irritable as I observed the exchange deteriorating into a kind of one-upmanship. I was reminded of my own past competing-for-status in that same realm. My irritation grew to an intensity that made me shift in my seat. The longer I listened, the more difficult it became for me to sit quietly and maintain my disguise. Contempt for them and their boasting swelled, along with my animosity, until I began looking for a way to attack, similar to a matador preparing for the final plunge of his rapier. It came as Glen Ford interrupted his own monologue regarding a recent trip to Paris, France.

He turned and spoke directly to me. "If you go nowhere else, you should try to get to New Orleans sometime, just for an exposure to something really different."

"I know all about this bullshit," I growled. "I have worked in the investment business, lived in New York and Chicago, and travelled all over the world. I left that life behind and came out here because I saw the hollowness in it all. Just like your trip to the mountains, you have visited a lot of places but you have never really been there, because you just throw money at

411

it until you get the thrill you are after, and fly away back to your glossy cushioned world of money and luxury."

They made no verbal response, of course, which left a kind of cold nothingness hanging over the table. The party didn't last much longer. As Glen paid the bill and we headed toward the door, I regretted undermining the image they had held of me, that they had found so pleasing to look upon. I realized too late that they had demonstrated a great respect for me, more importantly respect for my lifestyle, which they probably desired very much for themselves, a lifestyle I had been privileged to adopt. I tried for a warm and friendly farewell, which they tolerated with the withering goodwill that remained in their hearts, but something of great value had been destroyed. It would be a bleak drive home.

Blunt honesty regarding my personal history was an entirely unnecessary deflation of their memories and celebration. But worse, I had returned their generous respect and near veneration with bitter contempt and condemnation. It would be impossible for them, while riding home together in the same vehicle, I imagined with a nauseating sense of certainty, to look each other in the eye without standing on the common ground of condemning me as a fraud, aggrieved loser, and raving fool. I saw that my scornful reaction to their business success, wealth, and apparently good marriages was no more than envy and jealousy. I saw my disdain for their limited outdoor skills, and the pleasure they had gotten from a few refined menus along the way, as my own arrogant righteousness. Try as I might I could not justify my brutal disregard for them as decent people with whom I had enjoyed the trip of a lifetime, and for whom I had tarnished the memory.

In the emotionally excruciating aftermath of that episode, new awareness of my propensity for self-sabotage emerged. Not drinking, it became quite apparent, was not enough. I had discovered an almost unbelievable similarity between one A.A. co-founder's experience in the investment business and my own, while reading "Bill's Story" in the book *Alcoholics Anonymous*. It had represented a comforting identification for

412

me. But it yielded another insight as well, which had been supported and clarified with additional reading. The A.A. book suggested that alcoholics had reduced chances of creating anything good and lasting, despite being given the very best of opportunities, for several reasons that were not directly linked to alcohol consumption. Somewhere in those pages was the statement, "Selfishness – self-centeredness! That, we think, is the root of our troubles." And I had read somewhere else: "The first thing we had to learn was self-restraint."

Although I agreed with the weighty, wide-ranging truth inherent in the two assertions, I experienced immediate distaste for both as I contemplated their application to me personally. First, they were entirely foreign to my habitual pattern of reacting to the world around me. Even more daunting was the thought that changing my pattern of reacting was going to require enormous effort, if it was possible at all. I thought again of the trouble I had just caused myself and others, the similarly heavy prices I had paid in the past, and those I would continue to pay if something didn't change. New illumination fell upon the Step One contention: "that our lives had become unmanageable."

Over the next few miles, I became fearfully aware of how little I seemed to know about living life. Suddenly, anxiety arose concerning the legitimacy of my place in the fellowship of Alcoholics Anonymous. After all, I realized with increasing apprehension, a compulsive desire to consume alcohol had not manifested itself since my first two meetings. While I saw that I had experienced little trouble with stopping drinking, my heart raced at my comprehension of this enormous unmanageability. I so desperately needed help with that. Like a drowning man grasping at floating debris in a cold raging mountain river, I hoped my physical alcoholism represented sufficient qualification, that I would be given on account of it the opportunity to sort through my real problems, my overwhelming emotional and mental confusion, and someday reach a safe and peaceful shore.

Dignity? My actions were not dignified. I remembered that time in London when John Sargent had suggested I "get hold of myself" and I thought again about the term self-possession. I considered that my problem might always have been a lack of focus on a sufficiently elevated objective, with respect to self-worth, the worth of others, and those aspects of a good life that were beyond material wellbeing. Perhaps a belief in a Higher Power would somehow help raise the bar, lend new discipline in my battle against erratic and careless behavior. Almost everyone I knew seemed more dignified and self-respecting than I'd ever been, especially Celia, who had handled the many excruciating trials placed on her plate by our marriage. To preserve dignity, her first reaction was always to set aside her emotional and mental torment until it would not affect her speech and behavior. I began to crave that kind of composure, but could hardly imagine how I would acquire it.

I believed I had gained even more insight into the Franciscan's assertion that I may wish to do some additional work. Years of manipulating others in my continuous search for self-satisfaction, or overpowering them with brash controlling audacity and a loud barroom voice, would not be easy to change. It seemed that much of society was preoccupied with grasping after money and power, or visions of romance, and that loud, brazen individualism was a generally revered quality. But I had twenty years of evidence to remind me of the pain and disappointment I would incur by following that path any further. Completely oblivious of driving into the farmyard, oblivious of the entire thirty-minute drive home in fact, I went directly to bed, emotionally drained and mentally exhausted.

Lying in bed the next morning, I found myself re-evaluating the consequences of combining serious and ardent introspection with a little pretentious theorizing about my relationship with God. I could see it had landed me in a state of spiritual make-believe ('pink cloud' people in A.A had called it), and it appeared to be particularly delusional and hazardous in my case. In hindsight, old Will's assessment had been a fair warning that I did not heed. The fact that I was still acting to

414

satisfy my own perverted perspective of the world around me was a serious underlying problem, and it made a lark of the idea that I was guided by any kind of spirituality! Clearly, I was still governed by a condition the A.A. book appropriately described as "self-will run riot." I had embraced a fabricated intellectual progression that appeared to be an act of surrender when, in fact, it was one of recruitment. God, as I understood Him, was on my team, while I remained the captain.

Nonetheless, I felt a little happier and lighter inside than had been my experience in waking up over most of the previous forty years. I felt my life might have taken a meaningful turn. I remembered the mistake I had made the night before with lingering regret, but I had hope, too, that I could be free of such destructive behavior someday. Absent was the roaring numbness I had awoken to so often in the past, when horrific images flashed before my bloodshot eyes and I endured the inner terror of learning the truth about some social disaster, because I couldn't remember beyond a befogged sense of doom. I could see that I would continue to make mistakes. I hoped the moral devastation might be lessened by my efforts at 'doing the right thing' once in a while.

Following a delightful little Christmas party in mid-December, Celia had taken my daughter back east to spend the holiday with her family. I had received a Christmas invitation from my mother to share the day with family, but I had declined, preferring to immerse myself in A.A. at a clubhouse in the city. It had been thoroughly publicized; meetings were going on all day and a turkey dinner was being served free of charge all afternoon. The work I had done, opening up the past and looking at the unsavory aspects of my relationships, had cracked open some fault lines. I sensed that I needed to adopt a new attitude and discover a new foundation, but I did not yet know what that would look like and it left me feeling vulnerable. The anonymity of spending the day with a group of people that I could relate to in a meaningful but general way, and whose last names I didn't know, seemed the most comfortable choice for me. In the end, I did not regret it.

The couple that had first shown up at my local meeting about seven months ago, relieving me of my solitude, had taken me under their wing from that point forward. They invited me to celebrate New Year's Eve at their home. We had a truly relaxed and fun-filled time bringing in 1991, playing games, laughing a lot, and not drinking. The holidays had passed without a ripple of emotional turmoil or empty nostalgia, and that had been my objective. I hadn't felt threatened by the desire to drink, as many others in my position had talked about. I had simply wanted to step aside of the commercialism, the religious formality, and any social complexity.

In January, I began an earnest drive to increase my inventory of real estate listings. The market for farms, recreational property, and small ranches seemed to catch on fire once spring was in the air and, to capitalize on that, it was prudent to search out salable properties well in advance. With Barry looking after the daily feeding of cattle, I was free to divide my time between making money and my preoccupation with non-secular illumination.

When Celia returned with Elizabeth, for whom we had celebrated a second birthday a few months back, I soon found myself making an exception to the other two priorities. On my first trip to visit them in the New Year, Celia said, "Elizabeth is completely potty-trained now, and I have been wondering if you would like to take her back to the ranch with you for a few days. I know she would love that and it would give me a little time to myself."

In the midst of a messy blend of feelings, including delight because I truly adored my little girl, obligation because I felt truly grateful for Celia's selfless contribution, and staggering anxiety with trying to comprehend the potential challenges, I agreed. Celia began packing a few things for her and making a list to guide me in the care and feeding of a two-year-old. The next day, we drove off together and I found myself entering a small and wonderful kingdom that was to become a very precious aspect of my existence. She talked continuously, voicing her every thought, saying things that caused tears to well in my eyes over the beauty and simplicity. She was happy all the time, eating her breakfast, playing in the tub while having a bath, going to sleep in my bed while I read to her at night.

The only thing she demanded was my nearly constant attention, and I found myself regretting every single moment in which I had become otherwise distracted. It was hard work. There were moments in which she occupied herself by talking to her large green stuffed frog, or a teddy bear, and that helped. But the relief I felt, as she closed her eyes for her afternoon nap or finally fell asleep at night, was immense. In fact, the sense of relief was completely imaginary and temporary, because I almost immediately turned my mind toward fretting in some self-absorbed fashion in any case.

I had often heard the term 'insanity' discussed at A.A. meetings, at first thinking that it did not likely apply to me. Once I saw the senselessness of drinking to excess, and the repeated suffering and trouble it had caused, I admitted that I had been insane to that degree. Very gradually, I became more aware of the absolute craziness of much of my mental activity. I had to confess that my mental processes often ranged far from any concept I had of normalcy. Not that I was psychotic, I thought, but rather I was too often neurotic: overwhelmed by anxiety, carried away by grandiosity, or furious over some menial disturbance, all of which, I supposed, more balanced people did not experience. Or, maybe everyone occasionally experienced doubt with respect to the fine line between sanity and insanity, speculating anxiously about which side of it they were on. In any case, I detested the craziness that swirled through my mind at times and I wanted to be free of it. I had tried sitting quietly and meditating, but that only removed the merciful distraction of busyness and turned me into a sitting duck for attacks from my wandering, wanting, fearing, and angry mind. On that score, I should have thankfully permitted Elizabeth's sweet distracting playfulness to carry me away with joy. As I might crave an addictive substance, however, I was drawn by the notion of solitude, in which I could freely think my personal thoughts. I felt as though my time away from solitary thinking was somehow being wasted, an impulse similar to waiting impatiently for someone else to quit talking, for my turn to give verbal expression to my own cherished ideas. Fortunately, with a sense of the precious nature of her presence in my life as a guide, I did the right thing more often than not and participated in the little worlds she created.

In the months ahead, her visits became routine, every two or three weeks, and the duration grew from two days to five and more. One day, when I was driving her home, she asked how many days she had stayed with me, and I answered, "Three days."

"Daddy, next time I'm going to stay for eight days!" she exclaimed, trying to get as many fingers extended, and not more.

I turned my tear-filled eyes toward the window, unable to reply through the swelling in my throat. I often shed a few tears of joy in her presence, and sometimes even more over the sorrow of parting with her, as I drove back home alone.

Chapter 31

Someone at a meeting said, "I have been advised to reconcile myself with the religion of my childhood." It was one of those statements that stayed with me and occupied an increasingly important place in my thinking. I wondered how I could ever overcome the deeply entrenched animosity I had held for so long toward all things Christian. That was probably my biggest resentment, the most immediate focus of my anger and swearing. I remembered my high school friend Darren, and the first time he uttered the enormously blasphemous phrase, "Jesus fucking Christ." It had pleased me immensely to hear his expression of anger and rebellion, because it sounded so like my own. I tried the phrase out a time or two and we shared rounds of cynical laughter, as though we had just pulled a fast one on the guards and broken out of a prison.

There was an Evangelical Missionary Church two miles from the farm and I knew several of my ranching neighbors, people with whom I had become acquainted and rather liked, attended there regularly. On several Sunday mornings, I found reasons to drive past the modern but unpretentious white church, nestled among some very large spruce trees, with the manse a hundred feet away and similarly shaded. Observing the quite full parking lot, I deduced a large attendance and finally convinced myself that my presence may go unnoticed. I walked timidly from my truck toward the large open doors and experienced an eerie disorientation as I accepted the program from the smiling greeter. I was late enough that everyone was seated and only a few turned their heads in my direction, one a neighbor who smiled reservedly, for which I was grateful. My nostrils were seared with a familiar perfumed odor and I was reminded of those days long ago when my fainting had resulted in my release from attending the little church in town, a guilt free escape from obligation to my mother.

They sang a few hymns, still too high pitched for my participation, which my lack of familiarity with the words prevented in any case. We listened to a parishioner giving a reading from the Bible, the essence of which I don't recall. Two men moved along the aisles passing the collection plates up and down the rows, into which I placed a dollar amongst the tens and twenties. Finally, the minister approached the pulpit. He opened the large Bible to a previously selected page, placed his notes to one side, swept his paternal gaze slowly across the congregation gaining everyone's undivided attention in a long and seemingly grave moment of silence, and spoke boldly, "The man standing at the door of the brothel is looking for God." Those were the first and last words I recall from that experience and I was fascinated by them. I did not stay for coffee and fellowship as they invited everyone to do.

The following week the minister made a brief reference to the Twelve Steps of Alcoholics Anonymous and suggested that Christians may find their application enlightening. I considered that a sufficiently inclusive opening and, when the service had ended, found an opportunity to ask him if I could speak with him privately. He was open to my request, of course, and asked me to stop by his home for coffee the next afternoon.

Retaining a custom that seemed entirely appropriate to his six or seven decades of life, the minister wore a suit and tie even on his days off, but his manner was very casual and I felt warmly welcomed by him and his wife, who was delightfully attentive with coffee and cookies, but otherwise left us entirely alone. I spent a very comfortable two hours with him and shared a great deal concerning my life, my recent decision to quit drinking, and my even more recent inclination to re-examine Christianity. He impressed me as a thoughtful man who had a vast insight into the nature of humanity and sat in judgment of no one. Still, I was not explicit regarding my debauched history of misdirected romance, nor did I consider it important to expose the disorientation that still arose with my childhood memories.

He offered three suggestions for my consideration: first, that I read a book called *Mere Christianity* by C. S. Lewis, which he loaned me; second, that I attend a weekly men's breakfast meeting held each Saturday morning at a hotel in town; third, that I give some thought to a men-only workshop on relationships and sexuality that was to be held nearby in about five weeks.

I was hungry for answers and willing to read anything that might offer spiritual insight. As well, I was looking forward to further discussions with the kind and wise elder and mentor I felt I had stumbled upon. A note inside the book's cover informed me that C. S. Lewis had been a professor at Oxford University and an atheist for many years prior to his conversion and subsequent prolific writing on the subject of Christianity. My interest, and the credibility I allowed the author, rose sharply upon that discovery. His discussion of man's innate sense of right and wrong was fascinating, the 'Law of Nature' he called it, referring to it as 'Moral Law' interchangeably. The fact of the Moral Law's ubiquitous existence, he contended, was irrefutable proof of the existence of God. A sense of the Law of Nature was one of two characteristics all men had in common, the second being that they nevertheless did not abide by the first. On page fifty of *Mere Christianity* he suggested that men had always sought to be their own masters, apart from God, and stated, "And out of that hopeless attempt has come nearly all that we call human history – money, poverty, ambition, war, prostitution, classes, empires, slavery – the long terrible story of man trying to find something other than God which will make him happy." Well, I thought, I could check off several items on that list which pertained to my own case, and add a few that weren't there. His contentions had a tone of validity.

On page fifty-two he presented a case regarding Jesus Christ: "You must make your choice," he said. "Either this man was, and is, the Son of God; or else a madman or something worse. You can shut him up for a fool, you can spit at Him and kill Him as a demon; or you can fall at His feet and call Him Lord and God. But let us not come with any patronizing nonsense about His being a great human teacher. He has not left that open to us. He did not intend to."

I was puzzled by C. S. Lewis' certainty, and flipped back to reread his remark on page thirty-nine: "But, of course, being a Christian *does* mean thinking that, where Christianity differs from other religions, Christianity is right and they are wrong." I continued reading, but I felt increasingly like an oppressed victim of glib erudition. This highly intelligent author seemed to be laboring relentlessly at convincing himself of some rather easily comprehended ideas, and then invariably resorting, for proof of their authenticity, to a belief that "it was so because it was so." On page sixty-two he asserted, "We do know that no man can be saved except through Christ," and I was forced into a corner from which I leapt for mental relief. I simply was not ready to commit myself so specifically and laid the little paperback aside.

Responding to the issue of my reconciling myself with the religion of my childhood, Will, my A.A. elder, had suggested I read a book called *The Sermon on the Mount* by Emmet Fox. I found it in a bookstore and read it from cover to cover. It was a particularity refreshing read. In the first few pages Mr. Fox insisted that Jesus had proposed no theology, that his message was entirely spiritual and metaphysical, and that he was not intent on developing a limited man-like God or a religion. Those words substantially reopened the door for me by reducing much of the cluttered and confusing message that I had received during my childhood and adolescence to the status of rubbish. Emmet Fox wrote on page five, "But he teaches that we are only punished for – and actually punished by – our own mistakes; and he teaches that every man or woman, no matter how steeped in evil and uncleanness, has always direct access to an all-loving, all-powerful Father-God, who will forgive him, and supply His own strength to him to enable him to find himself again."

That sounded enormously compassionate to me, and uncomplicated by notions such as "original sin," "eternal torment," and the "Plan of Salvation," phases which Mr. Fox called "farfetched and very inconsistent legend." That kind of "unutterably horrible doctrine," he insisted, will not be found in the Bible. I concurred deeply and experienced a kind of profound liberation while reading his contention that such a God would be one "who conducted his universe very much as a rather ignorant and barbarous prince might conduct the affairs of a small oriental Kingdom." His "prince" sounded very like the God toward which I had directed my wrath and swearing all these years. My only very recently designated Higher Power had been specifically endowed with a complete absence of such rigid and pompous definition.

Tensions with Barry's fiancée gradually bristled toward a precarious state. The sulky bitterness I perceived in her, especially when she and I were alone in the house or crossed paths in the yard, I responded to with indignant obstinacy. She was a guest at my place, after all, and I would not let such behavior go unpunished. In the end, it was me who crossed the line one day, with some sarcastic remark. That led to Barry asking me what the problem was and, although I don't know how upset he was initially, my suppressed anger came to the surface and my words were not conciliatory. Barry's next words were a question. "Maybe Nancy and I should look for our own place?"

I heard an underlying challenge: that I could not manage the cattle without him. I did not entirely believe that, but more importantly, I could not have backed down even if I had. I greatly feared the conversation would end in an irreversible impasse when I said, "Maybe you should."

It was over. My little brother walked away. In the days ahead I relived the few moments of our last conversation many times and, as utterly sad and damaging as the outcome had been, I could find no alternative solution. I was surprised when, only three days later, Barry announced they had found a farmstead for rent that would accommodate his share of the cows. I wondered if they hadn't been contemplating a move prior to our confrontation. But that wasn't important right now, and I turned to the particularly distasteful thing I had to do next. I had talked to Will about the problems we were having and I knew his guidance was sound. I looked at Barry squarely and said, "I cannot let the cattle leave this place until we can arrange to remove your name from the land title."

Although the transition represented a gut-wrenching rift between us, I believe we both felt we had little choice, tried to do the right thing, and remained generally respectful, not allowing emotional and verbal impropriety to create deep-seated resentment. I did toss in a comment about his marrying Nancy and expecting a city girl to commit to a life of cattle ranching. But I had dropped the subject quickly and Barry had chosen wisely to let it pass unanswered. He possessed much more than I did in the way of social skills.

However, a few weeks later, when the legal matters had been sorted out and we met to sign an agreement that would release us from any further obligation to one another, it became clear to me that a difference in perspective existed. I was guilt-ridden at the prospect of emotionally disappointing and wounding my little brother, and hoped sincerely that everything was going well for him. Because of that, I decided to say something that would convey my sentiments and leave the door open to future brotherly reconciliation. Drawing some strength from the principle of doing the right thing, I looked at him eye-to-eye, inhaled deeply to overpower the hostility that was still close to the surface, and said, "I guess I have not been a very good brother in all of this."

"I guess you haven't," he replied with resignation.

I let the comment go by and turned to the business at hand, which we completed without further exchange regarding our relationship. I was disappointed, of course, but there was an element of closure in knowing that he felt wronged. Perhaps he believed he had not been fairly compensated for all the work he had done during our mountain adventure and around the ranch in the last two years. I, conversely, thought his cost-free accommodations and my help in setting him up with cattle of his own was more than a fair exchange and my thoughts were quite free of that issue. I had already gained some insight into the futility of playing the victim, the foolishness inherent in the notions of fair and unfair. There was satisfaction in knowing where we stood and I could leave it at that.

The very next day, Dennis, my second brother, called to say he wanted his seven cows, which he had purchased as an investment and left in our care, to be shipped with Barry's cattle. I had forgotten about those and, in a fog of surprise and further disappointment over the obviously broadening family rift, I missed some of his words. Clearly, however, there was no warmth in his voice, and there was emphasis in his suggestion that the cattle would thus be in better hands. I simply agreed to do as he wished and the conversation ended coolly.

I had also learned a little about the futility of prolonged self-reproach and I was trying to curb my inclination toward it. I wasn't at all confident I had handled things in the best possible way and thinking about the whole episode was dizzying. But I was certain I had been struggling to do my best, having taken the uncharacteristic precaution of discussing my decisions with my mentor, for a crosscheck on my thinking, before acting. Nonetheless, the call from Dennis had renewed my struggle, and it was further exacerbated by a letter from my mother.

I was shocked as I read the words and realized that she had clearly taken the side of my two younger brothers. Her words suggested that I had treated them unfairly and that I was solely responsible for taking action to restore good family relations. I thought of the countless letters she had sent me over the years, and the wonderful continuing connection with family they had usually imparted. I noted mentally that I had done my part in sending cards and letters in return, and calling her. I was saddened at her lack of impartiality, and I was angered at the realization that my brothers had made it a family-wide issue, creating a case and condemning me in my absence.

I decided I would do nothing to entangle myself in the messy bog that formed in my mind as I considered the prospects for useful dialogue. In their minds, I had been judged guilty and there would be no stepping back to take a reasonable look at things. Irritation with my father's convoluted methods of verbal combat resurfaced and, although I doubted he would involve himself in a tussle of this sort, I knew other members of the family had acquired a binding propensity for his style of engagement. I was hurt and angry but not yet motivated to act.

Looking to divert my mind, I attended the Christian men's breakfast, as the minister had recommended. I hoped Winston Holmes and other of my non-churchgoing neighbors, some of whom sat in the main dining area through which I had to walk, had not observed me entering the small conference room that had been reserved for the more righteous members of the community. As I paused in the doorway, the latter welcomed me with smiles that seemed exaggerated and I felt obliged to smile a big smile in return. I despised the dearth of authenticity, realizing at the same time it may have been my own projection. I felt at ease as I took my seat among them, though, and I don't think I was rattled visibly when I realized I had joined a Bible study. I swept away a wave of contempt and resolved to listen until I could determine the character of the conversation. Besides some of my rural neighbors, I knew an older gentleman sitting at the head of the table. He had served as a missionary in China many years previous, which he had made abundantly clear to me in a brief conversation following the church service one day. Another man, who I knew a bit about as well, had been a pastor somewhere, currently served as a counselor in town, and had a rather flamboyant blonde wife who worked for a competing real estate agency. I thought her ethics were not always biblically inspired.

We were trying to figure out what Jesus meant when He made a certain statement. I don't recall what He said, but I

426

couldn't avoid thinking that He should have been more precise. Why make it so difficult to understand? Then I thought: perhaps He had been clear when He said it, but something had been lost through unreliable human memory, before it was written down, or in the translation from Hebrew, or because the English we were reading was four hundred years out of date. In any case, the conversation segued to enemies of Christianity and someone expressed disdain for the multiple deities of Hinduism, of which I knew nothing but I concluded it wasn't wise to contribute a Buddhist slant on the conversation. The former missionary turned red in the face as he expressed his bitterness toward the communists who had taken control of China over forty years ago. No one seemed to think he was out of place with his apparently vigorous hatred, having had profound training in Christian ideals and a direct encounter with people who viewed those same ideals with contempt, I supposed. When he seemed content that he had thrown down the gauntlet to the communists, on our behalf, the conversation struggled to return to its previous more studious course. It never did, however, and we collectively concluded that Christ's message, because it was often woven into parables, was sometimes mysterious and beyond our comprehension.

Driving home, I wondered about the men's expressions of satisfaction regarding the meeting. I thought perhaps there was peer pressure at play which compelled them to have had a good experience without introspection. I smirked to myself at the thought of the missionary and his forty-year-old resentment; perhaps he needed to deal with it and could use A.A.'s fourth and fifth steps, as the minister had alluded to on Sunday. Then, winning a battle with my conceited, contemptuous predisposition, I surrendered to the fact that I was rather new at the spiritual game, and had best maintain an open mind.

I had the ranch and large house entirely to myself, since my brother and his fiancée had moved out, and I truly enjoyed coming home, lighting a fire, and tirelessly pursuing my new path in solitude. I also had the responsibility for feeding a hundred cows every day, as long as winter and early spring conditions kept the grass from growing. With Barry's consultation, soon after we'd moved there, I had bought a medium size tractor with a grapple-equipped loader and three-point hitch with a bale-handling attachment. It served well for many ranch chores and was indispensable when transporting the large round bales of hay and rolling them out on a white table cloth of untrampled snow, while the ravenous animals rushed in behind me to consume their daily ration.

The tractor did not have a cab and, when Elizabeth was staying with me, I sat in the seat with one arm around her as she stood alongside. "Hang on tight," I had to yell above the drone of the diesel engine and whine of the transmission whenever I needed both hands to shift gears or control the hydraulics. While we headed across the pasture in the cool air, she hummed and sang to her heart's delight, her voice resonating almost unnoticeably with the machine, her face beaming outward past the bulky turquoise hood of her winter coat.

It was difficult for me to ensure her safety on the tractor once we reached the stack of bales and I began rolling them out. So I usually found a place in the sun for her to sit and wait, leaning against a five-foot tall snow-capped hay bale, while I made the several necessary trips back and forth. She looked so small and vulnerable across two hundred yards of wind driven snow, her little pink face barely visible within the blue-green bundle of her two-piece outfit. I experienced moments of fatherly apprehension, and I stopped each time I returned to make sure she wasn't missing me or hadn't been frightened, only to discover her singing or happily sculpting the snow with her puffy purple mittens.

When I was done feeding, we walked into the herd and watched the cows eating. She assigned names to some of them, especially to a black, white-faced cow that was particularly quiet and showed not the slightest alarm at human proximity. I held Elizabeth's hand as she petted the fifteen hundred pound animal, which likewise demonstrated a complete absence of fear. Then, holding her securely in case we reached the old cow's limitations, I slid her onto its broad back, and she sat there beaming with glee. The big friendly bovine became known as "The Cow That Likes Little Girls" ('littow geos' phonetically), and we had to search her out every time from then on, summer and winter.

When I was with Elizabeth on days like that, the world beyond largely evaporated, as it had one spring day when my good neighbor, Winston Holmes, drove across the field to pay a random visit. He grinned with unsurprised delight at the sight of a little girl sitting on a cow and asked her if the cow had a name. "The Cow That Likes Littow Geos," she replied with certainty, and Winston's big belly shook with amusement. When she had returned home to her mother, and I was alone once more, I reflected upon those moments and I felt certain my life was richer than it had ever been.

Chapter 32

Quite often, when I was reading books with a spiritual focus, I experienced a wonderful emotional sense of release. Passages by Emmet Fox and other Christian writers suggested that adopting certain attitudes toward Christ could lift one up and place him beyond life's struggles, beyond the travails of the secular world. Descriptions of meditation in *The Heart of Buddhist Meditation* by Nyanaponika Thera, for example, implied a similar potential for transcendence. Such assertions never failed to have a magical, almost supernatural influence, but the effect was fleeting and produced no lasting change in my reaction to the world once I re-entered it as I was inevitably forced to do. I wondered if 'spiritual experiences' of that variety weren't described appropriately by the statement, "Frothy emotional appeal seldom suffices," found in the "Doctor's Opinion" in the book *Alcoholics Anonymous*.

I had been distancing myself from aspects of the secular world, especially anything I had an aversion for, through suppression and repression for forty years. What I really needed, I became quite certain, was more appropriately described by the phrase 'psychic change' which I interpreted as sweeping modification in the workings of my mind, which would alter my view of the secular world and provide me with a useful attitude toward it. I stumbled upon just such an awakening of insight as I read the first sentence of a book my younger sister had loaned me, *The Road Less Travelled* by M. Scott Peck, M.D.

"Life is difficult," he began. For a few minutes, I simply sat with the book in my lap, my head swimming with this new information, my mind unable to absorb another word. I couldn't have agreed more with his point of view, from a strictly private perspective. But I was temporarily doubtful about the relief I found in this sweeping assertion, doubtful of the permission it gave me to admit the truth of my personal experience. With everyone I had met since leaving home over twenty years ago, I had manufactured a glossy image of my idyllic country childhood, my exciting cowboy father, my enviable history of delightful days on horseback. I fully expected my listeners to drool with envy at the blissful perfection of it. I had worked relentlessly to paint the picture of a gifted life: blessed childhood, rousing adolescence, soaring career, financial success, world-traveler, and mountain man, all of it on easy street, all of it with perfect control. I had long since set aside the struggles and the pain of my youth because I thought they were inappropriate, that they should not have happened to me. I was certain that revealing such information would set me apart as odd, and disclose defective aspects of my character, because those same things had not happened to most other people. Excruciating defeat with repeated trading losses, the shame of sexual debauchery, the agony of drunken social embarrassments, and the many betrayals of trust – all of which had persisted through my adult life – I knew must be excluded where I sought to preserve the high regard of other people.

Dr. Peck continued, "This is a great truth, one of the greatest truths." In a footnote, he pointed out that the first of the Four Noble Truths taught by Buddha was, "Life is suffering."

I knew of Buddha's assertion, but I thought He was referring to conditions of poverty and disease and had rather overstated His case, at least as it pertained to our era; or that He had actually been referring to more subtle forms of discomfort, the sort of disquiet and lack of contentment that was not even perceptible to average humans, and had therefore overstated His case from a different perspective. I did not realize that He had been referring to cases such as mine, as though they were not at all unique among the countless billions of cases across unnumbered millennia and from shore to shore on all the continents of the earth, perhaps beyond.

I read on in *The Road Less Travelled*. "Most do not fully see this truth that life is difficult. Instead they moan more or less incessantly, noisily or subtly, about the enormity of their problems, their burdens, and their difficulties as if life were generally easy, as if life should be easy."

Once more I found myself at the threshold of newfound emotional freedom, but became halted in my tracks by a hazy incredulity. Not only was suffering common, so was the inclination to find it unacceptable. I saw that my pattern of objecting to this reality had been subtle rather than noisy; in fact, it had been silent. That was because, in addition to finding the condition generally unacceptable, I had judged it to be uniquely shameful. The walls that had held me captive for forty years received a solid battering.

Just then, old Will drove in the yard with his truck and horse trailer. I immediately looked forward to discussing my several spiritual forays with him. When he asked what I'd been up to, I brought up my church experience.

He said, "I've heard good things about that minister."

I expressed my frustration with the men's breakfast meeting. "I think they self-righteously believed theirs is the only answer, which would exclude over half the population of the world. I found the same attitude seeping through the pages of *Mere Christianity*. That's why I feel more comfortable with 'psychic change' than I do with phrases that sounded like 'religious conversion.'"

"That's good. You need to explore things. When it comes to the Higher Power, bigger is generally better." He had at once alleviated my concerns and placed a new guidepost along my path, without wasting words.

His voice was serene, his words certain, his facial expression unaffected, as though he had just observed that it was a good day for a horseback ride, which is exactly what he suggested with his next words. "I want to check on some cows and calves we moved to a remote pasture with a lot of bush. A neighbor reported seeing a grizzly wandering along a ridge that runs through the area. Bears will be kind of hyperactive right now after hibernation, looking to catch up on nourishment, and I'm not in the restaurant business. Why not catch your horse and come along?"

It felt good to catch and throw a saddle on Merlin again. I led him into the horse trailer and tied him next to the already saddled horse Will had brought with him. An easy flow of conversation continued as we drove out of the yard and turned west toward the foothills. Periods of extended silence were common when I was with Will and, realizing the extent of my initial verbal barrage that day, I deliberately refrained from talking too much, waiting for him to direct the conversation.

"What do you think of that Emmet Fox book? Have you read any of that?" he asked.

"Yes, I have," I answered. "I think it opens the door a lot wider than the church or the C. S. Lewis book."

"It's a good one for people like us who haven't always been churchgoers, more spiritual than religious. He says a person can get on track anytime, regardless of his past. He also says the world we live in is entirely up to us, an idea similar to the one laid out in a book titled *As a Man Thinketh*," Will added.

I was always amazed at how much reading he'd done. I also chuckled at his understatement, "haven't always been churchgoers," and I said, "That's what I meant when I said I preferred the phrase 'psychic change.'"

Will didn't respond, so I continued, "I started reading *The Road Less Travelled* by M. Scott Peck not long before you came along today. His first sentence is, "Life is difficult." That really turned some lights on for me."

We drove up to the barbed wire gate and I got out of the truck to open it. I thought to myself, "Man, I sure get going. I have to curb my long-winded responses and let him talk more." He pulled through the gate and into a clearing, where we unloaded the horses and snugged up the cinches. We strapped on chaps, tied oilskins behind our saddles, stuck rifles in scabbards, and mounted up.

433

With pent up energy, our fresh mounts pitched and pranced under us as we climbed up a small rise to join a trail that disappeared into the trees. Cool spring air sharpened the spicy organic aroma of the mixed poplar and spruce forest. As we rode free of the bush, into a large clearing, the midday sun blazed from a sapphire sky and bathed us in a tepid glow.

"Yes, life is difficult," my friend continued after at least twenty minutes had passed. "A lot of us never learned that, because we failed to grow up. Selfish and self-pitying, we never gained any real maturity, I mean."

The horses had settled down to a steady gait, walking side by side in the short grass. Feeling I had all the time in the world, I allowed several minutes of silence to pass until he began again.

"Life is not easy. On the other hand, once we understand that, and see that the same is true for everyone, two important things happen: our own life seems easier because we aren't resisting the truth all the time, and we begin to develop a little compassion for other people."

I absorbed his words and savored them, mindful of our vast, silent surroundings. Struggling against a constriction around my larynx, evidence of the respect and affection that suddenly welled up for this old rancher, and the thankfulness for his liberating insight, I said, "It amazes me that I know so little about life."

We crested the ridge and could see the cows spread out along the river in the valley below. Will gave them a onceover with a slow broad sweep of his binoculars before we rode down and through them. There was no indication of any trouble and, on the two mile loop we took in returning to the truck, we saw no signs of a bear. "Maybe he was just passing through," Will thought out loud.

I attended the two-day workshop the minister had recommended and I met several members of the local congregation there, one of them the man from the breakfast meeting who had been a pastor and was now a counselor. In his introductory talk, our facilitator explained that the program was designed for Christian men and the sessions were focused on past relationships with women, the shame and guilt that typically lingered, and on methods for freeing oneself from those inherently debilitating consequences. I thought of the people around me and doubted their records were anything like mine. The speaker asked for a show of hands, "How many have broken up with a high school sweetheart and still suffer feelings of guilt?" Probably sixty percent indicated they had. "How many have gone through a divorce?" About thirty percent admitted suffering that unsavory circumstance.

I concluded I was among those of the Christian community who felt a particular need for examining these issues. I was thankful they were not representative of the generally flawless church congregation. Still, although I had put up my hand in reply to both questions, I thought I had best use discretion regarding further disclosure.

The group leader's level of understanding and his articulation of men's suffering was enlightening and, once again, I found myself feeling less isolated with my own pain as I learned about that of others. As the two days wore on, I listened to personal accounts and gained more familiarity with the feeling of empathy. In spite of their relative innocence, compared to my debauched history, I saw that emotional damage was common ground among us.

One session in particular was memorable. After listening to the facilitator's prayer, "that our efforts would result in greater personal liberty and an expanded capacity to love others," we were instructed to make ourselves comfortable, close our eyes, and try to revive and relive the emotionally excruciating moments we'd been through. For perhaps thirty minutes, there was almost complete silence in the room except for occasional sniffles and even several instances of sobbing. I thought of Yvonne and Celia, way back to Jo-Anne, and then Yvonne again, and then I decided to stop inventorying names and merely focus on the feelings of regret and shame I still harbored. I thought of the other men in the room, and all the evidence in support of the contention that life is difficult.

At the end of the session, the facilitator asked us to focus on the fact that we had suffered as much as the women, possibly much longer because our suffering was often self-inflicted shame rather than a sense of victimization. He asked that we search for self-forgiveness by surrendering our transgressions to Jesus who had died for our sins, that we might find release. Then he prayed on our behalf again, "that we be immediately relived of our suffering." No doubt about it, I felt my burden had been lightened. I deeply desired to hold onto the liberated state of mind that seemed a tangible consequence of that day.

I attended services at the Evangelical church with some regularity over the next few weeks and I attended the men's breakfast meeting on Tuesdays. The minister's sermons usually contained some morsel of illumination, simply because he was a wise elder and had a large view of the world, to which he could effectively relate his spiritual message. I had less success gaining insight from various Biblical passages that were read on Sundays by members of the congregation, and I had no appreciation for hymn singing.

I remembered actually reading the King James Version of the Bible from cover to cover eight years ago, hidden away in the seclusion of my acreage on the outskirts of Chicago, sitting in front of the woodstove while large snowflakes floated down on the other side of my living room window. My objective then was more academic than spiritual, thinking I should have read it in order to more effectively reject it in support of my atheistic views. Even then, I was amazed and frustrated at the difficulty I had untangling the words of its numerous authors.

The deeper insight I anticipated from the men's Bible studies at our Tuesday breakfasts was not forthcoming either. We often reverently read segments of the Good Book only to become bogged down with understanding the message. With regard to parts that, if taken literally, were outside the range of current knowledge and customs, we relied on our missionary friend, or the former Chaplin, for interpretation. The missionary frequently opted for a hardline application to non-believers and other religions, while the Chaplin was inclined toward a more generally loving God, but the latter had to tread lightly for fear of being overridden. Too often I sensed we were engaged in defending Christianity and rationalizing its supremacy, rather than simply and securely searching for spiritual truth. The camaraderie was a lot more enjoyable than the discussion. Even so, I usually parted with the men in an agitated state of mind, chiding myself for not presenting them with arguments that I might have thrown into the mix in my more belligerent years; or berating myself for my contrarian attitude, even though I had contained it; or thankful that I had held my tongue, but wondering if I lacked integrity in doing so, for fear of risking their friendship.

I was drawn back into *Sermon on the Mount* because the message seemed more practical. Emmet Fox compared the Beatitudes delivered by Christ to the Eightfold Path of the Buddha and Ten Commandments of Moses, saying they were a general grouping of ideas, a summing-up of spiritual teachings. To take such an open-minded attitude I thought courageous and uplifting. He said they "had to do with mental states," and suggested Jesus was talking about right thinking leading to right action. A sentence on page eighteen, "Indeed, the whole current of His teaching is anti-ritualistic, anti-formalist," held sway in my mind.

I was compelled to read the book again. On page 109, I was drawn to the author's discussion of the Law of Life which led to his assertion that "the law of retribution is a Cosmic Law," and his quotation from Sir Edwin Arnold's 1885 rendering of the Hindu scripture, Bhagavad Gita, *The Song Celestial.*

> *It will not be contemned of any one;*
> *Who thwarts it loses, and who serves it gains:*
> *The hidden good it pays with peace and bliss,*
> *The hidden ill with pains.*
> *By this the slayer's knife did stab himself;*
> *The unjust judge hath lost his own defender;*
> *The false tongue dooms its lie; the creeping thief*
> *And spoiler rob, to render.*

It seeth everywhere and marketh all;
Do right – it recompenseth! Do one wrong –
The equal retribution must be made,
Though Dharma tarry long.

Mr. Fox then went on to say, on page 115, "In the Bible the term Christ is not identical with Jesus, the individual. It is a technical term which may be briefly defined as the Absolute Spiritual Truth about anything." Somehow, that opened a door for me and I suddenly felt less resistance. I found further clarity and validation when he asserted that THE CHRIST offers freedom from Karma.

It was only when I read his succeeding incredible claim: that no other source of freedom is available, that I suffered some dismay. I knew from other reading I'd done that Karma described an ancient Hindu concept, borrowed by Buddhists twenty-five hundred years ago. I immediately thought of the notion of Nirvana, which Buddhists certainly seemed to view as freedom from Karma, and I guessed that Mr. Emmet Fox hadn't completed his research after all. Therein resides the problem with too much analysis and discussion of spiritual matters, I concluded. Trying to unravel and define the mystery always leads from wonderful ethereal simplicity to frustrating, conflicting, and insufficient drivel. His was right about manmade religions, I thought. Too bad he came so close to violating his own taboos.

Chapter 33

One day I was browsing in a second-hand bookstore and *The Teachings of Don Juan: A Yaqui Way of Knowledge* by Carlos Castaneda caught my eye. Curled in front of the fire, I devoured the book because it was a refreshingly wild foray into the spiritual realm. Not once did I feel the urge to join in his curious, often bizarre, mystical journey. His wild wanderings were merely as wind under my own spiritual wings. I felt a sense of liberty that went to my very core, particularly with this excerpt from the book:

Anything is one of a million paths. Therefore you must always keep in mind that a path is only a path; if you feel you should not follow it, you must not stay with it under any conditions. To have such clarity you must lead a disciplined life. Only then will you know that any path is only a path and there is no affront, to oneself or to others, in dropping it if that is what your heart tells you to do. But your decision to keep on the path or to leave it must be free of fear or ambition. I warn you. Look at every path closely and deliberately. Try it as many times as you think necessary.

This question is one that only a very old man asks. Does this path have a heart? All paths are the same: they lead nowhere. They are paths going through the bush, or into the bush. In my own life I could say I have traversed long, long paths, but I am not anywhere. Does this path have a heart? If it does, the path is good; if it doesn't, it is of no use. Both paths lead nowhere; but one has a heart, the other doesn't. One makes for a joyful journey; as long as you follow it, you are one with it. The other will make you curse your life. One makes you strong; the other weakens you.

Before you embark on any path ask the question: Does this path have a heart? If the answer is no, you will know it, and then you must choose another path. The trouble is nobody asks the question; and when a man finally realizes that he has taken a path without a heart, the path is ready to kill him. At that point very few men can stop to deliberate, and leave the path. A path without a heart is never enjoyable. You have to work hard even to take it. On the other hand, a path with heart is easy; it does not make you work at liking it.

For me there is only the traveling on paths that have heart, on any path that may have heart, and the only worthwhile challenge is to traverse its full length--and there I travel looking, looking breathlessly.

His words echoed the A.A. Big Book's references to a "power greater than ourselves," and "God as we understood Him," and its declaration, "We found the Great Reality deep down within us. In the last analysis it is only there that He may be found." I was no less than jubilant as I recalled references to Buddha's insistence that there were 84,000 ways, each one only a finger pointing at the moon. It was evidently very easy, very tempting, and hopelessly distracting to become preoccupied with a specific finger, and lose sight of the moon. I became determined to close no doors, to wander along the broad hallway without restrictions on my heart, just open to the truth as it appeared each day. I had an appointment with the Monk at the Monastery in two days, and I believed the timing must have been inspired by that Power that was greater than me.

"Well, how are you? Tell me what has been going on." He invited me in with a big smile.

"I'm doing well, I think. I heard something about reconciling myself with the religion of my childhood, but I haven't made any progress on that. I've decided to relax in that

440

department and just keep exploring," I said as I sat down across from him.

"Are you working those steps and going to A.A. meetings?" he asked.

"Oh yes," I assured him.

He laughed, "That's good. If you told me that you had given those up because you had found the Lord, I wouldn't give you a snowball's chance in you-know-what."

I talked to him about the split with my brothers and the upsetting letter I had received from my mother. He reminded me that individuals, having chosen a radically different path, were frequently forced to temporarily disengage from family in order to establish a sound footing on their new course. The idea did not initially appeal to me because I viewed family cohesiveness as a priority, however loosely I defined it. But he suggested I give it some thought which, two weeks later, resulted in my decision to take the course he had prescribed. I compiled and mailed the following letter:

Dear Mother, Father, and Family,

This letter has been slow in coming because I didn't know what to say. It will be brief because there isn't much to say at this point.

There are only three pertinent points: (1) My life, although successful by some standards, and on the surface, has never been very rewarding. From day one, it has seemed I've had a feeling of emptiness and insufficiency, and I've spent too much of my life trying to fill these gaps. (2) There was no lasting solution in anything I tried, no philosophy of life or code of conduct that would remove the insecurities and hopelessness. (3) The program I am part of now is, doubtless in my mind, the answer for me. I feel better about myself, both assets and liabilities, and I am learning to accept others as they are. More often, as time passes, I feel deep down that "all is well."

So, do not be concerned about me. I have some peace of mind and a faith that everything is for the best. That is quite a

441

gift for someone who's not experienced it before. I sincerely want you to know I wish the very best for all of you. Mother, you mentioned forgiveness in your letter – do not be concerned. One great lesson I've learned is that I will have no serenity if I cannot and do not forgive one and all. It is not with anger or resentment, but with love and forgiveness that I say the following:

I don't know how long it will be or what will transpire to bring about a change, but today I am sure that I cannot be an active part of my family. I just want to excuse myself from social contact (and thereby excuse any lack of offers for social contact). I do not wish to avoid anyone where contact is prompted by a desire for open discussion or where I may be of some help. I am well aware of never demonstrating much of the above. However, as the letter states, I am trying to change my ways. There is much I have to do and I am not alone. The strength I have is sufficient for the job at hand. Beyond that, and pertaining to the future, I must leave things in the hands of a power greater than myself.

Take care all of you, Love, Richard

My A.A. friends, especially Dawson and Roger, who I had met at regular meetings but had gotten to know on a deeper level while travelling with them to district meetings and area assemblies, became a more integral part of my life. Conversations with them were wide ranging, including personal experiences that stretched back to our respective childhoods, along with rousing plans for hunting in the upcoming fall. Always present was an undertone of searching for meaning, growing beyond past wrong thinking, and following a new path, at the center of which was character building. They became very close friends of a type I had not previously known to exist. I visited them at home and they stopped by the ranch from time to time. There was always undisguised pleasure and goodwill in our greetings, because it seemed we knew each other at levels beyond typical human relating and had little to hide, as though there was little about

442

each other that we did not already know. The trouble caused by alcoholism throughout our lives had become a deeply meaningful common bond. The solution offered by Alcoholics Anonymous was good reason for joyful celebration. But more important than those two, in the process of dismantling barriers, was our common engagement in a commitment to carry to others the hope we had found in A.A. Through active participation in the affairs of the fellowship, our individual lives were made larger. The inherent selflessness of our efforts to serve in a realm beyond our own small worlds, without regard for personal reward, had indirectly infused our friendships with a spiritual quality.

I thought again about the depth of comprehension behind the statement in the A.A. Big Book: "Selfishness – self-centeredness! That, we think, is the root of our troubles."

I recalled how the meeting room had erupted with understanding and compassionate laughter at the desperate words of a relative newcomer. "I know this program is about getting free of self-centeredness," he had lamented, "but some days I am all I can think about." Everyone present had direct experience with the suffering brought about by self-absorption.

But not everyone had yet discovered the practical solution inherent in walking through A.A.'s Three Legacies of Recovery, Unity, and Service. Just as the sustained cessation of active drinking, as a result of working the Twelve Steps, remained a hollow aspiration unless and until one surrendered to doing the work, one could not learn about the liberating results of actively helping others without being specifically engaged.

At the same time, I knew my personal good fortune was not due to my extraordinary insight or intelligence. I had been guided by something beyond my own narrow awareness. My only contribution had been in making myself ready, with the accumulated pain that resulted from a life run entirely on self-will and self-seeking. I felt I had been the beneficiary of enormous good fortune, quite simply, and I stifled the temptation to further analyze my painful history, or to search for a grand meaning of life. Something unexplainable had brought me through the previous forty-one years and tossed me out at this desirable place. Making use of past good advice, I was content to leave it at that, keep an open mind, and stay clear of the debating society.

My enduring friend and former drinking buddy, Peter Kane, called and asked if I'd like to join him in travelling to a twenty year reunion of our undergraduate class. I had accepted his offer and was glad I did. It was the first time we'd been alone together since I had quit drinking, and I valued the long friendship we'd shared beyond that aspect of it, although alcohol had been a significant component of nearly everything we'd enjoyed. Still, the camping, canoeing, and travel we'd done during our youth were highlighted in my memory as fabulous exceptions to sitting in bars. Only in the final few years of my drinking career had we regularly congregated with 'lower companions' in a scuzzy establishment.

Across miles and miles of open road, my eyes devoured the beautifully vibrant and subtly varying prairie landscape, while, during the whole ten-hour drive to our destination, Peter did not have a single drink. Our conversation was relaxed and meandering, reminiscing and laughing about things we had done together over the years, catching up on news we could share about classmates with whom we'd had some contact, and speculation as to where the last twenty years had taken others. Peter had stayed in touch with more of them than I had because he had spent more time in the West. I had gone East sooner for my continued education, and stayed away longer with the stints in New York and Chicago. My more adventurous career had taken me outside the circle which, for many, had remained relatively small.

Peter reminded me that two of our graduating class of seventy had died in the interim. One was a woman, known to have committed suicide, and the other was a case of chronic bad health seemingly resulting from depression and excessive alcohol consumption. There was a brother of one our classmates, a man in the year behind us, who had taken his own life as well. We puzzled over the conditions that would lead a young person to that end, remembering with emphasis the vibrant youthful optimism we had typically observed among those same people during our college years.

Once we had been at the event a while, I found the enthusiasm I had formed for it was fading, intermittently, toward disillusionment. The questions varied little: "Where are you now?" and, "What are you doing these days?" I found myself wanting to observe rather than participate. Some were inclined to emphasize their superior progress since graduation. A few were more inclined to party than the rest. The wealthiest man there had stepped into the ownership of an inherited family business. Soon after graduating, he had married a classmate, the lady who committed suicide twelve years later and left him with three motherless children. He had since remarried and had thus rejoined the majority, which could be, as must be the case within any gathering of humanity, roughly described as normal. Those normal people had worked at stable, respectable jobs which had permitted them to buy houses, take attractive vacations, and participate in stable, respectable marriages which had resulted in children who likewise had promising futures – all of which they talked about in detail and at length. They wore neat casual clothes, sported trim conservative haircuts, conducted themselves with meticulous modesty, and were conspicuously deliberate in their consumption of a drink or two. I really couldn't decide whether I envied them or not. I thought their lives resembled pretty porcelain figurines and, although a few doors had almost certainly been opened to them while remaining closed for me, I could muster no enthusiasm for the monotonous reality they must have endured in the creation and maintenance of their flawlessness. I was reminded of my distaste for groomed cross-country ski trails, my preference for the roaming freedom of untrodden backcountry, my abhorrence of anything that felt like the 'hole in the donut.'

The merriest man present, on the surface at least, worked as a salesman for a small brewing company. His job kept him on the road, entertaining wholesalers and larger drinking establishments, and he laughed when he told us he had not found it convenient to stay married several times, several marriages that is, and several allusions to the topic as well. Only one man became entirely incoherent as Saturday evening wore on. I acknowledged privately that there would have been another in the same condition had I not found a way out for myself. Quite often in my past, after having a lot to drink, I had presumed that everyone must be similarly inebriated.

I observed that Peter was having a very good time while remaining reasonably sober; perhaps my presumptions had been in error? I remembered repeated instances of Peter remembering what we had done the night before when I could not, and I wondered if he had actually drunk as much as I supposed he had. At the end of the evening, he alleviated some of this uncertainty by slurring his senseless words as he staggered toward the car.

On the return trip, I touched lightly on some aspects of my abstinence and recovery, and the many benefits. Peter reiterated that Cindy, his wife of twenty years, had threatened him with eviction from their home if he didn't quit drinking so much, but he made it clear that he had no intention of following my path.

"I know a few guys who have quit on their own," he said, "and I drink that low-alcohol beer most of the time. Besides, I can't see buying into all the God stuff."

With that comment, I set aside any inclination for convincing him. After all, he had listened acquiescently while I repeatedly and boisterously professed my brand of atheism only a year and half ago. Still, I had heard stories about low-alcohol beer, and they always ended badly for real alcoholics. Something more, it seemed, had to change. I promised myself that, once I was home and alone again, I would embark upon an examination of the changes that had occurred in my thinking as a result of the new direction my life had taken.

I dug into a stack of paper that represented the journaling I had done over the last year. One attempt to describe my former thinking began with the heading, *"A process I learned from childhood – anger as a tool for tipping the scales in my favor"*

Hard work and dutifulness are essential in getting what you want. BUT: The world is an unfair place. You do not always get what you want, even when you've earned it.

Pleading your case on rational grounds or simply stating your wants, what you consider reasonable, does not work. BUT: Getting angry to intimidate or embarrass people, aggressively pinning them to their own guilt and asserting your version of fairness, does work.

FACT: The world is unfair and will try to make you feel you don't deserve the things you want. It will try to make you feel undeserving.

SOLUTION: Make sure you've earned what you want through "performance," then you are justified in demanding your share. If you run into objection, or are fearful of having to further justify what you want, get angry. That will tip the scales, transferring to your opponent any doubt you have, and you'll win.

That had struck me as an unpleasant approach to life, and I'd set out to graphically depict the ways in which my perspective had been altered. Several scrapped attempts finally led to the following:

BEFORE:

Pride---Insecurity
FEAR
(worry   anxiety   resentment   depression)

ANGER & HATRED
*Low self-esteem *Doubt that all is well, negativism,
pessimism
Result: Frustration

AFTER:

Humility------------------------------------Spirituality
COURAGE
(patience   tolerance   compassion   understanding)

SERENITY & LOVE
*Self-acceptance*Trust that all is well, positivism, optimism
Result: Happiness

I perused my work with substantial admiration for its academic appeal, while, intuitively, I suspected I had hardly scratched the surface in the progression I sketched. But a loftier inner voice argued that I must get beyond that restrictive view, place more trust in the spiritual guidance I was bound to receive as a consequence of my efforts. I began to journal in this haughtier vein, analyzing my past, assessing my progress, and defining my newly acquired living skills, perhaps to convince myself.

Before recovery I was on a treadmill, where romance and money led to power trips of self-righteousness and superiority. But there was always fear and, when the tide turned, I became self-pitying, resentful, and miserable. As the A.A. book insists, I lived within a cycle of excitement, anxiety, and depression.

Having hit a painful emotional bottom, I had two options: (1) build courage and self-esteem through honesty, self-searching, and humility; or (2) patch up my pride and ego, denying my wrong thinking with rationalization and justification, and return to the materialistic fray.

I now admit to the hopelessness of my condition and the mess I have made of my life. I choose the first option. I have discovered the difference between pride and self-esteem. I am finished with rationalization and self-justification. I am finished blaming others and the world for my cycle of anxiety, excitement, and depression. I want to change forever. Only the steps of A.A. could have brought me to this point. Anything else would simply rebuild the empty shell I had lived in for forty years. I did not know that I could feel as I do now. I feel a security that requires no buffering with anger, pride, or dishonesty. I feel love and compassion for mankind in general and I feel, for the first time in my life, I could have an intimate relationship based on spiritual, emotional, and physical balance. I am comfortable also that it will come. I am not planning or searching.

The way I am now: I see that selfishness is actually opposite to the love of self. I have found that love of one requires love of self, and love of self requires love of all mankind. Never before has courage and calm inner strength been mine! I do not need to worry about boundaries, because knowledge of myself tells me when to go ahead and when to walk away. And, I know my limitations. [I laughed at the thought of Clint Eastwood's line, portraying Dirty Harry: "A man's got to know his limitations." Spiritual indeed!] *As long as I am a force for good up to, but not beyond, my limitations I am happy. Life is joy. I no longer need diversions, and I enter into situations to bring happiness, not to derive it. I do not fear getting taken because I have nothing I fear losing. All fear is false pride. At the same time, my inner strength precludes prolonged abuse from others.*

Under the influence of my new vision, I decided to expand my circle of acquaintances by regularly attending a suburban

A.A. meeting I had visited a few times. It was attended by businessmen, well-dressed women, and a few professionals. I thought I might meet people more like myself there, more sophisticated than the friends I'd made in the rural meeting rooms nearer the ranch. Following the second meeting I attended I met Wade, a man of some refinement who related immediately to my background in the investment business. He said he had been in Alcoholics Anonymous for ten years. Here was evidence that sobriety did not mean giving up the finer things in life or subscribing to a humdrum existence, without affluence and the liberty to enjoy it. We quickly developed a kindred companionship and a few weeks later I asked him to be my sponsor.

He mentioned over lunch one afternoon that he was attending a four-day business seminar and convention in Cleveland. Then he remembered that he'd forgotten to get cash to pay for his plane ticket and asked if I had the money. It was with pride, and my recollection of those days in Chicago when my commodity-trading friends and I loaned each other money, back and forth on a handshake, that I said, "No, I don't have the cash. But here, put it on my MasterCard and I'll catch you later." Wade phoned me that evening to say he would return the card when we next met and I felt gratified that I could trust this man who obviously made his way in a moneyed world with the utmost of easy integrity.

I phoned a day later to say that I was on my way into the city and would stop by. Wade's wife answered and informed me that he had left on a business trip. I said I thought his plan was to leave in a few days and asked if he had left my credit card with her. She knew nothing about it except that something had come up and he had decided to leave earlier. It seemed strange that he didn't place more importance on our relationship and more urgency on restoring my credit card to me, but I concluded that he must have been under some pressure.

Only after two more days of waiting to hear from him did I become anxious and decide to call MasterCard, feeling all the time that I was acting unnecessarily, with a lack of trust in my new friend. There were forty-five hundred dollars in new charges, some in Akron and some in Cleveland, on my card. Some were from airlines and restaurants; others were for new shoes, dinners, and limousines. I asked that it be cancelled then and there. It was not stolen, I admitted, but was being used by someone I had loaned it to. Under those circumstances, they could assume no responsibility for the charges to date, the apologetic lady said.

I left messages for Wade and received no reply. The credit card statement came and revealed four days of extravagant partying, including huge bills at various nightclubs. I asked a few people about Wade and one man said he was a con and he doubted he had ever been sober two months in a row. He told me how Wade had been fired for abuse of an expense account, how he had even absconded with money from A.A. in one instance. For weeks, I remained too embarrassed to mention the episode to Will. I wondered how my lifetime of ruthless but practical suspicion had given way to such childish naivety. I found the latter far less comfortable to look upon because of its likeness to stupidity.

Finally, I told my old mentor the story. Will considered my words a little while and said, "People are in A.A. because they have problems. But we all have to learn to play by the rules of society. Go to a lawyer, get a judgment against him, and let it go. You can't get blood from a stone and you won't likely get any money back. But it is the right thing to do and the best way to put it behind you."

I paid off the forty-five hundred dollar MasterCard bill before the due date and proceeded to do as he suggested through the legal system. I made an appointment with a local lawyer, explained my case, and asked how much it would cost. "Three hundred and fifty dollars," he said. I instructed him to proceed. A week later I went in to sign some papers, and a week after that I got an invoice in the mail for $630.00. I stopped by two days later with a check for $350.00 and told the lawyer that I treated quotations for work seriously, to which he replied angrily, claiming that three hundred and fifty dollars didn't cover his costs. "Then you should have quoted me more," I said and left, not in the mood for another fleecing.

Another mover and shaker had moved to town and began attending my home group. I enjoyed the guy's company, his brash sense of humor, quick wit, and grandiose tales of intrigue and achievement. Old Jake had moved into the town to live with his mother, because she was very old and much in need of his kind attention.

One day he stopped by the ranch for a visit and shared with me a scheme he had in mind that was sure to make a lot of money. He explained how local governments were spending a fortune on road repairs in the backcountry, largely because beavers were damming streams and causing them to submerge roads and wash them out. I could envision the problem and listened while he described his innovative approach. Essentially it meant inserting a three-inch pipe horizontally through each damn to drain the water the beavers had planned to contain. The pipe would need to reach far enough into water to baffle them and discourage their blocking it, as they would do with any leak they could identify. The idea made a lot of sense and had several selling points, the most important being that the beavers would simply leave in frustration. That would be much more acceptable to environmentally conscientious groups that opposed shooting the animals or dynamiting their work.

If I was interested, Jake suggested, we would need to do some preliminary design work and some testing. He needed a partner to share in those development expenses, to manage the business, and eventually help supervise the crews that would perform the work. It sounded like fun, whether it became commercially viable or not, so I said I was interested. He had done some preliminary calculations and thought we would need to commit about fifty thousand dollars to get started. He said the first step was to find a metal fabricator and have him construct a long spear-like device that we could drive into the wall of a damn, using a jackhammer, to create a hole through which we could insert the pipe that would ultimately drain the dam. For the tests, we could probably rent some of the equipment, but we would need to purchase our own as the work proceeded. Jim was very excited and I felt fortunate that he had chosen to share his vision with me. I said I would give the structure of our partnership some thought and hoped he would do the same.

The very next day, I received a call from a local welder. He wanted to verify the instructions he had received to begin some development work and charge the costs to an account in my name. I hadn't had an account with him prior to that point and I was astonished to learn of the audacity of my new partner. I asked the welder to refrain from incurring expenses for the time being. Then I called Jake, who reacted with far less concern than I thought appropriate when I suggested there had been some miscommunication. I said I didn't want him spending money on my behalf, to which he replied with surprise. Then he disclosed that he had bought a few things at the farm supply store, where I did have a charge account, and he hoped that was alright. It wasn't, I told him, and I asked him to return them for a credit on my account.

I thought it necessary to draw the line clearly and said, "Jake, under no circumstances do I want you to purchase anything and charge it to me, period. I want this to stop right now."

He seemed a little indignant in the defense of his actions, and I felt like I was dealing with a child whose hand had been discovered reaching into the cookie jar. The recent credit card incident had left me wary and I doubt I would have reacted with the same certainty and finality had it not been for that.

I told Will about it that very afternoon. He said, "An entanglement like that could have become far more troublesome than the other one."

I said, "I have spent twenty years making deals with people, sometimes for millions of dollars, and I have always been alert to a scam. In fact, I have never met anyone like these two men, so blatantly inclined toward trickery, except one petty swindler in Morocco. I am amazed at my stupidity!"

"Early notions of spirituality can blind us to reality," he said. "Take a look at page eighty-seven in the Big Book."

I found the words that fit: "Being still inexperienced and having just made conscious contact with God, it is not probable that we are going to be inspired at all times. We may pay for this presumption in all sorts of absurd actions and ideas." That was a polite way of describing the spiritual make-believe that had befogged my thinking. I could see that my newfound 'faith' amounted to little more than the deluded expectation that a sound spiritual foundation inevitably guaranteed success in the material world. What had attracted me to these two men was my own lingering desire for a fast, high-flying lifestyle.

"It takes about five years around here to get your brains out of hock." Will's words echoed from meetings past. At first, I had scoffed at his insinuation of such sluggish progress. He had also insisted that I refrain from romantic involvement with women for at least two years. Recent evidence notwithstanding, I doubted my progress would be delayed to that degree. I saw little risk in permitting a local lady to join me for a weekend on horseback in the mountains, or in sharing a tent with her for two nights. That acquaintance faded quickly, without arousing my interest beyond that of test-driving a sports car I had no intention of buying, just to see if I could do it, and what effect it had. I wondered if I had contravened the terms of that mysterious release from sexual obsession I'd been granted a year ago, and had been grateful for ever since.

At the rodeo dance in late September, I met another lady, much younger than me, with long curly auburn hair. She loved to dance and made it obvious that she wanted to dance with me. Thankful for the lessons I had taken with Victoria, I enjoyed the evening without expectations. Around midnight, she suggested we go back to her place, which we did. Without delay we fell into her bed, where her lithe physical attractiveness and relaxed enthusiasm made it a memorable encounter.

In the morning, I discovered that she was the mother of two young children who lived with her in the mobile home she rented. But it wasn't that discovery that acted as a deterrent to further contact. Rather, it was her stirring sexual appeal that brought about my reluctance to get more involved. I knew that I had no other interest in her and would ultimately end the relationship, a pattern I had too often repeated in the past and felt bad about. It seemed that pursuing the activity would be a belligerent contravention of everything that had felt like progress since I'd first sought to change my life. I stopped by a few days later and politely informed her of my decision. I said I found her attractive but simply did not want to be in a relationship at present. Although I experienced wisps of regret over the foregone sexual pleasure, I felt rewarded with a sense of nobility, a first try at integrity.

Chapter 34

Except for short-lived glitches, my state of mind was usually close to euphoric, still riding the 'pink cloud' as A.A. friends who had been in the fellowship for a decade or more sometimes reminded me, reflecting on the earlier days in their own sobriety. I saw no reason for it to come to an end in my case, and I wondered if those who spoke of it in the past tense had ceased working the steps at some point, lost their spiritual connection perhaps.

At the same time, I still experienced bouts of anger, fits of rage even, and I reflected upon them with some bewilderment. The smallest thing, such as getting the tractor temporarily stuck, could send me into a raving cursing tirade. I didn't think these occurrences were evidence of advanced spirituality and I was always thankful that no one witnessed them.

During the three-day A.A. area assembly that fall, I once again experienced the kind of serenity that accompanies self-forgetting. The whole weekend, I was surrounded by people engaged in the business of Alcoholics Anonymous, everyone seemingly on a plane above their own small worlds, a sort of transcendence. In addition to eating lunches and visiting during breaks with Roger and Dawson, my circle of friends grew a little bigger and I felt a greater connection.

Elizabeth visited at least once a month for a week or so, and I always felt good about that. I still struggled sometimes, with giving her my constant attention and waiting patiently while she played inquisitively along the way. One frosty morning, we were preparing to go into town and get some groceries. She had been particularly tardy at rounding up her things and getting dressed. I had helped her with her mittens and her boots and zipped her coat, all of which seemed very tedious that day. Then she squatted down just outside the door to study a large insect making its way over some rough terrain. "Look, Daddy, a huge bug," she said, inviting me to retrace the fifteen paces I had taken while she was preoccupied.

Intent on getting a job done, I said, "Elizabeth, I am going into town. I'll see you when I get back."

With that, and my intention of teaching her a lesson about staying focused, I took another five steps, opened the truck door, and slid onto the seat. When I turned my head enough to inconspicuously check on her reaction, I saw that she had stood up. But she was obviously immobilized with disbelief and the fear that I would abandon her. I couldn't stand it. I slid back out of the truck and walked briskly toward her. Before I covered half the distance, I could see the large tears forming in her eyes and I rushed the final few yards with my arms open, preparing to enfold her.

"Daddy would never leave you, sweetie," I promised emphatically. "Don't worry and don't cry. Show me where the bug is."

She stared at me as I gently wiped her tears away, hoping with all her heart for sincerity in my words. In seconds, a glow of trust and joy returned to her pretty blue eyes. Then she turned slightly and began looking for the creature that had delayed her in the first place. "There he is, Daddy. Where is he going?"

We squatted together and watched as his laborious lumbering journey took him toward some entirely obscure objective, not unlike the life of a human being in miniature, I reflected.

"I'm not sure even he knows where he's going, sweetheart," I replied. Then, thinking out loud, I added, "I really wonder if any of us know where we're going."

"We're going to town to buy something to eat, aren't we, Daddy?"

A few days after I'd taken Elizabeth home, my elderly mentor, Will, drove into the yard. I had informed him regularly

457

of my progress at working the steps of the A.A. program, unavoidably, because his habitual response to any drawn-out tale of woe was, "What step are you on?"

On that day, he didn't wait for an opening before expressing his thoughts. "I've been thinking about you, and I wondered if you had gotten around to Step Eight yet, making a list of the people we've harmed and becoming willing to make amends to them all."

"I haven't put a lot of effort into it yet," I hedged, and then admitted, "In fact, no, I haven't done it at all."

"Well, it's a very important process if you do it thoroughly. I think the best way is to go right back, as far as you can, and have a look at all the relationships you've had with other people, beginning with your immediate family, parents, and siblings." He hadn't put that much emphasis on other steps and I listened carefully. "You see, a defect of character is really anything that separates you from other people. Behind most of those defects is fear, the fear of not getting what you want, the fear of getting too close to someone which is really fear of them getting to know you, and the fear of responsibility. In the end it's all about self-centered fears, you know." He paused briefly. "It can be a big job, but you won't find any exercise more valuable. And, don't worry about Step Nine, which is making the actual amends, while you are working on Step Eight. They are entirely separate processes."

He words suddenly generated a yearning to complete the step and, after I visited with him over a cup of coffee and he drove off again, I put together a plan. The ambiance of late fall inspired one last venture into the foothills before the snow flew. The next morning, I sorted out the necessary packing and riding gear, put together enough food and coffee for three days, loaded Merlin and Fitzsimmons in the trailer, and drove west. I parked the truck and trailer in a clearing, packed the panniers, duffle, and tent on the mule, and stepped into the saddle. I was captivated by the yellow splash of aspens that shimmered on a distant slope, and the sweetly pungent aroma of spruce that seemed almost tangible in the crisp tranquil air. My horse and mule were close companions, attentive while forever mute. Their only responses to my light hearted banter, which included praise for them, speculation about the weather, or curiosity with respect to our shared environment, were flicked ears. In that regard, I thought Fitzsimmons exaggerated sometimes, her long appendages flicking repeatedly, even in opposite directions, while Merlin maintained a degree of reserve befitting his leadership role.

Three hours later, engulfed by the whispering hush of the wilderness, I unpacked and unsaddled, hobbled Merlin and turned him out to graze, tied the mule to a tree to prevent too much wandering, set up the tent, and sat against another tree to enjoy a fresh chew of Copenhagen. I reflected upon the peaceful setting and the daunting task before me. In a switchback pattern, I had ridden down a quite imposing bank, before fording a broad but shallow stream, to reach a three-acre meadow that would serve as my home. The river's bank, on the side that bordered the meadow, was gentle and pebbled, and the crystal clear water rippled audibly at its edge. The area was defined by an even steeper ridge on its far extremity. A few scattered pine trees punctuated an abundance of grass. One of those trees, twenty-five feet tall and roughly three inches in diameter, was standing dead and provided a ready source of seasoned firewood. The camp was a self-contained paradise for horse and man. I delighted in my good fortune and noted the generosity of the Universe.

Over the next three days, except when rotating the two animals for bouts of grazing, building fires, cooking, and brewing coffee, I worked on my Step Eight. I started at the beginning, as Will had suggested, going as far back as I could recall and examining relationships with members of my immediate family. I looked at the part I had played in the unpleasant encounters I recalled, forgetting, for the time being, the harms others had done to me. I knew from my Steps Four and Five that regrettable aspects of my behavior were usually a result of the fears and insecurities that had dominated me. That cause and effect relationship, I had discovered, was really the 'exact nature of my wrongs,' knowledge which made it easier to make a detached appraisal of the effects my attitude and actions may have had on other people. I had long since accepted my powerlessness in the face of those fears and their consequences, and had forgiven myself on that basis. It was only important that I try to understand the harm I had caused.

From my earliest memories of interaction with my sisters, I could see that I had no sense of empathy and even less sympathy. At the very least, I had been inconsiderate. At worst, my own sense of victimization had led to morbid satisfaction in instances where they suffered or were punished at the hands of my parents. I was six years older than my first brother, Dennis, and had set aside little time for him at any point in his formative years. I was fifteen by the time Barry came along and I had already, by varying degrees, lost touch with my own childhood. I was therefore unable to share anything with him and my prideful preoccupation with adolescence precluded offering either of them the friendship, support, or encouragement they might rightfully have expected from their big brother.

I felt much respect and affection for my mother, but I had too often betrayed that sentiment with my brash grasping for a tough manly image. As an adolescent, I had preyed upon her desperation for continued good relations with her oldest son by including her in a self-serving strategic alliance, the sole objective of which was to manipulate my father. More specifically, it often involved the use of the family car on weekends. In that regard, I saw how my irresponsible attitude toward the vehicle, later exacerbated by my excessive drinking, was terribly disrespectful of the rest of the family and their need for transportation. If I had been in my father's position, with some insight into my son's behavior, I would probably have demonstrated a similar reluctance to hand over the keys. My self-centeredness, which the A.A. Big Book described as the root of our troubles, was pervasive. It blinded me to any consideration beyond my own immediate wants and it justified the narrow-minded sense of victimization with which I responded to any frustration.

While I worked away at identifying my part in difficulties, which I had hitherto perceived as being entirely the fault of others, including my omissions in situations where others had probably reasonably expected more of me, a strange awareness developed. I began to see that other people had often been very kind to me, but that I had been unable to receive kindness. Actually, I had been unable to perceive kindness or even subscribe to its existence. I had faced every situation as though my personal security was at stake. I had spent too much of my life seeking after an advantage, clinging to my share, and grasping for more of everything, in a world I perceived as perpetually hostile. I reflected back and forth over the years and was deeply saddened at my frequent refutation of the affection, trust, and generosity that had been offered so freely by family members and countless acquaintances. Perhaps, in some cases, it was not offered unconditionally. But I had typically viewed each and every instance as potentially manipulative and self-interested.

When I began to develop relationships with women, I was usually free of that enormous hindrance during a brief phase of infatuation. But, at the slightest cause for suspicion, I became guarded and began instinctively to withdraw, unconsciously assuming the position that 'the best defense was a strong offense.' From that point on, I sought for every advantage, taking all I could get, knowing with a certainty that an end was unavoidable, even desirable.

I remembered a friend of mine saying in an A.A. meeting, "All of my character defects were based in some vague idea of self-preservation." His words had seemed to me a rather shallow generalization at the time, but I suddenly felt the depth of his contention as it applied to my own case. The accuracy of the term, for describing the fear that motivated my thinking and actions, was profound. I had been reacting to a threat that could only be defined as potential non-existence. If this, or, if not that, I will cease to exist. I will cease to have an identity, a

461

meaningful state of being. I recalled vividly, from ten years ago, the dreaded abyss that seemed to await me when I had contemplated quitting smoking. Listing the pros and cons of an obviously insane habit, I had discovered that dark aspect of my addiction. But I had not seen at that time how my whole life was permeated by similar trepidation. I had grasped after and clung to numerous sources of emotional relief with a life and death urgency and gravity that were unwarranted.

Out of the same distorted need to establish my existence came the big-shot image I felt compelled to project upon family and friends. It must have hurt my parents and siblings when I discounted improvements they had made to the farm while I was far away. I vaguely remembered my little brother leading me into the living room to see the new furniture, during one of my whirlwind visits, and my shrugging it off as being beneath my standards. The persistent tolerance of my friends, in the face of my exaggerated business success stories, was equally hard to look at.

My business associates had put up with irresponsible use of my expense accounts, demands for special profit-sharing arrangements, and outright deceit about the potential for schemes I sometimes invented. Their tolerance of my behavior was almost unexplainable, much of it owing to no more than the loyalty inherent in friendship, as in the relationship I had with my long-time mentor, Noel Hyman. My business scruples had declined over time as well, reaching an all-time low when I used my own good record and the well-earned reputation of Sherry Mason, my loyal assistant from many years prior, to gain a business development contract with her present employer following my most recent return to the West. A hot clammy wave of discomfort engulfed me as I realized I must go directly to Daniel Fox, the man who had hired me on that basis and paid a handsome sum in advance for work that never materialized.

This thorough review of my past had occupied more than twenty hours, spread over the three days I spent in my solitary camp, and included more than twenty pages of names, followed by a brief description of my actions and the effect they probably had on my victims. At last, I had gone back over the list and added one more column in which I outlined, across from each name, the actions I might take in making amends. That was leading into Step Nine, but there remained no reservation in the willingness I had developed to set matters right if I could. As I saddled Merlin, loaded my belongings on Fitzsimmons, and headed back down the trail, I felt that I had walked through a door that led to a new maturity. I was prepared to assume a new level of accountability for my actions, while simultaneously taking some responsibility for the wellbeing of others. When I got home, I opened my journal and recorded the following:

Once again, I see how my defective psychological machinery stood in the way of my happiness. For I wronged people, not with any specific intention, not targeting any one individual to receive the brunt of my anger or self-pity, because I often wanted to love these persons, to care for them, and to have them love me. My actions and my thinking were completely self-centered, driven entirely by unidentified fears within me. No doubt this is still the case. Higher Power, help me.

Resolute in my commitment to make amends, I drove into the city the next day and went straight to the office building where I had agreed to work but merely cashed a fat check. I asked if Daniel Fox was in and waited while his secretary called him. I recalled the enthusiasm with which he had greeted me more than three years ago and the optimism he had displayed regarding our agreement. I wondered if he would exhibit an outward resentment over my betrayal of his goodwill. I enjoyed a fleeting and futile ray of hope that he may not have noticed. Then I continued realistically, to prepare for the unsavory task at hand. I was determined to remain sincere and to openly admit to the serious undermining of trust and friendship my actions had probably caused. I vaguely decided to leave the exact wording of my amend in the hands of a Higher Power as I understood it, which, in that moment, was no more complex than a faith anchored in 'doing the right thing.'

The handshake he greeted me with was hearty enough, but his half-smile revealed a justified hesitancy. "I haven't seen you for a while," he said indifferently, as he ushered me into his corner office and indicated an elegant chair on the visitor side of his large executive desk.

I began directly. "Daniel, I am here to admit that I behaved irresponsibly and disrespectfully following our business agreement. You trusted in my reputation, and in Sherry's faith in me, and I abused that trust by not following through with the kind of effort we both know was required for the task. My first regret is that I undermined the possibility of a good relationship with you, a man I intuitively respect. The second problem is that I took money from your company and did not provide an equitable effort in return. I consider myself in breach of our contract and I am willing to return the fifteen thousand dollars."

His pensive expression was impossible to interpret as he leaned back in his big chair. "Perhaps he will construe my words as those of a man defeated by the secular world, a weak man depleted of all self-esteem," I thought anxiously, "or worse, of one who is conniving for a further handout." I felt sheepish and wished I had not entered into this foolish endeavor.

"Rick," he said finally, "you have no idea how much your words mean to me. Forget about the money. A lot of time has passed and I wouldn't know how to account for it on the company's books in any case. Water under the bridge. It is the fact that you are here that I am so thankful for. I could never understand what happened and I instinctively felt that you had more integrity than that. But you have not only cleared your own name, you have quite honestly restored my faith in humanity. Just tell me what inspired you to make this visit, which I think must have taken a lot of courage."

I hadn't planned on telling him I was a member of A.A., but his earnest enquiry and his kind, sincere expression encouraged me. "I discovered that I had a drinking problem and

I joined Alcoholics Anonymous. One of the Twelve Steps of recovery suggests that we try to set matters straight in cases where we might have harmed other people."

I thought I detected a moistening of his eyes as he responded to that revelation. "I'm not a religious man," he began, "but I can understand the benefits of such a challenging exercise, especially for a person who is trying to overcome addiction. As it turns out, I'm glad you are here for another reason. My brother has continually destroyed his life by drinking, and seems unable to stop. Nothing we have tried seems to help. I understand that A.A. members are quite committed to helping others. Would you be willing to talk with him?"

Swelling with gratitude at his words, I wrote my phone number down and handed it to him, offering every assurance of my willingness to help if I could. We talked for another twenty minutes, without ever touching on the business aspects of our lives. Although his abiding by all the rules for good behavior had apparently yielded him a life of unqualified success, I felt that he sought after something I had. As I drove home, I reflected upon the passionate nature of his personal curiosity. I believe, for myself, I had unearthed new courage by surrendering to spiritual values.

My heart still thankful and euphoric, I wrote in my journal that evening:

Growth, then, is measured by an ever-increasing ability to surrender our instinctive demands in the service of God and our fellows. But, at any given time, we are where we are. We cannot see beyond where we are and we cannot act in some dimension in which we do not exist. The responsibility to grow is ours. However, there is also a responsibility to live as we believe God would have us today. Since we are incomplete we make mistakes. Largely, that's how we grow.

God has happened to me in A.A. I have learned much from other sources, some enlightening ways of viewing things. I have also confused things by exploring too far from my source,

Alcoholics Anonymous. I will probably continue to expand my knowledge, but I must remember that My God is God as He has revealed Himself to me as I worked the Twelve Steps, God as I understand Him. There can be no more than that for me, today.

I prefer the pain that prompts me to work the steps rather than the pain of disorientation and despair I experience when I forget who I am, or when I try to be something I'm not, or when I try to make God something I do not understand because He has not revealed Himself to me in that fashion. That makes everything unmanageable again.

That evening after supper, I searched through a small stack of books I had not yet read, all spiritual in nature, some I had purchased and some that had been loaned to me by new acquaintances that were on a path of their own. I picked out *Approaching Hoofbeats: The Four Horsemen of the Apocalypse* by Billy Graham and began to explore the contents.

Paraphrasing a passage from the Bible, the world renowned evangelist wrote, "Don't let the world around you squeeze you into its mold, but let God remold your mind from within, so that you may prove in practice that the plan of God for you is good, meets all His demands, and moves toward the goal of true maturity."

I relaxed, letting the book rest on my lap, and considered the remarkable wisdom of those words, the utter desirability of living in a way that felt as though that process was taking place. I reveled in the uncluttered spiritual freedom promised by his message. It seemed that very thing had taken place very authentically in Daniel Fox's office. I continued to peruse.

Mr. Graham cited these words from Romans: "…creation waits in eager expectation for the sons of God to be revealed. For the creation was subjected to frustration, not by its own choice, but by the will of the One who subjected it, in hope that the creation itself will be liberated from its bondage to decay and brought into the glorious freedom of the children of God."

I thought of the bitter old missionary who attended the men's breakfast meetings. He would agree entirely with the intimidating rigidity of that message. Even as I read it, it left me with a sense of being coerced, hoodwinked, and deceived. I remembered this proposition from some other book I'd read: the pain, suffering, and frustration of life is simply God (Jesus) knocking at the door of our hearts. Such suggestions as these certainly provided an all-encompassing explanation for my life to date, I concluded, if I wished to adopt them. I wondered, however, with growing dismay, "Why in Hell would any God who loved me, a God of true compassion, devise such a revolting scheme?" The thinking behind these assertions seemed more attuned to the narrow objectives of a hoodlum gang that subsisted on fear and aggression, not those of a benevolent, enlightened, and all-pervading divinity.

I began to leaf through the book with reduced enthusiasm until I focused on the catchy name D. Martyn Lloyd Jones, whom the author had chosen to quote: "Blessed be God who has undertaken our salvation and our perfection and who, having started the work will go on with it, and who so loves us that if we will not learn the lessons voluntarily, will chastise us in order to bring us into conformity with the image of His dear Son."

"Jesus Christ!" I cursed with revulsion and no connection between my exclamation and the material I had just read. I continued expressing my aversion aloud. "I cannot read any more of this constricting, stifling rubbish. It is in direct conflict with the spiritual path I have been on all day, the path with heart!" I sat quietly a while, until free once again of the dogmatic severity. Then I went to bed and slipped into a sound and contented sleep.

That fall, I gave my spiritual research a bit of a rest while I turned my attention to hunting. Roger and Dawson were accomplished moose hunters, while I, being a prairie boy, was not. Along with Brad, a master bow-hunter who was struggling with drinking related problems of his own, they took upon themselves the task of educating me in the art. For forty days we hunted, commencing with Brad shooting a large bull from ten yards away after calling him in with the grunting beckoning of a cow, satisfying a tag for Roger and completely filling his freezer. I hunted with them and, when not with them, I spent many days alone, practicing the intricate teachings I'd received from Dawson. I followed tracks through two and three feet of snow, trying to predict where a cow, calf, and bull would be lying before the trio sensed my approach and went crashing through the bush too far beyond me for a clear shot. At other times they disappeared silently, so far ahead that only fresh scat and their beds in the snow remained as evidence of their spectral passing. I once stood powerless in knee-deep snow and glimpsed from fifty yards distant, through the leafless bush that separated us and ensured their safety, a wraithlike departure of their huge forms, soaring across the tops of willows eight feet tall and disappearing into a heavy covering of spruce. I never did get a shot at the mature bull or cow, although I had an opportunity to take the calf and passed it up, but I will not forget the intimacy I experienced. Alone in the muted wintry stillness, where time itself seemed to terminate its march, where I trudged across frozen creeks and felt the cool trickle of snow down my neck as I brushed beneath laden boughs, I came to constantly feel their primordial presence. But I could not sufficiently advance my skills to compete with their prescient instinct for survival. In that way, I came to see more clearly that fulfillment is found in the seeking, and that arrival may be most precious while still shrouded by apprehension.

By the end of hunting season winter had enclosed the ranch in earnest. I filled many days reading in front of the fire, an activity that may have become wearisome had it not been refreshingly interrupted for two hours each afternoon with starting the tractor and rolling out bales of hay for the cattle.

Elizabeth's monthly visits continued and remained delightful. I attended several A.A. meetings each week and enjoyed occasional visits with my A.A. friends. Life had become routine, comfortable, and I think I might have been happy to live out my days without further volatility had I been able to relish the ordinary and familiar, had I found security in circumstances of contented stability, had I not always yearned to drift with each shift in the wind, like the proverbial tumbleweed.

Part VI
Darkness and Light

Chapter 35

Many people knew I had horses for sale. I didn't need a herd of fifteen after my brother left and we weren't in the packing and guiding business any longer. One day in March, a lady who introduced herself as Samantha called and asked if any of them were suitable for kids. I told her that several would make ideal kids' horses and she said she would stop by to look at them that afternoon.

She was an attractive lady, about my age, and obviously knew something about horses. Between us, a casual friendliness developed almost immediately. It wasn't a lustful interest I developed, but rather the idea that here was a lady I could be partners with. I learned that she worked as a nurse, and was also an accredited animal health technician. She had three children: a boy, seven, a girl, fourteen, and a boy, sixteen years of age. We went for a walk because she said she loved the outdoors and would like to look at the cattle. I discovered that her familiarity with large animals went beyond her professional training, as she had lived on a ranch with her ex-husband until three years ago. She didn't buy a horse that day, but promised she would accept my invitation to bring her kids over and let them ride a few so they could choose for themselves.

Two days later she called and asked if Saturday worked for me, because the kids would not be in school. "Of course," I said. "If you have time, we'll all go for an afternoon ride." She seemed pleased with that suggestion.

Her children were exceptionally polite and well-behaved, all three quite attractive and seemingly very bright. Over the next two months, she stopped by a few times, we met in town occasionally for coffee, and I was invited for dinner with the family on several evenings. They came over to go riding a second time and we had a nice picnic. When I announced that my daughter was staying with me at the ranch, Samantha asked if they could meet her. "Why don't you bring her for dinner tomorrow night?" she suggested. I said I would.

Being just short of three and a half years old, Elizabeth immediately idolized Samantha's teenage daughter, Vanessa, and responded with delight to the special attention she received. The boys, Paul, the oldest, and Alex, were polite as usual but were not a feature in Elizabeth's eyes. Nor was Samantha, despite her rather soapy appeals for my little girl's attention. It was a pleasant evening but, as soon as we had said goodnight and climbed into the truck, I felt relieved to be alone again with my beloved daughter. She snuggled in beside me and, five minutes into the drive home, fell asleep. I glanced down at her little blonde head and thought about the richness of her presence in my life. This time, she had brought me a birthday card, which she had made from scratch as she had done with other cards I'd received for Father's Day, Christmas, Easter, and Valentine's Day. All of them were precious reminders of the innocent admiration she had for her dad. I would do nothing, ever, to harm this relationship.

Celia announced that she had made plans to take Elizabeth east for the summer holidays. She felt they needed to spend some time with her family in Connecticut and would be staying for a month on the New Jersey coast, where her parents kept a summer home. I knew I would miss my daughter, but I could hardly express dissatisfaction in light of Celia's overall selflessness. "You'll both enjoy that a lot, and so will members of your family, I'm certain." I assured her of my acquiescence. I drove them to the airport two weeks later and said goodbye for two months, hugging Elizabeth close to my heart and encouraging her to call me anytime.

I began spending more time with Samantha and her children. Alex liked to sit on my knee and rewarded me with questions that stirred within me the deep satisfaction of mentorship. Vanessa threw herself at me with enthusiastic hugs when I arrived and departed, often noticeably pressing her rapidly developing body against mine. I was surprised to the point of uneasiness one evening when, saying goodbye, she had kissed me fully on the mouth. I assigned it to a combination of adolescent exuberance and naivety. Paul remained more distant, being a little older and having more vivid memories of his father, but he was friendly and polite nevertheless. I was enthralled with her children, if not overly enthralled with Samantha herself. She was very accommodating, however, and before long I accepted her invitation to stay the night.

Thoughts about us combining our lives began to surface, in a conceptual fashion. I owned and lived alone in a four-bedroom house with three bathrooms, while they were cramped in a rented mobile home. I could hardly justify continuing to own such a large house unless it was being utilized. I had a cattle herd to look after, and Samantha was familiar with ranching and trained in animal health. My home life was empty, except for occasional visits from Elizabeth, and Samantha's children gave me a warm fuzzy feeling. I had been selling real estate to augment a meager ranch income and help meet expenses, which included servicing a sizable mortgage on the property. Samantha earned a good income and could divert the dollars she paid in rent toward utilities and the upkeep of our home. In fact, she quite specifically mentioned one day that she was earning a good income and was in a good financial position with no debts. I craved getting away from the sales job to spend more of my time on the ranch, riding in the mountains, and hunting. The vision I created in my mind was persuasive. I began to look upon it as a gift, perhaps a direct result of the effort I had devoted to my spiritual journey. On those terms I felt assured that my Higher Power had been, and would continue to be, my guide. Therefore, I decided, I need not worry too much about details at this point. It was obviously meant to be, and only a coward would turn away from the fulfillment it offered.

I knew I did not feel a powerful affection for Samantha, but I rationalized that to be a positive feature in our prospective partnership. She had many very respectable qualifications. After all, the passion that had obscured reality and lured me into so many past relationships had not lasted long. I concluded that they had fallen apart because they were not founded upon a fundamental pragmatism. The idea of joining forces with Samantha seemed intensely practical and I began to pursue my vision. One day I offered to mow the lawn for her and while doing so I sculpted it, leaving the uncut grass in the shape of letters that spelled 'I love you.' Paul, whose attention I had directed toward my work, literally bounded toward the house to report the breaking-news headline to his mother. She was suitably impressed and new doors opened immediately.

We got around to discussing marriage quite soon after that, including her intention of changing the children's names to Nelson, so that we would be more distinctly a family. I thought it was going further than necessary and wondered how their father would feel. She was so adamant about doing it. Prior to this, I'd been disturbed by degrading comments she'd made about the children's father in their presence. I observed the subtle ways in which she obstructed his attempts to visit his children and her steadfast attendance whenever they talked with him over the phone. In the end, I decided it wasn't my affair. I was more concerned that Samantha had yet to meet any of my friends.

I invited her to take a drive one day, to visit with my good A.A. buddies, Roger and Dawson, along with their wives whom I had come to know quite well. Although I had informed Samantha quite early in our acquaintance that I was a member of Alcoholics Anonymous, to which she had responded with little apparent interest, I had not disclosed the membership of my friends. I introduced Samantha as my fiancée, an announcement that resulted in much easygoing openness and, within a half hour of our arrival, I'm sure the basis of my acquaintance with the two men had become quite clear.

We had all gotten together at Roger's home, where we drank coffee and talked for much of the afternoon. During the whole time, however, the encounter felt odd to me. Roger and Dawson had been warm and welcoming toward Samantha. Their wives, I thought, had done their best to engage her in conversation. But she remained aloof, almost impolite or unfriendly toward them. On the drive home, I emphasized that I held them in high regard because of their openness and honesty. Samantha said they were not the kind of people she imagined me associating with. I didn't know what she meant, but said no more about it. I merely hoped she would come to see their good qualities and get over the fact that they were not highly educated, or whatever her objection was if not that.

Two days later Dawson called me and wanted to meet for coffee in town. After some brief general discussion, he leaned forward, looked me straight in the eye, and said, "I have something I feel I must say, and I'm warning you, it could be upsetting. You may even get upset with me personally, but it is something I must say as a friend."

I braced myself and said, "Let's have it. I trust you as a friend."

"And I trust my wife's judgment because she is a smart lady," he said, and then continued with intensity, "She pleaded with me to talk to you. Her impression, a very strong intuitive reaction that she cannot put aside, is that the woman you are thinking of marrying is a gold-digger. She thought your friend Samantha seemed on edge and very defensive, as though we somehow threatened her relationship with you."

I accepted Dawson's warning as the caring gesture of a man I was certain I could trust. But, immediately after I parted with him, I brought into play several arguments to discount the importance of his words, not the least of which was my conviction that spiritual guidance and assurance had been instrumental in Samantha and me getting together. Deliberately rejecting all complicating and counterintuitive thoughts, willfully preventing them from taking root in my consciousness, I held steadfastly to my vision of a satisfying outcome. It was a puzzle with all the pieces in place, the ranch intact, the house amiably and usefully occupied. It was meant to be.

One day near the end of July, Samantha said rather abruptly, "The kids will go back to school in little over a month. If we are going to get married and move the family into your house, we had better do it soon. I don't want them faced with changing everything after the school year begins."

Inside, I reacted with fright toward her urgency and toward the brevity of the interval involved. Then I thought I was perhaps not being sensitive to her concerns for the children. In the end, we decided to speak with the aging neighborhood minister. We picked a date with which he agreed and committed to be married thirty days hence. The kids flew into a state of ecstasy at the news, reacting as though they were the jubilant servants of a princess who was about to be carried off by a knight in shining armor. I wondered again why they were not burdened at all with a lingering affection for their biological father, with whom they had previously lived for some time. In any case, on a succeeding afternoon, the five of us drove to the ranch where they began choosing bedrooms and taking possession of their new home, which I found deeply gratifying.

I asked Roger to attend the small wedding as my best man. Only Samantha's sister would be there on her behalf, along with the three children. When Roger came to the house, around ten in the morning on the big day, he found me sitting on the front step and he could hear the ranting and whaling that emanated from inside.

"What's going on?" he asked with obvious concern.

"She's in a kind of crazed state, overreacting to everything," I said hesitantly.

He sat down beside me and we said nothing more for a little while. It felt good to have him near. Roger was a strong personality, naturally cynical after years of hard drinking, but in his voice was sincerity and caring. "Maybe I shouldn't say this," he began, "but it's not too late to back out of this. It will be too late a few hours from now and you might be making a big mistake."

Without arguing or attempting to justify my actions, I said simply, "I have made a decision and I cannot back out now."

Even as I murmured the words, my body experienced a benumbed immobility, the same state I had experienced during those bouts of bullying in high school, the same dazed rigidity with which I had born the punishment of markets that moved against my positions and sapped my finances when I might have acted to stop it. Seemingly, I had been unable to act in a self-preserving fashion, both then and now, because I resisted putting myself at odds with the way things were apparently 'meant to be.' No matter how strangely wrong I felt about my situation, I would not have to face being wrong if I did not cave in and admit it. External evidence of unacceptable circumstances was no challenge for pride turned inward, where my very survival seemed to depend upon holding some obscure but self-determined course. No matter how painful the potential consequences, how gloomy the prospective outcome, it did not take me long to reject the unpalatable alternative.

Samantha and I were married that day. Her sister stayed with the kids while we spent a few honeymoon days at a mountain resort. She was in a surly mood from the beginning and complained that it wasn't much of a honeymoon, while I fought with my desire to have it end sooner than it would. The kids greeted us with happy smiles when we returned and Samantha told them we had a wonderful time. I often puzzled over their tendency to focus admiring attention on her happiness and wellbeing, to listen to her stories and historical accounts with fascination, as though they were the adults and she was the child. But they seemed happy enough, and her demands for attention appeared short of insatiable, so I chalked it up to my own lack of understanding.

The first significant battle between Samantha and me began with my inadvertent discovery of her financial situation, or perhaps she fully intended the discovery, which must have inevitably taken place. As she opened her mail one day, she placed face-up on the kitchen table a statement which made clear, at a single glance, that she had an outstanding bank loan for fifty-five thousand dollars. A further cursory investigation, trying to keep my research inconspicuous, indicated that she was obligated to make payments of more than fifteen hundred dollars per month, including principle and interest at nine percent. That was in sharp contrast with her premarital claim of no outstanding debt. I stifled the urge to address it immediately. Instead, I waited until the children were present and brought it up calmly, setting a snare of inescapable design, hoping that her reaction would remain both civil and truthful. "The fifty-five thousand dollars you owe the bank, that's a large sum. It is a surprise to me after hearing you say you had no debts outstanding. What was it for?"

She lied, "I didn't say that. I meant that I had no large credit card balances owing. That's what the loan was for, to consolidate my credit cards, plus money I borrowed to buy my car."

"You lied," I said, "an outright lie. You are in no position to contribute a fair share of expenses and you married me, at least partly, to escape a financial crisis. I see the real reason for your impatience now. It wasn't because of the kids going to school, but because you could not take care of them and handle the expenses by yourself."

"Don't call me a liar," she shot back. "You are mean and the children don't like you. They are afraid of you."

What ensued was the first of many occasions during which she physically and socially sequestered the kids. She simply rounded them up with a single command and went down to the T.V. room, placing me in solitary confinement until I learned my lesson, I supposed. The feeling of isolation added only marginally to the devastation I felt with respect to our combined financial condition. Still reeling, I picked up the ringing phone and muttered hello.

"Hello, Rick? I am calling because I was given your number as a member of A.A. I'm in bad shape from drinking and I need to talk to someone. Could I come and see you?"

Not now, for God's sake, I thought, as I dutifully replied, "It would be better if I came to your place. Where are you located?" I understood that I had no choice about helping another alcoholic. It was something I had to do, the right thing to do. He gave me his address in town and I left immediately, utterly relieved that I had somewhere to go, and some purpose that would dilute the effect of my distressing thoughts.

Tom was in bad shape, as he had said, hungover, remorseful, and he told me he was ready to look at a different way of doing things. We sat and drank coffee together for two hours while he related the details and accumulated costs of his drinking career. I shared a little of mine, along with the hope I had for turning my life around. When his wife came home we included her in the discussion, with less introspection perhaps, but it increased the dimension as she related her view of Tom's problem. Despite all that had been said previously, Tom thought he probably wasn't that bad, that he might stop, or at least control his drinking, without measures that were too drastic. He did not want to give up playing in a band, which he admitted often performed in saloons and necessitated staying overnight in other towns. It was too much of his identity, he said.

After I left them in their unhappy home, my thoughts circled round the slimness of his chances for recovery, given his inability to admit the hopelessness of his condition. I found myself caring about Tom and fearing he would not be motivated enough to perform the arduous work necessary for continued sobriety. As a consequence and immediate benefit, my personal problems, which had loomed so large upon my departure, seemed much less significant on the return trip. By turning my focus toward helping someone else, I had transcended their effect. I looked down upon the circumstances of my world as though it were a fleeting, floating series of events, rather than an unconditional and finite catastrophe. My mind was more relaxed and largely freed of its previous heavy burden.

The initial domestic disturbance in my home blew over eventually and the household assumed a stable routine. Samantha prepared meals while Paul and Vanessa helped. I was kept busy with fall farm work and little Alex often followed me around outside, or sat in the same room talking about his day and asking questions. I adored his company.

Celia called one day to announce their return. Then she handed the phone to Elizabeth and we talked for five minutes about her summer vacation, before she finally asked, "Daddy, when can I come and stay with you again?"

"Soon," I said, with more exuberance than necessary, while my whole body became drenched with the dread of explaining my new circumstances to her and Celia. "I will come and get you very soon."

I announced that my daughter would be visiting and reminded Vanessa that we had discussed the sharing of her room with Elizabeth, whom I intended to make feel entirely at home among this new family. They'd developed a mutual admiration on those several previous occasions and Vanessa did not appear to have developed any objection in the meantime. The shock came later, after her children had taken themselves downstairs to the T.V. room, when Samantha turned to me and said, "You are going to have to let go of Elizabeth, you know. This is your family now."

I was so stunned I had no response. I simply turned toward the door, overcome by nausea, and walked out into the yard. The mild contempt I harbored for my new wife gave way to abhorrence. I felt vulnerable and trapped. I got in the truck and, without a specific intention, drove the twenty miles to Roger's place. His big grin was a welcome sight. He said the coffee was on and asked how I was doing. I told him of the words that had dominated my mind for a half hour and hovered above my existence with the finality of a guillotine blade.

"Jesus Christ!" he said with disgust.

"Yup, it's bad, Roger," I admitted.

"Women are like horses," he said. "There are a lot of good ones, but every once in a while, you get a real fucking knot-head."

I wouldn't have put it that way, but it was the first time anyone but Alex had caused me to laugh out loud in weeks, and I let myself go on, enjoying the enormous relief I felt.

He went on, "You can't get rid of a dicey woman as easy as a rank horse, but you can't give in to her either. You'll have to set her straight, show her who wears the pants."

We talked for another hour and he hugged me as I left. I felt strengthened and assured that I could see it through with the help of friends like him. But I knew it wasn't going to be easy, nor was it likely to be pleasant much of the time. When I got home, Samantha asked with a tone of interrogation, "Where have you been all this time?"

"It's none of your business," I replied in the manner of throwing down the gauntlet. That instance of definitive defiance had a noticeable effect and there was an end to her directly confrontational remarks.

Elizabeth came for a visit, following a face-to-face talk with Celia wherein I explained to her shocked visage that I had gotten married while they were away. She had only rather sadly stated, "I think Elizabeth would have loved to be a part of the wedding, since it was an important event in her father's life. You'll need to make sure she doesn't feel alienated in any way."

I paid specific attention to all interactions, and believed her visit went well. Vanessa was pleasantly welcoming and they played almost incessantly with her collection of unicorns, their long, silky manes and tails mesmerizing for my little four-year-old daughter. On the return trip, I talked a lot about her special place in my heart and my hope that she would enjoy being part of a larger family. She said, "I like Alex and Vanessa, Daddy, but I like it when I spend time with you, just me and you sometimes." Tears welled in my eyes, with feelings only she could arouse, and I swore it would always be as she wished.

Several days later, around nine in the morning, I received a call from Cindy Kane. Her voice was near breaking as she informed me that Peter had crashed his car and was killed. We talked only briefly, until I said I would drive into the city that afternoon. My longest standing and closest friend was dead, driving while drunk. His low-alcohol beer experiment had obviously failed and I wondered why I was able to accept a solution that had not been within his reach. I was alone in the house and glad of it, as I packed a few things to take along in case I stayed overnight.

Cindy and Peter's three girls gathered near me when I arrived, temporarily ignoring the presence of close relatives, as though I was their closest family member. Peter's brother was there and related to me the details of his death. He had gone to a bar after playing softball, gotten quite drunk, and had driven off a curve in the road on his way to their summer cottage where he planned to spend the night because Cindy had warned him not to come home if he'd been drinking. The car had rolled several times, throwing him out of the window, and had finally come to rest with Peter beneath it.

Several references to their father revealed the girls' anger at being abandoned through his drinking and irresponsibility. Cindy, as well, displayed as much resentment as she did grief. I thought it was fortunate that she seemed to suffer no regret for denying him a place beside her in bed when he'd been drinking. His oldest daughter, who was married and had a child of her own, took the responsibility of asking me to give her father's eulogy. As I drove home again, I was struck by the matter-of-factness the family had displayed. There had been sorrow, but it had been without much compassion, somewhat bitter and subdued by the trials of living with an active alcoholic. In my heart, I hoped there would be more evidence of affection as time passed, because I identified with my friend and his lack of choice concerning alcohol.

Three days later I returned, with the intention of preparing Peter's eulogy based on comments from his family, including his mother, sister, and brother. I asked each of them to describe their relationship with him and to share some of their fondest memories. Everyone participated and I thought the exercise itself was beneficial. It had brought out the best qualities of my friend. It reminded his family that he was, except for his drinking, a truly kind, generous, and likable man. I believed I could do one last thing for Peter by imparting what I'd heard to those attending his funeral two days hence.

Returning home on the day of Peter's burial, I felt as though the five days that had passed since receiving the news of his death had represented a nearly complete suspension of the balance of my life. Samantha had not participated in the process, largely because I had not invited her, but she had been respectful of my sorrow and detachment. In the days that followed, my outlook on life assumed a broader and deeper perspective. I felt more compassion generally and the grief I experienced over the death of my long-time pal transformed itself into sorrow concerning all the struggles and turmoil that arose between living beings, including the family that shared my home.

At least partially moved by that sentiment, after I had been sitting for a while, drinking coffee, and contemplating a collection of spiritual readings I regularly employed in the morning to set a positive course for my days, I decided to go back to bed with the intention of making love to Samantha, if she was in the mood. On several occasions, she had rather vulnerably expressed a longing for affection. On others, she had presented more demanding arguments, stemming from the fact that we had not had sex at all in the many weeks since we'd been married. I had merely declined to engage in a discussion of the matter, finding it impossible to explain that I was denying her desire because I felt no romantic attraction for her.

She was physically appealing, however, with large breasts and a fit body. So, on that morning, my physical desire for sexual release stirred me and I decided to engage her. I crawled under the covers and snuggled against her, put my arm around her. After she got over the initial surprise, she responded without delay. She only paused to mention that it was the time of month when she was most likely to become pregnant. I was on a predetermined course and dismissed her concern, thinking that such an unfortunate outcome was unlikely with one brief engagement.

Despite that uncommon, while admittedly unexceptional, encounter, our relationship grew colder as time ground slowly onward. I perceived on several occasions that the children withheld the enthusiasm they had once demonstrated for their new father, despite Samantha having completed the legal change of their last names to match mine. The withholding phenomenon seemed especially evident when their mother was present, and I concluded she was trying to get at me through them. Seven-year-old Alex hadn't changed, however, and I supposed he was too young to be effectively manipulated, although, one particularly distressing incident concerned him as well.

Elizabeth had come for another visit and, while the others were in school, she and I spent wonderful hours together. During a trip to the local aquatic center, however, large tears began forming in her eyes and she asked, "Daddy, do know what Alex told me?"

"No, my little darling, what did he say?" I replied with pain striking at my heart.

"He said that you were his dad now and couldn't be my dad anymore." She started to sob and reached for me as I brought the truck to a stop at the side of the road.

I held her and said over and over again, "Elizabeth, my one and only little girl, I will always be your daddy and no one will ever come between us, forever and ever. You must believe me, sweetheart; nothing will ever change between us." Tears streamed from my eyes as well, and we held each other for a long time.

Finally she said, "Daddy, will you come in the swimming pool with me?"

Despite the strong aversion I had overcome each time, I had always gotten into the pool with her. I said, "My sweetie, that's just one more thing that will never change." We drove on and had a terrific day together. She adored the pool and water slide, giggling wildly when I went down with her lying on my back or feigned panic while she straddled my abdomen. As I drove her back to her mother at the end of her visit, I made a decision. I announced that I wanted to stay with them a few days and nights, from time to time, to add to Elizabeth's feelings of security. In Celia's heart, Elizabeth's welfare always came first and she encouraged me wholeheartedly.

Back with my new family, there were days when I felt lonely in my own house, although Alex remained as affectionate as ever, particularly when Samantha was not nearby, and Vanessa continued to express a kind of magnetism. Then a shocking incident took place concerning Vanessa, who had now turned fifteen. The three kids and I were watching the movie *Man from Snowy River* for the third or fourth time, sitting together on the big couch in the downstairs T.V. room. As usual, Vanessa had curled up next to me, lifting my right arm and placing it across her shoulders, which allowed her to nestle closer. I always enjoyed the affection she displayed. My right hand rested upon the back of the sofa, until she began toying with it. That kind of passive frolicking wasn't unusual either. But, at some point, it seemed that a new objective had formed in her mind. She quite unmistakably attempted to place my hand upon her right breast. Although I experienced a fleeting temptation to let her do as she wished, to maintain a disinterested passivity, I was simultaneously shaken by a blaring internal alarm. The disturbing notion that she might have been somehow encouraged to do this raced across my mind. Several times I pulled my hand back and, as many times, she gradually tugged it towards her again. In the end, I removed my arm completely from its position behind her and sat up straight. For days afterwards, the event accelerated my already growing paranoia.

I found it less confusing, though still unusual, when Samantha displayed an attitude of friendly support for my hunting activities. As bow-hunting season approached and I began preparing for it, she asked if she and the obviously fascinated Alex could join me in some way. It was noticeable that the older boy, Paul, had no interest in things of that nature and declined my offer to include him. In any case, I selected a promising blind near a popular mule-deer trail and decided it might be helpful if my two volunteers acted as beaters, beginning a half mile back of my position, to push the quarry toward me and to provide a distraction. Despite our concerted efforts on three frigid mornings, I had no success with my bow. Hunting alone, after rifle season opened, I shot a nice buck and mounted the antlers for Alex, who was delighted.

Chapter 36

One a relatively mild day in early winter, while I was busy building a cattle shelter some three hundred yards from the house, I noticed Samantha drive into the yard and begin walking toward me. Five minutes later, she was facing me and sharing the news that she was pregnant. I listened with friendly and attentive interest. Internally, I knew I had arrived at a point of no return and my knees nearly gave way. In the days following that announcement, Samantha's attitude shifted to that of peacemaker. She seemed to adopt a longer-term, more constructive view. In an undoubtedly conciliatory mood she asked one day, "Would you be interested in seeking counseling together, so we can begin to make the best of this marriage?"

"Yikes," I reacted inwardly with revulsion, while I said, "That's probably a very good idea. In fact, I know of a minister who acts as a marriage counselor and who Roger has recommended, because he and his wife received a lot of help from the man."

She agreed with my contribution and suggested I call the minister to arrange an appointment. At our first meeting he asked a few general questions and gave us a little talk about marriage. Then he asked what we thought was wrong with ours and asked a few probing questions of us individually. At the end of the session, he said he wanted to see us separately and we set up appointments for the following week.

My one-on-one session with him had a different tone, right from the beginning. It was a man-to-man discussion in which he began by saying rather bluntly, "Although Samantha seems to harbor a lot of insecurity, I believe you are probably ill-prepared for a relationship."

He talked about the relevance of sex in a loving relationship and, responding to his direct enquiry, I gave him a substantially curtailed history of my sex life. I informed him of my conclusion that sex was not an important aspect of a lasting commitment. He said my thinking was typical of an addicted person, the pendulum swinging from one extreme to the other, and gave me a contact number for Sex Addicts Anonymous. He assured me that anonymity was a top priority in that fellowship, hence the contact number but no meeting information. Further, he promised he would not divulge any part of this discussion to Samantha. I was greatly relieved by his concern for confidentiality and, overcoming my initial aversion to the unsavory implications, I felt strangely enticed by the notion of investigating S.A.A., possibly a consequence of the relief I had experienced in A.A.

The man I talked to on the phone asked a few questions, largely to ascertain that my motivation to attend meetings was strictly to do with recovery from sexual obsession. I gave him the name of my source, which reassured him, and he gave me the address and meeting time for a group of Sex Addicts Anonymous. My enthusiasm waned as I parked the truck and walked toward the door of the meeting room. I began to doubt that my problem was any more serious than a robust sex drive, as the college counselor had described it twenty years ago, but I decided to go in. It was a men-only meeting and several of the members welcomed me personally, with brotherly warmth that surpassed even that of members in Alcoholics Anonymous. Prominently displayed was a framed version of The Twelve Steps, with some of the wording adapted to fit the specific needs of this fellowship.

The meeting opened in a familiar manner, a moment of silence to reflect upon those who still suffered followed by a few readings. Then personal sharing began and progressed from one to the next of the dozen men present. Members introduced themselves as powerless over their sex addiction and I listened as they talked about Step One for my benefit, once again the newcomer in the room. Gradually, my focus on their words shifted from an interest in the varied and specific manifestations of their common affliction, to a heartfelt connection with the pain they had endured as a result.

I saw before me a group of well-dressed and otherwise well-balanced gentlemen, who had been entirely defeated by powerful and perverse mental twists, most far more devastating and far less socially acceptable than any I had ever experienced. The man I had spoken to over the phone stayed after the meeting and we talked a while longer. Following his suggestion, I bought a book from the supply of literature they had on hand, *Hope and Recovery: A Twelve Step guide for healing from compulsive sexual behavior.*

On the drive home I felt entirely detached from problems in my own little world, while my heart led my mind in the search for an explanation, some justification for the agonizing and unremitting suffering I had witnessed in that room. I knew, as a result of my own introspection, that uncontrollable mental twists had coerced me into actions that were harmful to my wellbeing, repeatedly. As well as sabotaging my efforts to build a comfortable and satisfying life, many of my actions had been harmful to others. Fortunately for me, obnoxious drunkenness and uncontrolled promiscuity were not legally prohibited, or even considered taboo by the society in which I lived.

As I drove into the farmyard, my anger soared. The mongrel bitch that Samantha and her kids had brought with them was harassing the cattle again. The problem had begun two weeks ago, right after I brought the cowherd home for the winter from a summer pasture. There was no one else around, meaning Samantha and the kids had gone somewhere and had again ignored my instructions to tie the dog up before they left. I caught her, gave her a whack, and fastened the light chain to her collar. I suddenly had a strong urge to visit Will, my old mentor, who had not been coming around as much since my marriage. My wife reserved a cool reception for my friends and it was inconvenient to sit in the kitchen and have a coffee most of the time.

It was a relief to set eyes on him again and I felt a calmness settle over me. He had once briefly attributed my getting married to loneliness, so I had since been content to leave it at that. But I brought up the recent dog problem, expecting him to advise handling it with care to avoid another battle.

Instead he said, "That's like having a tack in the sole of your boot. You'll have to get rid of the dog, if she won't, before the cows go through a fence, or worse, slip on some ice. I've seen cattle splay their hind legs on ice and cripple themselves with damage to their hips and backs."

We had coffee and visited a bit more before I drove home again, with strengthened resolve. By the time Samantha returned, I was ready with a concrete decision. "That dog was chasing the cattle again," I said sternly, "and, if the kids cannot look after her and keep her tied up, you will have to give her away."

She said she would talk to them again and make sure something was done about the problem. That same afternoon I began to observe another bewildering trend: Vanessa occasionally hanging around, when I was working alone outside, and making a concerted effort to promote the finer qualities of her mother. "Mommy is pretty, isn't she?" for example. She mentioned the dog occasionally, too, and how cute she was.

Over the next week all was well, but then the tendency to ignore their canine pet returned. Either they left her roaming and getting into trouble or, if they did tie her up, left her for too long without food and water. On several occasions I gave in and took care of her needs, but my patience was waning, and I resented their lack of practical concern and respect for my instructions.

On a snowy day in December, I called Elizabeth to say hello and to ask her about her fifth birthday party, which was coming up on the weekend. I had not planned to go, thinking it was for her little friends and that my presence would go largely unnoticed in any case. "Who is coming to your party?" I asked.

"You could." She said the words slowly, with the sweetest tone of hope in her voice, but not the slightest hint of a demand.

My heart melted and, without any consideration of other plans I might have had, I said, "Well, then, I will be there."

I merely told Samantha I was going and allowed no opening for reproach or senseless argument. Before the big day arrived, another two feet of snow had fallen and the roads were a little treacherous. But I never doubted that I would go, and it turned out to be a wonderful day, perhaps of greater benefit to me than Elizabeth. Following the snowstorm, the temperature had soared and much of the accumulation had melted. But then it dipped below freezing again, covering everything in ice. It was only an hour before dark when I returned home from the birthday party and I decided to roll out a couple of bales to hold the cattle overnight. I didn't see the dog and wondered if they had finally found another home for it.

The next morning Paul, the eldest boy, went out to the barn and I realized they had tied it in there overnight. She followed him to the house where he fed her and I said nothing about it until they were leaving for school, with the dog running loose in the yard.

"You had better take the dog with you," I said to Samantha, "because I have no more patience."

"I think she has learned not to chase the cattle," Paul said.

"If there is any more trouble, I'll do something," Samantha assured me.

I contained the rage I felt over their obvious, somewhat antagonistic disregard for my concerns. I did not want a bigger mess. They drove away and I walked over to check on the horses. I went back in the house to enjoy a cup of coffee in solitude. For ten minutes, I sat in the quiet of my old sanctuary, my thoughts happily occupied with the details of the day before. One of Elizabeth's friends, a little girl her age, with reddish hair and big blue eyes, had seemed a little overwhelmed by the raucous gathering of eight or ten others at the birthday party. I had taken an opportunity to smile at her and ask her name. Her response indicated that she was more comfortable speaking with an adult than joining in the fray, so I had indulged her for ten or fifteen minutes, and she remained my best friend for the duration of the party, sitting on my knee occasionally and bringing me extra birthday cake.

I heard the dog barking and looked out the window. I could see cattle milling around in the direction of the barking and went out to investigate. I was just in time to see two heifers skidding their way across the icy corral, the dog barking and running behind them. One slipped badly and barely tucked her hind leg under her before she fell. It might have been a disaster. I caught the dog and tied her in the barn. I considered my options, and I made up my mind. It was time to demonstrate that I did not take what I said lightly, that I was a man of his word and would not accept repeated disrespect. I walked back to the house, breathing deliberately, re-evaluating and trying to shine the light of reason on my decision, thinking about doing the right thing. I knew my neighbors, all cattlemen, would not hesitate to do what I planned. I wouldn't have either, except that it could have extremely undesirable repercussions. The other parties involved had chosen not to sympathize with my position, perhaps, in fact, to use the issue at hand as a weapon of defiance, assigning it a significance well beyond its practical reality. I determined that fear was not a valid excuse for refusing to do the right thing. This was merely a test of my courage.

Being completely preoccupied with remaining objective and emotionally calm, I had been almost entirely oblivious to the uninterrupted progress of my physical actions. Upon regaining presence of mind, I was surprised at the degree of certainty I felt as I continued back across the yard and consciously slipped the ammunition clip into the .22 caliber semi-automatic rifle that rested with familiarity in the fold of my arm.

There was no violence in the 'spit, spit' of the two rapidly released head shots which killed the dog instantly. Only while

I stood waiting for the final twitching of limbs to cease did I begin to feel an urgent desire to remove the carcass from the barn and drag it well back in the bush before Samantha returned. No one would be going there before spring, well after the coyotes and ravens had completed their janitorial work.

As it turned out, she didn't return until late afternoon, when she brought the kids home from school. They were there an hour before anyone realized the dog hadn't run up to greet them. I heard some muttering and then Samantha asked, "Where is the dog?"

"Gone," I said with finality, and braced myself.

"You didn't shoot it?" she asked.

"I did, most humane thing to do, all things considered," I replied.

I thought she would be angry with me, but probably remain quite subdued while the kids were present, since the reality of the situation could hardly have escaped her completely.

"HE'S KILLED A MEMBER OF OUR FAMILY!" she screamed repeatedly with blood curdling insanity in her voice.

I remained surprisingly calm inside as I observed the feigned state of dread she employed in rallying her troops and marching them downstairs to the fictional safety of the T.V. room, ostensibly before I killed yet another member of the family. There they stayed, and there I was content to leave them, while I had a bite to eat and got ready to leave for my weekly A.A. home-group meeting. I did not feel a need to discuss the issue. My relief at having taken charge of my affairs was quite complete.

I joined Roger and Dawson at a restaurant for coffee after the meeting. My friends responded to my handling of the dog issue by assuring me the kids would get over it, the matter hardly being outside of ordinary. They interpreted Samantha's reaction as indicative of someone who could use some help.

By the time I arrived home, the entire family had gone to bed. The next morning I went out to the barnyard quite early and, by the time I returned to the house, Samantha had left for work, taking the kids to school as she went. I was working in my office when they returned in the afternoon and little Alex came into the room with a sullen but not unfriendly expression on his face. I pushed my chair back and reached my right arm outward, inviting him in. I lifted him on my knee and asked how his day was. He threw his arms around my neck and hung on silently while I hugged him in return.

Then he leaned back a little and said, "I talked to my friend Cory and he told me they've had to get rid of two dogs at their place. He said it was always sad. But he said I would get over it pretty soon."

"WE WILL NEVER GET OVER IT, ALEX!" Samantha's voice reverberated from the kitchen as she continued, "Come out here this minute."

I hugged the little fellow again, before he responded to his mother's command. "She's nuts," I thought to myself, "and her craziness has nothing to do with the welfare of her kids." I developed a desire to speak with the Monk at the monastery, to seek a fresh and more spiritual point of view regarding my marriage. Besides, I was too often suffering from painful regret and severe self-criticism with respect to the future I had constructed for myself. I was often irritated, too near rage actually, even when alone. I frequently felt unstable, despite my daily readings and morning contemplation, which usually resulted in measured responses and the demonstration of a reasonable attitude.

It was snowing lightly as I drove up to the familiar old monastery, and a half-inch of accumulation crunched under my footsteps as I approached the entrance, beyond which I had been repeatedly guided toward greater peace and wisdom. I sat across from him, in the presence of his welcoming smile, and answered his general query regarding my progress. "I have a problem," I began and proceeded to outline my new circumstances. I expanded upon certain points at his request, most frequently as they pertained to Samantha. Much of the conversation involved issues I had intended to circumvent on the basis that, if I was disturbed about a person, place, or thing, there was probably something wrong with me and the way I was looking at it.

During an extended pause, near the end of my tale of woe, he asked, "Do you know if Samantha has a history of abuse?"

I said, "I don't know about anything like that, except she was a resident in a convent in her formative years and she expresses a lot of bitterness toward nuns and the church. She doesn't like to discuss anything regarding my recovery or spirituality. She has even been critical of my going to A.A. meetings and expresses contempt for my A.A. friends."

"Well, based on the things you have told me about her, her obsession with controlling things and so on, I began wondering, that's all. What you have just said adds to my suspicions. To be honest with you, however, it is your wellbeing that causes me more concern. I think you have a big decision to make." He let that thought hang in the air for a moment before he continued, "As I see it, there are three possible outcomes for you. One, you can join in the insanity, playing the game on her terms, largely giving up your spiritual journey, competing for the children's affection, and trying to carve out a life for yourself. But I don't think you will stay sober for long if you choose that option. Then she will have the upper hand for sure. Two, you can attempt to detach yourself from the insanity and continue to follow your recovery program, but that is highly unlikely to work because you simply have not been sober long enough. The ground you are standing on is not as firm as you might think. You can probably sense already that your Higher Power as you understand Him is a changing phenomenon, and Alcoholics Anonymous is the only stable part of your life. She may instinctively fear your stability and continue to undermine it."

He paused, giving me time to absorb the essence of these first two alternatives. "And what is the third?" I asked with trepidation.

His conclusion was clear. "If sobriety is your priority, get free of the marriage. I am quite familiar with the Catholic Church's views on the topic of divorce, but your present situation does not have a constructive future, in my opinion. Each of you will be better off living separately, and so will those children, regardless of economics."

His words were a source of enormous relief. Even though I had previously wished that dissolving the marriage was an option, I had argued against the idea on the basis that it was, at once, a legal impossibility and a spiritual transgression, God's will having been somehow satisfied by its formation. On the drive home I continued to struggle with that issue, still not seeing that any God worth his salt would be unlikely to insist on human suffering where a rational and legitimate alternative was available. At home, and in Samantha's presence, I found myself in a new state of mind in which I was no longer simply conniving and striving for position, while capitulating to a life sentence. Instead I looked upon her as a prison guard who was unaware of the tunnel her ward was constructing beneath the wall. It was a Friday, past business hours, and I decided I would call a lawyer Monday morning, probably the one I'd employed while purchasing the ranch five years ago. He had impressed me as a personable man with whom I could discuss my position and options without immediate pressure to proceed on some legal course.

During the weekend I sought relief by rereading segments of my favorite spiritual volumes and searching for insight into my dilemma, for guidance that would support a right attitude and, therefore, right action. On page forty-seven of the book *Twelve Steps and Twelve Traditions* I read, "But in A.A. we slowly learned that something had to be done about our vengeful resentments, self-pity, and unwarranted pride... We learned that if we were seriously disturbed, our first need was to quiet that disturbance, regardless of who or what we thought caused it." Further along, I was jolted into a less palatable clarity with these words: "The perverse wish to hide a bad motive underneath a good one permeates human affairs from top to bottom. This subtle and elusive kind of self-righteousness can underlie the smallest act or thought."

I knew that my part in the two of us getting together in the first place included self-serving motives and unthinking irresponsibility. I could not blame Samantha for my predicament. I had been motivated by a self-centered vision of my future on the ranch, of which financial scheming had been one aspect. I had never, except in the shallowest ways, given any thought to the welfare of her children, and I had not thought of the fallout for Elizabeth. I had not even heeded Samantha's warning regarding the conception of the child that would be ours in a few short months. I was baffled by the stark realization of these facts. How had I misled myself to that degree and suffered such a dearth of common sense?

I was no stranger to delusions arising out of reckless and rationalizing selfishness. But two new phenomena had served to further confound me by removing my last defense, the threat of self-injury. They were 'spiritual pride' and a resurrected version of the 'Santa Claus God,' the one that willingly and regularly grants your wish list, which I had deliberately discarded around age eighteen. I had duped myself with the kind of thinking highlighted by Emmet Fox in *Sermon on the Mount* when he quoted from Matthew VI: "Lay not up for yourselves treasures upon earth, where moth and rust doth corrupt, and where thieves break through and steal. But lay up for yourselves treasures in heaven where neither moth nor rust doth corrupt, and where thieves do not break through and steal. For where your treasure is, there will your heart be also."

I remembered saying to Will one day, as we drove along a country road, "Sometimes I think I should sell the farm, get free of all material attachments, and spend my life in a spiritual search, doing A.A. service, and carrying the message of recovery. That's when I'm happiest."

He turned his head to look straight at me, a skeptical look in his eye, and then, turning back to the road, said, "That sounds like a calling, and I don't think you're ready."

That day I had burst with laughter at his ruthless honesty, and I often chuckled to myself in solitary reflection at the silliness of my words. But wishful thinking reinforced by Fox's addendum to the above Biblical quotation – "But seek ye first the Kingdom of God, and all these things shall be added unto you" – had led to foolish expectations based on misplaced pride in my spiritual progress. I had factored into my matrimonial decision a restoration of the Santa Claus God, a divinity that rewarded people directly for their good behavior, while, as the assumption must necessarily be, depriving or punishing those who have acted badly. (He knows who's been naughty and nice.) I had been a victim of the idea that I was acting in line with God's will for me, all because the vision I constructed during the initial unfolding of events had been so agreeably promising to me. As a back-up, and further justification for acting irresponsibly, I had deluded myself with the belief that God would make everything right, in spite of wedding day indications to the contrary.

I had forgotten the feet-on-the-ground wisdom of a catchy Arab axiom I had come across, "Praise Allah, but tie your camel to a tree." To me, that meant many Biblical contentions were applicable, in a literal sense, only if one was living in a monastery. Otherwise, there was risk of spiritual pride, or spiritual stupidity perhaps, a problem that occurs when one's concept of his Higher Power leads to severing his connection with earthly reality.

In any case, as with misreading a road map, one must simply return to doing the right thing and, where retracing previous steps is not an option, he must set a new course. In that regard, page eighty of *Sermon on the Mount* was instructive: "You must get rid of all sense of resentment and hostility. You must change your own state of mind until you are conscious only of harmony and peace within yourself, and have a sense of positive good-will towards all." On the next page, Fox continued, "With a new difficulty of any kind, it is the reception that you give it mentally, and the attitude that you adopt towards it in your own thoughts, that completely determine its effect upon you."

Will had often asked, "What step are you on?" Because I was still working on Step Nine, making amends to those I had harmed, I decided on Sunday to review my Step Eight, the extensive list of people I had determined were in that category. I selected the name of my former friend from Chicago, Troy. We had spent countless good days together and, in the end, I had betrayed his friendship with a resentful and negative report to the managing partner regarding Troy's performance at work. He had been let go that afternoon, a decision I believed had little to do with my input, but I feared, nevertheless, that my words may have been relayed to him. We had not spoken since. I drafted a letter to my estranged buddy, admitting my lack of loyalty and the unwarranted resentful state of mind that perpetrated it. I expressed the gratitude I felt for his past friendship and included my sincere wishes that the course he had taken since had been rewarding and fulfilling. I sealed the envelope and would mail it on my next trip to town. The effort had been constructive and compassionate, performed with no expectation beyond the hope of lessening Troy's anguish, and it had thus provided an uplifting distraction.

Monday morning, after everyone left, I phoned the lawyer and made an appointment to see him at eleven o'clock. "You have a very large problem," he said in response to my story. "You must be very careful, because she could quite easily have you removed from the home, given the circumstances. And, to make matters worse, a judge could order you to continue to make the mortgage payments."

I was stunned by his words, seemingly turned to stone right where I sat. Speechless, I merely looked at him with despair in my heart.

"Is there any chance of her leaving?" He searched for a slim reed.

"Not very likely," I returned. "I have friends who believe she was after the ranch from the very beginning. What exactly are you getting at?"

"Well, if she were to leave and take the kids, even for a few days, just long enough to demonstrate that she had other options for accommodation, you might hold onto your property," he said.

501

He was a kind man and we talked a little longer. But I left with little hope that I would find a satisfactory escape. I resolved to make the best of the miserable life I had created for myself, despite the hopelessness with which the Franciscan monk had viewed my chances.

Mr. Alex Webber was another name on my list of amends owing. On Wednesday I decided to drive out to his guiding operation in the mountains and meet with him. Our relatively good relationship had ended badly because of my drinking, rash behavior, and promiscuity. That was four and half years ago, but I remembered it vividly, and I expected he would as well. I thought he had unfairly altered the conditions of my employment while I was in transit and had given no consideration to our incompatibility when he assigned my brother and me to team up with the scheming Audrey and irascible Luke. But I accepted that my part in the trouble was the full extent of my remaining concern in the matter.

He was plainly not happy to see me as I entered the building where everyone met for breakfast or to eat their bagged lunches. He did his best to ignore my presence in the midst of several of his employees, all of whom I remembered, and all of whom returned my greeting with extraordinarily subdued acknowledgment.

"I want a private word with you," I said as discreetly as possible to Mr. Webber.

"I don't see what you could say that would interest me," he replied, glancing from beneath his large black Stetson while he stepped deliberately toward the door that led into a large barn. As he continued walking away, I followed him. "Whatever it is you want, the answer is no," he said over his shoulder.

When he stopped and began to sort through some tack, as though I was not even there, I began, "I have come here to admit that my conduct while I worked for you was unacceptable." He did not react as I continued, "That is the only reason. I am not looking for anything from you. I have quit drinking by joining Alcoholics Anonymous and one of the steps requires that I set straight past situations, especially where my drinking and behavior were destructive."

He obviously lacked the inclination to participate in that train of thought and merely said, "What are you doing these days? I heard something about your guiding and packing venture."

"Yes, my brother and I had fun with that, but I have since switched to raising cattle and doing a little real estate business," I said, deciding any conversation was better than silence. Then, returning to the task at hand, I added, "Anyway, it is important that I take responsibility for my part in the way things went between us and I'm glad to see that your business seems to be doing well."

The resentment he had apparently been harboring appeared far from appeased, and the full extent of his efforts to understand was to utter, with some condescension, "It's too bad you hadn't stayed with the futures business. You could have made a lot of money at that."

I thought the best I could do was leave before I risked muddying my primary objective by engaging in that diversion. I did not know if he had absorbed what I said or not, but I believed, given time, he would understand what I had done. That was the important thing and, if he chose to hold onto his resentment, that was his affair.

"Well, that's what I had to say. Thank you for listening," I said, offering to shake his hand. He declined and I turned toward the door of the barn in which I had once assumed responsibility for saddling thirty horses on cool mountain mornings.

"Have a good summer," he added, addressing my back without noticeable enthusiasm.

"You, too," I said over my shoulder, feeling that the best possible outcome had been achieved. I felt great relief as I drove away, having done the right thing. I spent the balance of the afternoon touring mountain back roads, stopped for a steak supper, and took my time travelling the hundred and twenty miles between there and home. I felt fortified by my efforts, as though I had made another installment on my membership in a club which operated on a plane above the turmoil of my despairing home life.

It was 10:00 p.m. when I walked into the house and I was immediately confronted by Samantha. "Are you going to tell me where you have been all day?" she asked threateningly.

Sharing where I had been and what I had done would have had its own nauseating repercussions. Her tone only made it easier to ignore her and continue to my study. She followed me soon afterwards and addressed me in the same tone. "This environment is not good for the kids, never knowing what to expect from you. If you don't change the way you are, I am leaving and taking them with me."

I gazed at her, stone-faced as possible, while I reacted internally with utter disbelief. Rather than the hopeful astonishment I felt, and could hardly contain, my words were couched in disdainful skepticism. "You won't leave," I said, "you don't have the guts to leave," and I turned my head to address the papers on my desk. I didn't view my actions and words as those of a spiritually advanced being. I felt, rather, that I might finally be tying my fucking wayward camel to a tree.

Thursday morning I left very early, without reporting in, and I returned to the farmyard only after everyone had gone for the day. I drove twenty miles to an A.A. meeting that evening and stayed late, drinking coffee until ten. When I returned, I noticed some boxes stacked by the door and went to bed with a hopeful heart. I made a good effort at being cheerful Friday morning, saying nothing about the mounting material indications of their pending departure. Nor was there any comment in that regard from Samantha, who was obviously punishing me with the silent treatment. The kids dutifully followed instructions as well, remaining mute in the face of my greetings, eye contact confined to the conveyance of scorn.

I drove over to visit with Roger that afternoon and accepted his invitation to stay for a supper of moose steaks. I brought him up-to-date on the circumstances surrounding my marriage and we concluded that it was a hell of a mess, no matter what the outcome. "She is putting pressure on you to change," Roger said.

"But she doesn't even know what it is she wants changed," his wife added, concurring.

Afterwards, we went together to an A.A. meeting and I didn't get home until ten-thirty. The house was empty of people. Hardly anything else had been removed, but the family and the few boxes by the door were gone. They had left no forwarding note. If I was expected to suffer feelings of abandonment and some version of hopelessness, nothing could have missed the mark by a greater margin. I went to bed with a guarded sense of elation, mixed with painfully hesitant anticipation, punctuated during the night by semiconscious flashes in which I doubted the accuracy of my memory with respect to recent developments.

My first thought after waking up was I must get in touch with the lawyer and ask his advice following this sudden turn of events, which I had assured him would never occur. But it was Saturday and I decided to wait until mid-morning to track him down. Around eight-thirty, the phone rang and my anxious premonition was accurate.

"Well, do you believe me now?" Samantha asked. "Are you ready to talk?"

"Where are you?" I asked, hoping to convey concern and glean useful information at the same time.

"George and Vivian invited us to stay with them," she shot back, "until it is safe for us to return home."

She had apparently launched a character assassination program to establish my guilt. George and Vivian had been Samantha's neighbors before she moved to my place. I nevertheless had had some prior and unsatisfactory acquaintance with them, and I thought she had made a good choice, a good alliance, under the circumstances. Their own lives were often in turmoil and George had contemptuously rejected the idea of getting help in Alcoholics Anonymous, stopping by several times to argue with me about it. Vivian told me she thought there were a lot of really screwed up people in A.A. and George did not need to associate with that sort. I had suggested she might look into Al-Anon and that only led to a more incensed enmity.

"I asked if you were ready to talk?" she repeated.

"Well, not yet, I guess." I hoped to stall things without riling her further.

"Well, then, you had better start packing your things and get out of my house," she threw down the gauntlet and hung up.

I was stunned to learn that she had taken the battle to that level so soon. Apparently, we had both been thinking well into the future and, apparently as well, property was at the core in both cases. The warning Dawson had passed on a few months ago, gold-digger, rang menacingly in my ears.

I was a little surprised, a few minutes later, when the lawyer answered his office telephone. "Just sorting through a few things while it's quiet around here," he explained. "What's up?"

"My wife has taken the kids and is staying with friends," I told him, "and she has threatened to take the ranch."

He hesitated only briefly, while I confirmed for him that Samantha had not stayed in the house the previous night and that she was not there now. "Change the locks immediately. It's your house. Then, inform her of the action you've taken, right away, and tell her you will call the police if she tries to return. That should keep her away a few more days, long enough to formulate the next step."

I drove into town and bought new exterior door hardware. I rushed home and replaced everything Samantha had keys for. My heart was racing the whole time, and it didn't slow down while I phoned her with this new information, hoping to quickly stall any plans she might have for returning. Once I had her on the line, I repeated the lawyer's words without allowing for additional conversation, and ended the call. Even two hours later, it was all I could do to remain calm. A neighbor drove into the yard, one of the men from the church and the breakfast meeting, a man I had quite high regard for. He was already aware of the problem and had stopped in with the hope of being helpful, intending ultimately, it soon became apparent, to negotiate a happy reconciliation.

I appeased his wishes by admitting that things had reached an ugly impasse, that I did not think it would be easy to straighten them out, but that I was willing to try. He suggested that we arrange a meeting for the next day, including him and me, my wife, and his sister-in-law with whom he believed Samantha had a friendship. I agreed to that and he agreed with me that a little time apart might be beneficial for everyone, help defuse tensions. I felt like I was locked into an all-night, very high stakes poker game, it was just past midnight, and I was up a bit.

I drove over to visit Will, desperate for the calm that I usually experienced in his presence. I doubted he would have anything to contribute regarding my current circumstances, but I knew, even if we talked about cattle and grass conditions, it would help. Briefly interrupting the task of making a pot of coffee, he had glanced over his shoulder several times with a slightly pained expression as I brought him up-to-date.

When I finished, he turned slowly to say, "Just don't make a loser out of anyone, especially a woman. Making a loser out of someone else never makes you a winner. Try to respect the dignity of the other person at all costs and you won't pay for it later." We talked for more than an hour and, although he offered no strategic advice, his parting words were an unmistakable guidepost, "Remember, be polite."

By 1:00 p.m. Sunday, Samantha was conversing with his sister-in-law in the master bedroom, while my neighbor empathized with my concerns and fears as we sat around the alcove in the kitchen. He said that a few church members had met that morning after the service and had demonstrated their willingness to help Samantha with expenses. One family had even offered the use of a second house, in which she and the kids were welcome to stay until we sorted things out. He therefore agreed to present the idea of an interim separation to his helpmate, who in turn presented it to Samantha, who submitted without protest. Arrangements were then made to transfer those of their possessions they would need to carry on a normal life for the next month or so.

By that afternoon, with the help of several other church members, it was done. I had to stifle the ludicrous notion that some universal governing force had finally moved over to my side. I smiled instead at an example Roger had used to convey his contempt for such thinking. "Yup, God was sure looking after me!" he had mocked the declaration of a self-righteous person who had missed getting on a plane that crashed and killed two hundred other beings.

The lawyer suggested that, although a major hurdle had been crossed, I was still vulnerable to a property action down the road. Although I could probably expect some delay because Samantha was now past seven months in her pregnancy, he thought I should propose paying a reasonable level of child support, even begin early to establish some good will since that was an inevitable responsibility in any case. Later that day, I drafted a letter and included a check, post-dated for one month, as proof of my good intentions.

In addition, with no intention of following through, I offered a red herring based on our combined destitute financial situation. I told Samantha over the phone that I thought I should begin proceedings to subdivide the house and yard from the rest of the ranch, sell it as an acreage property, and buy a house in town where she and the children could live. She thought that was a stupid idea and insisted that she would be moving back to the ranch, whether I was there or not. Her objective remained intact, in spite of her maternal condition.

Feeling we had suddenly become comrades in desperation, I thought of her former husband, whose phone number I had in my possession, and called him up. "She will be after legal possession of the ranch," he said calmly, among other unflattering recollections, "or she will bankrupt you in the process."

There was nothing to be gained by burying my head in the sand. I needed to consider actions to divert further disaster and impossible future financial obligations. At the same time, I felt a desperate need to stay on track with my sobriety and my spiritual journey. I was beginning to accept that a ruthless application of whatever secular tactics were available to me was not necessarily inconsistent with continued progress along a spiritual path.

Chapter 37

An A.A. friend loaned me a book about relationships by Barbara De Angelis, *Are You the One for Me? Knowing Who's Right and Avoiding Who's Wrong.* Certainly a pertinent question, and a promise of insight, I read with hungry enthusiasm. The book listed many dos and don'ts, of course, but it was her "going home syndrome" that fascinated me. She wrote, "As human beings, we gravitate toward the familiar... Returning to the familiar is a basic instinct that gives our lives a sense of continuity and safety in a chaotic and changing universe." As I explored in more detail just how this idea applied to my relationships, I concluded the following in my journal:

There are two ways in which a dysfunctional childhood environment might affect the choice of a mate:

(1) Pick mates (with loving nurturing characteristics) and then re-create my HOME environment by imposing it upon them: 'Now you know what I went through!'

(2) Pick mates (with characteristics of a nasty parent or parents) that will re-create my HOME environment for me.

For me, HOME was arguing, bickering, criticism, belittling, anger, self-pity, no play or fun, just work, lack of trust, deceit and denial, emotional distance, guilt and shame, never good enough; close intimacy was actually dangerous.

All my previous partners and relationships are explained by Category #1, all rejected and hurt by me. That was a consequence of growing up with my angry unavailable father.

People attempt to give you love and you hurt them, reject them, and make them work hard for love.

Samantha was different; she re-created my early family environment.

I had changed my approach for selecting partners. Perhaps I could no longer conscientiously treat people as I had in the past (thereby creating that environment), so I found someone who would make me feel at home by subjecting me to my HOME environment.

That discovery was hardly a solution for anything in the present and, although it might be helpful in future choices, I doubted that I would remember to apply it specifically along with all the other dos and don'ts suggested by the myriad self-help books I'd been reading. Besides, I was no longer sure that my family was entirely to blame for my childhood experience, or my perception of it. I put the book aside, viewing the insight as nothing more than interesting and quite academic at that. I suddenly felt completely overwhelmed by all the conundrums of life. Without any complicating qualifiers, I simply wanted my freedom back, unencumbered.

I decided to drive into the city and attend another S.A.A. meeting that evening. Not looking for answers, rather I wished to gain more familiarity with the puzzling human condition. I had been reading the book I'd purchased from the men there and I had experienced a bewildering blend of freedom and despair as a consequence. Both men and women had written openly about their personal stories of confused childhoods, disconnected adolescences, and despairing lives of acting out on compulsions and obsessions that were strangely beyond their cognitive control. Whether the stories concerned a woman's sexual encounters with a hundred men, a man's voyeurism or exhibitionism, or the more acceptable and less hazardous promiscuity to which I had subjected myself, the results were (to varying degrees) the annihilation of social, emotional, and spiritual wellbeing.

511

Hitting closer to home over the past several months, I had paid particular attention to the arrest of a family man from a small town a few miles away. At thirty-nine years of age, he had long been a solid member of the community and had established a good reputation as a minor league boys' basketball coach. Why had he suddenly pulled the world down around himself by engaging in "sexual invitation and sexual touching with the boys he was responsible for," as the newspaper had defined his transgressions? I had been deeply saddened to think of the pain it caused his family, parents, friends, the boys he was involved with, the boys' parents and, of course, himself. His life must appear to be at an end.

From further afield, again of particular interest to me because of my heightened awareness, was news of a thirty-six year old married mother of two children who had carried on a sexual relationship with a fifteen-year-old boy over a three-month period, until the boy's mother twigged to the goings-on and brought in the police. The legal implications were much less severe in her case, and so probably was society's judgment, but she, her children, and her husband must have suffered a great deal. Not unique, I thought, are the causes and conditions which gave rise to these behaviors in the first place. A.A. literature employs the rather innocuous phrases "instincts out of control" and "self-will run riot" to explain the crazy behavior of the practicing alcoholic. That is probably as accurate as anyone could be, no matter how technical or psychologically sophisticated the terminology, in describing something that is really entirely undecipherable.

The hollow unthinking phrases "this too shall pass" and "everything happens for a reason" echoed in my mind, sounding even more absurd than usual. One might just as well say, "It doesn't matter, your trouble is unimportant." But it did matter, I thought, to each and every person connected with these catastrophes. At the same time, I was quite certain I did not know how or why.

I could see that the wrath and internal revulsion I once directed toward the perpetrators, upon hearing news breaks of this sort, especially when children were involved, were based on ignorance. My reactions most recently had been reeling bewilderment at the deranged undercurrents that blight human existence, and the singularity of some people's exceptional misery and distress. That is why I was attending the S.A.A. meeting, because there was something going on in those rooms that had a much deeper and more vital spiritual significance than present events in my life, no matter how tumultuous they threatened to become.

I perceived that pride was absent in the meeting, as was any discussion of objectives pertaining to the material world. The objects of their gratitude did not include social recognition, increasing bank accounts, or new houses and vehicles. Sometimes they were thankful not to have lost contact with a few family members who had found it within themselves to understand and forgive, but they were most often hesitantly thankful and hopeful that the devastating compulsions that had ruled their lives, and often ruined them, could be held at bay through ruthless introspection, spiritual surrender, and intimate fellowship with the mutually desperate. I hadn't been to prison, suffered social disgrace, or had my self-image crushed by a shameful stigma, but I found relief among these men through a common touchstone of anguish and sorrow nevertheless. Perimeter walls came tumbling down and permitted searching at liberty, as though my vision was no longer limited by commonly acknowledged horizons.

I considered a recent report of suicide, a churchgoing family man, a respected member of his community, who owned a prosperous farm. "Why on earth did he kill himself?" was the question asked by many. "It's very hard to understand," others replied.

It might not be so difficult to understand, I reflected silently, if you really knew him. Not I, nor anyone else, dared speculate aloud; better to bury him with an unsoiled record which, perhaps, had been his own final desperate motive. Some of us, like me, have had a long familiarity with the darker side of things. At the same time, it appeared, many have not. For those, to discover at some point how close they are to the edge may be more than they can handle. Perhaps he had crossed some invisible line, only to find himself on an ugly and slippery slope, which he feared he could not manage. He was possibly not as well equipped as those of us who have trained since childhood to live two lives simultaneously.

I shuddered with anxious gratitude that I had been able to handle my lot, and that I had not been handed the burden of the member who was sharing his story at that moment. He had been expressing his thoughts on the frightening futility of time spent in a prison psychiatric ward because of his obsession with and his acting out of violent sexual aggression. Presently, he was tearfully expressing his joy at attaining something like a spiritual release from this powerful and devastating handicap, through working the Twelve Steps and staying close to the S.A.A. fellowship. That's why I was there, I concluded, to participate in miracles. The image I saw, of the man sitting across from me in the room and relating his story, was that of a powerless and innocent little boy. Completely absent was the repeated brutal offender.

By the end of the next week I had been served with notice of a legal action to gain spousal support and child support for her three existing children in addition to the one as yet unborn. Early the following week I was served with a property action. War had been declared. To make matters worse, she had engaged the lawyer with whom I had squabbled over the $630.00 fee he attempted to charge me for gaining a judgment against the slippery, swindling, would-be-sponsor who flew off to Ohio with my credit card. As a result of several social encounters over the intervening year, I was certain the lawyer had nourished his resentment and, just as certain, that he would be overjoyed at this fresh opportunity for retaliation.

Allan, an A.A. member with whom I had a good personal connection, had talked one day about his long and brutal domestic court battle, referring several times with admiration to the lawyer he employed. The friendly lawyer I had spoken to earlier, who gave me good and practical advice in the initial stages, had made it clear he was focusing on contract law and wanted to steer clear of unsavory domestic cases. I went to see Allan to get more information about his lawyer.

"She was quite a lady, works with a firm in the city," he said, "very clever and a bit ruthless, not cheap, but well worth the money."

When I left him I had her phone number in my pocket and was resigned to spend whatever it took to fight a good battle. On the way home, I stopped in to see a local horse-trader, the same one my brother Barry and I had bought eight horses from almost five years ago. He hadn't changed: dry cracked lips that explained his minimal smile, a whiff of whiskey on his breath, amiable enough if not pressed.

"I need to get rid of those horses I bought from you back in the spring of 1989. What are they worth now?" I asked.

"Same as you paid for them. About nine hundred a piece, wasn't it?" he drawled, adding, "How many?"

"Ten, I guess, if you want them," I said.

He nodded affirmatively. I knew horse prices were up a bit, but the horses were now five years older. It was a fair deal and we shook on it. That was my first step in unwinding the life I had built for myself on the ranch in the foothills. I had made the decision without much prior thought, propelled by a subconscious acceptance of the inevitable. I knew in my heart that other similar decisions would have to be made, until, I feared, nothing remained of my dream but memories.

I made an appointment and drove into the city to meet my new lawyer, Catherine, who I eventually referred to as Catherine the Great, respectfully if not always affectionately. Pleasant, attractive, stylish, and smoothly deliberate, she inspired the kind of confidence that left me feeling grateful that she was not on the opposing team. After listening to a brief description of my circumstances she asked me to put together an extensive list of information and records.

"Are you aware that this could take several years and cost you a lot of money?" she asked. I hesitated, wishing it weren't so, and she continued, "The reason I ask is to ascertain that there is not a more palatable solution, such as mediation. We can try that, you know, even though I agree with your assessment that it does not seem a probable course. Here's what I propose: I will make a thorough review, once you supply me with the background material, and I will contact her counsel to investigate the possibilities for a mediated settlement."

"I am not going to settle for paying support beyond what is reasonable for my child and I am not going to settle for any sharing of property that I owned before the marriage, which actually exceeded in value the sum-total of all property remaining today," I said, without a modicum of doubt running through my mind. There was more involved than money and I was taking a stand.

"Your position is reasonable. There is a very good chance of that being the court's conclusion, but I expect we will not achieve it without litigation." Her straightforward honesty impressed me and I let her go on. "I'll need a fifteen thousand dollar retainer, regardless of the short term outcome."

I gave her a check that day. Two weeks later she called to confirm that, having presented my position to Samantha's lawyer, mediation was not a viable alternative. I suspected that Samantha's ability to leave a retainer was seriously limited and that her lawyer, a second antagonist in any case, was working against a percentage of her property settlement, perhaps even encouraging her to do battle. Scenes of wearying frustration and despairing impediments to progress, as portrayed in Charles Dickens' tragic portrayal of the legal system in *Bleak House*, drifted menacingly through my mind. I went to an A.A. meeting that night and drank coffee with Roger until ten-thirty.

"Oh, it will be an endurance test before it's over," he said. His tone merged foreboding with determination. "I'll stick with you, call any time," he promised, and I left him, feeling less alone.

Chapter 38

Praying to any reasonable God for partisan support in a fight against a pregnant woman and three kids seemed entirely impractical – revolting in fact. And yet, I felt in serious need of spiritual guidance. I vaguely recalled a passage from the book I had borrowed from the Kowloon Hilton seven years ago, *The Teaching of Buddha*. When I got home I looked it up, read it, and then wrote it out, with insertions to personalize the message:

"The (MY) world has no substance of its own. It is simply a vast concordance of causes and conditions that have had their origins, solely and exclusively, in the activities of the (MY) mind that has been stimulated by ignorance, false imagination, desires, and infatuation. It is not something external about which the (MY) mind has false conceptions; it has no substance whatever. It has come into appearance by the processes of the (MY) mind itself, manifesting its own delusions. It is founded and built up out of the desires of the (MY) mind, out of its sufferings and struggles, incidental to the pain caused by its own greed, anger, and foolishness. Men who seek the way to Enlightenment should be ready to fight such a mind to attain their goal."

That was the truth: my best thinking had brought me to this place! My life was a disaster by every secular measure; it wasn't anything to crow about spiritually either. My past was an accumulation of debauchery and pointlessly squandered opportunity. I had no current contact with my family of origin.

I would be in court, potentially for years to come, fighting an agonizing battle to establish a reasonable outcome for a misguided domestic disaster. The nauseating scene that formed in my mind's eye, as I surveyed the wreckage of every vision and opportunity I'd ever had, resembled in every respect the smoldering ruins of a derailed train.

Innocent little Elizabeth never mentioned that we had the whole place to ourselves again; nor did she seem concerned with what had become of the others. She was obviously and simply content with the new status quo, and my gratitude for her presence in my life often soared to joyful tears. Inspired by deep appreciation for her support, I decided to give Celia some more money. There were at least two practical arguments for doing it as well. First, she had recently opened a small culinary store in the resort town where they lived and I knew she could use some help. Second, I sometimes wondered about the fairness of the financial terms in our separation four years earlier. I questioned whether I had been sufficiently generous in light of her cooperative attitude back then, and the generous good will she continued to display. Also spurring me to do it was the notion of reducing the size of the target at which Samantha and her lawyer were aiming their artillery. I wrote a check for fifteen thousand dollars, adding a bit to the nine thousand I had received for the horses, money I wanted to make a memorable use of for sentimental reasons, rather than let it disappear into unpleasant legal expenses. Celia was, as always, grateful in return and I felt certain I had done a good thing.

Another meeting with my lawyer led to several decisions. We would file a petition for a divorce; I would not contest the issue of custody, believing that visiting rights ought to be agreed to voluntarily, with a child's welfare the primary concern, if any real benefit were to accrue; I would sell the ranch, to effectively remove another target from the property suit. I was going to be too strapped financially to maintain ownership of it in any case. While digesting the last of these decisions, I was suddenly overwhelmed by the conviction that I could best handle my losses and avoid inevitably burdensome liabilities by running off to the mountains and becoming a recluse, maybe in Peru.

I decided to visit Allan, the A.A. friend who had referred me to Catherine the Great, and I turned onto the road that led to the ranch he had salvaged from his matrimonial confrontation. Somehow the conversation turned to my horse-packing adventures in the mountains, in response to which he expressed such immense personal enthusiasm that we decided to take a little trip together in two weeks' time. I had not sold Merlin or Fitzsimmons, and my friend had several horses of his own. It would be a welcome diversion from my crumbling world.

I stopped to visit with Will, to bring him up-to-date on my affairs. "Too bad it has to go that way," he said. "My wife was so glad to get away, she easily settled for a bit of money. She left the ranch alone because she knew the boys would end up with it anyway. This marriage of yours has been rough going all along. It will be easier if you consider that sometimes we need to go into the darkness to see the light."

When I got home, I phoned a realtor and invited him to list the ranch for sale. Then I phoned Roger and talked for a half hour, still frantically fending off the stark reality of my decisions, the wretched sting of facing them in solitude. Finally, the time had come.

While I sat alone that evening, tears occasionally welling in my eyes, I reviewed my history on the ranch. There had been much sadness and struggle during my years there. My faithful dog, Perro, had been lost; Victoria had departed, unable to tolerate my insanity; Barry, my little brother, and I had suffered our falling out; and a dozen other calamities had occurred. Through blurry eyes, along a line of sight that passed from the living room where I sat, through the kitchen, and into the large front entranceway, my focus settled on the gun rack. Which would be my choice? The .22 magnum was hardly big enough; the 30-30, the .308; or should I make absolutely sure with the 12 gauge shotgun in my mouth? I thought of the several friends and acquaintances that had arrived at this irrevocable finality, and I felt a wretched empathy. From that gloomy state I was drawn to consider the release they must have craved. Perhaps it was all too much, and there just wasn't any point in suffering further. Besides, it would bring bitter retribution to those who had made my youth so desperately miserable.

In the same instant, I knew I would not do it. I had failed, by all the standards of the society in which I lived, and I would have to endure the fact that my general demise was laughable to anyone who cared to comment on it. But once more, that old powerful will-to-live influenced the course of my thoughts. My habitual grim determination to see-it-through held sway, and further mental meandering on the subject of suicide was choked off by the ensuing nausea.

Regretful things had happened. But I had sobered up in this place, too, and had begun a life changing journey, much of which had taken place while I sat gazing thoughtfully into the glass door of a crackling woodstove. The cattle and horses, Elizabeth's visits, baby calves in the springtime, a spectral herd of elk moving through in the fall, simply sitting on the deck and looking out across the land, all those had contributed precious moments. Most of my grief, when I was honest with myself, was over the loss of a vision, something that had drawn me to this setting in the first place but had not materialized. Whatever it had been, I saw that I had now acquired a new vision, or rather, an ethereal longing. I recalled a passage from the *Dhammapada*, a poetic account of the Buddha's wisdom I had found soothing and elevating on other occasions.

He is awake
And finds joy in the stillness of meditation
And in the sweetness of surrender.
Hard it is to be born,
Harder it is to live,
Harder still to hear of the way,
And hard to rise, follow and awaken.
Yet the teaching is simple.
Do what is right,

Be pure.
At the end of the way is Freedom
Till then, patience.

Sometimes, the greatest peace could be discovered in statements dealing with things unknown. As it was with religious dogma of all sorts, there were edicts among certain Buddhist sects that I found pointless and unreasonable: not eating meat, for example, and not squashing a mosquito when it is biting your arm. But I quickly brushed aside this academic distraction, for, beyond those few shallow dictates, I often sensed that I was very near a path with heart. Most certainly it remained beyond my grasp, but I was comforted by believing such a path was there. With my mind resting in an abyss that separated two worlds – my secular dreams on the one side and a spiritual yearning on the other – I slept peacefully that night. I dreamed I stood alone upon a hilltop, in hazily shrouded nakedness; that material possessions had been denied me, here and hereafter, and that no one knew of my existence. As I looked upon myself from a distance, I saw that I was serene, smiling, and that I did not want more than I had in that moment.

The next morning I sat staring blankly out the window into the receding darkness of early dawn, only remotely aware of the restorative effect of my first cup of coffee. From time to time throughout these last weeks, as with all the days of my life, anger had rushed up volcanically from deep in my gut and fear had swirled round me and swamped my mind. Overwhelmed, I sometimes reeled with bewilderment. I was not free of the bondage of self; nor, in those moments, did I necessarily believe I wanted to be. Deep within, however, following further reflection, I knew I did really want that freedom. At the same time, I did not want to be bound to a religious code or to be induced with an external panacea for my salvation, for which I experienced no deep inner connection. The truth, it seemed, was much larger than that, and I needed to remain free to roam among the eighty-four thousand paths, forever yielding to that which my heart might embrace.

I am not a poet, but in a sudden moment of clarity I reached for a pen and wrote these words in my journal:

The Nature of Things:
To all who tread upon its surface,
The earth makes itself available without judgment.
To all who breathe the breath of life,
The air makes itself available without distinction.
To all who quench their thirst in its coolness,
Water makes itself available without partiality.
To all who seek its light and warmth,
Fire keeps its comforting glow from no man.
To all who fall within its vast inclusiveness,
Humanity excludes not by sex or nation or color or race.
Why, then, should I?
For all who are swallowed by its quaking and eruptions,
The earth lets its character be known without mercy.
For all who meet their demise in its gales and tempests,
The wind remains mercilessly impartial.
For all who are lost to its tides and torrents,
The water spares no one.
For all who are robbed and scorched by its searing rage,
Fire changes its nature not one iota.
In its long history of brutal and bloody corruption,
Humanity has dispensed no immunity.
Why, then, should I?
Do earth, air, water and fire feel benevolent,
Less than they regret their cruelty, or relent?
Creatures like horses and cattle serve and nourish,
While grizzly bears and sharks ravage and devour.
Drawn by the scent and beauty of the rose,
Admirers are pricked by its thorns.
Will humanity, of which I am but a molecule,
ever surrender the violence in its nature?
Why, then, should I?

Feeling liberated by a fresh and profound sense of belonging and inter-being with the universe, and at ease with my indistinct part in all the chaos and suffering that typified the human condition, I nevertheless felt I had managed to ask a very large question that led nowhere. The words on the page embodied thoughts that wavered tentatively before me like a mirage, elusive as puffy cumulus clouds flying before a blustery prairie wind.

I went outside and wandered into the nearby pasture, out among the cattle, their eyes following me with distinctly bovine indifference, and I stood quietly for a while. I turned slowly, allowing my gaze to take in the full panorama. As the sun crept above the horizon, its crimson hue paling to passionate orange then shimmering yellow, its soft rays imparting a pastel glow on the fringes of all forms in its path – the great spruce trees that lined the long driveway, the fences I had constructed with painstaking forethought, the mother cows nursing newborn calves, the horse and mule throwing long shadows as they drank at the creek bank, the lush pasture glistening with a heavy dew, and the grand old hip-roof barn that Peter Kane and I had sweated at reinforcing one hot summer day – my mind remained calmly suspended. I saw, as though I had not really seen before, each detail for which I had great affection. As I dropped slowly to my knees on the moist turf, an immense sense of freedom flooded my being. However hesitant I was to believe in its permanence, my unknowing became knowing. My heart swelled, thankful to some mysterious nameless vastness for this moment, and the balance of the poem drifted gently into my consciousness:

Am I unique among the elements that surround me?
Born into such a mix, did I choose my character?
And yet, I alone have the power to think thus,
To be mindful.
Aware, I see that my nature alone is not unalterable.
This is the truth.
From tiny insects to all the Gods of history,

Ethereal beauty and nurturing benevolence,
Give way to murderous toxicity and hell-fire.
No surprise that I am inherently thus,
No surprise if I remain thus,
Surprising only that I may come to know,
And by knowing, find my destiny in greater purpose.
Mine alone is to quest for a higher state of being,
To search for what is right,
To do what is right.
Mine alone is to pursue a path with heart.